FRENCH ENTRÉE 18

CHAMBRES d'HOTES

BED AND BREAKFAST IN FRANCE

FRENCH ENTRÉE 18

CHAMBRES d'HOTES

BED AND BREAKFAST IN FRANCE

PATRICIA FENN and ROSEMARY GOWER-JONES

Quiller Press

Important Note

Readers are encouraged to send in their comments and suggestions but please address these to Rosemary Gower-Jones – c/o Quiller Press, 46 Lillie Rd, London SW6 1TN.

First published 1998 by Quiller Press Ltd
46 Lillie Road, London SW6 1TN

Line drawings: Rosemary Gower-Jones
Area maps: Helen Humphreys
Front cover picture: Tim Jaques

ISBN 1899163 36 0

Printed and bound in Great Britain by
Biddles Ltd, Guildford and King's Lynn

Contents

The Regions and Departments of France

Tips for Beginners

Maps and guides: Good maps add so much to the enjoyment and success of a holiday that it seems unnecessary to insist that they should be essential companions. I must stress that those in this book are intended only as an indication of where to find the entries. They should be used in conjunction with the appropriate Michelin maps, which are models of clarity and comprehensive cover.

The red Michelin, apart from all its other virtues, has useful town maps. Its cost is justified if it directs you to even one good meal, I believe. In the areas already covered by French Entrées I like to think you won't need any other guidance. That said, chambres d'hôtes landladies are experts on their immediate locality and have regular feedback from their guests, so take their advice.

Currently in print are: FE8 – The Loire, FE17 – Normandy, FE 10 – The South of France, FE11 – Paris, FE 19 – The North of France, FE13 – Provence, FE14 – Brittany Encore, FE16 – The Gardens of France, all published by Quiller Press.

Booking:
Sunday lunch is the Meal of the Week, when several generations settle down together to enjoy an orgy of eating, drinking, and conversation that can well last till teatime. You should certainly book then and on fête days. Public holidays are as follows:

New Year's Day
Easter Sunday and Monday,
Labour Day, 1st May
VE Day 8th May
Ascension Day
Whit Sunday and Monday
France's National Day, 14th July
The Assumption, 15th August
All Saints Day (Toussaints) 1st November
Armistice Day, 11th November
Christmas Day

Make good use of the local tourist bureaux, where you should find some English spoken. Let them do the booking for you if you have problems. This is the place to pick up maps and brochures.

Take with you:
Depends where you're heading. If it's the S category that interests you pack some soap, and a decent towel if you can't stand the risk of a handkerchief-sized baldie. Shouldn't be necessary in M and L grades. In the latter group you can expect to find freebies like shampoo, bath oil, hair dryers and even trouser presses, but a total blank when it comes to a bedroom clock, so consider taking a travelling version. A small iron is a precaution, except where we specifically mention laundry facilities.

I would always advocate using the local markets for self-catering but it's worth taking tea if you don't like stale teabags, marmalade (good for presents, too), biscuits and cereals if you have favourites – all of which are either hard to locate, expensive or horrible.

Bring home:
The list of Best Buys doesn't change much. Obviously wine – you should be able to buy it for half the price you pay back home if you stick to the cheapos and the medium-priced bottles. There is far less differential on the vintage wines and sometimes they are cheaper here. Be a lager lout by all means, stock up on coffee, plain chocolate, ironmongery, kitchen gadgets. Best of all are impulse buys in the markets.

Closing times:
If you can't beat 'em, join 'em. Accept that not a cat stirs between 12 noon and 2.30 p.m. and that if the rest of the population is eating then you might as well join them. Even the markets snap abruptly shut – forget impulse picnics after midday. At the other end of the day it's a joy to be able to find shops open until 7 p.m. Mondays are almost as dead as Sundays, so if it's a long weekend you're planning, try and add on the Friday instead. Sunday dinner and both meals on Monday can be a real problem.

Breakfasts:
Usually a strong plus point for chambres d'hôtes. The breakfast that is normally included in the price tends to outclass those served in hotels and should certainly be taken into account when comparing prices. Many a farmer's wife will throw in morning-collected eggs, a slab of home-produced butter, and a selection of home-

made preserves. On the other hand don't expect the budget stops to offer expensive pâtisserie and fresh orange juice and if your lodging is excessively remote it may not be possible even to arrange for that French breakfast staple – the fresh baguette. A trend of which I do not approve is that practised by some of the more upmarket chambres d'hôtes – of charging extra for breakfast. This is a sneaky way of upping the charge, since you are hardly likely to drive from your rural château into the nearest town for a cup of coffee and, without the self-catering facilities that tend to be the preserve of the M and S groups, you have little choice but to add another 100f to the bill. They could of course argue that 'chambres d'hôtes', unlike its British so-called equivalent 'bed and breakfast', makes no mention of food, but the ploy just adds fuel to the hotel keepers' claim that chambres d'hôtes are just small hotels with fewer taxes.

Telephoning:

Bearing in mind how few rooms are available in each chambres d'hôtes and how much rural navigation is often involved in finding them, it makes sense to telephone ahead – the landlady will switch on the heating if she's sure of a customer – and if you are planning on eating in, a reservation is usually essential. Every chambres d'hôtes owner that I asked reckoned that they could handle a telephone booking, however meagre their English. If you have difficulties, use a bar – inevitably the customers will rally to your aid if you look helpless enough. The public phones in France actually work.

To dial within France use the **ten** figures given in the guide
e.g. **Châtillon-la-Borde** page 262: (0)1.60.66.60.54.

To dial France from UK:
00 33 followed by the 9 figure number given in the guide (omitting the (0) shown in brackets in the text)
e.g. **Châtillon-la-Borde** page 262: 00 33 1.60.66.60.54.

To dial UK from France:
Dial 19 44 then STD code minus 0, then number.

Emergencies:
Fire 18; Police 17; Operator: 13; Directory Enquiries 12.

Introduction

The second edition of a guidebook like this has to be better than the first. In 1995 Bed and Breakfast in France was a pioneer, in that, without accepting payment of any kind Rosemary Gower-Jones and I investigated chambres d'hôtes throughout France and reported our conclusions in terms far more comprehensive than those of the usual symbolised guide. We plumped out the bare facts with the carefully-observed details that make all the difference. The view, as in all French Entrées, is that we paint the picture, you decide if it is right for you, armed with all the information that only a personal inspection can supply. It has been said that consulting our guide is like asking a knowledeagble friend's opinion; we may not necessarily agree with all that friend's priorities (Rosemary's and mine are sometimes different!) but we read between the lines as well as along them, and make up our own minds, well briefed.

It was a huge enterprise for just two of us to undertake and there were many occasions subsequently when, reinforced by the immense assistance of readers' comments, we longed to amend some of our findings and to include some mouth-watering new discoveries. Now we have the opportunity to do this, and offer a newer, leaner, more authoritative guide.

For the first edition the initial inspections were shared between Rosemary in the southern half of this vast country and myself in the north. This time all the legwork has been covered by the stalwart Rosemary, ably abetted by her patient husband John, who drives, translates, and is the only one of our team who can transpose our accumulated wisdom on to a computer.

Like a dog bringing home a succession of luscious bones, Rosemary has dropped into my lap the results of her year's checking and investigating. And for those who say "What a lovely job" let me tell you that driving round the often dark and dirty countryside searching for an elusive, misleading address, only to find that the lady of the house has gone shopping, is less fun than it may seem. So is writing up the findings of the day in the light of a French one-watt bulb when you're dead tired and longing for bed.

The entries in this book are the stars, the sifted, the true and tested, but there were an awful lot of others that had to be eliminated first.

Let's face it - b. and b. is not for everyone. If your idea of a holiday is having the bed turned down with a choc on the pillow, cocktails in the lounge and not having to chat to strangers, you're reading the wrong book. If, on the other hand, you feel you might be missing something in not exploring the natives as well as their country, then you should give the chambres d'hôtes a try. Sceptics might be surprised to find that they are often more comfortable than a hotel, with more freedom, more space, more interest, and all at half the cost.

Ask yourselves why your hosts started b. and b.ing in the first place. To augment their income for sure, but odds on too, because they like people. Liking people in this case means making sure they are happy - like seeing they are warm and comfortable and that they know a bit about the region and get most out of its attractions. Not a bad recipe for a host-guest relationship.

The spread of chambres d'hôtes has been phenomenal. Since I first tentatively included a few specimens in the early French Entrées (and was surprised at the enthusiasm they invoked), they have mushroomed. Many a farmer's wife has augmented her income by accepting government grants to restore outbuildings; many a châtelaine of a stately but crumbling home has found that an agreeable way to fund a new roof or central heating is to tack on a few bathrooms to existing spare rooms and capitalise on inherent spaciousness and graciousness. Many a widow, left with an oversized empty nest, has combatted loneliness by filling her offspring's vacated bedrooms with appreciative (and no doubt tidier and more profitable) guests.

As we, the customers, have demanded higher standards, so have prices risen accordingly. But not much. With the delightfully favourable current exchange rate, you will be paying less, not more, than last year.

Fellow guests will be pot luck. If you do not wish to get involved, elect to eat out in the evening, which is the sociable time. Most b. and b. dinners are eaten round one long table, with the hosts officiating. But you'd be missing what is usually a bargain. While the food will not be sophisticated, it will be home-cooked, frequently from home produce. Expect at least three courses, usually with wine included. The conversation will be at worst interesting, and as the wine flows, at best hilarious. Experiences will be shared, friendships forged.

It does pay to book ahead. With only a few rooms to allocate, the more popular beds are grabbed early. Basic telephone English has usually been mastered. Don't even think of turning up on spec on busy weekends and fètes. Have the courtesy to phone again if you are delayed, thus strengthening the entente cordiale. Don't bank on an evening meal unless it's prebooked - this is not a hotel with a big freezer, thank God. The ideal time to turn up is late afternoon, giving Madame a chance to do her chores and shopping and allow you to get your bearings and relax. Odds are you'll get a welcome cuppa.

Categories.

French Entrée grading has always been L for Luxury, M for Medium and S for simple; it has worked well with the hotels and restaurants and now it's working for the b. and bs. In this case **L** probably means a château or manor house, with a bill for two, including breakfast, of 500-800f. When you consider you're getting an inside view of a stunning building, meeting charming, well-educated, probably English speaking hosts, enjoying spacious rooms, surrounding grounds, tennis court, pool, for a fraction of what you would pay in a similar hotel, count yourself lucky if you end up in one of these. Furniture will probably be family heirlooms, meals will be served on fine china and silver, towels and carpets will be thick. The owners realise that they are part of the attraction and make an effort, no matter how unpromising their guests, to appear, even if only for an apéritif, though I notice the trend is increasingly to opt out of the communal meal. Dinner will be elegantly served and you will be abusing the hospitality if you turn up in a T shirt and trainers. Count on upwards of 140f. Breakfast should be a treat, though I deplore the trend of charging extra - bed and breakfast should be just that - including fresh orange juice, croissants and often ham and cheese for their Scandinavian and German visitors who favour this category. You could economise on lunch.

M covers the majority of entries. They could be houses currently too big for their owners, old farmhouses beamed and full of character, modern villas in a particularly attractive situation, mills, monasteries, townhouses. The rooms and bathrooms are likely to have been contrived out of existing bedrooms, so they will differ in size and price. Expect to pay between 250f and 500f. You might have the choice of single or double beds, bath or shower, so specify. Evening meals will not always be on offer - one hostess told me she preferred to sit and chat with her guests over an apéritif than slave single-handed in the kitchen - but good nearby restaurants will be recommended. Breakfast usually include croissants as well as bread and perhaps home-made jams.

The **S** group represents the best and the worst, and more selectiveness was essential here to choose the ones we could confidently recommend. the kind of 'simplicity' that means discomfort - cold lino, lumpy mattresses, meagre hot water - is just not on. Most of our range have bathrooms either en suite or perhaps across the corridor; if there are family rooms together they may well share a bathroom. Many S chambres d'hôtes are on farms and are particularly suitable for families - plenty of diversions and little cost. The rooms will often be custom built, perhaps without a good deal of character but clean and wholesome, and excellent value at between 170 and 250f. You could get lucky with breakfast here, involving farm produce and quantities to satisfy rustic appetites. Paradoxically this can be the worst group (it is budget after all) for breakfast, with the dread foil packages and yesterday's bread toasted. The busy farmer's wife usually finds time to serve an evening meal that is astonishing value. 60-90f will buy plain but satisfying three courses, plus home-grown veg and salad. Cider is often offered in Normandy and Brittany, and wine in other regions (don't blame me if it stains your teeth!).

Arrows. The arrows indicate the bullseyes. They are the paragons, tried and tested, that fulfil admirable at least two of the criteria - good value, welcome, comfort, special situation - and preferably all of them.

Generalities

Prices are for two people and include breakfast.

Opening times: year-round unless stated.

Parking: one of the big pluses - safe, free and enclosed unless stated otherwise.

Directions: We aim to save you the hassle of bumping down the wrong cart track by giving clear and detailed directions. The maps are mere indications - you would be foolish to travel without the appropriate Michelin.

Payment: Cash. Plastic money occasionally in the L class.

'Compris' means fully inclusive. i.e. for diner - *apéritif*, wine and coffee are included in the price we quote.

'En suite': I hate the pretentious term and it does make very boring reading to add it to each entry, but it is useful shorthand and you will find sometimes it does creep into the text. Generally the assumption is that unless stated otherwise, a bathroom is included in the deal. Padding along cold corridors, illuminated according to the whims of those wicked French time-switches is no longer acceptable.

ALSACE

Départements: **Bas Rhin**
Haut Rhin

Situated in the north east corner of France, this region is separated from Germany by the river Rhine. The German influence is still very strong, noticeably in the architecture, the language and the food. The houses are more like Swiss chalets, heavily timbered and everyone speaks not only German and French but a tongue of their own, Alsatian.

Since the Franco-Prussian war of 1870, all Alsace and part of Lorraine, the sister region, belonged to Germany until after the 1914/18 war, and again in 1940 Alsace became totally German (not just occupied); this meant the young men had to join the German army or suffer concentration camps.

The Vosges mountains in the west form a natural boundary with Lorraine.

The region is divided into two *départements*, **Bas-Rhin** and **Haut-Rhin**, the former, in the north, is on low lying land, the *préfecture* of Strasbourg, once a tiny island on the river Ill in 800 B.C. is now a vast city, housing part of the European parliament. Hops are grown in the neighbouring flat lands, and very good beer is produced both here and further north at Hochfelden. Don't miss a visit to the lovely little town of **Saverne** north-west of Strasbourg. Many locals prefer it to Strasbourg for shopping. The *pietons* (pedestrian precinct) leads down the centre of the town where the Mairie is flanked by two very old houses. At the foot of the town the Marne-au-Rhine canal runs past the Château-de-Rohan. Once owned by the well-known Rohan family, taken over by Napoleon III, the black railings still surmounted by large gilt 'N's. Now belonging to the State, you will find the Syndicat d'Initiatif up in one of the gatehouses. Closed from 12 to 2 p.m. but then everyone is having lunch outside the restaurants in the *pietons* where you can relax peacefully and enjoy a full meal or a light *tarte à l'oignon*. The town is twinned with Leominster and, for the homesick, a gift of a red British telephone box in working order sits outside the boulangerie/café.

The southern department of **Haut-Rhin** has the attractive city of Colmar as the county town. The great wealth of Alsace comes from the vineyards covering the eastern slopes of the Vosges. The Wine Route begins at Marlenheim in Bas-Rhin and extends south, running west of the main roads and railways, to Thann, south of Colmar. Extremely pretty little medieval villages, decked with flowers, line the

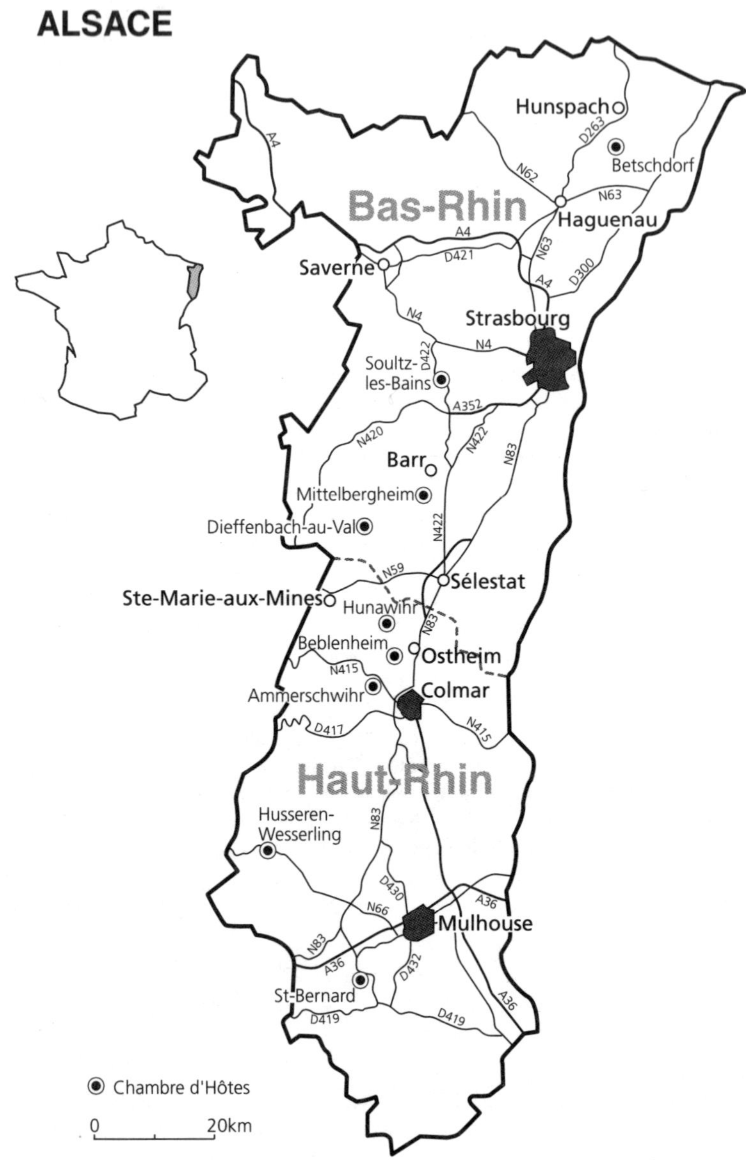
ALSACE
Bas-Rhin
Haut-Rhin
Hunspach
Betschdorf
Haguenau
Saverne
Strasbourg
Soultz-les-Bains
Barr
Mittelbergheim
Dieffenbach-au-Val
Sélestat
Ste-Marie-aux-Mines
Hunawihr
Beblenheim
Ostheim
Colmar
Ammerschwihr
Husseren-Wesserling
Mulhouse
St-Bernard
A4
D263
N62
N63
D421
D300
N4
D422
A352
N420
N422
N83
N59
N415
D417
D430
N66
A36
D432
D419
Chambre d'Hôtes
0
20km

route, and many happy days can be spent exploring them, and
ucts. Mostly white wines are produced, a choice of seven different va
after the grapes of their origin. A small amount of eau-de-vie and fruit lique
produced in the Dieffenbach valley.

Food-wise, Alsace is famous for copious dishes of *choucroute*, based on pork sausage and cabbage, and *baeckeoffe,* a stew of beef and lamb with potatoes, but the crowning glory is the *tarte flambé*, savoury or sweet and the *tarte à l'oignon* a close second. There are rich varieties of *charcuterie*, and of course the *kugelhopf*, a light yeast cake with a scattering of raisins and almonds, always baked in a fluted mould. The only cheese of note is Munster, common to both regions. The sheep producing the necessary milk graze on the high slopes of the Vosges.

The emblem of Alsace is the stork. To have one nesting on your roof is a sure sign of good luck. Many buildings have cart wheels fixed on their chimneys to encourage them to nest. Since they are now becoming scarce, parks have been set up to breed them, one notably at Kintzheim, where a little train will take you round.

Alsace is at its best in September and October during the *vendage*. The villages are a riot of colour from the hanging geraniums and the streets pleasantly alive with tourists, mostly Scandinavian, American and German; the British don't seem to have cottoned on to the fact that this is the best time of the year to visit. The Alsatians, though busy with the *vendage*, are very welcoming, unlike some parts of France where chambres d'hôtes close at grape picking time.

In Alsace hardly any chambres d'hôtes serve evening meals. However, a great many have a kitchen corner, or access to a larger shared kitchen.

BAS-RHIN

BETSCHDORF. 67660

44km NE of Strasbourg. From Haguenau N of Strasbourg take the D263 northwards; in 10km turn right to Betschdorf.

The village of Betschdorf has been noted for its pottery since the beginning of the 18th century. The grey pots with strong cobalt blue and highly glazed designs are widely known. There are many potters in the village; the trade has been handed down over the generations. The village, now three kilometres in length, has typical Alsatian houses on either side of the road all half timbered. Just a drive through the length of the village is quite a feast for the eyes. Stop off near the beginning of the main street at:

…oelle Krumeich (M)

…3.88.54.40.56. fax: (0)3.88.54.47.67.

… ell … gar- … lowers. … s back th… s of potters and … ly lessons in pot mak… very attractive accommodatio… Three rooms have been tastefully and interestingly furnished, two have a sunny west aspect where you can relax before going out to an evening meal in a local restaurant, the other has its own kitchenette. Breakfast is taken in the comfortable salon on the first floor, of course served on their own pottery. Your hosts are such natural and charming people that even if you arrive with no interest in pottery you will find yourself succumbing to their charm and having a go at 'throwing a pot'. Highly recommended in an area where there are few interesting chambres d'hôtes. Joelle speaks English, and credit cards are accepted. Rooms from 200f to 290f according to size and amenities. 30f extra for use of the kitchenette.

DIEFFENBACH-AU-VAL. 67220

48km SW of Strasbourg. 10km NW of Sélestat. A quiet village at the foot of the Vosges mountains in the Valley Kirsch where Eau-de-Vie and other liqueurs are distilled, west of the *Route-des-Vins*. Sélestat, nearby, badly damaged in the last war, is now rebuilt; it is a commercial town useful for banks, supermarkets and petrol. Dieffenbach is not the usual pretty flowery village of the *Route-des-Vins* but worth a detour because it has a very good chambres d'hôtes.

Take the road from Sélestat to Villé (D424), in 7km turn left (signposted Neubois) on to the D697 and it will lead you to Dieffenbach. The house is well signed off the main road, left up the Route de Neuve-Eglise.

M. & Mme Serge Geiger. "La Romance" (M)

17 Route de Neuve-Eglise. (0)3.88.85.67.09. fax: (0)3.88.57.61.58.

The quality and decor of the house is impressive, with marble floors and staircases. Madame is very artistic and has painted many of the paintings on the walls.

All the bedrooms, each with shower and bathroom, are thickly carpeted. On the ground floor 'Bluet' has two single beds, 'Lavende' overlooking the hills behind, has a double bed; on the first floor 'Rose' with its own little tower sitting room has a double bed and 'Pine', also double bedded, has a mezzanine suitable either for a sitting room or as an extra family bedroom.

The Geigers have a young family, so there are swings and a lawn for youthful guests. Altogether they provide really good value, considering the luxury they offer. Double rooms cost 300-350f.

Breakfast is served in the large marble-floored salon, but no evening meals. However in the village is *le Hühnerstall*, a restaurant they recommend as being 'correct', which usually means good food at reasonable prices (Closed: Mon).

MITTELBERGHEIM. 67140

20km SW of Strasbourg. A pretty little village, south of Barr, dominated by the wine house of Boekel. Turn right off the main road to:

M. & Mme Dolder (S)

4 rue Neuve. (0)3.88.08.96.08.

A large house approached by a wide drive. Over the rear garages are three chambres d'hôtes, off-putting from the outside, but inside quite different. The pleasant simple rooms have fresh green and white decor and pine furniture, are carpeted, centrally heated, and have excellent lighting. Large windows look south-west over vineyards to the tree-lined slopes of the Vosges mountains. Tables are set on the wide landing for breakfast, where there is a mini-kitchenette with fridge. Good parking below windows, and *dégustations* on the spot. Rooms 230f.

There is a choice of three restaurants in Mittelbergheim, or 1km north in Barr where *La Fleur d'Or* has local specialities at very reasonable prices and a jolly patron.

SOULTZ-LES-BAINS. 67120

20km SW of Strasbourg. This would be a very peaceful retreat from the bustle of a day in the city of Strasbourg. A visit is essential, however much you dislike cities.

The European parliament in modern buildings is on the outskirts.

For *centre ville* there is a good underground car park in the Place Gutenberg within easy walking distance of the cathedral, tourist office and museums, which are all in the same square. There are some very old houses here, like the Maison Kammerzell, now a restaurant, and also the oldest chemist in France.

The great crowd-puller is *'l'Horloge Astronomique'* in the cathedral; it chimes daily at 12:30 pm because the clock is half an hour slow. The body of the cathedral closes at 12 noon and admission to see the clock in action is by ticket only. Figures of the twelve disciples pass the Christ figure and bow, a cock crows three times at St. Peter's turn, various other things happen, but you need to be six foot tall or take your stilts along to get a good view - the small area of the cathedral by the clock is jam packed. They weren't joking in the tourist office at a quarter to twelve when they said "You had better hurry if you want to see the clock working", though only one minute away, the queues were extensive even then.

There are some lovely windows in the cathedral, a very interesting carved pulpit and a sculpture of the Mount of Olives. Somehow the noise of so many people talking was more like a cocktail party than a church, and the constant loud speaker reminders to 'watch your handbags and wallets' was most off putting (and this wasn't in August). A pity really - it is a lovely cathedral. It was here that Marie Leszczynska married Louis XV by proxy.

Walk down the side streets from Place Gutenberg to La Petite France where the small tributaries of the river criss-cross the tiny streets, and the medieval houses dip into the water. There are plenty of restaurants to choose from here in the prettiest part of Strasbourg.

It was the Mayor of Strasbourg who suggested to a young officer Rouget de Lisle that he should compose a rousing song for the army of the Rhine in 1792. The result was what is now the Marseillaise.

From the N4 at Marlenheim take the D422 south (SP Molsheim) and in 6km look for signs to the farmhouse on the right, quietly situated down a side road.

NEW **M. & Mme Schmitt. Ferme Biblenhof** (M)

(0)3.88.38.21.09. fax: (0)3.88.48.81.99.

Combined with an *auberge* this is one of the few chambres d'hôtes in Alsace which provides an evening meal.

The old farmhouse is lovely with larger and more gracious rooms than those across the courtyard above the *auberge* dining room. However, all ten are en suite and decorated with an attractive assortment of antique and modern furniture. Rooms 220/260f. Evening meal 70/100f, drinks not included.

In the high season this could be a little crowded but at other times I think it would be extremely good value. I didn't meet Mme when I visited, but Monsieur gave me the impression he cared about his guests, and certainly everyone I spoke to was very pleased with their rooms in the old farmhouse.

HAUT-RHIN

AMMERSCHWIHR. 68770

12km NW of Colmar. At the southern end of the *Route-des-Vins*, this prosperous wine village was almost destroyed in the German retreat of 1944 but luckily the old part survived to tell the tale. It has been tastefully rebuilt combining old and new. Many viticulteurs live here and offer upmarket *dégustations*. Just up the road is Kaysersburg, the birthplace of Albert Schweitzer, surprisingly not spoilt by the hordes of tourists intent on finding his house. Seek out the fortified bridge and many lovely old houses and shops where prices are reasonable. Colmar, the *Préfecture* of Haut-Rhin, is only a short distance away. A busy town with some fine buildings and open squares, good shopping facilities, some under cover, and best of all the adorable *Quai-de-Poissonerie* where the flower-bedecked bridges straddle the canal in the old town, very peaceful after the hubbub of the commercial centre. There are plenty of restaurants beside the water, where small punts are moored. It is possible to tour the town by a little train, but never between 12 and 2pm!

Return to Ammerschwihr and make for the old part of the town, where a stork nests on the stone gateway, and you will find the home of a *viticulteur* at:

M. & Mme Thomas (M)

41 Grande Rue. (0)3.89.78.23.90. fax: (0)3.89.47.18.90.

Elegant Mme Thomas is highly organised. She has studios, apartments or just plain rooms, for two, three or four people, well furnished but facing across the narrow street. Better to ask for a room on the first floor, which is lighter. If you feel like self catering, choose a studio complete with kitchen. *Boulangerie*, *épicerie* and restaurants can all be found in the village.

A new breakfast room has been added since my last visit, and even more studios. A sunny terrace and private parking are all welcome amenities. Rooms and studios vary from 245f to 275f.

BEBLENHEIM. 68980

13km N of Colmar. Looking for somewhere central to stay in the southerly part of the Route-des-Vins where the villages come up thick and fast sometimes only a mile apart, presented a problem. The larger towns had no exciting chambres d'hôtes and the prettier villages offered more frills than basic comfort. However busy little Beblenheim, totally absorbed in the *vendage* at the end of September, seemed just the place. It is central for visiting **Ribeauvillé**, a town situated at the foot of the Vosges mountains. Delightful nooks and crannies lead off the main pedestrian precinct in the centre. Shops and pleasant restaurants line the street. From the 13th-century *Tour-des-Bouchers* near the *mairie*, there is a good view of the three castles, one a ruin, ancient homes of the Ribeaupierre family, whose Counts once owned vast lands around here. The town is noted for its festival of strolling players at the end of August. Lots of pottery and Alsatian wine glasses selling at reasonable prices; the shops often stay open from 12 noon to 2pm. The parking is excellent, under shady trees at the entrance to the town.

Much fighting went on here in the German retreat of 1944. Ostheim nearby, an old town, was totally destroyed at that time; just one remaining wall in the village square has a stork's nest on top of it. The town has been rebuilt in modern style, losing all its character.

Up the road is Riquewihr known as the 'pearl' of the wine route. Certainly there are many very old and colourful houses in blue, red, mustard and green, all timber-framed. The main street leading down from the gate tower, where there is a museum, is heavily cobbled and thronged with tourists. Although this is a wine village there is not much evidence of the *vendage* in *centre ville* - too busy with the tourist trade - prices are high in the shops. There are numerous restaurants here and plenty of *dégustations*. It will cost you 10f to park outside the walls of the village.

In September in Beblenheim you will be dodging trucks of grapes as you wander through the flower-filled streets (but the village is not inundated with tourists). The wine here has a good reputation. Turn right by the fountain into the rue Jean Macé and the rue de Raisins, a cul-de-sac, is immediately on your right.

M. Klein. "Gambrinos" (M)

4 rue des Raisins. (0)3.89.49.02.82. fax: (0)3.89.49.05.41.

Hidden behind large gates, this 16th-century house has a cosy courtyard. An old wood staircase leads to rooms on the first and second floors, comfortably furnished. Enjoy the window boxes and fresh flowers in your room. An extra bedside lamp was brought at once on request. 290f b&b. There are now two very pleasant new apartments on the second floor, two adjoining rooms, double and two singles, sharing a bathroom and kitchen corner with a washer/drier. 270f for two without breakfast, 350f for four, seems a good option to me, let on a daily basis, with a *boulangerie* and an *épicerie* close by.

Well-worn stone steps (for residents, the public have another door) lead to a

Winstub (wine cellar) an added bonus, where from 6pm *tartes flambés*, cooked in a wood oven, served on a wooden platter and eaten with fingers, are quite the best I have tasted. Cheerful Jean-Jean, Jack of all Trades, does everything. The elusive owner M. Klein, an antique dealer, was not so elusive on my last visit. Young and dynamic, he keeps his eye on this very popular chambres d'hôtes. A hearty breakfast is served by a *femme de menage*.

Parking is outside the gates in the small cul-de-sac.

HUNAWIHR. 68150

14km N of Colmar. This is a small unspoilt village bedecked with flowers, on the Route-de-Vin. Where the small church still has its surrounding fortified walls commanding a view of the whole valley. (The church is used by Protestants and Catholics alike.)

NEW **M. & Mme Seiler** (M)

3, rue du Nord. (0)3.89.73.70.19.

This large house in the centre of the village has a spacious courtyard car park overlooked by a disused *chai*. There are five rooms in a separate building, three on the ground floor with kitchenettes have tiled floors - 310f; two above are warmly carpeted and cost 250f for two. Some rooms overlook the village road, but all have showers and loos.

Monsieur Seiler is German and speaks English so there are no language problems here. No evening meals, but plenty of interesting restaurants in the vicinity.

HUSSEREN-WESSERLING. 68470

34km NW of Mulhouse. 41km SW of Colmar. Take the N66 from Mulhouse to Epinal and in 29km turn left at Ranspach to the village. The house is on your left on the road to Mollau, at the foot of the Vosges mountains.

Mme Herrgott (S)

4 rue du Gare. (0)3.89.38.79.69.

In this long 18th-century house on the roadside are four guest rooms; all have a kitchenette, most have an extra bed, complete with luxurious feather duvets that are favoured in this area. The three rear rooms overlook the lovely garden now boasting a superb swimming pool; heated and covered, it is in use year round. Nice Mme Herrgott serves generous breakfasts of just about everything you could wish for - three kinds of bread, orange juice, cereals, cheese. Altogether a recommended stay. Parking just off the road by the two garages, one for guests. Rooms 280f for one night, 250f a night for longer visits.

SAINT BERNARD. 68720

53km S of Colmar. 13km SW of Mulhouse. Within easy reach of Colmar. Dual carriageway on the N83 south to the junction with the D466, then in 9km at Spechbach-le-Haut turn right. Signed in the village by the restaurant "Cheval Blanc" in the rue Principale.

Mme Bairet (S)

13 rue de l'Eglise. (0)3.89.25.44.71.

A very warm welcome here from accommodating hosts who have built guest rooms over their tobacco drying sheds. Their pleasant house is in a quiet road not far from the church. Of the four simple rooms, only one is en suite, with a private fridge; others share facilities and a fridge on the landing.

Quiet and friendly, in an area where the choice of chambres d'hôtes is limited. Rooms 190/210f for two. 10% discount for four nights.

LORRAINE

Départements: **Meurthe-et-Moselle**
Meuse
Moselle
Vosges

Often Alsace and Lorraine are clubbed together, presumably because they are both in the north-east corner of France, and the area round Metz was part of Alsace after the Franco-Prussian war.

Geographically and culturally they are very different. The natural border of the wooded Vosges mountains stretches from Franche Comté in the south tailing off into the Parc Régional des Vosges du Nord at the German border in the north. 1,000 small glacial lakes are hidden in the folds of these mountains, the highest peak being 1,424 metres. These peaks are rounded and treeless, aptly called *Ballons*. Skiing here in winter and sheep graze in summer, producing milk for the Munster cheese.

Lying on the western side of the **Vosges**, Lorraine has four departments. Mountainous Vosges in the south, where Epinal is the *préfecture*, a town I found unexpectedly pleasant, spanning both banks of the river Moselle. **Moselle** in the north bordering Bas-Rhin, Germany and Luxembourg, where Metz with its beautiful gothic cathedral is the county town, is more industrial. Further south **Meurthe-et-Moselle,** stretching a finger north to the Belgian border, has Nancy, the capital of all Lorraine, as its *préfecture*. Never miss an opportunity to visit the beautiful Place Stanislas in the centre of the old town (see Maizières, p.14). Lastly (or perhaps first if arriving from U.K.) **Meuse,** the most westerly department, borders on the Ardennes and Belgium. Unremarkable Bar-le-Duc is the main town, but further north is much fought over Verdun, and close by the *Ossuaire* (War Memorial) overlooking the surrounding countryside where many bloody battles took place in the 1914-1918 war.

The cultural difference between the two regions is striking, especially when flitting from one to the other over *Cols* or through the one tunnel in the Vosges. Whereas Alsace has the affluent busy attitude of a Germanic society, Lorraine is totally French, resolutely laid back, and only in the north-east is German spoken.

Small farms with livestock and fruit fields, cover the land. The tasty little mirabelle plum is a great favourite, made into pies, jams, liqueurs etc - almost a

LORRAINE

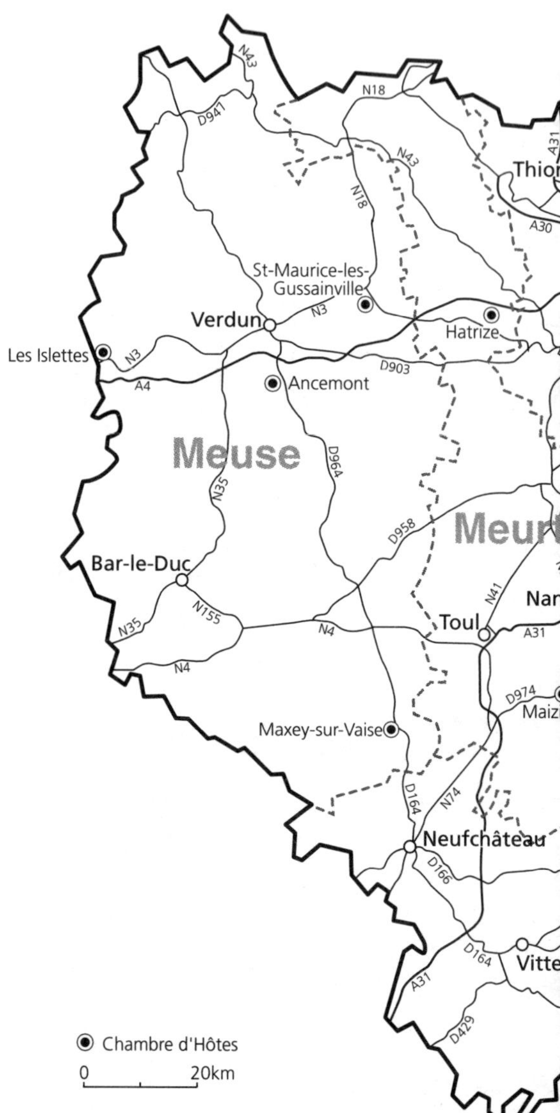
N43
D947
N18
N43
N18
A31
Thion
A30
St-Maurice-les-
Gussainville
Verdun
N3
Hatrize
Les Islettes
N3
D903
A4
Ancemont
Meuse
D964
N35
Meurt
D958
Bar-le-Duc
N41
Nan
N155
Toul
N35
N4
A31
N4
D974
Maizi
Maxey-sur-Vaise
D164
N74
Neufchâteau
D166
D164
Vitte
A31
D429
Chambre d'Hôtes
0
20km

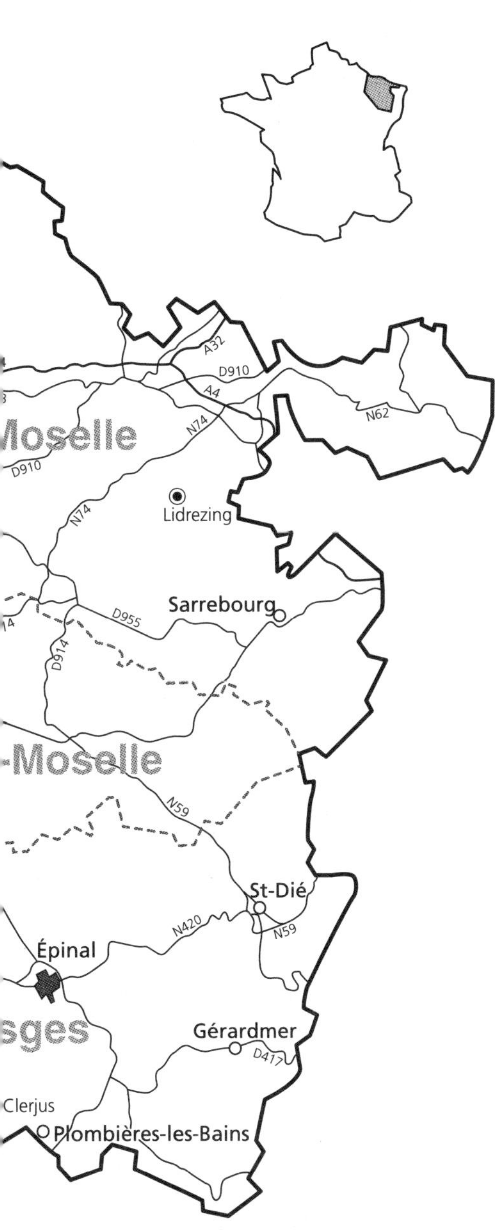
A32
D910
A4
N62
N74
Moselle
D910
Lidrezing
N74
Sarrebourg
D955
D914
-Moselle
N59
St-Dié
N420
N59
Épinal
sges
Gérardmer
D417
Clerjus
Plombières-les-Bains

rival speciality to the famous Quiche Lorraine. Some light industry near towns supplies work, as do towns like Vittel, where you can visit the spas and taste the water.

Roman remains of an amphitheatre at Grand, in western Vosges, are being excavated. The region was a Duchy until the death of Stanislas when, under the marriage agreement between his daughter and Louis XV, it reverted back to France.

Joan of Arc was born here, Louis XVI and Marie Antoinette were caught in Lorraine trying to flee the guillotine. History is kept well alive in the various villages.

MEURTHE-ET-MOSELLE

HATRIZE. 54800

25km NW of Metz. In the northern part of the department, a village with easy access to the A4 has an isolated up-market chambres d'hôtes on the N103 just north of the village.

M. & Mme Arizzi. La Trembloisière (M)

Route de Briey. (0)3.82.33.14.30. fax: (0)3.82.20.15.55.

When the Arizzis were on the point of retiring they visited their first chambres d'hôtes in Brittany and were so impressed they decided to keep their large, well-furnished family home in two hectares of enclosed land, and take in guests. Expansive double-glazed windows overlooking the countryside and the A4 allow you to watch the traffic glide silently by. A very handy stop, where you will be made most welcome. Three rooms, a choice of double or single beds for 270f. Parking in the garden behind locked gates. Sadly no longer offering evening meals, but there are 15 restaurants within 5km, Madame assures me.

MAIZIERES. 54550

13km SSW of Nancy. A perfect place to stay for visiting Nancy, the capital of Lorraine and *préfecture* of Meurthe-et-Moselle. Though 1000 years old, the city really prospered under the rule of Stanislas Leszczynski, the ex-king of Poland who was given the Dukedom of Lorraine by Louis XV when the king married his daughter, Maria. The previous Duke, François III, had left Nancy to become Holy Roman Emperor after his marriage to Maria-Theresa in 1736.

Stanislas set about making Nancy one of the loveliest cities in France. To this day the Place Stanislas is superb. Beautiful wrought-iron gates, railings, balconies and fountains surround the square, painted in black and gold. Floodlit at night it is like fairyland. An *Arc de Triomphe* leads from the square to the Place de la Carrière and the Ducal Palace, now a museum. The rue Maréchaux close by, where Victor Hugo's father was born, has many small restaurants with reasonable prices, but on a first visit you won't be able to resist a table outside one of the larger restaurants facing the square. The Hôtel-de-Ville, the Théatre and the Grand Hotel all magnificently overlook the Stanislas statue in the centre. On the other side of the town is the Church of Notre-Dame-de-Bon-Sécours. Stanislas and his wife are buried here. The church is almost entirely of marble, floors, walls, statues and altars. Wisely Louis XV insisted that the Dukedom went back to France at Stanislas' death.

A day in Nancy will be complemented by a stay in the lovely home at Maizières of:

➤ M. & Mme Cotel (M)

69 rue Carnot. (0)3.83.52.75.57.

Easy to find, on the right-hand side of the road coming from Nancy. Large gates lead into the long courtyard of this large, terraced house, once the bishop of Toul's palace.

The three rooms are delightfully furnished; overlooking the quiet green garden behind ensures tranquillity. A family room has a charming extra alcove bed. Comfortable armchairs and thick carpets, modern shower rooms, matching drapes and pretty flowered wallpaper complete the picture. Evening meals in front of a log fire are imaginative and beautifully served, while an enormous portrait of M. Cotel's great-great-uncle in Napoleonic uniform watches your every mouthful. Your farmer hosts will give you all information of the area, where to park in Nancy and easiest ways of getting there, etc.

Evening meals, if reserved, 70f. Wine not *compris*, but not thrust upon you.

Rooms 200/220f. This really is a charming place; you will want to stay many nights. Arrowed for good value.

MEUSE

ANCEMONT. 55320

10km S of Verdun. Visit the cathedral which was badly damaged in the First World War; but fared better in 1939-45. It has a canopied High Altar, held up by four gigantic barley sugar marble pillars and some very good stained-glass windows, particularly the rose window above the organ.

North of Verdun is the largest beer museum in Europe, at Stenay on the river Meuse. The Meuse rises near Domremy-la-Pucelle and flows north to Verdun and eventually over the border to Belgium, heading for the North Sea at the Rhine delta - a restful narrow river, sometimes flowing along canals with small boats cruising peacefully and tying up at villages en route.

From Verdun follow the D34 south along the Meuse, turn right in the centre of Ancemont and the château is on the left.

M. & Mme Eichenauer. Château-de-Labassière (L)
(0)3.29.85.70.21. fax: (0)3.29.87.61.60.

A very impressive château, with plenty of space for parking in the forecourt, and a covered garage. The pleasant garden at the side now has an inviting swimming pool. Over the years the village seems to have encroached on the lovely building, but inside the château has maintained its former glory and the large rooms are very pleasant, one on the ground floor richly furnished with a luxury bathroom, others on the first floor include a suite for six. M. Eichenauer, who speaks perfect English, prefers guests on demi-pension basis, and does a special rate of 300/325f, per person, all drinks and wine *compris*. Reduced rates for children. Good value for all the amenities. A very pleasant place to stay if you want that little extra atmosphere of days gone by.

LES ISLETTES. 55120

27km W of Verdun. 55km N of Bar-le-Duc.19km north of this village is Varennes-en-Argônne, the town where Louis XVI and Marie Antoinette were caught trying to flee the country. They had to pass through a small archway over the road, it was here, M. Drouet, a good revolutionary, drummed up support to stop the coach as he felt sure it was the king's. It was near midnight on 20th June 1791 and they held them in the village, while they investigated. Two years later a memorial tower was built on the spot, but in the First World War the whole village was destroyed. The tower has been rebuilt, but no archway over the road. A pleasant village with a large American memorial to the 1914-18 war and a small museum where the arrest is depicted exactly as it happened.

From Bar-le-Duc take the N35 north, the *Voie Sacré*, so called because it was the road by which all the reinforcements and supplies were taken up to Verdun in the First World War. Branch off at Erize-la-Petite on the D998, and head for Clermont-en-Argônne and Les Islettes is on the N3, just on the border with Ardennes. On the right at Les Vignettes the next hamlet, you will find:

M. & Mme Christiaens. Villa les Roses (M)

Les Vignettes. (0)3.26.60.81.91. fax: (0)3.26.60.23.09

Two houses, one 18th-century the other 16th-century, furnished in keeping with the age of the house, stand in a large park. In the main house Madame has four rooms, the good news they are now all with private facilities. In the older house is one family room with kitchen and bathroom, and another for two on the ground floor 250/270f. Everything for the baby supplied. A very comfortable lounge for guests.

No evening meals generally, but Madame is a very congenial and relaxed person who will give you a meal if you are stranded. Restaurants nearby. Breakfasts more than adequate - ham, cheese plus ample jams and home-made bread. Spacious parking, guarded by two Alsatian dogs. All credit cards accepted.

MAXEY-SUR-VAISE. 55140

60km SE of Bar-le-Duc. 10km N of Domremy-la-Pucelle. The nearest chambres d'hôtes to Joan of Arc's birthplace at Domremy-la-Pucelle. The house with flagstone floors stands empty beside the church where she was christened and took her first communion. Next door is a small museum, mostly of old manuscripts (6f entry). On the hill above, a Basilica has been built in her memory on the spot where she first heard the voices of Saint Cathérine and Saint Marguerite telling her to fight for France.

The peaceful Lorraine village of Maxey is quite charming, embellished by the small River Vaise being channelled into a canal dividing the wide street, a shallow stretch of water teeming with trout. It is the trout maternity home of the region, fishing absolutely forbidden! The people are very honest, occasionally feeding the fish. A fascinating place to spend an hour peacefully gazing into the water, a mother duck and her chicks thought so too.

Mme Cardot (S)

La Grande Rue. Vaucouleurs. (0)3.29.90.85.19. fax: (0)3.29.90.82.88.

Young Madame has a very large house overlooking the river, and has turned the granary into two simple rustic rooms, each en suite, for three or four. A salon with kitchen facilities for light meals has the original sink and an ancient *petrin*, a wooden bread-making trough used on the farms in years gone by. Rooms 230f, for two, 280f for three, reduced to 200f for a three-day visit. No evening meals; unfortunately there is no restaurant or café in the village, but there is an *épicerie* making self-catering an option; swimming pool for guests, ready for 1998.

SAINT-MAURICE-LES-GUSSAINVILLE. 55400

23km E of Verdun. For visiting the battlefields of the First World War, this would be one of my first choices. The most interesting areas are round Douaumont which lies off the D913 east of Bras-sur-Meuse. The *Tranchée des Baïonnettes* is a reconstructed trench which forms the graveyard of the men of the French 137th Regiment who were killed here in June 1916. The *Ossuaire-de-Douaumont* is a magnificent memorial to the 130,000 French and German soldiers killed on the battlefields of Verdun in the Great War, whose bodies were never identified. On the first floor is a chapel and two galleries, each 140 metres long, containing 36 sarcophagi. The walls are covered with memorial tablets dedicated to individuals and regiments. In the chapel there are two tombs, that of Monsignor Charles Ginisluy, Bishop of Verdun, and Ferdinand Noël, chaplain to the Ossuaire who ministered to the bereaved. Mass is celebrated daily at 9 a.m. (10.30 on Sundays). The Ossuaire is dominated by the 46 metre high '*Tour des Morts*', and in front is the National Cemetery with the graves of 15,000 French soldiers marked by simple wooden crosses and red rose bushes. On the ground floor is the usual shop and a cinema with an audio-visual presentation of the battles. Shows last about twenty minutes and are given in French, English and German.

At **Fort-de-Vaux** (5km north-east) are the remains of an outpost defended to the last by 250 French soldiers under the command of Commandant Reynal, against ferocious gas attacks by the Germans from 1st June 1916 until their surrender seven days later. It was from here that Reynal sent an appeal for help, by carrier pigeon, his only method of communication. Despite the hazards of gas and smoke, the pigeon got through on 4th June, dying on arrival at French H.Q. The fort was retaken by the French in November 1916. To this day there exists a society which commemorates this brave pigeon.

The pleasant drive along the N3 to Etain gives you time to reflect and brings you back to the world of today.

This chambres d'hôtes is signed at Etain or can be reached by the autoroute A4 exit Frensne-en-Woëvre, then the D908 north to Etain and the house is 7km on the right.

M. & Mme Valentin. Le Ferme des Vales (S)

(0)3.29.87.12.91. fax: (0)3.29.87.18.59.

This modernised barn didn't look too promising beside a busy road, but on inspection, it proved to be a charming house with a huge salon and log fire burning merrily in September. The rooms are on each corner of the first floor, reached by a galleried balcony, overlooking the salon. Sunny and light, with double glazed windows, they are furnished with great taste in different colours. One could be a bridal suite, with white lace *ciel-au-lit*. Monsieur, an ex Air Force pilot, has rebuilt the barn himself, keeping all the old character but installing modern conveniences. Evening meals *en famille* with local produce from the farm opposite are 120f, including wine and coffee. Parking at the back of the house. Good value here, and a swimming pool being constructed on my last visit.

Rooms 240f for two, extra bed 50f.

MOSELLE

LIDREZING. 57340

56km ESE of Metz. 46km NE of Nancy. This low lying area of the Moselle is very peaceful, with small isolated farms and hamlets almost surrounded by water. Take the D999 from Metz to Morhange, continue to Conthil and turn left on to the D79 and then the D79c.

M. & Mme Mathis La Musardière (M)

Morhange. (0)3.87.86.14.05. fax: (0)3.87.86.40.16.

A very warm welcome and family atmosphere awaits you in this charming little farmhouse, whose three guest rooms offer every comfort. All are decorated artistically, one even has a jacuzzi bath, another has independent ground-floor access. In the peaceful garden are thirty aromatic plants, herbs and organic vegetables. Evening meals of regional dishes or vegetarian taken together add to the enjoyment of your stay. 110/150f, excluding wine, on reservation. A popular place. You need to book well ahead. A chambres d'hôtes well worth a detour.

Rooms 310f.

VOSGES

LE CLERJUS. 88240

16km. N of Saint-Loup-sur-Sémouse. 16km. W of Plombières. A quick drive through the spa town of Plombières a few years ago did nothing to attract me; but reading how Josephine (wife of Napoleon Bonaparte) used to visit it regularly to take the waters, I decided to give it another try. It proved well worth a visit. Situated in a deep valley between wooded hillsides it is a compact little town with many reasonable restaurants and attractive pavement tables. The original Stanislas Bains is opposite the house Josephine stayed in, 4 rue Stanislas. Look for the plaque on the wall. The waters are now taken in a more modern building further down the street.

You can't miss the angelus echoing from the tall church spire; inside are many brilliant stained glass windows. The church was rebuilt in 1863, dedicated to the Virgin Mary, who has protected the town through two world wars. Not a house was damaged in either, so all the old balconied buildings still exist. I think the *Vierge-Marie's* good-will must extend to the surrounding hamlets as it was near Le Clerjus that I discovered this chambres d'hôtes.

From the main Chaumont to Luxeuil-les-Bains road, the D417, turn north on to the D64 (SP Le Clerjus), at Le Clerjus keep on the D12, bearing left then right to the little hamlet of Sous-les-Bois, signed down the hill to the second house on the left.

NEW ➤ **Mme Nazon** (S)

3 Le Buisson, Sous-les-Bois. (0)3.29.30.15.07.

Idyllically situated on a hillside, this beautifully renovated farmhouse has much style and interest, plus a swimming pool boasting 24°c in June. A large salon/dining room with stone walls and heavy beams, furnished with many interesting old pictures, was once the granary.

On the first floor are two guest rooms with independent entry from a raised part of the garden. One small double has a shower and loo and a large sunny window overlooking the garden. The other room, for three, stretches across the house; divided by a curtain it has small floor windows at one end but light from an interior window comes in at the other. Luxurious shower, and wash basins and loo are hidden in different alcoves, not only carpeted but the accommodation has thick mats as well. Lots of lovely extras, boxes of tissues, hair dryers etc. 240f for two.

Lively Mme Nazon cooks a superb evening meal, beautifully served and a copious breakfast is served on red and white tablecloths. Nothing forgotten here, from the welcome drink to the sad farewell wave. Parking under your window.

Evening meal 80f wine *compris*, less for children. A definite arrow.

AQUITAINE

Départements: **Dordogne**
Gironde
Les Landes
Lot-et-Garonne
Pyrénées-Atlantiques

From Bordeaux on the Atlantic coast to the Pyrénées on the Spanish border lies the region of Aquitaine, stretching inland to Gascony in the east and the Dordogne in the north. Romans and Visigoths have occupied it at some time, but it became part of the Frankish Empire in the 8th-century and eventually a Duchy, owing allegiance to the Kings of France.

The leading light in this area is undoubtedly Eleanor of Aquitaine. She inherited the whole Duchy in the early part of the XII century. At that time the Duchy extended as far north and east as Périgord, Limousin and Poitou. Such an inheritance meant that she was courted by many. She eventually married Louis VII of France and had two daughters by him. However her light hearted manner and conduct did not endear her to the French court and Louis was persuaded to divorce her in 1152. Her dowry, the Duchy, was returned to her and she promptly married an old boy friend, Henry Plantagenet of Anjou, who became king of England (Henry II) two years later. The Duchy renounced its allegiance to the French and together Eleanor and Henry ruled the whole of England and Wales and all of Western France. They made their home at Poitiers and rarely visited the British Isles. When Henry died in 1189 his son Richard (the Lionheart) succeeded, and he too spent only a few months of his reign in our country.

The English control of Aquitaine was fairly weak, which led them to follow the example of their Languedoc neighbours in building fortified towns called *bastides*, whose inhabitants were granted several privileges to ensure their loyalty.

The French were not happy with this state of affairs, especially when Edward III claimed the French throne on the death of Charles IV in 1328. This led to the Hundred Years War and the English were finally defeated at Castillon-la-Bataille in 1453.

The five departments of Aquitaine are:

The Gironde in the west, with the large port of Bordeaux, is famous for its production of wine. The vineyards are situated in many areas and produce different types of wine, determined by the soil and vines. Despite their differences they are all known as Bordeaux, whether red or white. The reds are often called claret by the British.

Les Landes, once a long sandy coastal strip stretching from Arcachon to Bayonne with a marshy hinterland, has now been rescued from the encroaching Atlantic sand by draining the land and planting huge forests of pine trees. The coast from Biscarrosse Plage to Bayonne is 200km of sandy beach, backed by dunes and pines. The Dune de Pilat in the north is the most notable.

In the south the **Pyrénées-Atlantiques** is sub-divided into Béarn and Pays Basque, bordering Spain. The Spanish influence is strong here; all town names are in French and Basque. The old coastal resorts so loved by the Victorians grace the coast - Biarritz, St. Jean-de-Luz and Bayonne, which is on the estuary of the river Adour. The Pyrénées and the foothills to the north had been left very much to their own devices when France regained Aquitaine. Valleys run towards Spain climbing abruptly up into the mountains. The weather is mild here even in winter.

Pau, the high town in the Béarnais area, is the *préfecture* of the department. An area ruled over by the d'Albret family, ancestors of Henri IV.

The other departments of Aquitaine lie inland.

To the north the **Dordogne,** so well beloved by the British tourist, is dominated by the river Dordogne running through its very pretty undulating country. Périgueux in the centre, with its many-towered cathedral and modern squares, is the administrative town. There are still Roman remains around the old town.

The ancient name Périgord dominates the whole department, dividing it into four sections, Périgord Vert, Blanc, Noir and Pourpre. Besides the river the main attractions are the prehistoric caves and archaeological sites, near Montignac and Les Eyzies.

Last but not least is the department of **Lot et Garonne**, south of the river Dordogne, also a large vine growing area. Some of the best *bastides* can be found here. Agen in the south is the *préfecture*, a busy, uninspiring city. The western area is mostly flat with pine forests - a continuation of Les Landes.

I am told Lot et Garonne is one of the few departments where people have the right to be buried in their home ground!

DORDOGNE

LE BUISSON. 24480

29km W of Sarlat. 10km S of Le Bugue. Often linked with Cadouin just up the road, where there are remnants of the Holy Shroud in the Abbey. For years this brought great wealth to the Abbey, but modern science has cast doubts on its authenticity. The Abbey is open mornings and afternoons from Feb. to Dec. Le

AQUITAINE

Gironde
Landes
Pyrénées
Atlantiques
Bordeaux
Castelnau-
de-Médoc
Lapouyade
Arcachon
Mimizan
Mont-de-Marsan
Magescq
St-Lon-les-Mines
Ondres
Biarritz
Sare
Itxassou
Bidarray
St-Jean-Pied-
de-Port
Montory
Lay-Lamidou
Oloron-
ste-Marie
Pau
Boeil-
Bezing
N215
N137
A10
N10
D1
N89
A63
N113
A66
N250
A62
D932
N134
N124
D924
D933
D934
N117
A64
D93

Champagnac-de-Belair
D939
N21
Cherval
Verteillac
Périgueux
Dordogne
N89
N89
N21
Proissans
Paunat
Trémolat
Bergerac
Sarlat-la-Canéda
D933
Monbazillac
Le Buisson-de-Cadouin
Domme (Nabirat)
Baleyssagues
segur
Douzains
Cancon
Marmande
Lot-et-Garonne
Villeneuve-sur-Lot
Agen
A62
N113

Chambre d'Hôtes

20km

Buisson lies along the Dordogne just before it is joined by the river Vézère.

Leaving it rather late to book a room at 5 p.m, we looked for the Office de Tourisme and found it closed. On advice from the *boulangerie* we landed up in a little dress shop where two charming ladies joined in the search by ringing round likely chambres d'hôtes. After the first choice was complet, we were delighted to find a room at La Coste, a tiny hamlet outside Le Buisson with the promise of an evening meal. The ladies duly directed us to take the D25, direction Cadouin, turn left just as we left the town, where there was a double signpost to La Coste, go straight up the hill past a left turn to La Coste and we would find La Feuillantine on the left.

➤ **La Feuillantine** (M)

M. & Mme Donval. La Coste. (0)5.53.23.95.37.

A very smart newly-built Périgord house with vast views over the countryside. Three well-furnished ground-floor rooms with every comfort have patio access through double-glazed doors.

We shared dinner with two other guests. Monsieur and Madame both beavering away in the kitchen producing a really fabulous meal. Soup, *mousse de saumon*, *brochettes-de-boeuf* with *pommes noisettes*, cheese, and ice cream *chantilly* with meringue. Bergerac wine was not *compris* but shared with other guests. This was one of the best meals I have ever had in a chambres d'hôtes, and beautifully served. M. Donval, bought up in a *patisserie*, is a very keen chef and takes great delight in producing good food. He and his wife joined us over coffee.

Rooms 260f. Evening meal 100f. Good value both for quality of room, food and *accueil.*

Another option in the area:

4km out of Le Buisson on the D29 to Lalinde turn left to the tiny hamlet of Gavernat and the farm is on the right.

NEW M. & Mme Lambin. La Ferme de l'Embellie (M)

Hameau de Gavernat. (0)5.53.22.95.43.

This pretty little Périgord farmhouse with a flowery garden is easy to find. Rooms are in a separate adjacent building. Pick your own grapes from the picturesque overhanging vine. Rooms for two or three and a family suite, all with tiled floors but efficient electric heating. The salon/dining room is in the main house, where you can watch Madame preparing the evening meal, which is the *pièce-de-résistance*

here. The menu is displayed on the long table, with a list of guest's names. Madame, an accomplished hostess, introduces you to fellow-guests over the *apéritif* and you sit down to five or six courses for 90f. Apéritif and coffee *compris*, but wine and bottled water charged for, about 30f a head.

Madame lights up a surreptitious cigarette towards the end of the meal. Anti-smoking brigade beware, smokers rejoice!

This place is popular with all nationalities, so book well ahead.

Rooms 270f. Demi-pension 225f each. A *taxe de séjour* is now imposed by the *mairie* of 5f per person, from15/5 to 15/9.

CHAMPAGNAC-DE-BELAIR. 24530

3.5km NE of Brantôme. 25km N of Périgueux. Great limestone rocks overhang the approach road to nearby Brantôme, now benefiting from the new bypass. Almost an island, on a loop of the river Dronne, its a serene little town, full of history. An excellent tourist office supplies information on the old Abbaye and other lovely buildings. Stroll round in the evening and choose one of the many restaurants on the river bank. Nearby St. Jean-de-Côle is also well worth a visit. In fact for an interesting holiday, both geographically and historically, the area in this part of the Périgord takes some beating, and a stay at this château would perfect it.

Follow signs left as you enter Champagnac-de-Belair from Brantôme on the D83. Just outside the little village is:

NEW M. & Mme Duseau. Château de Laborie-Saulnier (L)

(0)5.53.54.22.99. fax: (0)5.53.08.53.78. Open all year, by reservation only from November to April.

An imposing château built originally in the 14th-century, and owned by the present family for 20 years. Past history is vague but the owners will delve into it with you. There is a possibility that the second wife of John Lackland may have lived here; certainly it was owned by the Marquis de Taillefer in 1873.

The château walls enclose a small courtyard dominated by the dungeon tower. A dual flight of steps leads to the front door. In the large entrance hall your eyes light on an English high pram containing a toy phantom - "The château ghost", laughs Madame Duseau.

A tour through the vast rooms, where moquette lines some walls and an original Napoleon III carpet covers most of the floor, leads through the salon to a most attractive dining room where large and small tables are draped with long blue cloths and breakfast croissants are served on a gold and silver platter. The most striking thing about this château is the warmth of these vast rooms. Madame Duseau makes sure her efficient central heating is switched on, even in the autumn and spring. I don't think I have ever found such a large château kept so comfortably warm.

Three high-ceilinged bedrooms on the ground floor overlook the park.

The blue room, boasting a genuine Napoleon III bed-head, can be combined with an adjacent room to form a suite. Choose it if you prefer a shower - the yellow and blue rooms have baths, the latter bright blue on claw feet - 450f. Upstairs two slightly smaller turquoise and grey rooms, also en suite, 350f.

Evening meals are served rarely and only on reservation; the cost is 200f and wine is extra, but foie gras is on the menu.

With a pleasant modern swimming pool in the grounds, this represents good château value, especially combined with the warm family atmosphere.

CHERVAL. 24320

40km S of Angoulême, 18km N of Riberac. From the D 708 17km N of Riberac. Les Pouyades is signed.

NEW M. & Mme Truffeaux. Les Pouyades (M)

(0)5.53.91.02.96.

A drive of oaks and chestnuts leads to an elegant, towered 19th-century *maison-de-maître* on a cereal farm, standing in two hectares of parkland.

The square entrance hall extends right across the house, dining room on one side and on the other a small salon leading to a comfortable lounge, all shared with the family.

Upstairs one room stretches across the house; double aspect windows, warm carpets, a double bed and a large gleaming white bathroom, bath and bidet - it's all there for 400f for two. The second, smaller room has a charming red check *ciel-de-lit* and a shower room. 300f. Both worthy of the price. No evening meal, restaurants in Vertaillac 7km away.

DOMME. 24250

8km south of Sarlat. Domme is an absolute must when visiting the Dordogne - a most attractive *bastide* built on a rocky crag during the Hundred Years War to keep the English out. They may have succeeded then, but not to-day. In summer there are more British cars here than French. Approach from Vitrac and enter by the Porte des Tours, the best preserved of the three old gates, where prisoners were once kept in the tower. Their graffiti is still on the interior walls. Follow the signs to large car parks on the Belvédère de la Barre *(payant)*. A new viewing platform on the terrace gives a panoramic view of the valley below, where the river Dordogne flows towards Beynac. Wander round the many little streets with pretty limestone houses bedecked with flowers. Finish up in the Place de la Halle, beside the covered market. Built in the 17th century, it has a wooden balcony and deep caves underneath where the people hid in times of trouble. Shops, restaurants, cafés to suit all tastes. Sit outside and watch the world go by; if possible avoid July and August when it does!

For a recommended chambres d'hôtes take the D50 east from Domme to Groléjac; at the lake, turn right SP Liaubou-Bas and in 3.5kms Le Jaonnet is in the hamlet on the left. Alternatively from Sarlat in the north take the D704 to Groléjac and turn right at the lake, then first left, following signs to Le Jaonnet.

NEW **➤ Mr. & Mrs. Holleis. Le Jaonnet** (M)
Liaubou-Bas. Nabirat. Tel & fax: (0)5.53.29.59.29.

Le Jaonnet, called after a Guernsey Bay, is a 200-year-old converted farmhouse, an unexpected find hidden away in a well maintained hamlet of sandstone houses. The Holleis give a warm welcome to all their guests.

The galleried salon has a striking stone fireplace with carved figures. The piano here is often played by guests and many a musical evening develops. The dining table has hosted many a party, as Konrad, an Austrian-trained chef, has worked and taught in Guernsey for many years, so you will be sure of a sumptuous meal. He and his wife Elizabeth speak French and English - no language problems here.

In a wing of the house two comfortable attractive double rooms, 'Saints' and

'Moulin Huet', share a shower and wc; in the others the facilities are adjoining. 'Icart' sleeps three people, as does 'Fermain', with a private terrace, and 'Portelet' is a suite for four, approached from the courtyard. Prices vary from 250-350f; 60f for extra beds.

Evening meals are 95f, all drinks *compris*, with special rates for small children.

Even better demi-pension rates - 200f each. Evening meals are not obligatory, but I am sure you will find no better value meal in the Dordogne. In the high season a two nights stay is no hardship and you will probably wish you had booked a week.

MONBAZILLAC. 24240

7km S of Bergerac.This small village on a hill has a large château surrounded by vineyards. It gives its name to the famous sweet white wine produced here.

From Bergerac follow signs to Monbazillac via the N21 south. In the village past the château bear right and the chambres d'hôtes is well signed,

NEW M. & Mme Gaubusseau. La Rouquette (M)

(0)5.53.58.30.60. fax: (0)5.53.73.20.36.

A 'Belle Chartreux', overlooking the château with views towards Bergerac, this stately home is set in two acres of green lawns and flower beds. It has been a chambres d'hôtes for some time; but has changed hands recently and the present owners have been lovingly redecorating and making some very comfortable rooms for guests, complemented with a warm welcome.

The dining room and the lounge/games room are vast rooms with natural stone walls and good views.

Four rooms each have their own bath and loo. 'Roxanne' sleeps four, boasts a balcony with magnificent view, and is spacious and light. 'Muscadelle' has double aspect windows, padded bed heads and pretty curtains. 'Belvédère' sleeping three, decorated in yellow, has an even better view of the Château de Monbazillac, whist the aspect of 'La Treille', a pretty green room, is appropriately over the vineyard. The tiled floor of the fifth room, entered from the garden, keeps it cool in Summer; behind its baldaquin are stairs to a mezzanine with a double bed suitable for children.

Prices are determined by size of room - from 300-500f.

No evening meals but there are three restaurants close by, one at the château, where menus are from 135f and wine from 70f.

PAUNAT. 24510

42km S of Périgueux. Within easy reach of Les Eyzies and Montignac, on the north side of the river Dordogne, the countryside is gentle and undulating, with dotted farmsteads and private houses.

Not in Paunat, but a turn-off from the Le Bugue to Bergerac road (D703) at the cross-roads from Saint-Alvère (1km before the village of Pezules), follow signs left for 1km.

NEW Mme Simand. La Maison des Bois (M)

Tel & fax: (0)5.53.22.75.74.

FE friends of Mme Simand who visited her in Normandy at Nonant will have to drive south these days to find her hidden in a wood in the Dordogne, but they will still recognise some of her many possessions which have moved with her and now decorate the two guest rooms in her wooded hide-away and the welcome is just as warm as ever.

A suite of rooms - two singles and a double bed - share a bathroom and have access to the garden. The other room is a small double in a separate building, en suite, and looks through the wood to the swimming pool below. Madame Simand will produce an evening meal on request for 100f, and there is now a corner kitchen for guests to self-cater and eat in her conservatory. The pool was ready in May when I visited, temperature 17 degrees and rising steadily, and brave guests were venturing for a swim before breakfast. Room prices for two: 1 May to 30 Sept. 300f. 1 Oct to 30 Apr. 250f extra bed 100f.

PROISSANS. 24200

8km N of Sarlat. 17km SE of Montignac. An ideal place to stay for - not to be missed Sarlat. Lovely old buildings, the Boétie house by the tourist office, the Cathedral the *Lantern des Morts* and many others will fill a whole day and more. The different squares and cafés are a delight, (parking in the largest). Just north of Sarlat is Ste. Nathalène where the Moulin de la Tour, built in the 16th-century, is still making oil from walnuts in exactly the same way as it did 400 years ago. You can watch the whole procedure - fascinating - and buy the finished product decanted into journey-proof tins. Also within easy range is the very famous *Grotte-de-Lascaux* at Montignac, where the prehistoric paintings of animals were discovered in a cave in 1940.

To find Proissans go north on the D 704 from Sarlat turn right in 4km (signpost La Val d'Ussé); in 2km turn right again (SP Les Chanets). L'Arche is 1.2km on the right. If you book ahead you will receive a card with exact instructions from all directions.

➤ Mme Jeannette Deleplace. L'Arche (S)

(0)5.53.29.08.48.

This old house, completely restored in 1992, overlooks rolling countryside, in a hamlet of only three houses. The six rooms, one for a family are all most attractive, with beamed ceilings. 200f for two.

Really interesting meals, beautifully served, are taken in the owners' lounge/dining room, with log fires on cold nights, 75f. Drinks are not *compris* but litre *pichets* of local wine at 18f (or a choice of others at a reasonable price). Excellent breakfast, fresh bread and croissants, home-made jams, no plastic packets of butter here. A really charming home in which to stay. Some English spoken. Maintains an arrow.

TREMOLAT. 24510

30km E of Bergerac. 37km S of Périgueux. A rather pretty small honey coloured village, close to the Cingle-de-Trémolat another of the loops for which the river Dordogne is noted.

From Périgueux take the D 710 to La Bugue, then the D703 and the D31 west. In Trémolat turn right at cross roads leading to the cemetery then turn left, the house is on the right with a large open garden.

NEW Mme Moulin (S)

Le Bourg. (0)5.53.22.81.28. Closed 1 Nov-Easter.

This is a purpose-built modern house on a small cereal farm on the fringe of the village. Three spotlessly clean bright rooms are on the first floor, all have private facilities; but only one is completely en suite. Rooms are simple; but warmly carpeted, and well furnished for two or three persons and a choice of single or double beds. Breakfast

and dinner in the dining room where there is a small sitting area for guests. Madame is no newcomer to chambres d'hôtes, she has been running this one for seventeen years. Evening meals 100f with Bergerac wine. Rooms 250f for two. Good value for this area.

GIRONDE

CASTELNAU-DE-MEDOC. 33480

21km N of Bordeaux. The Médoc area is renowned for its vineyards north of Bordeaux, Château Lafite, Margaux and many other well-known names flash by as you drive along the flat roads; *dégustations* galore are available in these most prosperous properties. The Médoc can be reached by a ferry from Blaye to Port Lamorgue (100f for two people with a car) or take the dual carriageway N10 round the north of Bordeaux. Exit 7 on to the N215 north SP St. Médard then right on to the D1 to Castelnau.

From here it is easy to visit the Dune de Pilat, the highest sand bank in Europe, which overlooks Pyla-sur-Mer, a holiday resort with sandy beaches spreading into Pilat-Plage. The road suddenly turns inland and heads for the Dune, 117m high, stretching for 2.7km along the coast and 500 metres wide. It has been forming since the 18th-century with a little help from man to prevent the sand slipping down into the forests. Well worth a visit although now capitalised as a tourist attraction with large car park, little shops and cafés lining the route to the wooden *escalier* which takes you nearly to the top. It is worth the climb of 187 steps, in sets of twelve, with a small platform between. Even the *Troisième Age* were making it to the top. Once on the last step it is wise to take off shoes and trudge up the remaining rise of sand to enjoy the aerial view of the surrounding wooded countryside, Arcachon with the Atlantic on one side and the whole width and breadth of the sandbank around one.

The *escalier pour descendre*, as it is euphemistically called, is non-existent, just a quick easy run down the bank, sinking in up to the ankles.

The chambres d'hôtes at Castelmau is on the Sainte-Hélène road (N215) just outside the town on the right.

NEW M. & Mme Pery. Domaine de Carrat (M)

Route Ste-Hélène. (0)5.56.58.24.80.

A warm welcome from Madame after you drive up the tree lined drive to a large house with enormous integrated stables. A previous owner had many carriages.

Rooms are furnished with taste with pretty flowery wallpaper. Two with en suite facilities can be let separately or combined with two smaller rooms for a family. Another very pretty room on the ground floor opens on to the extensive garden. Breakfast is taken in a large comfortable salon.

No evening meals, but a kitchen for guests has access to a pleasant sunny terrace.

A most attractive old house, full of character. I think a winner for the area.

Your hostess is charming and the price is right at 260-300f for two and 460f for four.

LAPOUYADE. 33620

30km N of Libourne. From the N10 about 44km north of Bordeaux, take the D145 east to Bédenac and Veyrines then right at the second cross-roads to La Petite Glaive. The village of Lapouyade is further on.

NEW M. & Mme Bonnet. 'La Glaive No 2' (S)

(0)5.57.49.42.09. fax: (0)5.57.49.40.93.

Book ahead and receive directions. Rather tricky without a good map.

Hidden in a clearing in the forest this little *ferme auberge* is a refreshing oasis after the busy *Nationale*. It has beautifully modernised rustic rooms, all with showers, for two, three or four in a separate building. Each has its own enclosed terrace and a communal sitting room, with a fire in winter, and parking outside. The room for three stands alone up a flight of stairs. The room for four has a second double-bed on the mezzanine. Rooms 230/260f, extra bed 70/90f. Madame was happy to produce an evening meal when we rang at 6 p.m. though we were the only guests. It cost 90f, local specialities and carafe of wine *compris*. In the season the dining room may be used by non-residents.

An attractive place, which now has a swimming pool, and resident guests are well cared for.

MONSEGUR. 33580

14km from La Réole. 9km from Duras. Take the D668 from La Réole to Duras, leave it to climb the hill to Monségur and just at the top outside the centre of the town you will find the château entrance. The Bastide of Monségur has strong English connections, as it received its first charter from Eleanor of Provence, wife of Henry III of England.

M. & Mme Ledru. Château de la Bouche (M)

(0)5.56.61.80.22. fax: (0)5.56.61.85.99. Closed: 1/11 to Easter.

If you feel like staying in a château but can't afford astronomical prices, this 19th-century edifice is just the place. M. Ledru has done it up from scratch over the last few years.

Château de La Bouche

There are two square towers at either end, one housing a bedroom, and a round central tower which was originally a hunting lodge and now has an attractive stone staircase. M. Ledru has thought of everything. There are four rooms for two or three, one of which has been adapted for access for the handicapped. On the second floor up a private stairway is a suite with two rooms for a family. Lovely views from most rooms over the valley of the river Dropt. There is a lounge to gather in before you join your hosts for dinner. Evening meal 100f with *apéritif*, wine and coffee or *tisane compris*.

Rooms 280f for two to 400f for the suite.

SAINT-MARTIN-DE-LAYE. 33910

12km NE of Libourne. 46km NE of Bordeaux. Up a track from the D22 between St. Martin-de-Laye and Bonzac.

➤ Mme Garret. Gaudard (S-M)

(0)5.57.49.41.37. Closed: 15/10 to 15/4.

On the northern fringe of the wine-growing area of Bordeaux is this very comfortable home, not far from Pomerol and St. Emilion. We rang ahead to ask if it was convenient to arrive early one Sunday afternoon and found comfortable loungers and sunshades ready for a siesta in the hot September sun. I felt sorry for the other guests who arrived just in time for dinner.

Situated in large, grassy lands with a perimeter of trees, this restored farmhouse of honey-coloured blocks looks very plain from the outside, but don't be misled. The large high-ceilinged rooms have beams and independent entry through french windows. Our room faced south and had a palatial bathroom. A second room in a detached building is carpeted and spacious. A smaller room facing north is 180f, others 250f, 5% reduction for a stay of 3 nights or longer.

Sitting on the terrace in the setting sun we enjoyed an excellent dinner with our attentive hosts M. & Mme Garret and other guests. Shrimp salad, roast guinea fowl with repeated helpings of chips, good selection of cheese and the local dessert called *Millas* rather like *Far Breton*.

The delightful salon, where breakfast is served, has many lovely pieces of antique furniture, collected over the years. Dinner costs 85f, *apéritif* and wine inclusive (not available from 15/7 - 31/8).

Good shady parking and M. Garret, a retired farmer, helps you with your luggage. Good value, so an arrow.

LES LANDES

MAGESCQ. 40140

14km NW of Dax. A nice little town within easy reach of all the Basque towns like Biarritz and Saint-Jean-de-Luz which are just over the *département* border. Leave the village by the D150 to Herm, which crosses over the N10 and in about 300 metres Le Cassouat is on the right.

Mme Desbieys. Le Cassouat (M)

(0)5.58.47.71.55.

Ringing up late one evening we were delighted to find a room in this ultra-modern house, situated in a large park of pine trees, complete with lake. I have often seen pictures of this place, but nothing I have read about it really does it justice. A very warm welcome awaited us.

Two rooms upstairs share a luxurious bathroom, good for four friends or a family as they are up a private staircase. One has pleasant views from the enormous ceiling-to-floor window looking over the back garden and lake. Two ground floor rooms have their own small balcony with tables and chairs. A 5th room since my last visit is en suite. 265f for 2 for one night, 255f for a longer stay.

An excellent breakfast started with the 'house' speciality, a mixture of fruit juices and honey, all beautifully served at one table but every couple having their own special tray of butter, jam, coffee, etc. The village, with a choice of four restaurants, is under a kilometre away, so no problem about an evening meal.

ONDRES. 40440

6km N of Bayonne. From Ondres *centre ville* on the N10 turn at the sign to Ondres Plage. The chambres d'hôtes is on the left just before a Tourist Information kiosk, within easy reach of Biarritz and all tourist spots on the route to Spain. The vast sandy beach is only a few steps from the excellent parking bays. There is no promenade, just one café and restaurant. As all along this coast the Atlantic waves can be dangerous.

NEW ➤ M. & Mme Puyravaud. Le Bout-des-Landes (M)

Avenue de la Plage. (0)5.59.45.21.87. Open all year.

This chambres d'hôtes is perfect for a holiday by the Landes coast. I can't praise it enough. It is a modern villa in a residential avenue leading to the beach, the small garden boasts a swimming pool. There are two large lofty rooms in an independent building, furnished in pine, decorated in peach and blue. Each has a private terrace through large patio doors, overlooking the forest behind, and a spacious well equipped shower room. Choice of double (with *ciel de lit*) or single beds. No smoking allowed in rooms. 290f.

Between the main house and the rooms, in a small garden, is the swimming pool.

Your hosts are friendly and helpful; their daughter lives in England, so English is understood. Breakfast here would put many a large hotel to shame. Cereal, eggs, cheese, yoghurts, orange juice, fruit, croissants, home-made jams, etc begins to read like Mole and Ratty's picnic in *The Wind in the Willows*.

No evening meal but an excellent fish restaurant, 'La Plancha', is on the beach, within walking distance for the fit. A pizzeria is nearer in the other direction, or there are restaurants in Ondres. Book well in advance in summer to avoid disappointment. A well deserved arrow.

SAINT-LON-LES-MINES. 40300

13km SW of Dax. Take the D6 from the Dax ring road and turn right at the sign to the château just before the village.

NEW M. & Mme de Lataillade. Château de Monbet (M-L)

(0)5.58.57.80.68. fax: (0)5.58.57.89.29.

Dating from the 17th/18th century this is a real family château with a well-used relaxed feeling. Approach is via a long drive overlooking peaceful countryside. Charming hosts, Madame speaks good English.

A comfortable lounge catches all the sun. The little courtyard at the back is a favourite spot for summer breakfasts.

There are two large bedrooms with polished wood floors and spacious bathrooms, overlooking pleasant country aspects, for 500f, and a smaller room with shower costs 300f. A family suite with sloping ceilings is on the second floor, 450f. Perhaps the rooms are a bit pricey but the warm welcome helps.

No evening meal, restaurant in the village.

LOT-ET-GARONNE

BALEYSSAGUES. 47120

22km S of Ste. Foy La Grande. 2km NW of Duras. From Duras take the road to Marmande. After the château first right to Baleyssagues. At the bottom of the hill take the third turning right SP Baleyssagues D134. After the bridge straight on for 2km. At small crossroad Savary is signed, second house on the right.

NEW M. & Mme Schaepman. Savary (M)

Tel. & fax: (0)5.53.83.77.82. Closed: 30/9 to 15/4.

A very pleasant quiet place to stay, south of the river Dordogne yet near enough to

visit all the well-known sites.

Three rooms are all in brown and pine, overlooking the garden from large windows and have excellent modern shower rooms.

A very pleasant swimming pool has views over the open countryside, and there is shady parking with gates locked at night.

Your Dutch hosts speak excellent English and will gladly direct you to places of interest. Breakfast is Dutch - cheese, ham, eggs, etc - but not obligatory. Rooms are 240f, breakfast 30f each, making the B&B price (for two) 300f very good for such a nice place.

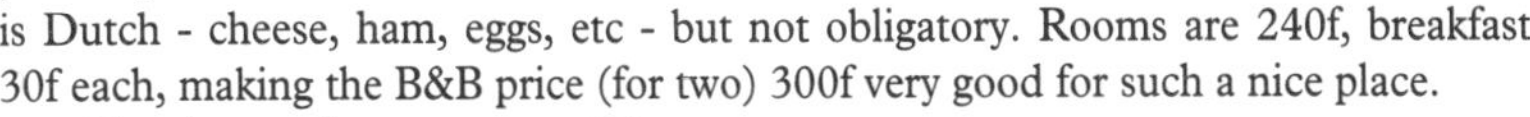

Evening meals on request, 80f.

CANCON. 47290

40km S of Bergerac. 19km NW of Villeneuve-sur-Lot. This area of Lot et Garonne is most interesting historically. There are some lovely bastide hill villages to mull round, many built by the English in the 100 Years War. It is within easy reach of all the Dordogne attractions and close to the last stretches of the river Lot, before it flows into the Garonne.

From Cancon take the N21 towards Villeneuve-sur-Lot for 3km and the sign to the chambres d'hôtes is on the left; the turning up a long narrow lane is on the right.

NEW M. & Mme Vrech. Manoir de Roquegautier (M)

Beaugas. (0)5.53.01.60.75. fax: (0)5.53.40.27.75.

A lovely surprise awaits you here. The manor house, originally built in the 13th-century, rebuilt in the 18th, has been completely restored by the young owners over the last ten years. The lawned terrace and the swimming pool below have a superb view of the surrounding valleys. Climb the wood and stone steps in one of the four towers to find four enchanting guest rooms. Suitable for year-round occupation with carpets and central heating and well modernised shower/bathrooms. One with a charming *ciel-de-lit* for two has a bathroom in a tower. Another, a small suite with

o single beds in an adjoining tower room is most attractive. Climb o more rooms, a small double with adjoining room for three with single rough a low archway in the tower again. The use of tower rooms and the ure of ancient and newer beams gives much character to all the rooms and windows of varying shapes and sizes keep them light and airy.

There is a small T.V. room downstairs for guests and meals are taken in the high ceilinged dining room or out on the terrace in warm weather.

Evening meals (on reservation) are 98f, all drinks *compris*.

Rooms 379/400f for two; 595f for three; 635f for four. Annexe rooms I didn't like so much are for July and August only. 305f. Interesting picnic snacks are offered by the pool if you fancy a lazy day in.

DOUZAINS. 47330

3km SW of Castillonnès. 30km S of Bergerac. From Castillonnès take the D254 to Douzains. Le Capy is on the right just before the village.

Mme Jacquot. Le Capy (S)
(0)5.53.36.83.68.

The small village of Douzains is very quiet - just a church and a few houses. Close to the N 21 at Castillonnès, it is an easy run to Bergerac and Monbazillac.

The large old farmhouse has seen better days but we were somewhat reassured by a welcoming wave from a man in the front garden, who turned out to be Mme Jacquot's son.

Motherly Mme Jacquot was at the door to show us to our room, one of many off the 27 metre long corridor, well-furnished in keeping with age of the 1850 house, with french windows to the garden and flowers by the bed. An adjoining bathroom must once have been another bedroom; the marble washstand is still in place. Towels and cupboards are in generous supply. There are two other rooms, one for a family.

Son and family live at one end of the house and run the farm. This must have been a very palatial house when it was built! Repairs are slowly taking place to counteract the wear and tear. Terraces run the length of the house on both sides. A homely place, good for children who will enjoy exploring. 180/200f.

We joined Mme Jacquot, a widow, for dinner in the dining room with views to the bastide town of Castillonnes. Real farmhouse cooking here. Soup, mixed vegetable salad, hot cheese and tomato tart, followed by pork chops, courgettes and

spaghetti, then a choice of local cheese and
clafouti! With wine and coffee *compris*, excelle

PYRENEES-ATLA

BIDARRAY. 6478

17km NNW of Saint-Jean-Pied-de-Port. This small rom Saint-Jean-Pied-de Port, the celebrated Basque town, teem *commerces*, which is the border town for pilgrims to Saint-Jacques-de-Compostelle where their passports are stamped, a must when visiting the Pays Basque.

Coming from the north on the D918 turn right over the river Nive to Bidarray. The tiny village is on the left. Ignore this and turn right and in about 200 yards the chambres d'hôtes is on the left.

NEW **➤ Mme Haran. Gaztanchoania** (S)
(0)5.59.37.70.37.

This spotless little chambres d'hôtes has an unpronounceable name but is easily found by the roadside.

The rising sun catches tips of the surrounding peaks of the Pyrénées before it bursts on this well-kept farmstead where Languedoc cattle graze peacefully beneath your windows. M. & Mme Haran have converted four large rooms into comfortable guest rooms, some with baths. Two have balconies, all are warmly carpeted - 230f. 50f for an extra bed.

This was a peaceful oasis late one evening after a heavy day of visiting chambres d'hôtes. Madame was quite happy to give us a meal and a very pleasant room with a view of the Pic d'Iparla. We joined other guests relaxing in comfortable arm chairs in the dining room for an aperitif before a meal of local specialities such as leek tart, *poulet Basque*, Pyrénées cheeses and gâteaux maison, all for 75f *apéritif* and wine included. Children 35f. Lively young Mme Haran presided over the meal, while her husband was out supporting the local team, playing *pelote*, a very serious game in this part of France.

Open all year, with central heating. Spacious parking in the garden.

Excellent value for a farmhouse chambres d'hôtes. Arrowed accordingly.

BOEIL-BEZING. 64150

[illegible] The Pyrénées Atlantiques has two distinct areas, the Pays Basque [illegible] At one time when the Basque area was independent, there was a strict [illegible] between the two, with customs posts. In Béarn, Pau, the chief town, was [illegible] seat of the d'Albret family. Henri d'Albret married Marguerite d'Angoulême, sister of François I, King of France, and their grandson later succeeded to the French throne as Henri IV. The Béarnais are still proud of their history and royal connections.

Coming from Pau on the D938, in about 15km at roundabout take exit SP Boeil-Bezing to centre of the village, turn right and in 1km just past the Medical Center turn right again. Well-signed.

NEW **Mme Minot. La Lanne de Bezing** (S)
(0)5.59.53.15.31. fax: (0)5.59.53.15.21.

Quite the best chambres d'hôtes I have found for families with young children. This old building has been beautifully restored in the garden of the original house where the Minots live. There is a large salon on the ground floor for meals, and a kitchen which guests may use. Outside there are plentiful toys for small children. The house is on the fringe of a thriving village, well off the main Pau road.

Sunny first-floor rooms are named after flowers: Mimosa, Primula, Edelweiss, etc. - and are decorated in their respective colours, all with showers. Every amenity available for babies - baths, changing mats, cots, etc - and, best of all, at the end of the corridor, a delightful nursery with comfortable chairs for Mum and Dad while they watch the little ones play with the numerous toys supplied; even a cot here for the youngest. Madame has young children of her own and has thought of everything.

Evening meals are 75f, wine not *compris* but a *pichet* of local wine costs only 22f. Better *crus* if wanted. Evening meals are not obligatory, so parents can visit the local restaurants after feeding and bedding their offspring, taking advantage of the baby-sitting service. I am sure this place will soon have an arrow as a speciality chambres d'hôtes

Rooms 230f May to September, 240f 11th July to 24th August, and 210f out of season.

COSLEDAA. 64160

23km NNE of Pau. Not in the village, situated on the D227 west of Boast, well signed.

NEW M. & Mme Lautecaze. La Noyeraie (S)

Tel & fax: (0)5.59.68.02.90.

"This is a modern farmhouse on a large mixed farm, ducks, pigs, turkeys, cows, fruit and maize. The facilities are good. We had a large room for four (two singles one double) with a bathroom attached. Breakfast was excellent and dinner consisted of all farm-produced ingredients and was very good and very lively" - Christopher Wensley.

This busy farm is certainly all go. You name it they grow it, even nachi the new pear/apple from the Far East. In a huge cave under the house Monsieur makes jams, bottles fruit and hangs his geese.

Three simple rooms, one downstairs, are all en suite for 200f. From July to September the evening meal is obligatory - no hardship! Your generous hosts include all drinks for demi-pension at 180f each. Half price for children under 7 years.

GER. 64530

12km W of Tarbes. Tarbes airport, Lourdes and the Pyrénées are all close by. 11km from Tarbes on the Pau road (N117) look for signs to the chambres d'hôtes on the left after the roundabout. Ignore the signs to Ger on the right, the house is not in the village.

Mme Clède. 'Maitechu' (S)

7 chemin La Hourcade. (0)5.62.31.57.10.

This modern house in large shrubbed garden, with pristine clean swimming pool, is only 1km west of the Greenwich Meridian. It has two large adjoining rooms upstairs with 3 double beds and a double downstairs. There is also a fridge, hair dryer, bathroom scales, etc.

You will be treated as truly personal guests of the family. Madame does not usually provide evening meals, but if you do eat here it will be excellent value with fresh garden produce, local specialities and best Bordeaux wine.

M. Clède can tell you the temperature and pH level of his pool at any time of the day; you will not be flavour of the month if you go jumping in without first taking a shower, but you will find the pool-side shower nicely warm, so use it!

Rooms 230f. Extra bed 30f.

ITXASSOU. 64250

20km SE of Biarritz. 35km from Cambo-les-Bains. A little Basque village just off the main road in the shadow of the Pyrénées. From the D918 (Route-des-Vins), 35km from Cambo-les-Bains, after the long bridge turn right to the village of Itxassou and immediately right under another bridge climb to the château.

NEW Mme Regerat. Château Soubeleta (M)

(0)5.59.29.78.64. or (0)5.59.29.22.34.

Rebuilt in the 19th-century this little towered château overlooking the river Nive has been in the family since 1886. It is just the place to stay if you want to self-cater in peace and quiet. The owners no longer live here. They have a cereal farm a short distance away and run the château as a separate chambres d'hôtes. There are four large airy rooms for two, three or four, with modern shower rooms. A dining/sitting room and a modern kitchen where young cheerful Madame Regerat makes you breakfasts, then allows you to use it for the rest of the day.

A wild walled garden has washing lines, and there is large terrace with tables, etc. For a family with children this would be ideal, tucked away from main roads.

Rooms 260f, good value, on a pleasant site.

LAY-LAMIDOU. 64190

4km S of Navarenx. 26km S of Orthez.Take the D2 out of Navarenx and the house is well signed in Lay, a level village with distant views of the Pyrénées.

NEW M. & Mme Desbonnet (M)

(0)5.59.66.00.44.

This house is one of many well-established dwellings which have been in the village since the 16th-century. There is an old bread oven at one side, now a decoration in the kitchen. The large flat walled garden with green lawns, bushes and island flower beds, has open fields behind.

We were given a warm welcome on arrival, gathered into the garden for a cool drink on a hot September evening, introduced to family and other guests before being taken to a charming room, elegantly furnished in Louis XV style, with pretty floral pink curtains and bed cover. The attached shower room and separate wc in marble tile had everything for comfort. Dual aspect windows overlooked the road and courtyard making it very light and airy. Mme Desbonnet's acquisitions from antique sales decorate the room with great taste.

Another room with a garden view, has a quaint corner wardrobe, corner wash basin to match and an en suite shower. Room three comes complete with a very large bathroom, all on a private corridor. 260f. for two.

Elegantly served breakfast, and evening meals at 90f, make this a must for a visit to the Béarn. You really do feel you are private guest of the family here. Mme Desbonnet is an accomplished binder of quality books. How she finds the time for such an exacting occupation I don't know.

Awaiting confirmation for an arrow.

MONTORY. 64470

20km SW of Oleron-Sainte-Marie. Deep in the country, this is just the spot for keen fly-fishermen or anyone wanting perfect peace. From Montory take the D749 to Haux and follow the signs for 3km.

NEW **M. & Mme Ruata. Maison Villeneuve** (S)
(0)5.59.28.59.69. Closed: 15/11 to 31/03.

Built in 1806, this rustic little chambres d'hôtes was once the Customs House between Béarn and the Pyrénées Atlantiques, and was recommended to me by a French lady who stayed there. Madame Ruata was as charming as predicted. The simple beamed rooms with wood polished floors have modern showers, and views

over the Pyrénées. There were fresh flowers in all the rooms, even though Madame Ruata was not expecting us to call. A pleasant salon opens on to a rural garden, and there is a courtyard for meals outside. M. Ruata will instruct you in fly fishing.

Evening meals 80f with wine *compris* are also recommended.

Rooms 230f for two.

SARE. 64310

9km SE of Saint-Jean-de-Luz Situated on a hill, this is a less pretentious village than nearby Ascain but with a natural charm of its own, dominated by a huge *pelote* wall.

From the A63 exit 3 or the N10 take the D918 to Ascain, then the D4 over the Col Saint-Ignace. Look for a chambres d'hôtes sign on the left about 1km before the village. It's a typical red-painted Basque house, easy to miss from the roadside.

NEW M. & Mme Garbisco. Ibar-Gaina (S)

(0)5.59.54.21.89.

I couldn't believe my luck when I discovered this charming house. A south-facing terrace for breakfast has a fabulous view over the Pyrénées, as does the delightful room above, which has a large balcony, plenty of room for three and an en suite shower and wc. Another room at the back, for three, has a bath, no balcony but a pleasant view of the countryside. Cosily furnished, both have warm carpets and attractive decor. I can't wait to return here for a few days. Why do I always find these lovely spots too early to stop for a night?

Madame is equally charming, even when we disturbed her at the unforgivable time of 12:45 p.m. No evening meal; but there is a restaurant in Sare.

Rooms 250f for two. Parking in front of the house.

AUVERGNE

Départements: **Allier**
Cantal
Haute-Loire
Puy-de-Dome

The Auvergne derives its name from the 'Averni', a Gallic tribe who, under the leadership of Vercingetorix, strongly resisted Roman control. Julius Caesar finally conquered the area and executed the valiant Gallic chief in 46 BC. The region then became a flourishing Roman province, and evidence of this period of the region's history remains in such sites as the Temple of Mercury at the summit of the Puy-de-Dome. The local place names ending in -ac, and -at (Aurillac, Carlat, Mauriac, etc) indicate their origins as Roman settlements dating from this period.

After the collapse of the Roman Empire the Auvergne passed through a troubled time politically, being fought over by the Merovingians, the Carolingians and the Dukes of Aquitaine, who finally gained control. The line of defences, 11th and 12th-century châteaux along the eastern edge of the Puy-de-Dome, marks the border between Aquitaine and Burgundy. After the marriage of Eleanor of Aquitaine to Henry II of England in the 12th century, the Auvergne was part of England, and was the scene of many battles in the Hundred Years War (13th/14th centuries). The Bourbon family, which ruled France from 1589 until the Revolution, originated from Allier, and this part of the region is still known as 'le Bourbonnais'.

The area often referred to as the Massif Central is dotted with extinct volcanoes. It is mainly agricultural with mixed farming producing cheese, but some industry is concentrated round the central capital Clermont-Ferrand.

Allier in the north is fairly flat farming land, cold in winter but often dry and hot in summer. It is dotted with Limousin cows, small châteaux and villages. Three large towns here Bourges to the north-east, Montluçon south-west and in the east Vichy, which was the seat of the French government after the fall of France in the Second World War.

Driving south one enters the real volcanic area of the **Puy-de-Dome** department. High rounded peaks, with a typical dip in the middle and plateaux with many good roads spanning out from the *préfecture*, Clermont-Ferrand, which is overlooked by the Puy-de-Dome peak, 1465 metres high. For up-market chambres d'hôtes in old family houses you are spoilt for choice in this area.

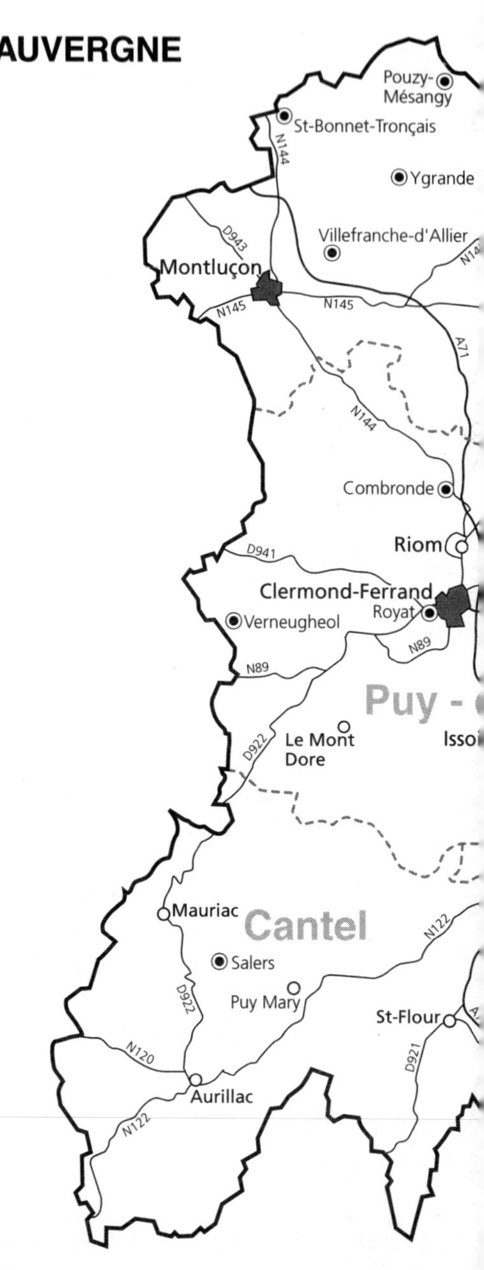
AUVERGNE
Pouzy-Mésangy
St-Bonnet-Tronçais
N144
Ygrande
D943
Villefranche-d'Allier
Montluçon
N145
N145
A71
N144
Combronde
Riom
D941
Clermond-Ferrand
Royat
Verneugheol
N89
N89
Puy -
D922
Le Mont Dore
Mauriac
Cantel
N122
Salers
D922
Puy Mary
St-Flour
D921
N120
Aurillac
N122

D973
N79
N7
N7
N209
Vichy
D906
Thiers
Vaulx
Ambert
D906
La Chaise-Dieu
Vieille-Brioude
D906
N88
Haute-Loire
Yssingeaux
N102
Mazeyrat
d'Allier (St.Elbe)
Le Puy-en-Velay
Seneujols
N88
Chambre d'Hôtes
0
20km

The Mont Doré and Bourboule area further west is totally geared to the tourist trade, with many lakes, hotels, camp sites and purpose-built flats etc, but very few chambres d'hôtes. Have fun looking for the source of the Dordogne at the Puy-de-Sancy (1886 metres), reached from Mont Doré by *téléférique* in fine weather. Orcival is a delightful little village nesting in the hills west of the Puy-de-Dome. It has a fine Romanesque church, a real picture floodlit at night. Saint-Nectaire also boasts a lovely Romanesque church as well as producing the famous cheese. At Ambert an old paper mill is still producing paper by the same method used at the end of the 16th-century.

Haute-Loire to the south-east is a gentle undulating *département*, but is still pretty high with fields of the lovely wild narcissus in May. Some of the best farm chambres d'hôtes in the whole of France are hidden here, excellent value for a holiday or en route - they are never far from main roads.

The church of Saint-Paulien in Le Puy-en-Velay was built in the 5th century and is one of the official starting points for the annual pilgrimage to Santiago-de-Compostella in Spain; but the largest Romanesque church in the Auvergne is the Basilica of Saint-Julien in Brioude, dating from the 4th century; it was completely rebuilt with many different stones in the 11th and 12th centuries.

The **Cantal** to the south-west of the region does feel less populated, with its sweeping hills and less wooded countryside. It has its own extinct volcanoes. The Puy-Mary (1787 metres) and the Plomb de Cantal (1858 metres) can be visited during most months of the year when there is no snow. Some lovely old houses with the Lauzes tiled roofs make the villages most attractive, notably Salers.

The river Allier crops up all over the region; rising in the Lozère it joins the Loire near Nevers in Nièvre; but not before its salmon and trout have been tickled and caught by ardent Auvergne anglers. The Loire (known as the Royal River in France), also passes through the region, rising at the foot of the Gerbier-de-Jonc in the Ardèche then flowing through valleys in the Haute-Loire and the Puy-de-Dome. The mineral waters of the Auvergne such as 'Volvic' and 'Vichy' need no introduction.

Bleu d'Auvergne is probably the most famous cheese of this region.

Locals have their own vineyards and wine is made and consumed on the premises. Not a lot of Auvergne wine sells outside the region, and there are not many *dégustations*.

ALLIER

POUZY-MESANGY. 03320

60km SE of Bourges. 34km NW of Moulins. 17km N of Bourbon-l'Archambault. This central area of France was the birthplace of the Bourbon dynasty of French kings. The ancient little town of Bourbon-l'Archambault is delightful, with much history to pursue.

Take the N76 SE from Bourges to Sancoins, then for about 1km the D951, branch on to the D40, SP Lurcy-Lévis, which becomes the D1 as you cross the border into Allier, continue on the D1 to Pouzy-Mesangy. Take the D234 out of the small village in the direction of Le Veurdre and in 1.5km the farm is signed on your left.

NEW **Mme Raucaz. Manoir 'Le Plaix'** (S)

(0)4.70.66.24.06. fax: (0)4.70.66.25.82. Open all year.

Early pictures I received of this manor house failed to express its charm. A treat awaits you here, it really is quite lovely.

The farmhouse dates back to the 13th-century when it was a fortified defence post. It has been carefully modernised losing none of its old and interesting appeal, and is now a working farm for dairy cows and sheep. M. Raucaz has retired but his son carries on, living acrosss the farmyard.

The immense fireplace extends from the dining room into the bedroom above. The guests salon opens into the garden. There are five guest rooms, approached by the original stone spiral staircase in the tower, and just a few steps up is a double room with one extra bed for a child. You must stay for one week in this room to qualify to use the small adjoining kitchenette. Up another turn are two more rooms, beautifully furnished, having shower rooms and a choice of double or single beds, one with the giant fireplace. On the second floor at the top of the tower are two larger rooms, each with a bath. These are particularly nice, but all are so interesting that choice is difficult. 200/240f.

Evening meals 80f, wine *compris*, with farm produce.

This makes a very handy night stop on the way south, not far from the Bourges to Moulins *Nationale*, but I am sure you will regret not staying longer. There are many places to visit from here and four hectares of land to roam over.

Book you must, and discuss your preferences with Madame. I feel this one warrants an arrow, so do write and tell me.

SAINT-BONNET-TRONCAIS. 03360

56km SE of Bourges. Right in the middle of one of the largest oak forests (Forêt-de-Troncais) in Europe.

From the A71 south of Bourges leave at exit 8 SP St-Amand-Montrond, take the D951 SP Charenton-du-Cher, to junction with the D953 SP Cérilly; in 9km take the D39 to St. Bonnet.

NEW M. & Mme De Pomyers. La Beaume (S)
(0)4.70.06.83.76. fax: (0)4.70.06.13.46.

This house was built just after the Revolution as a dwelling for families who worked at the Forge, which supplied some of the cables for the Eiffel Tower in Paris until 1920. It is now a small homestead, with sheep, chickens and a large vegetable garden. Don't let first impressions with the house, hidden behind another building, put you off. The three rooms on the first floor are very comfortable and spacious and warm. One for three has a single bed round the corner en route to the shower and separate loo. A sunny west window awaits afternoon arrivals, and a tray of tea and biscuits on arrival, brought up to your room, if desired, is the ideal welcome. Other rooms have a bath or single beds, 210f.

Evening meals with the family - 70f, wine *compris*, are very satisfying, using all their own produce, and honey for breakfast comes from their own hives. Monsieur is happy to give you directions for tours of the forest, or will even accompany you.

VILLEFRANCHE D'ALLIER. 03430

21km. E of Montluçon on the D16 between Cosne d'Allier and Montmarault.

Mme Siwiec (S)
23, Ave. Louis Pasteur. Tel & fax: (0)4.70.07.46.62.

This small market-town has a well-restored 19th-century tavern in the centre, with three cosy chambres d'hôtes rooms on the first floor for two or for families. Windows at the front might mean a bit of traffic noise. Parking is in the open courtyard behind. Mme Siwiec welcomed us with tea in front of her log fire.

Evening meals 65f are good value, with local specialities. Croissants for breakfast with new bread.

Rooms 230f.

YGRANDE. 03160

38km NE of Montluçon. 14km NE of Cosne d'Allier.The true centre of France is in the small village of Vesdun about 20 miles west of Ygrande, where there is a large circular plaque in the centre of the village giving directions and distances to all the capital cities of the world.

From the village of Ygrande, which is north of Cosne d'Allier, take a small road left by the school. You will find Les Ferrons well signed from here, about 2km away.

Mme Vrel. Les Ferrons (M)

(0)4.70.66.31.67. or (0)4.70.66.30.72.

Hidden in the country, about 200 yards from the main farmhouse, stands this lovely old *maison de maître* in its own spacious wooded grounds. Four large carpeted rooms, pleasantly decorated, have views over the countryside. 240f. The house is entered through a porch into a long narrow room. At one end is a cheerful log fire, arm chairs and T.V. At the other are dining table and kitchen facilities.

Mme Vrel is there in the morning to serve a very good breakfast consisting of orange juice, cereal and cheese as well as the normal fresh bread and various jams. She will now provide an evening meal on reservation. All this is excellent value for money, with plenty of freedom and very quiet, as is her sister's chambres d'hôtes at Mainneville in Normandy.

CANTAL

SALERS. 15410

47km N of Aurillac. Built on a layer of basalt, this medieval village was founded by the Baron de Salers in 1069 and in 1428 Charles VII authorised its fortification against the English and the 'Routiers' (roving bands of highwaymen, not today's lorry drivers). Under Henry II in 1550 the town became the seat of government of the Royal Bailiwick of the High Mountains of the Auvergne (*Bailliage Royale des Hautes Montagnes de l'Auvergne*). The Knights Templar had close connections with Salers and the museum in the Maison des Templiers is worth a visit. Little remains of the really old town apart from the church door, parts of the walls and some street staircases but there are lots of cottages and artisan shops in the village. 1km outside the village on the Route de Puy Mary you will find:

➤ Mme Vantal (M)
(0)4.71.40.74.02.

M. and Mme Vantal, dairy farmers, have given up the first floor of their house to five of the smartest guest-rooms I have seen for a long time. Nothing fancy about them, in fact not an ornament in sight, which comes as a relief after an overdose of bric-a-brac. There is a choice of rooms, with baths or showers, single or double beds, one family room for four, all prettily papered and painted, with good central heating, plentiful hot water and nice views, Lovely white cotton sheets and at least four fluffy white towels and flannels. 230/250f.

You can be spoilt by having breakfast brought to your room, or you can opt for it downstairs or outside in summer. Orange juice, a huge slab of farm butter with fresh bread and croissants and a selection of jams and honey are all beautifully served. A salon for guests is a further attraction.

There is a good choice of restaurants in Salers. I can recommend the Restaurant des Templiers where the 65f menu will give you *pounti* (a local speciality - a leek soufflé), *poulet volaille* with a selection of vegetables, and cheese or sweet. Menus at 89f and 120f just give you more food, not better. As Mme Vantal said the next morning, 'All our regional specialities are calorific!'

I really loved this one. The welcome was so friendly and young Mme Vantal is such an animated hostess who thinks of everything. A nice situation too en route to one of the highest peaks in the Auvergne.

HAUTE-LOIRE

Le Bouchet St. Nicolas 43510 - see stop press page 346.

MAZEYRAT-D'ALLIER. 43300

46km NW of Le Puy. Leave the N102 26km S of Brioude, signposted St. Eble but before you get to the village look out for a cup and saucer sign on your left to Chamalières

➤ M. & Mme Sdei (S)

Chamalières, St. Eble. (0)4.71.77.12.26. Closed 30/9 to 15/2.

If you feel like a bit of pampering head for this chambres d'hôtes, so hidden in the country you can easily miss it, to find up-market rooms unspoilt by excessive prices. Three rooms have very high vaulted ceilings, and a mezzanine platform on which are two other single beds, offering space for four people if needed. They open on to a sitting area with comfortable armchairs and T.V. - 220f.

The garden is prettily terraced with lawns and flowers, all very private. M. Sdei conducts tours of panning for gold in the nearby river Allier. Worth a try, you might be lucky! He is really knowledgeable on the subject. Meals are taken in the old farm dining room. Evening meal - 60f, all drinks *compris*. except Thursdays and Sundays. A most attractive chambres d'hôtes and full of character. Arrowed for exceptional *accueil.*

SENEUJOLS. 43510

18km SW of Le Puy. Old houses in Haute-Loire are often built with the rather dull dark-grey volcanic stone and this is typical of many in the area.

From the autoroute south of Clermont-Ferrand exit 20 take the N102 to the junction with the D902 at Coubladour, follow the D902 for 17km to St. Christophe and turn right on the D31 to Seneujols. The farm is on the right as you enter the village.

NEW

M. & Mme Boyer (S)

(0)4.71.03.19.69. Closed 1/11 to 31/3.

"The Boyers live in a converted farmhouse and have refurbished an adjacent building to provide spacious and comfortable accommodation on the first floor. The energy and enthusiasm they bring to their business is an example of how an ideal chambres d'hôtes should be run. Nothing was too much trouble here, all meals oversupplied, using their own fresh vegetables and meat from relative's farms

and all prepared to a high standard. Highly recommended." - H.Coe.

So I went to find out for myself. Certainly the welcome is very warm here. There are three rooms, simply furnished, one for a family with one double and bunk beds, another leading directly on to a new terrace over the garages which are used as a games room in summer. In the guests' salon is a kitchen area for preparing picnics and drinks. If staying for a few days Madame will even pop your washing in the machine for 15f. A welcome budget stop on the way to the Cévennes.

Rooms 200f for two, 240f for three and 260f for four. Evening meals with the family 60f, wine *compris*.

VIEILLE-BRIOUDE. 43100

4km S of Brioude Just off the N102 at the northern entrance of Vieille-Brioude, on your left near the sports stadium.

Mme Chantel. La Coustade (S)

Chemin du Stade. (0)4.71.50.25.21. fax: (0)4.71.50.20.45.

On the outskirts of the lovely old village of Vieille-Brioude, in flat country surrounded by hills, is the modern farmhouse home of young M. and Mme Chantel. Purpose-built at the back are five smart rooms named after flowers, each with different coloured wallpaper, matching bedspreads, etc. Meals are taken with the family in their large modern dining-room overlooking a terrace and there is a comfortable sitting-room for guests and play area for children. Here are the amenities of a motel with the friendly atmosphere of a chambres d'hôtes.

Rooms 180/200f, for two, according to season and length of stay. Evening meal 60f with four courses and wine *compris*. You wouldn't get that in a motel!

PUY-DE-DOME

COMBRONDE. 63460

10km N of Riom. Leave the A71 at Riom (Exit 13) and drive north on the N144. Turn right, SP Chaptes, just before Combronde and follow signs to the chambres d'hôtes.

NEW **Mme Beaujard** (M)

Chaptes, Beauregard-Verdon (0)4.73.63.35.62.

A very warm welcome is waiting for you at this lovely old house which was built at the time of the Revolution and has been in the same family ever since.

Original floors, fireplaces and stairs of volcanic lava are still in place. Most rooms face south with views to the Puy-de-Dome, overlooking the sunny lawned garden. Amenities here include a covered terrace with a fridge, for picnics, and enclosed parking, and a pleasant salon / dining room for breakfast. Three guest rooms on the first floor are large and elegantly decorated, with matching bed linen, some with *ciel-de-lit*. Just one room faces north, but has a country view. 300/350f. Extra beds 100f, but free for a baby.

No evening meals but Madame tells me there are many excellent restaurants in Riom.

COURPIERE. 63120

14km SE of Thiers. I am inclined to agree with Georges Sand that Thiers is a black town. Sprawling up a hill, it is divided by the narrow, relentless N89 with shopping precincts on either side and certainly as you leave the town on the east side the tall houses look ill-kept and pretty miserable. But park in the covered car park (payant) near the *mairie* and descend down narrow streets to the *vieille-ville* and you will find much more of interest. (There is a free car park by St. Génis church but a bit difficult to find in the maze of narrow streets.) Almost every other shop is a *couterie*. At nearby Monnerie knives in all shapes and sizes are produced in profusion. The Sabatier factory is here. There is also a museum of knives in the old town. So don't dismiss Thiers with first impressions. It has more to offer.

Don't try to find this château from Courpière, easier to head for Thiers, leave by N89 in an easterly direction, in 9km turn right on the D7 to Celles-sur-Durolles, past the village, still on the D7 towards Sainte-Agathe you will pick up a discreet sign to the Château on your right.

➤ M. and Mme Dumas de Vaulx. Château de Vaulx (M)

Ste-Agathe. (M) (0)4.73.51.50.55. fax: (0)4.73.51.54.47.

Such a gem of a château, set in parkland, with four towers and a moat, looking like a fairy-tale castle yet still a real family home with every room in use. Originally built in the 13th-century it has had its ups and downs but remained in the same family.

Such sensible use has been made of all the tower rooms, kitchen, butler's pantry, bathroom but best surprise of all, through the library, is a charming circular chapel licensed by Pope Leo XIII for mass and all the other sacraments, with a really ornate altar and even a child's *prie-dieu.* Your charming hosts will gather you in for a cup of tea in the kitchen as though they had known you all their lives.

Two rooms are in the château, one enormous, with modern bed and monogrammed white sheets which belonged to Madame's grandmother and still going strong. The bathroom attached to this room is in a tower and the bath stands regally on clawed feet. Excellent lighting and hot water. The other room, circular, is in one of the front towers, entered by a dressing room with wash basin and the private shower and toilet, is adjacent. Fun sleeping in a tower. Before you complain about lack of luxury carpets remember that you are going up to bed up the same stone stairs the family have used for hundreds of years and looking out at the same view down the valley from a château where the English defended Aquitaine from the Duke of Burgundy. Sometimes an evening meal is available in the kitchen with the family - no pretensions, just real hospitality. Before dinner you may be invited to inspect the cellars, where the family hid a priest during the Revolution. Down here Monsieur has made a little bar where aperitifs are sometimes taken. Huge parkland round the castle to explore. No high château prices - 300f for bed and breakfast for two and evening meal occasionally from 60f each, all drinks *compris*.

Arrowed for good value.

JOZE. 63350

20km NE of Clermont-Ferrand.On the D1093 only a short distance from the A71 and the A72.

M. Masson (M)

Loursse. (0)4.73.70.20.63.

This beautiful *maison-de-maître*, which has been in the family for years, would make a wonderful relaxing stop on the way south; but arrive early, or better still stay a few days and enjoy the exceptional ambience of the house and parkland, with sweeping lawns to the river Allier, a salmon fisherman's delight.

One large double bedroom with a modern, comfortable bed overlooks the garden. The adjoining bathroom leads to a smaller room, probably once a dressing room, now with one or two extra beds for children - a family suite or just a room for two, 280f or 470f for three.

Fishing permits can be bought in the village of Joze, which also has a couple of restaurants.

Do book well ahead. With only one room you haven't much chance arriving on spec. M. Masson prefers a reservation and will then give you full instructions how to find the house.

ROYAT. 63130

5km W of Clermont-Ferrand. A town only a few kilometres from the Puy de Dome which has a toll road almost to the top. On a clear day one can see for miles in all directions. A great tourist attraction - parking, restaurants, '*table d' orientation*' - it's all up there.

From Royat follow signs to the golf club at Charade, D5f, and the château is next door.

NEW Mme Gaba. Château de Charade (L)

(0)4.73.35.91.67. fax: (0)4.73.29.92.09.

Our closest chambres d'hôtes to the capital of the Massif Central.

You will have a very friendly welcome from the young owners who bought this 19th-century château three years ago and have been steadily restoring it. It now has six guest rooms, a salon with a large billiard table and an adjoining dining room.

The grounds, with many rose bushes and bowers, are large and pleasantly shady, bordered by the lane leading to the local golf club (9 holes). Keen golfers can slip that extra round in while the rest of the family relax at the château.

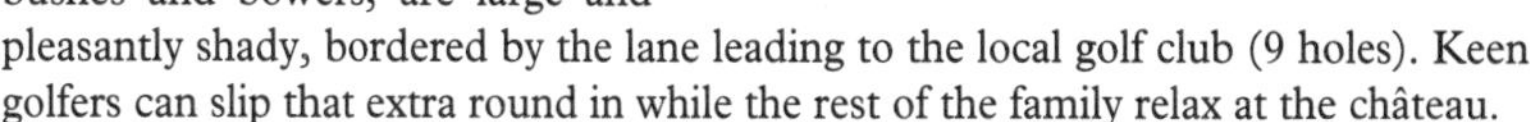

Three large rooms on the first floor are furnished in keeping with the age of the château - polished wood floors, flowery wallpaper and velvet Victorian chairs, but modern plumbing is all en suite. Some rooms have a small adjoining tower room, others duel aspect windows. *Chambre bleu* has a vestibule with separate bath and loo, *chambre vert* comprises two adjoining rooms for a family sharing facilities. On the second floor beamed high ceilings make the rooms very light. I liked the yellow room facing south. Every sort of accommodation catered for here, 390/460f, includes breakfast in the garden or in the dining room in inclement weather. Extra bed 130f.

No evening meals; but a small restaurant close by produces light meals, or *gastronomique* if reserved; plenty of choice further afield in Royat.

VERNEUGHEOL. 63470

40km E of Aubusson. 60km W of Clermont-Ferrand.Take the D941 from Aubusson towards Clermont-Ferrand, in 35km turn right on to the D82 towards Herment. Before the village turn right on to the D240 to Verneugheol and the chambres d'hôtes is signed in the village.

NEW **M. & Mme Thomas. La Glufareix** (S) (0)4.73.22.11.40.

A quiet country farm near the hilltop village of Herment, between Aubusson and Clermont-Ferrand.

"We arrived about 6pm to be welcomed by Madame with a big smile an a large jug of orange juice. After the preliminary greeting, etc, we were shown to our accommodation, a large first-floor bedroom containing two large double beds, a huge wardrobe, bedside tables and a writing desk. Ample lighting, wooden beamed and carpeted. The adjoining shower room was light, modern and very inviting. All spotless. The farm is 18th-century, recently renovated but maintaining its original character. Huge dining room with a massive fireplace in stone, wooden beams, etc. The sitting room with TV is similar. Madame is a great cook. Plenty of good solid regional home cooking, five course dinners with a different menu each evening beautifully presented and wine included, 65f each. Prices reduced September to May. M. Bernard is a busy man, 100 cows to be milked morning and evening, he is also the Mayor for the region and a host without equal" - J.C. Thomas.

After such a glowing account I just had to visit, and agree entirely. There are five rooms, including a suite for six. 200/250f for two. Extra beds 70f include breakfast. In the salon there is an interesting display-case of tools for making sabots. Proof of my visit!

BRITTANY

Départements: **Côtes d'Armor**
Finistère
Ille-et-Vilaine
Morbihan

Accompanying guide - 'French Entrée 14 - Brittany Encore'

One third of France's coastline is to be found in Brittany, and that's a lot of sand, rocks, surf, headlands, fishing villages, bays and beach resorts. The snag here is that, unlike its more sophisticated Paris-fed neighbours - Normandy and the Loire - Brittany tourism dies for the whole winter. Toussaints (November) to Pâques (April) is the normal closure, but October to May is a distinct possibility too. This, after all, is the cold windswept north, and the heating bills make landladies think twice before incurring them. When you reckon that there's rarely an unoccupied bed to be found in this No. 1. bucket and spade region during school holidays, that doesn't leave much of the year to take pot-luck.

It's worth the effort to plan ahead. Brittany, land of myths, ghosts, will-o'-the-wisps, legends, is pure magic. You can sense it most powerfully in the central Forest of Brocéliande, the home (so say the Bretons) of the Arthurian legend, and in the far north-west in wild Finistère, where the miracles worked by local saints, many of them monks from Britain, are still revered, and pagan spells are accepted side by side with colourful Christian traditions. This is Brittany at its most Breton - home of the unique enclos *paroissiaux*, astonishing church enclosures crowded with amazingly elaborate carvings of triumphal arches, calvaries and ossuaries, parish vying with parish over several centuries to produce the most glorious combined effect, working with the rough, local granite. At the most famous in Guimiliau are 200 figures depicting Passion stories... It is in the south, in Morbihan, that you are most likely to catch another Breton phenomenon - the Pardon, an impressive local religious procession, where the *coiffes*, collars and costumes handed down through the generations are brought out and proudly paraded. The principle *Pardons* are listed in FE 14, along with another treat - the markets. In this land of superb fish and vegetables, they are exceptionally attractive to supermarket-weary eyes.

I can never decide which is my favourite area - Côtes d'Armor with its fantastic coastline, marvellous beaches, pink granite rocks, the beguiling river Rance, and

BRITTANY

Roscoff
Lannion
St-Martin-des-Champs
Morlaix
Trégrom
Jaudy
N12
D786
D767
Brest
Finistère
N165
D887
N164
Plonevez-Porzay
Douarnenez
D765
Quimper
N165
St-Yvi
D785
Nevez
Guidel
N165
Lorient
N24
Larmor Plage
La Trinité-sur-Mer
Quiberon
Chambre d'Hôtes
0 20km

St.Briac-sur-Mer
St-Malo
Pleslin-Trigavou
Plouër-sur-Rance
Dinan
Boussac
St-Ouen
St-Pierre-de-Plesguen
Fougères
Ille-et-Vilaine
Rennes
Ploërmel
Le Grand Fougeray
Elven
D4
N176
D768
D155
D766
N12
N137
N175
N164
D178
N157
N24
N166
D177
D163
N165
euc
rmor
rbihan
annes

two of Brittany's most attractive towns, St. Malo and Dinan, or the south, with the astonishingly Mediterranean-like Gulf of Morbihan with an island for every day of the year. I love the twists and turns of the river Belon and picturesque Pont Aven, I love the seaside resorts of Finistère, like Benodet, and the fishing villages of the west, like Douarnenez and Concarneau; I would not neglect exploring the interior, particularly the canals and towns like Josselin and Dinan. Nowhere is very far from the feature that dominates the landscape and the character of the Bretons - the sea. Nowhere is sophisticated - forget your nightclubs and smart clothes - everywhere is very, very beautiful.

Because this is essentially a region where tourism is a top industry, Brittany has one of the largest crops of chambres d'hôtes to choose from. They range from severe, granite châteaux - there is a cluster of three beauties in the Côtes d'Armor whose owners are exceptionally friendly - to simple farm accommodation. Many a Breton farmer has blessed this supplement to his income in agricultural hard times.

There is so much to see, so many things to do, so many new experiences to savour that I wager the first visit won't be the last.

COTES-D'ARMOR

DINAN. 22100

30km S of St. Malo. 20km S of Dinard. A gem of a town, probably the most interesting and attractive in the whole region and not to be rushed through on any account. Penetrate into the heart of the old town with cameras well loaded, to record the photogenic crooked gables, pillars and beams of the houses built for 15th-century merchants whose trades are echoed in the street names: Cordeliers, Merciers, Lainerie, Poissonerie. The rue d'Horloge is one of the most picturesque, with its strange 15th-century clock-tower enclosing four bells, one of them a gift from the ubiquitous Duchesse Anne.

Stallholders used to sell their wares in the shelter of the arcades formed by the stubby granite pillars supporting overhanging upper stories - as practical today for keeping off the Breton rain as ever was. Visit the fish market, open every day in the narrow rue de la Chaux, part of a tangle of little streets round the old market. The main market takes place on Thursday on what used to be a mediaeval fairground, the Places du Champ and du Guesclin, full of cars on other days.

When the delightful meandering round the old town is complete, take a closer look at the port, where the pleasure boats take off for a fascinating trip up the Rance to St. Malo in summer, by walking down one of the most beguiling lanes in Brittany. It leads from the English Garden, via the rues du Rampart and Michel, into the rue du Jerzual and its extension, the rue du Petit Port, winding through the 500-year-old Jerzual Gate, between the elegant house now owned and restored by craftsmen, right down to the water.

Make for the Port on the Rance at Dinan below the town on the D2, and the rue de Petit Fort is just opposite the *Pont Gothique*. Ignore signs for pedestrians only and bravely drive up the cobbled hill. The Logis is on the right for off-loading, parking is further up the hill in a public car park just after the *Lavoir*.

Mme Ronsseray. Le Logis du Jerzual (M)

25 rue du Petit Fort. (0)2.96.85.46.54. fax: (0)2.96.39.46.94.

A very large garden meanders up the cliff-side behind the house, terraces of lawns and apple trees with views over Dinan, a paradise for adventurous children.

This 15th-century house is devoted to guest rooms on different levels, overlooking the street below. Rooms are full of character and the furnishings with old Breton beds and *ciel-de-lits* are in keeping with the age of the house, but all have private modern facilities, though a suite shares a loo on the top floor - 350/380f for two, reduced after three nights.

Energetic Mme Ronsseray, whose husband is an architect of Historic Buildings, welcomes you cheerfully. They live next door a few steps across a wooden bridge. There is a small dining room and sitting area for guests.

No evening meals but many local restaurants - one right opposite.

Another choice for Dinan:

NEW Mrs. Lockwood. 55 rue de Coëtquen (S)

(0)2.96.85.23.49.

This bijou little town house is right on the road side, but parking outside is possible, as it is such a quiet little street; a larger free car park is close by. With only one room here, you will be assured of a warm welcome as a very private guest from the English owner who has lived in France for thirty years. Mrs. Lockwood can offer you one en suite double-bedded room - with a bath - for 200f. Stay a week and you get one night free.

There is a little patio and garden on the cliff-side behind the house. Altogether a charming little chambres d'hôtes, almost in the centre of Dinan.

No evening meals, but all the restaurants of Dinan are within walking distance, give or take a few hills.

PLÉLO. 22170

20km NE of St. Brieuc by N12, exit Plélo. In lovely unspoilt countryside:

➤ Le Char-a-Bancs (M)

(0)2.96.74.13.63. fax: (0)2.96.74.13.03.

The Lamours are a remarkable family, working together in total harmony to run several projects in one. Their home is an old mill, whose raftered dining room overlooks the millstream. Tables are rugged millstones or long polished boards and the effect is effortlessly rustic and quite unique.

They are best known as a *crêperie*, and indeed their *crêpes* and *galettes* are excellent, but for a more substantial meal try the famous *potée*, a thick stew that simmers continuously in a huge iron pot on the perpetual fire. All its ingredients are home-grown vegetables, pork and I-dare-not-ask. They also grow much of the cereal, to make the flour, to make the pancakes.

Parisians like the rural set up so much that they make the four-hour journey just to spend the weekend here, leading their children on the house ponies and paying for pedal rides on the fast flowing river.

Herein lies the only snag - since I last wrote about the restaurant in FE5, it has become very well-known and perhaps too popular. One otherwise enthusiastic report deplored the increasing emphasis on the playground theme. However, generally readers have been charmed.

One of the Lamour daughters is an interior decorator and has furnished the converted old building 500 metres down the drive in harmonious country style as a chambres d'hôtes. Another daughter is responsible for looking after the guests' welfare - "I am a *femme de ménage*," she declared.

The rooms are more sophisticated than one might expect, each with its own theme - La Chapelière has straw hats as decoration (500f), Les Oiseaux has birdcages (350f), La Musique features simply a music stand (420f) and l'Horloge must have a clock but I can't actually recall it. You can opt for a bath or a shower.

The rooms may seem unduly expensive compared with the simplicity of the crêperie, but both offer value for money in most unusual settings. The arrow firmly stays.

PLESLIN-TRIGAVOU. 22490

22km S of Saint-Malo. 9km N of Dinan. 9km S of Dinard. Perfect for visiting the beach or the charming town of Dinan.

From Dinan take the N176 northwards and in 7km turn on to the D766 towards Dinard. In about 2 to 3km turn right on to the D28 (SP Trébéfour) and the chambres d'hôtes is signed left round a corner.

NEW M. & Mme Morel. Le Val Garance (M)

Trébéfour. Tel & fax: (0)2.96.27.83.57.

First impressions of this 1830 farmhouse tucked away in a small garden and semi-detached are not exciting, but don't hesitate - the rustic effect inside is very pleasant, and the friendly hosts and their large family would make this a good place for children. There is a long comfortable lounge/dining room with a large fireplace and a colourful collection of liqueur bottles fill one windowsill. Two different staircases at either end of the house lead to guest rooms, some with natural stone walls, all warmly carpeted, with shower rooms. There are a family room for four, another in pretty green with single beds for three, a pink room with two single beds and a cot and so on, all attractive and differently furnished, sometimes with a velux window but mostly with views of the garden. 250f for two, extra bed 60f.

Your hosts join you for an evening meal which is 80f, all drinks from *apéritif* to *digestif* included.

PLOUËR-SUR-RANCE. 22490

25km S of Saint-Malo. 9 N of Dinan. A favourite area, blissfully little-known. There are fabulous views over the wide and wonderful Rance and good walks on both sides of the river. Plouër boasts a marina, so there is usually plenty of colourful activity and at La Hisse you can hire boats for river explorations.

From the D176 from le Mont-Saint-Michel to Saint-Brieuc take the D12 (SP Dinan) at Super U, drive past the village, and the house is on the right in 1.5km.

NEW Mr. & Mrs. Robinson. La Renardais (M)

Le Repos. (0)2.96.86.89.81. fax: (0)2.96.86.99.22.

Five years ago your Scottish hosts bought this fine sturdy house, which was once a café/bar/épicerie and have completely renovated it, effectively keeping the old granite fireplace in the large lounge, interspersing local stones with smooth white walls, and incorporating the stable to create a dining room which opens on to a very English patio and rear garden.

Up the original chestnut staircase are five beamed guest rooms, warmly carpeted. Choose between singles, doubles with king-sized beds, and a family room, bath or shower, all with many extras like hair-dryers. Four have en suite bathrooms, the other has a basin with a private loo/shower on the corridor. So book well ahead and ask for your preference. 260/300f according to size.

Evening meals sound good value for 90f, quality wines from 40f to 100f a bottle, or by the glass; clientele is a good mix of French and English.

Parking in the gravelled front garden.

POMMERIT JAUDY. 22450

9km S of Tréguier by D8 and D6. The valley of the river Jaudy is a particularly green and pleasant area of northern Brittany. The rugged coast is not far away, but the scenery here bears no relation to its harshness. All is lush and gentle.

➤ Comte & Comtesse de Kermel. Château de Kermézen (L) (0)2.96.91.35.75.

Comte de Kermel used to be a coffee planter in Africa before he returned to claim his inheritance of the 15th-century château that had been in his family 550 years. The colonial tradition of hospitality is still evident. If you ever felt intimidated at the thought of being entertained by a count and countess, forget it. This hostess patently enjoys sharing her gorgeous home with guests, many of whom have become friends. It's hard not to be friends with the ebullient Comtesse de Kermel, who is the unstuffiest comtesse imaginable. She claims that she was pushed (by the energetic François de Valbray at Briottières) into b. and b. business but, given no option but to get out the paint brush and start decorating the rooms that had been empty for the past forty years, she typically buckled to and made the best of what has proved to be a very good job.

The bedrooms are all lovely. Mine had twin Directoire beds, rose-covered fabric on the walls and at a tall window looking directly down the drive flanked by two solid *pigeonniers* - 460f. Next door was larger, with attractive green toile, panelling painted pale green and a *lit-matrimonial* - 550f. To reach them involved climbing a winding stone staircase, slippery and crooked enough to necessitate hanging on to a rope with unengaged hand, so this one is not for the handicapped.

To reach what is probably the nicest room of all involves another similar flight and encumbered as always with excess baggage, it seemed an unwise choice for me. More prudent packers should consider this charming yellow room, with bigger bathroom (550f), whose aspect is south down towards the river. Leave time for a walk here. Mme Kermel, who loves nothing better than organising, will distribute maps. It was early spring for me, the banks of the lane that follows the rushing river were covered in bluebells, Ragged Robin, wild garlic, primroses, buttercups, violets, star of Bethlehem, wild cherry blossom. The willows were at that brief moment before the green takes over, when their flame foliage would indicate autumn rather than spring.

This is a lovely place to stay, with the kindest of hosts. You'll want to go back and back. No evening meals but a superb restaurant nearby at la Ville Blanche.

TRÉGROM. 22420 PLOUARET

25km NW of Guingamp by N12; take the Louargat exit, then D33 to village. Trégrom is a pretty sleepy hamlet of grey stone houses covered in roses. In the centre opposite the church is:

➤ Mme Nicole de Morchoven. L'Ancien Presbytère (M) (0)2.96.47.94.15.

Open the blue door on the village street and discover a magical secret garden. A courtyard, flowery, enclosed and deeply peaceful, fronts the 17th-century presbytery, a lovely grey stone building with blue shutters, exuding an extraordinary atmosphere of serenity.

I like everything about le Presbytère - the warm kitchen with old porcelain stove and bunches of dried flowers hanging from the ceiling, and all the bedrooms - the peach one with a big bathroom and tub (300f), the twin-bedded one with beams an blue *Toile-de-Jouy* fabric (250f with shower), the red *Toile-de-Jouy* (ditto). Most of all I like the atmosphere of a comfortable family house presided over by nice Mme de Morchoven. She is well known for her evening meals (125f - must be reserved) which include lots of fresh vegetables. A winner.

FINISTERRE

NEVEZ. 29920

5km SW of Pont Aven.12km SE of Concarneau south-west of Pont Aven at Nevez take the D77 to Port Manech. Turn right to Raguenès before you go down to the Port and almost immediately turn left down a small lane to Kérambris which will be signposted on the main road.

➤ Mme Gourlaouen. Kérambris. Port Manech (S)

(0)2.98.06.83.82.

This farmhouse is in an excellent position away from the main road down a private lane, a short walk to the cliff paths across Kérambris' fields. One mile to the nearest lovely sandy beach. There are garden chairs and tables in a large orchard. Mme Gourlaouen is a young charming hostess always on hand to help you. The six rooms, with independent entry from an outside staircase, are very compact with efficient shower rooms and W.C. en suite. They look out over farm buildings and fields. Breakfast is a real treat here, not only fresh bread and huge croissants, but also a local speciality such as *Far Breton*, all served at a long table in Mme's dining room. This is a wonderfully central place to stay for visiting the coast from Concarneau to Pont-Aven. There is a super beach for children at Port Manech. Good restaurants and a crêperie are only a mile away. There are also three large gîtes at one end of the farmhouse, very safe for children away from the main road.

Double room 240f. Secure parking. Some English spoken.

PLONEVEZ-PORZAY. 29550

12km NE of Douarnenez. 21km NNW of Quimper. From Douarnenez take the D107 to Plonevez-Porzay. Drive right through the village and after a roundabout on the other side you will find a small side-road on your left with a chambres d'hôtes sign which leads you to the farm Bélard-Huella.

Mme Fertil. Bélard-Huella (S)

(0)2.98.92.50.73.

Only a mile from the beach this old farmhouse has been turned into six bedrooms, three up and three down, all with showers and loos. One room especially is very

rustic, with a granite fireplace, as it was the original kitchen. Double room 230f. Breakfast is taken in the new farmhouse across the parking area. Two other rooms not en suite in the main house are 180f. A very comfortable place to stop and not expensive. Plenty of interesting things happening on this farm; children would have loved the new litter of piglets which were born when we stayed there. Locronan is close and has excellent restaurants. Try the Grimaldi where a very jolly rotund patron will often join you for a coffee and chat if he has time. A lot of the locals eat here.

ST-MARTIN-DES-CHAMPS. 29600

25km SE of Roscoff. Morlaix is set in a steep-sided valley, where the rivers Jarlot and Queffleut join, and dominated by a giant viaduct. It's a pleasant colourful town, with many yachts tied up at its entrance. Traces of antiquity remain in steep cobbled streets and 16th-century mansions like Duchesse Anne's house, one of the town's showpieces.

In a suburb north-west of Morlaix. Coming from Roscoff on the D58, at the first roundabout at Morlaix before going under the N12 motorway take the first exit and at the next roundabout take the third exit signposted to the chambres d'hôtes Kéréliza.

Mme Abiven. Kéréliza (S)
(0)2.98.88.27.18.

Situated in large grounds not far from the Morlaix by-pass. This makes a very comfortable overnight stop for the Roscoff ferry. The attractive house has been tastefully renovated by the young owners and the five rooms all have very smart new shower rooms and with loos. Double rooms 220f. There is a pleasant sitting room and dining room where an excellent breakfast is served. Some English spoken.

SAINT-YVI. 29140

15km E of Quimper on D765 towards Quimperlé.Well-situated for visits to the lovely southern Finistère coast and Concarneau, but in peaceful, hilly, forested countryside.

M. & Mme Le Gall Kervren (S)

(0)2.98.94.70.34.

Turn left at St. Yvi and follow signs for 2.5km. Don't be misled, as I was, by thinking you've arrived when you come across a chambres d'hôtes sign on a modern house on the left. This is where the Le Galls live themselves. The one you are looking for is a completely separate building up the hill on the right; it backs on to a working farm, and has spectacular views over the surrounding countryside. Although the long low building is new, I suspect it may have been built with old stone and certainly blends into the Breton scene very well. The rooms, with flowery curtains and pastel paint, are modern, cheerful and comfortable, with good showers in the bathrooms and the owners have made the effort to make them all individual. 240f. A very pleasant garden, with children's swings, would invite breakfasting outside, but there is also a large salon, with open fire for less clement days. A good safe choice.

ILLE-ET-VILAINE

LA BOUSSAC. 35120

8km SE of Dol-de-Bretagne by N176 and D155. Lovely green countryside. 2km from Boussac by D155.

Mme Briand. Le Moulin du Brégain (S)

(0)2.99.80.05.29. fax: (0)2.99.80.06.22.

I have to use that word again - there is no other but idyllic for the setting of this converted watermill set in a deep green valley, surrounded by trees, with stream running through the grounds and a lake for fishing (rods supplied). The Briands have young children themselves, so could certainly cope with other people's.

The rooms have slanting wooden roofs with velux windows, but the sun penetrates well and they are pleasantly decorated in pastel shades. Two communicating rooms are in blue and pink with the bathroom between them. Two others have showers. 250f for two, 350f for four, 400f in the suite. Evening meals with your hosts are pleasantly relaxed, starting with an *apéritif* in the garden in suitable weather. Mme Briand, once an air hostess, is un-fazed as she copes with guests arriving for breakfasts at different times, getting children off to school and the inevitable phone.

LE GRAND FOUGERAY. 35390

39km S of Rennes The village is only 4km from the N137, just north of the Forêt-du-Gavre where mushrooms can be picked; once a year at the beginning of the season there is someone there to check your spoils are edible.

From the village square take the D57 (SP Besle), turn left to Chère and the mill is about 2km further on, well signed.

➤ Mr. & Mrs. Spendley. Moulin de la Chère (S)

Tel & fax: (0)2.99.08.30.86.

This lovely peaceful watermill situated at the end of a lane in 16 acres of woodlands and rivers, was once the largest mill in Brittany. An ideal spot for fishing and bird-watching.

The tall house straddles the river and is unique in that the building is in Ille-et-Vilaine but the terrace and garden are in Loire-Atlantique, a situation which means the owners pay taxes to both *départements*. A lever controls the flow of water from the river under the house. Nothing in the picture they sent prepared me for this idyllic spot. The terrace outside the dining room overlooks a wide expanse of river, where, in utter peace, you can watch the ducks leading their young in convoys, while the Spendley's friendly goats look on. I had a job to tear myself away from the enchanting view from the terrace.

The English owners, who once ran a large hotel at home, are well versed in hosting guests. They have six guest rooms - doubles, twins or family rooms - all with private facilities and centrally heated. Rather steep stairs requiring tall people to duck for beams, lead to five rooms on the top floor, eye level with the birds in the surrounding trees; there are views of the river or countryside from all of them. A very large family room is on the first floor beside an extremely comfortable lounge with a log fire in winter. Here Mrs. Spendley's collection of paper-weights add to the decoration.

In the dining room the circular workings of part of the mill have been made into a splendid interior fish pond. Your hosts share the cooking and alter the menu to suit nationalities. Evening meals are 75f on reservation. Wine is not included; but there is a very reasonable choice, starting at 10f a bottle.

There are swings and a couple of go-karts for children who are also very welcome.

It all exceeded expectations and, at 225f for two, 50f for an extra bed, exceptional value, deserving an arrow.

A 10% deposit is required on booking, but your hosts are happy to accommodate you for just one night or much longer.

ST. BRIAC-SUR-MER. 35800 DINARD

16km W of St. Malo by the D168 across the barrage, then the D603. My favourite seaside resort in the area happens to have a chambres d'hôtes worthy of it. St. Briac is blessed with a variety of beaches, some just coves, some sizeable stretches of sand, facing in virtually all directions, so that there is always one sheltered. Whichever way you look there are vistas of rocks, islands, bays, boats, begging to be painted. Lovely walks, lovely picnicking, either on the beach or on one of the benches along the St. Brieuc road, with super views over the water.

➤ Jean François Stenou. Manoir de la Duchée (M) (0)2.99.88.00.02.

Some 3km from the village, from the D168 between Plouabalay and Dinard take the D3 to St. Briac, well signed from here. You end up in deepest countryside, with only the birds for company.

Well worth the effort. This one is a winner. The little 16th-century manor has been converted by M. Stenou and his sister, 'les jeunes' as their neighbour fondly calls them, into a picture-postcard home, covered in roses. The rooms, named after flowers, have been tastefully decorated in country style, coronets of muslin hang over the beds, and bold colours have been cleverly introduced so that the old stone never seems gloomy; good bathrooms come with each of the four double bedrooms and one suite. There is even the luxury of two bathrooms with Rose - 600f if you want them both, Lilac has a balcony, but Camelia - 500f - with salon and hidden alcove bed particularly delighted me; all are lovely, each with TV and hair dryers. Rooms 350f and 500f and worth every sou. The place exudes rural calm, but the comforts are there too.

The new breakfast room in a 'Jardin d'Hiver' is now complete and is as agreeable as the rest of the ensemble created by the Stenous.

No evening meals, so make for Saint-Briac.

ST-OUEN-LA-ROUERIE. 35460

18km S of St Michel, 25km S of Avranches by D40. From Pontorson take the N175 and turn left on to the D97. Signed from there. Set in pleasing, wooded countryside.

M. & Mme Barbier. Château des Blosses (L)

(0)2.99.98.36.16. fax: (0)2.99.98.39.32.

The 19th-century home of the Barbiers was the very first château chambres d'hôtes I ever sampled. It was the hospitality and interesting experience of staying with such appealing hosts that at first led me to investigate many other examples of the genre.

I liked its unpretentiousness then - it may be a château but the childrens' muddy boots furnished the hall - and although those children may now be grown up, there is still an informal atmosphere.

The château stands in ten hectares of grounds, with the border of Normandy and Brittany running through, and a six hole 'swing golf' track. There are now seven comfortable bedrooms, spacious, light and elegantly furnished, with bath and loo, costing from 550-800f. Breakfast, featuring home-made conserves, farm butter and fresh eggs, is a *petit déjeuner gourmand,* as M. Barbier puts it. Book before 2p.m. for dinner, costing from 240f depending on the wine, which is included in the deal.

SAINT-PIERRE-DE-PLESGUEN. 35720

13km E of Dinan by D794 and N137. Take the St. Pierre-de-Plesguen exit, turn right towards the village, turn left on to D10 for 2km. Do not get confused by two other chambres d'hôtes signs on the same road. It's a very pretty drive at the edge of the forest.

➤ Mme Michel-Québriac. Le Petit Moulin du Rouvre (M) (0)2.99.73.85.84.

There's no doubt that there's something very romantic about old watermills. The first time I visited Le Petit Moulin for FE5, some 10 years ago, there was a honeymoon couple in the next bedroom and now I find a photographer busy taking wedding photos of another bride and groom. Undoubtedly the setting for the converted 17th-century mill is highly photogenic, fronted by a huge lake, with vast mill wheel still intact.

The file has been unanimously enthusiastic about the Petit Moulin and Mme Québriac's welcome. She has been doing b. and b. for twenty years now so she should be pretty good at it. Her evening meals have been particularly well received and I can understand why. She describes her cooking as '*familiale*' but that's a bit modest. The menu on my last visit was soup made from her own vegetables, rabbit terrine, fish with *beurre blanc* sauce and apple tart, for 100-120f.

The rooms are small, cosy and extremely comfortable, each with a private bathroom - 350f. The furniture is mostly antiques, with colourful plates on the stone walls, and a big salon for the guests' use. With a strong track record, Le Petit Moulin comes highly recommended, but make sure you book - it's now in plenty of other guide books.

MORBIHAN

ELVEN. 56250

16km NE of Vannes by N166. Vannes is a delightful town on which to centre a holiday that could combine a lot of water, inland and marine, with unspoiled countryside and urban delights like good restaurants, shops and market (Wed. and Sat.). The canalised waterway from the lovely Gulf of Morbihan drives into the heart of the town, lined with masts and rigging, so that the charm of the place is immediately obvious. It becomes increasingly so as you progress to the main square, full of café tables, and then through the 17th-century St. Vincent's gate into the shade and calm of mediaeval town. Lots to see here, lots to admire, lots to photograph, all flowery, extremely pretty. Easily accessible from Elven:

Mme Engel. Kergonan (M)

(0)2.97.53. 37.59.

Tucked away at the end of a lane with several acres of woodland surrounding a river. In the old barn dining room with enormous stone fireplace, guests eat at one long table - 80f for dinner including drinks.

Two double rooms have showers, one on the ground floor has a bath, as does the family room, sleeping four-six. 230f for two, 50f for each extra person.

Kergonan has changed hands since the last edition so first-hand reports would be particularly welcome.

GUIDEL. 56520

11km SE of Quimperlé. An ideal situation, only a short drive from the coast. The chambres d'hôtes is actually 4kms N of Guidel, near the forest of Carnouet.

Take the Guidel exit from the Nantes-Brest autoroute, follow signs on the right. 'Locmaria-Guidel', turn left at T junction, and at 300 metres look for sign on the right.

M. & Mme Hamon. Ty Horses (M)

Route de Locmaria. Le Rouho. (0)2.97.65.97.37.

A large luxurious modern house with thatched roof. The horses in the house's name refers to the Hamon's main occupation - a stud farm, with twenty horses when I was there. The guest rooms, named after Breton islands, are in a separate building from the main house, modern, cheerful and spotless. They are all different, some twin beds, some double, and with individual colour schemes - 250/280f. Breakfast is taken in a room with big glass windows making the best of the view of the countryside, or indeed outside on the terrace, weather permitting. Scattered under the trees in the garden are plenty of expensive recliners and tables, indicating a real concern for guests' comfort and relaxation. I like this one very much.

LARMOR PLAGE. 56260

3km S of Lorient by D 29. The village still has an appealing unsophisticated air about it, in spite of Larmor's popularity as a dormitory suburb for the Lorientais, and the new development along its southern beaches. This has opened up a new promenade of restaurants and bars, and it is indeed very pleasant to sit here, catching all the sun and dipping into the water whenever feasible. This beach is fine sand, as is the original town bay, curving round to face the fortifications of Port Louis across the estuary. Spare time to visit the Gothic church, with some remarkable 16th-century Apostle statues in its side porch.

M. & Mme Allano. Villa les Camelias (M)

9 rue des Roseaux. (0)2.97.65.50.67.

From the town follow the Route de Kerpape, which becomes the rue des Roseaux. The house is on the right.

Les Camelias is well named - when I visited in spring the shrubs surrounding the house were studded with exotic pink and red blooms. It's a lovely garden altogether, ideal for recuperation after a hard day on the beach. The white, modern house is bigger than it would seem from first impressions - from the road it looks like a bungalow. Two guest rooms have french windows opening directly out on to the lawn - good for the handicapped - and have baths - 260f; those upstairs, slightly smaller, have showers and are more rustic, at 240f, but all are charming, fresh and comfortable.

Mme Allano makes every effort to please her guests and I thoroughly recommend a stay here, particularly for a family, who could have buckets and spades in action within ten minutes.

LA-TRINITÉ-SUR-MER. 56470

30km W of Vannes on the Quiberon peninsular. The wide estuary of the river de Crach, reminiscent of Salcombe in Devon, is a yachtie's haven. Hundreds of masts align themselves in the marina, transatlantic maxis are dressed overall, and it is an intriguing pastime to stroll up and down the jetties peering down on the boats' occupants and guessing their nationalities. The town itself is new and fairly boring, with its row of souvenir shops and bars, none of them with the benefit of afternoon sun (drive a fewkms west to Carnac Plage for that), but all round are wonderful sandy bays, waiting to be discovered. On no account miss the walk round the headland from the yacht club to the point - half an hour's pure delight, with aspects of sands, rocks, river and, ultimately, sea. Le Latz is a grey stone hamlet on a finger of the river. To one side are unattractive mud flats but around the corner, where stands the Maison de Latz, there is always deep water to accommodate the bobbing boats.

➤ Mme Le Rouzic. La Maison du Latz (M)
(0)2.97.55.80.91.

3km from La Trinité, very well signed from the town. Try and beat this one - combine an idyllic setting on the water's edge with an extremely comfortable bedroom, a charming intelligent hostess in one of the most interesting parts of the coastline and you have La Maison du Latz.

La Maison du Latz
La Trinité-sur-Mer 56

Nicole is both efficient - the modern house is spotless, the chambres d'hôtes well run - industrious - the almond cake for breakfast is baked before she goes to bed - and thoughtful - nothing is too much trouble to help her guests enjoy their holidays.

Little touches abound. As well as lots of thick towels in the bathroom, there is a dumb valet to tidy overnight clothes, the lights work and the windows open (on to a view of the river, boats and utter calm).

Classical music wafts. Tea is automatically offered if guests arrived looking in need. My downstairs room had white cane bed-heads, white covers, pastel curtains and plenty of space, with adjoining bathroom - 350f. Upstairs is a suite highly desirable for a family at 400f and two at 290f.

A glass verandah runs round the side of the house and breakfast here is a treat well worth getting up for. Apart from the excellent almond cake and the usual croissants and bread, there are yoghurt, ham and eggs and five kinds of home-made jam - mirabelle, fig, apricot, sweet orange and green tomato.

Understandably popular and you should book weeks ahead.

PLUVIGNER. 56330

11km from Auray by D768. A hilltop village with 12th-century church dedicated to Our Lady of the Nettles (must be a history there).

At Pluvigner take the D102, direction Languidic, then follow the chambres d'hôtes signs.

M. & Mme Grèves. Chaumière de Kerreo (M)

(0)2.97.50.90.48. fax: (0)2.97.50.90.69.

I found this one by accident. Quite lost in a maze of country lanes, looking for Le Cosquer Trélécan from what proved to be the most obtuse directions, I came across another sign. A happy chance, because this one is a treasure. Apart from the fact that it is an extremely pretty thatched 16th-century cottage, with decorative old beams, big log fire and pleasant garden, the big bonus is that Gérard is a professional cook. He used to be chef at the prestigious Moulin des Ducs and was also an instructor at the hotel school, so you can rely on eating well here, not only at breakfast (nothing plastic - *crêpes*, eggs, real butter and home-made jams) but also at dinner, when he offers a *repas du marché*, on reservation, for a modest 90f, wine included (six days a week).

He and Nelly have been in the b. and b. business for only a few years. They started with three bedrooms with showers, well fitted and country-pretty 280f. There is now a fourth room - Niniane - a spacious double, with a bathroom - 310f. Gérard was building a new terrace for summer lazing while I was there, which should be ready by now. For the more active he tells me that there are several good golf courses nearby.

BURGUNDY

Départements: **Côte d'Or**
Nievre
Saône-et-Loire
Yonne

The very name suggests good living, good wine, richness, generosity and mellow fruitfulness. Like the Burgundian hills, there is a rounded dignified quality implicit - nothing hurried - sleepy villages, slow-flowing water, time-honoured traditions, centuries of history sun-baked in old roofs and placid squares, and everywhere the cult of the grape.

Viticulture now may be highly scientific - has to be - but the views over those vine-covered hills can't have changed much since Roman times. The Romans knew a thing or two about wine and lost no time in planting the south-facing gravelly slopes with the vines that would keep them well supplied. Names like Vosne-Romané commemorate their dedication. They found the result greatly to their liking.

As did the monks in the Middle Ages, who continued the tradition. They created vineyards like Le Clos de Vougeot eight centuries ago. Pope Gregory XI accepted thirty barrels from this vineyard and was so impressed that he made the abbot a cardinal in recognition of his talents temporal if not spiritual.

The Kings of France preferred Burgundy wine to any in their realm. Madame de Pompadour's favourite tipple was Romanée Conti, while Napoleon preferred Chambertin. By the 18th century the superiority of the wine was recognized throughout the civilised world, new markets opened up abroad, and Beaune became the first trading centre for Burgundy wine, followed by Nuits St. Georges and Dijon.

Today, mercifully recovered from the 19th-century ravages of phylloxera, thanks to the clean American vines grafted on to French stock, benefiting from the latest oeneological research, the wines have never been finer, and the opportunity to taste the (often) superb results and to buy some to take home should not be resisted. To drive through unassuming villages with great names like Nuits St Georges, Pouilly, Mercurey, Vosne-Romanée... is like opening a wine catalogue.

Even without the vines it would be attractive countryside, rolling, wooded, expansive, and dotted with the distinctive, white Charollais cattle that for me are as

BURGUNDY
Sens
Yonne
Villefargeau
Auxerre
Chevannes
Cosne-sur-Loire
St-Révérien
Nièvre
Nevers
A5
N6
N60
D905
N77
A6
D965
N151
N7
D971
D978
N81

Chambre d'Hôtes
0 20km

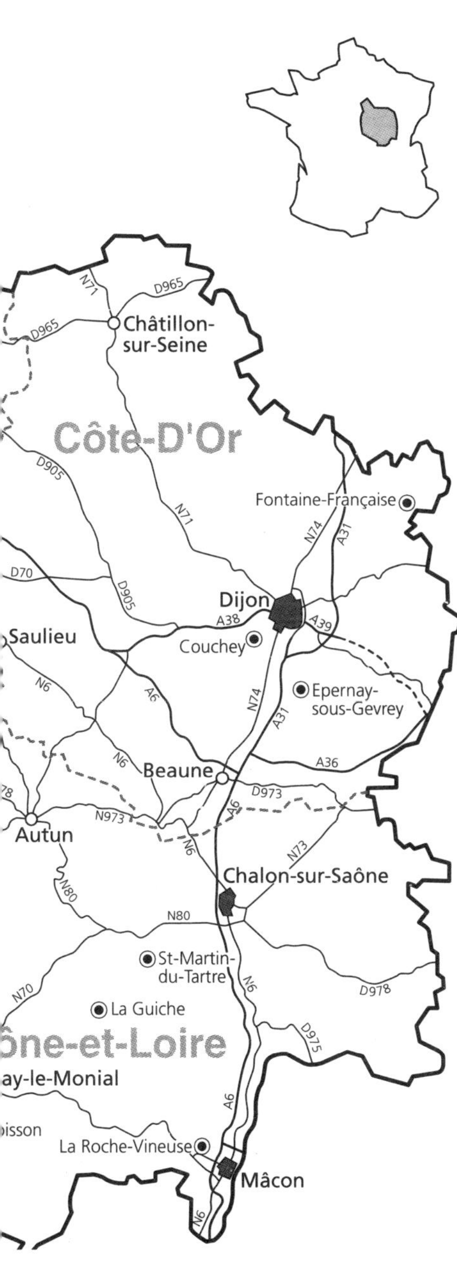
Châtillon-sur-Seine
Côte-D'Or
Fontaine-Française
Dijon
Couchey
Saulieu
Epernay-sous-Gevrey
Beaune
Autun
Chalon-sur-Saône
St-Martin-du-Tartre
La Guiche
ône-et-Loire
ay-le-Monial
isson
La Roche-Vineuse
Mâcon
N71
D965
D905
D70
A38
A39
N74
A31
N6
A6
A36
D973
N973
N73
N80
N70
D978
D975

good as a sign saying You have arrived in Burgundy. It is threaded with rivers - the Saône, the Seille, the Yonne, the Loire - and canals, particularly the Burgundy and the Nivernais, providing plenty of variety for cruising. The tempo of a barge holiday seems exactly right to view this region.

Burgundy's appeal as a tourist area does not stop with its wine. As a medieval and Renaissance art and architecture centre it is unrivalled in France. Since Roman times the duchy has been a crossroads for travellers, who brought their skills and knowledge to Burgundy, and the enlightend Dukes of the 15th century encouraged artists and sculptors from Paris and Flanders to live and work there, leaving behind unique examples of their talents. The Romanesque buildings of the 11th and 12th centuries alone would merit a journey - Tournus, Cluny, Paray-le-Monial, La Charité sur-Loire, Autun are prime examples, but hundreds of small villages have stunning Romanesque churches as their hearts - don't miss any opportunity to dive inside and marvel at the length of time that has passed since their builders laboured to affirm their faith.

A century later Vezelay was the beginning of a new look, known as the Burgundy Romanesque school, more elaborate, leading on to the Gothic, like Notre Dame in Dijon, and subsequently to the Renaissance classical revival - look at St Michel in the same city.

Burgundy was a bit slow to realise the potential of the b. and b. market but it is fast catching up and there is no shortage of choice now. As the two major autoroutes used by the holidaying Brits pass through the area, and as it is a comfortable drive back to the ports to catch an afternoon ferry, a lodging here makes good sense. It may only be one night the first time, but it would certainly be a shame not to spend longer and taste more of the delights of the region on the next occasion.

COTES D'OR

COUCHEY. 21160

14km N of Nuits-Saint-Georges. From the A31 (Sortie Dijon Sud) take the D122A to the N74 south for 3km. Turn right on to the D122B to Couchey.

In the heart of the vine growing valley south of Dijon. Your hosts' vineyards surround the village.

NEW **M. & Mme Brugère** (M)

7 rue Jean Jaurès. (0)3.80.52.13.05. fax: (0)3.80.52.93.20.

Drive through the village and you will find No 7 well signed beside the dégustation *Marsannay of Domaine des Courtes Charrières*. The 300-year-old house is sideways on to the road in a small courtyard garden full of roses. Once a cuverie where bar-

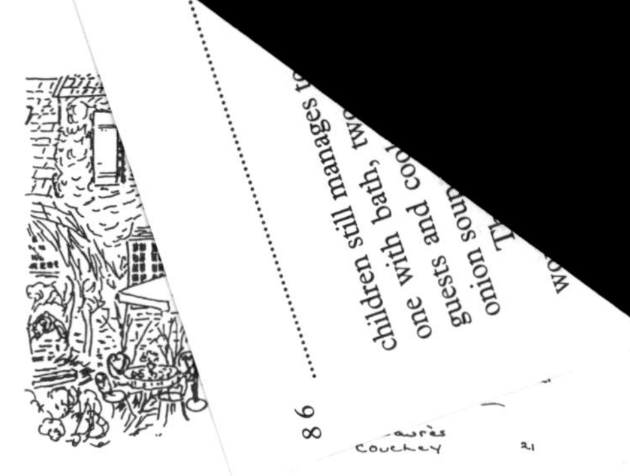

rels were made, it was bought by the Brugère family thirty years ago. They have maintained all the lovely old features of stone arches, heavy beams, huge fireplaces and meandering rooms. One suite has an independent entry from the road with bedroom and separate luxury bathroom (sunken bath, two wash basins, etc.) 300f. In the house one room has Regency striped green walls with en suite shower and w.c. Two others have baths, 280f and two more have private bathrooms across the corridor, 250f.

These sunny rooms all face south-west over the garden and are quite delightful, as is the welcome from a charming hostess. Monsieur, who speaks English and German, will conduct you round his cellars for *dégustations* on the spot. Recommended highly. Book well ahead, especially at weekends. I was *désolée* to find it *complet*.

EPERNAY SOUS GEVERY. 21220 GEVREY CHAMBERTIN

12km from A31, exit Nuits St George, 22km S of Dijon. From Dijon take the D996, turn right onto the D25 at Corcelles-les-Citeaux and Epernay is 6km, near the Route du Grand Cru. Ideally situated in fact for visits to all the great wine villages, and Dijon and Beaune. It's a quiet little village, in whose tree-lined square is to be found:

Jules and Jane Plimmer. La Vieille Auberge (M)

Grande Rue. (0)3.80.36.61.76. fax: (0)3.80.36.64.68.

It may have been *vieille* once, but the Plimmers have completely restored the old farmhouse, re-surfaced the crumbling walls, installed new, brown shutters, put on a new roof and generally spruced the place up inside and out, so that you might be forgiven for thinking it was brand new. Jules hails from Dartmoor and Jane from Folkestone, so those nervous of airing their school French should feel quite at home here. I admire their courage and enterprise - Jane with two young look after five rooms (functional, clean, all with bathrooms, family rooms: 300f a double, 350f for three), welcome their an excellent 100f dinner six nights a week. For us it was French , roast lamb, and almond baskets with strawberries from the garden.

here are swings, a paddling pool and Plimmer children to play with, so this uld make an ideal family holiday.

FONTAINE-FRANÇAISE. 21610

37km N of Dijon. 70km W of Vesoul. Exit "Til-Chatel" from the A31. Right opposite the château on the D960.

NEW M. & Mme Berger. Le Vieux Moulin (M)

Tel. & fax: (0)3.80.75.82.16.

Rustique in the extreme is this old mill-house beside the main road. The old mill workings jostle for space among the more modern furnishing of the salon/dining room. Brisk M. Berger dabbles in a brocante shop on the roadside, but at the rear of the house six guest rooms are in a *mélange* of corridors.

Two in the main house overlook the river and mill pond, one with an ornate carved bedhead and matching bedside tables. Another, for a family, with a charming view over the river and swimming pool, has a large bathroom across the corridor. Two others in separate buildings are not so nice but have the advantage of small kitchens and TV. A separate little stone house contains a very compact double room, en suite with shower, and has a delightful private terrace, I rather liked this one. All are close to the small swimming pool beside the house. Parking is in the public car park which is down a lane leading to the back garden and river bank, easy for off-loading. Evening meal 95f, wine *compris*.

Rooms 280f, 330f for ones with kitchen.

NIÈVRE

ST RÉVERIEN. 58420

On the D977 between Cormery (15km) and Corbigny (17km). A little Nirvernais village with an important Romanesque church. Spare a moment to appreciate its lovely 12th-century ambulatory and the 16th-century frescoes. Nearby the Etang de Vaux is a popular excursion, the Vaux lake for fishing and the Baye lake forsailing.

Mme Bernadette Burgi. La Villa des Près (M)

(0)3.86.29.04.57. fax: (0)3.86.29.65.22.

'This is not a chambres d'hôtes - it is a maison d'hôte,' says friendly Mme Burgi. In other words the whole house is open for guests' use. And a very nice house, too - very French, white shutters, iron balconies, in the village, but quiet, with a lovely garden sloping down to an unexpectedly dramatic view of the surrounding countryside.

Madame Burgi, who speaks some English, stresses that this is a house of quality, pointing out that the sheets are linen and hand-embroidered and that the mattresses are new and not cheap ones, thus justifying the price of 300f for a very pleasant double room with shower. There are actually six rooms in all, but the three more modern ones on the top floor are only used in the summer, because of high heating costs.

The breakfast room has a splendid view, the terrace even better. There will soon be a *cuisine* (Madame emphasised that I should not call it a *cuisinette*) for the guests to self-cater, and a barbecue, too, as easy alternatives to eating at the restaurant in the village.

I think this one is a good safe bet and if you stay six days you get the seventh thrown in for free.

SAÔNE-et-LOIRE

LA GUICHE. 71220

15km NE of Charolles by N79, D983 and D27. Truly in the middle of nowhere, high on a rocky plateau, La Guiche is the only sizeable village for miles around.

➤ John and Rosslyn Binns. La Roseraie (M)

(0)3.85.24.67.82. fax: (0)3.85.24.61.03.

Through the village, signed on the right. No language problems here. Since John Binns, an airline pilot, is away from home so often, his nice wife Roslyn finds her guests keep her company. I met an English couple staying in their gîte, alongside the main house, who couldn't speak highly enough of her kindness.

The house is an elegant, bourgois residence, cream walls, white shutters, flowery garden, lime tree approach, all immaculate, all very nice indeed. Fresh, frilly, white curtains flutter at the windows. Four bedrooms are decorated in Laura Ashley style, each with its own bathroom, some with their own terraces for private sunbathing, a bargain at 350f. The evening meal is good value too, at 120f.

Nothing but praise from satisfied readers, so an arrow.

SAINT-MARTIN-DU-TARTRE. 71460

30km SW of Chalons-sur-Saône. 25km N of Cluny. An excellent place to stay for visiting Cluny. Tucked away in a valley is the famous old Abbey, which was built in the 11th and 12th centuries, and was a thriving community until the Revolution when it was systematically destroyed, taking nearly as long to dismantle as it did to build. Now in the ruins is a college for engineers. In 1806 Napoléon decided to revive the National Haras (stud farms) and one was built here of stones recovered from the old abbey. The church of Notre Dame is an imposing building in the centre of the town, and has a rather puzzling Second World War memorial alongside it. Little remains of the abbey but the old pillars of the narthex and the flight of steps. The shopping precinct appears to be pedestrianised but, beware, it is only half so and constantly there is a flow of fast cars along the narrow pavement, making sure of their half of the right to use it; no give and take here, the cars win.

The huge stables of the National Haras are a joy to visit. You can wander freely and stay as long or as short a time as you like. Most of the horses are in loose boxes, well filled with clean straw. The large stud draught horses were in different stalls open at one end and luckily well tethered as they were kicking impatiently as the groom brought round their oats, but instantly quiet when he tipped in their feed at mid-day. There are beautifully groomed riding horses, small Connemara ponies and Arab steeds all looking wonderfully healthy. The riding horses are particularly friendly and seem to enjoy being peered at.

Taizé is a tiny hill village north of Cluny now world-renowned since Brother Roger Schutz started a small ecumenical religious community here in 1940. The community is self-supporting and concentrates its spiritual work on young people. The movement has grown every year and is now known in about twenty countries world-wide. An ultra-modern church has been built and there is hutted accommodation for all who come to join in the worship and companionship. The original tiny village church is still there.

NEW **Mme Bergeret** (S)

Maizeray. (0)3.85.49.24.61. Closed 15/10 to 1/04.

You would never find this lovely little chambres d'hôtes accidentally, tucked away in the tiny hamlet of Maizeray. The restored farmhouse has a flowery balcony overlooking the small pretty garden. Utterly peaceful, well away from the main roads.

The salon on two levels is just for guests, and up a few steps are two charming countrified guest rooms, pretty pink flowers or dainty forget-me-nots adorn the walls. Both have baths and separate loos, little baskets of necessities beside the wash basin. Double/single beds with duvets. One room is large enough to take an extra bed for a child, 65f. Nothing has been forgotten. 300f.

You will love Mme Bergeret, an artist in her spare time. She does everything to make her guests feel welcome and will cook you an evening meal if you reserve ahead - 95f, wine *compris*.

Well worth a detour. Write and tell me how much you like it.

A copious breakfast can include eggs, cheese, home-made cakes and jam.

POISSON. 71600 PARAY-LE-MONIAL

8km S of Paray-le-Monial by D34. In the village follow signs to Charolles (D458). Paray-le-Monial has become one of the great centres of Christianity, the home of the communities of many religious orders. In 1873, 30,000 people made the first pilgrimage to the town and dedicated France to the Sacred Heart, a policy advocated by Sister Margaret-Mary, a 17th-century nun, who received many visitations here. A vow was made in 1870 to build a church dedicated to the Sacred Heart - the realisation of which can be seen by visitors to Paris on the hill in Montmartre. In Paray the lofty Basilique du Sacré Coeur stands on the right bank of the river Bourbince, approached by a promenade lined with weeping willows.

➤ Mme Edith Dor. Château de Martigny (M)

(0)3. 85.81.53.21. fax: (0)3.85.81.59.40. Closed: from Nov-Easter.

Perhaps some of the sanctity and devotion has spilled over from Paray to Poisson. There is certainly an indescribable atmosphere, intangible yet powerful, that permeates the old house. Martigny is more house than château, more home than just a house. Mme Dor has filled it with lovely possessions, decorated the bedrooms with perfect taste, and welcomes, really welcomes, her friends to share her treasure. She is the kind of lady that naturally assembles friends around her - the sort of gathering that used to be called a salon. They stay for weeks on end - artists, musicians, actors arrive and practise their arts in her converted bar.

Stay here and you too will be in no hurry to leave. I for one certainly count an early morning swim in the pool, with a view over the valley swirling in mist, doves, peacocks and swallows providing the company, as my fondest Burgundian memory.

The choice of room was difficult. Not the twin-bedded Laura Ashley blue room, pretty though it is, because I prefer bath to shower, not the pink suite because while I was dithering a Swiss couple quickly bagged it, not the Chambre d'Honneur, although it is the largest and most impressive (550f) and the bathroom most sybaritic, because I was a bit over-awed by twin baths (I should have thought one big one would be more fun). But I could not fault '*Rubans*' named after the enchanting green and pink ribboned wallpaper, the green picked out in the paintwork, double and single beds (500f). It felt as though the lady of the house had actually slept here herself in order to decide where the lights should be (most effective bathroom ever), dressing table, hangers... quite perfect. All the rooms have an extra single bed and 650f for three.

Dinner (160 inclusive) is eaten at one big table and was the best sampled in a chambre d'hôtes. Charolais melon, home made terrine, Bresse farm chicken, vegetables organically grown in the potager, salad, cheese, strawberries, home-made ice cream, apricot flan and coffee and lots of wine for 160f. A very special place.

LA ROCHE-VINEUSE. 71960

8km W of Macon, east off the D79. Some of the loveliest Burgundian countryside is to be found in this area, vines in the foreground, views of distant mountains, and a series of old villages with pink stone houses covered in roses.

➤ Mme Eliane Heinen. La Tinailler d'Aléane (M)

Sommeré. Tel & fax: (0)3.85.37.80.68.

The hamlet of Sommeré is about 2km from the pretty wine village of La Roche-Vineuse, well signed. The road climbs up a hill, and the chambres d'hôtes is on the left; you have to ring the bell on the high iron gate, not knowing what might lie behind it.

Nice Madame Heinen swings open the gate and reveals a very pleasant surprise. Inside is a charming courtyard, fountain playing and a big colourful garden;

the ancient L-shaped stone house, is covered in roses and creepers. To the left is the old bakery, now used as a breakfast room, in which there is a kitchenette for the guests' use, and room for them to picnic - typical of Mme Heinen's concern for their well-being. There is a stunning view from the garden of the highest mountain, La Grange du Bois, on the distant horizon.

The nicest room is on the ground floor, with old furniture, including a four-poster (newly vacated by a honeymoon couple when I was there) and a good bathroom (bath) for a very reasonable 280f. The two other double rooms, one with twin *bateaux* beds and one with a double share bathroom (shower) for 270f, and there is one more with a shower for 250f. Madame speaks good English, so there is the possibility of discussing the options when telephoning.

She offers an evening meal only in winter, by special request, observing very understandably that she prefers to welcome her guests, offer them an *apéritif* and chat a while, rather than absenting herself in the kitchen.

This is one of my favourites, with a well-earned arrow.

YONNE

CHEVANNES. 89240

8km SW of Auxerre. Leave Auxerre by the N151 and immediately right on to the D1. As you enter the village look for sign left to the rue de Ribourdin. The château is on your right.

NEW M. & Mme Brodard. Château-de-Ribourdin (M)

Tel & fax: (0)3.86.41.23.16.

M. Brodard has a history of this château dating back to the 15th-century for guests to peruse. The name Ribourdin appears in the 15th century as a group of fortified houses round Chevannes. Philip de Chuin was the Seigneur in 1517, and the property was left to his grand-daughter, who, despite being a Huguenot, fell in love with a Roman Catholic. Nevertheless the property still remained hers and her descendants, until it was sold in the 18th century. It lapsed into disuse in 1841 then it was sold in 1897 to M. Leroy, whose daughter still lived here until 1952 when it was sold to the present owner.

The main château is occupied by the family but the equally large stables opposite have been restored and converted into chambres d'hôtes, so there is not a lot of family contact.

Five smart functional rooms (one for the handicapped on the ground floor) are very pleasantly decorated in different colours; all are spacious with king-size or single beds and very modern bathrooms, with a choice of baths or showers, 350-400f. The two larger rooms can take an extra bed for 70f or 100f for two beds, including breakfast.

In the field-like garden is a small swimming pool. Separate tables for breakfast have pretty cloths and matching napkins. Paintings, adorning the walls, by local artists are for sale.

No evening meal, but 'La Chamaille', a one star Michelin restaurant, is within walking distance.

MONT ST SULPICE. 89250

12km E of Joigny, by D91 and D43 or 16km N of Auxerre by D84 and D43.

Very watery country. St Sulpice is between the rivers Armançon and Serein, not far from the Yonne and very near the Nivernais and Burgundy canals.

➤ Françoise and Didier Brunot. Domaine des Morillons (M)

(0)3.86.56.18.87. fax: (0)3.86.43.05.07.

Easier to find from Brienon. Heading for Auxerre on the D84 cross first the Burgundy canal, then the river, then after 200 metres take first left, opposite the Restaurant d'Armançon. The Domaine is not signed (deliberately) so look for the name on the gate.

If there is a more friendly, more entertaining couple in the b. and b. biz than Françoise and Didier I have yet to meet them. The fact that Didier is a wine lover helps. Whatever other mistakes you make, do not fail to have dinner Chez Brunot. The first splendid bottle of Aligoté arrives on the table on the lawn for *apéritifs*, and then another. 'Come and see my cellars,' says Didier and, after a highly educative tour, it is time for another *petit verre*.

Dinner is both copious and simply delicious - for us a salad of smoked duck, salmon with leeks, salad, two superb local cheeses, raspberries and strawberries picked from the garden. Between courses Didier will disappear and return bearing yet another prize bottle, culminating with a Ratafia for *digestif*. 160f inclusive!

Thanks to the Brunots' fluent English, the conversation flows as liberally as the wine.

After midnight we managed to stagger across the gravelled courtyard to our comfortable beds in a converted granary. For 350f we got a large, luxurious bathroom, supplied with all manner of desirable extras like hair dryer, good soap, thick new towels, his and her loos and washbasins and the kind of shower you can turn around in while directing a torrent not a trickle.

There are three other good rooms in the old house, where Brunots have lived for 300 years. I liked the one with rose-patterned paper and a balcony best.

Didier will arrange all manner of activities in this area which he knows so well. You can cruise the canals on a barge for a day or a week, you can take a wine tour in the very best vineyards, you can be guided through the region's most interesting Romanesque churches. You can leave your car safely in his courtyard while you swan off or be met at Paris airport and be transported wherever thereafter. He is yours to command. But best of all, just stay and eat at Les Morillons. The 2 nights minimum stay will be no hardship.

'97 news is that there is now a swimming pool amongst the amenities. Not hard to see this is one of my absolute favourites. Arrowed of course.

VERMENTON. 89270

22km S of Auxerre. A rather dull little town condemned by the heavy traffic of the N6 continuously thundering through. Take the N6 south from Auxerre. Just before Vermenton there is a long low wall on the right. At the end of the wall turn sharp right down a lane signed Le Moulinot.

NEW Ms. Robertson & Mr. Wooton. Le Moulinot (M)

(0)3.86.81.60.42. fax: (0)3.86.81.62.25.

Hidden behind trees below the busy N6 (heard rather than seen) this old mill house is in an idyllic position yet it is only a short walk from the town.

A welcome pot of tea from Gael Robertson, who runs this chambres d'hôtes, while Leigh Wooton, the owner, takes people for luxury cruises on the canals, and arranges balloon flights.

The tall house is entered by a salon/dining room with delightful views of the mill pond. Excellent breakfasts are served in here. Evening meals can be arranged if enough people book in advance; but there are simple restaurants close by and better ones in Auxerre.

Six very different guest rooms on two floors, quietly carpeted, all with private bathrooms even if the odd one is on the landing. A charming room for three stretches across the house overlooking the mill pond (310f). Others with a similar view have dual aspect windows. 260/310f according to size.

You will meet mostly English and American guests here. Not a place to improve your French. I liked it even on a wet night.

VILLEFARGEAU. 89240

6km W of Auxerre.From the A6 exit Auxerre (Nord), take the N6 (SP Auxerre) and in about 1km turn right on to the D158 (SP Perigny & St. Georges-sur-Boulche). At a major cross roads turn right on to the D89 and in 2km fork left on to the D22 (SP Les Bruyères). The chambres d'hôtes is on the right as you enter the hamlet.

NEW **M. & Mme Jouillié** (L)

5 Allée de Charbuy. Les Bruyères. (0)3.86.41.32.82. fax: (0)3.86.41.28.57.

This house in one hectare of fragrant garden was once a factory but over the last 35 years it has been completely restored. The ivy-covered exterior with Burgundian tiled roof doesn't really prepare one for the luxurious interior. Friezes of dark wood carvings of grapes adorn the stair wells. The Italian style loo on the landing with ornate pillars and painting on the walls is only a taste of things to come.

Tread the thick pile carpet into bedroom number 1, which is a replica of one slept in by Madame de la Vallerie in the 17th century; it has fabric-padded walls matching the baldaquin. The ceiling is studded with tiny sunflowers set in squares, with larger ones at every corner in memory of the Sun King. Step into the luxury blue bathroom where fleecy towels and robes await you, gold tapped bath and basin, all complemented by pillared corners. 700f.

It is almost a relief to cross the thickly carpeted corridor to Madame Maintenant's room, with dark green ciel-de-lit and a small bathroom where the shower rains down on one between the basin and the loo. Does it really work in practice? 500f.

The pièce-de-resistance is room three which stretches across the house, comprising a sleeping area decorated in deep salmon pink with a gold and white circular inset carved ceiling and a salon of pure Versailles. Portraits of Molière, Boileau, La Fontaine and Racine look down from the architraves whilst pillars of angels playing various musical instruments support the corners, a centre round table with 18th-century chairs and a mantelpiece adorned with a collection of 80-odd china cats, and from all this a door leads to a bathroom where panels of cloudy blue sky beam down on you in the bath. 900f buys this one!

If you are wondering about your hosts by now, they are absolutely charming. Monsieur speaks English well and Madame is a cookery writer who will produce an evening meal, if reserved, for 200f; wine not *compris* but of excellent quality, produced from their vast cellars, partaken with your hosts at the very long dining room table, if so desired, or in solitude if preferred. Breakfast is so copious, English, French, everything offered, I doubt you will need an evening meal, certainly not lunch.

Monsieur will take you mushroom-gathering in their woods where there are many varieties. For rainy days there is a vast salon under the eaves without windows where on long couches you can relax watching television or videos in all languages, browse through their library or play chess. On fine days wander round the garden and indulge yourself eating delicious red cherries straight from the tree.

Though the decoration of the rooms was very much over the top, the comfort was too and I enjoyed the company of the Jouilliés the longer I stayed with them. Prices are high; but compare them with hotel prices in U.K. and the luxuries outweigh them, plus the exceptionally friendly accueil which, after all, is 90% of a good chambres d'hôtes. I think you will vote in favour here.

CHAMPAGNE-ARDENNE

Départements:	**Ardennes**	**Marne**
	Aube	**Haute-Marne**

Companion guide to the area: 'French Entree 19 - The North of France'

Champagne is a unique area, visited by thousands of tourists every year principally to sample its famous eponymous product. Although grapes are grown throughout the area, the champagne industry centres on Epernay in the Marne *département*. A visit to the world-renowned cellars here is a must for any itinerary in the area but I would not devote more than a couple of days to the town, which is otherwise without interest. Reims is much more rewarding, with its glorious cathedral, and some memorable restaurants, thanks to the patronage of the wealthy champagne-growers.

The Marne is a mighty river, which ought to be more picturesque than it turns out to be. Little capitalisation, other than that of industry, has been made of its green and pleasant banks.

Much the most appealing *département* scenically is the Ardennes, with a capital, Charleville-Mézières, that deserves to be better known. A truly delightful town, with vast central market square bordered by delightful old buildings. This is a territory that has been fought over and on for many generations and it has affiliations way beyond its borders. The Ardennes spill over into Belgium and so do the principal rivers, the Meuse and the Semoy, carrying picturesque barges throughout the watery Northern European network. If you are looking for an inexpensive, away-from-it-all, scenically attractive holiday you should certainly consider the Ardennes, but I fear that chambres d'hôtes are few and far between. Any discoveries would therefore be particularly good to know about.

ARDENNES

BRIENNE-SUR-AISNE. 08190

20km N of Reims. Follow the river Aisne along the N925 from Soissons through quiet little villages to Neufchâtel where the D366 from Reims joins the D925 and round a bend is the nice little village of Brienne-sur-Aisne.

CHAMPAGNE / ARDENNE

M. & Mme Lériche (S)
(0)3.24.72.94.25.

A warm welcome at this restful farmhouse on the far fringe of the village. Three rooms full of character are on the first floor of the adjoining building, two of which have sitting-rooms and beds on the mezzanine above, accommodating a family of five. So many amenities - indoor games for children, bikes for hire, and a washing machine for 10f, a pleasant garden and country views from the windows. No evening meals but a shared well-equipped kitchen with microwave (15f extra per day). Very useful if you don't want the expense of eating out, but there is an excellent restaurant *À la Bonne Volonté* at the other end of the village (1km away). We ate well there; menus at 70f and 96f and wine *en carafe*. Most attentive service.

The Leriche's 10-year-old son has made an interesting museum of fragments of shells, cooking utensils, etc, remnants of the First World War found in the surrounding battlefields. Good breakfast. A bargain at 180f for two.

AUBE

PLANCY L'ABBAYE. 10380

37km N of Troyes. Exit from autoroute A26 at Arcis-sur-Aube, then N for 1.5km on N77, turn left on to D56 for 13km.

Plancy is a pleasant, sleepy village grown up around a large, open square, centring on an old, iron bandstand. Tourists rarely venture in this direction, as prices indicate. On one side of the square is the blank apricot-painted facade of an old presbytery. Looks good but not half so good as the garden side.

➤ **Mme Violette Misswald** (M)
1, Place du Maréchal Foch. (0)3.25.37.44.71.

A secret garden, cool, shady, colourful, runs right down to the river Aube. There are tables dotted about the lawns and on a little terrace at the water's edge. The house, facing south, presents a sunny honey-coloured aspect, grey shutters enclosing deep windows, mellow old roof tiles. Utterly charming.

At present there are three good chambres d'hôtes, all with bath or shower and loo and view of garden and river, approached by an outside staircase. A kitchen is available for guest's use, as is the charming salon. Outstanding value at 250f a dou-

ble, and an evening meal at 70f (on reservation). Mme Misswald and her delightful daughter Mme de Bonade, who helps her mother, would like to convert another room, but they need a few more tourists to discover their gem before they can afford to carry out the work.

Even if you do not intend to stay here (big mistake), at least cross one of the bridges to the opposite bank for a superb picnic. Willows dip into the river, fast-flowing here because of the defunct lock gates which funnel the stream, plenty of shade, and even a little beach. A magical place altogether.

Arrowed for lovely house, kind hosts, superb position, good value.

POUGY. 10240

120km S of Reims. 25km W of Troyes. This small village is close to Longsols where there is the oldest wooden church in France. Water sports on the Lake Aube and the Reservoire Seine-et-Marne are nearby. Exactly halfway between Calais and the Mediterranean. 15km from the A26 (Exit Arcis-sur-Aube).

NEW M. Antoine Morlet. Château de Pougy (M)

Grande Rue. (0)3.25.37.09.41. fax: (0)3.25.37.87.29.

This 18th-century château is quite charming. As you enter the gates there are neat parking bays on either side of the circular lawn. A shady hectare of lawns and trees surrounds the property.

In the same family since the Revolution it has now been handed down to young M. Morlet; but his parents help out on occasions, his mother still cooks the evening meals. The rooms, with modernised facilitiies, are furnmished in their original style, using good-quality family furniture.

When I visited it was full of wedding guests; but the groom's sister, related to all the guests, cheerfully knocked on all the doors and whisked me round the rooms. Bewildered guests in their various stages of finery had no option! Large rooms with high ceilings, fireplaces, oak floors, a pretty green room has a vestibule and a large shower room, the blue with a bath, double bed. A family room with bunks in a side room shares the ensuite facilities. Two smaller rooms in another wing of the château, one very pink, are both en suite with showers. Quickly opening doors to showers and bathrooms I was brought up short by finding one room not an expected cupboard but a minute chapel having a lovely statue of the Virgin Mary backed by a blue window with a small *prie-dieu* in front. Two rooms can be a suite; shut off from the main corridor, but each has private facilities. 250f for two; 310f for four with bunks.

A pleasant salon is on the first floor with semi-circular windows overlooking the garden. The dining room is downstairs, where at seperate tables breakfast and evening meals are served by Monsieur. Dinner 90f, wine *compris*. All excellent value.

FRANCHE-COMTE

Départements: **Doubs**
Jura
Haute-Saône
Territoire-de-Belfort

A region lying east of Burgundy, nestling against the Swiss border. There are four *départements*, Haute Saône and Territoire de Belfort to the north, Doubs in the east and Jura in the south west.

Haute-Saône is low agricultural land and not quite so interesting as the other *départements* though it is trying to promote itself as a holiday area and many lakes and holiday sites have been constructed. Vesoul, the *préfecture*, lies at the foot of La Motte, a hill dominating the valley of the Durgeon. So damp was this valley that it was only in 1854 that the church of Notre-Dame was built on top of the hill in thanks to God for having rid the town of cholera. It is possible to drive to within 200 metres of the top, then it is shanks' pony to the church from which there is an excellent view of the surrounding country.

A very small part of Haute-Saône, bordering Burgundy, produces wine at Champlitte from mostly Chardonnay and Pinot Noir grapes, the white being the most renowned.

In the north at Fougerolles is the centre of the wild cherry growing, the source of Les Griottines, cherries soaked in kirsch and eau-de-vie. A striking feature of the small villages is the number of high arched windows and doorways, a relic of the times when they were the entrance to the granary. There is hardly a house without two or three.

Territoire-de-Belfort is a big name for one of the smallest *départements* of France. It lies in the north-east of the region, bordering on Alsace. Fairly flat farming land surrounds the industrial *préfecture* of Belfort, which is famous for railway engineering.

Doubs is altogether a different, more sophisticated *département*, having the old Roman town of Besançon as its *préfecture*, a town well worth visiting with large bridges spanning the surrounding river Doubs. Park in the large shady car park by the Pont de Brégille and you will be within walking distance of the fascinating old town. In the Square Castan is the remains of an old Roman theatre among surrounding trees. Victor Hugo was born close by in what is now the Place Victor

FRANCHE-COMPTE

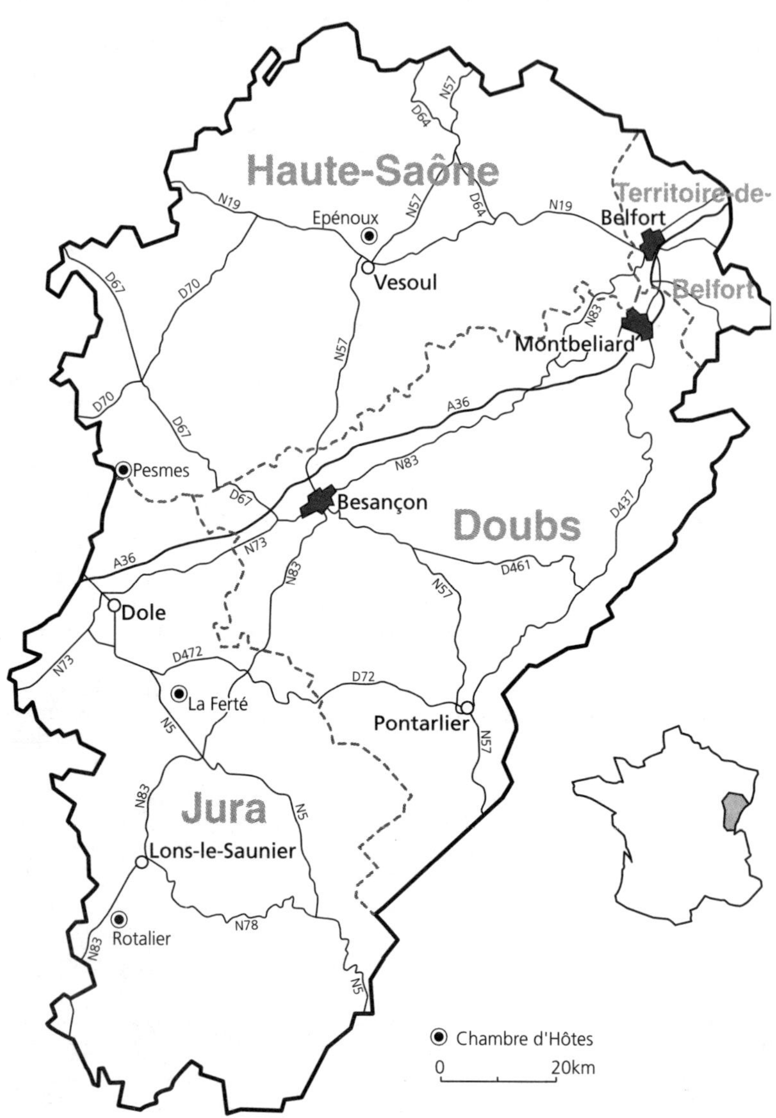

Hugo; a plaque is over the door of the house. Going up to the cathedral the road passes under the lovely 2nd-century Porte Noire; the road leads up to the Citadelle, which is 118 metres above the town of Besançon. In Roman times it contained a temple. When the Spaniards conquered this part of France they built a fortress here in 1688 and the French went on building when they regained possession. It has been a state prison, a barracks for officers and cadets in the time of Louis XIV and a place of execution for many patriots shot during the Second World War. Now it is owned by the city of Besançon and is a leisure and cultural centre, with zoo and aquarium. Good parking and a large restaurant at the top outside the ticket office.

Jura by far the best known by name of all Franche-Comté departments, takes its name from the mountains between France and Switzerland. The wine produced along the Burgundy border is well known in France, but not a lot is exported.

The countryside varies from vineyards on the western slopes to high plains and thickly wooded mountains in the east. Some of the tallest trees in Europe are on the slopes of the Jura mountains.

Dole is a busy little town, the birthplace of Louis Pasteur - he had his laboratories at Arbois, a town surrounded by vineyards.

Lons-le-Saunier in the south of the department is the *préfecture*, a pleasant town with a dominant railway station. A quiet drive through this region makes a pleasant change when heading for the Rhône Valley.

JURA

LA FERTE. 39600

24km SE of Dole. Take the D405 south from Dole. After 10km turn left on to the N5 to Vaudrey, then fork right on to the D469 to La Ferté. The chambres d'hôtes is well signed in the village on the left.

NEW **M. & Mme Peseux. Le Moulin** (S)
(0)3.84.37.51.83.

This is an ancient mill house. There are millstones everywhere, one still working but producing electricity instead of flour. A branch of the river Cuisance gurgles under the house, turning the wheel.

A family room and one other upstairs are neatly furnished and the modern en-suite shower rooms sport hair dryers. Friendly hosts will produce an evening meal for 100f, d'Arbois wine *compris*, and you will enjoy a quiet night well off the road with easy parking.

Rooms 230f for two, 280f for three.

ROTALIER. 39190

12km S of Lons-le-Saunier. Follow the N83 and in 11km turn left to Rotalier. The château is well signed.

NEW M. & Mme De Boissieu. Château Grea (M-L)

(0)3.84.25.05.07.

In the family since 1758, this charming house is situated on a hill surrounded by vineyards. A large sheltered courtyard leads to the front door where you will have a very warm welcome from Mme De Boissieu. This is a homely 'L' shaped château with the comfortable salon leading to a terrace. On the first floor is a large but cosy bedroom with good views, an adjoining correspondingly large bathroom with bath to wallow in has an adjoining room with bunks for children, all so light and airy. The second bedroom on a floor above is smaller but very prettily decorated in pink, with a double bed for two, shower and wc. Madame will provide a light meal on your first night, but afterwards you have the use of a full kitchen leading to a terrace. Breakfast is in the adjacent dining room. A really comfortable happy home here. The price of 350/400f is warranted.

HAUTE-SAONE

EPENOUX. 70000

4km N of Vesoul. As you enter the village of Epenoux from Vesoul, the château is on the left.

Mme Gautier (L)

Château d'Epenoux. Route de Saint-Loup. (0)3.84.75.19.60. fax: (0)3.84.76.45.05. This more than compensates for the lack of chambres d'hôtes in the department. The compact little château is situated in 3 hectares of parkland where the oldest weeping beech tree in Europe stands supreme. Some well worn shutters at the back are misleading - the four rooms are charming, with polished wood floors, central heating, marble fireplaces, pretty drapes, some *ciel-de-lits*, and huge, carpeted, modernised bathrooms. One is a suite of two rooms for a family, on the second floor, where on the way up you will pass a very old etching of Paris in the 19th-century, spanning the wall.

A lounge, furnished with antiques but with comfortable modern armchairs, is a delightful place to meet your fellow guests before dining together. Madame does all the cooking.

A tiny chapel stands in the front garden; it even has a small balcony (perhaps for the servants?) and an old dalmatic hanging by the altar. The château was once used as a leave centre for Army officers serving abroad.

Demi-pension only is 760f for two people, but wine is extra. Should be worth a detour to stay here. Unfortunately, I had to visit in the morning and was miles away by nightfall!

PESMES. 70140

39km E of Dijon. 37km W of Besançon. This little hill village overlooks the River Ognon. From Dijon A39 exit Auxonne then D20/D112 to Pesmes.

NEW M. Hoyet. La Maison Royale (L)

Tel & fax: (0)3.84.31.23.23. Closed 30/9 to Easter.

No difficulty in finding this one, on the left as you enter the village. It was once a fortress guarding the village, visited by Henri IV, but until ten years ago it was a roofless shell. M. Hoyet has completely restored the tall oblong building and it is now a very spacious chambres d'hôtes, flying the 'Fleur-de-Lys' flag. Almost a hotel, but the friendly welcome from such a courteous host and Lydi, his charming partner rather belies this.

The vast salons and stairways have many mementoes of M. Hoyet's time spent working in Japan. One has space to stand back and admire the varied artefacts in the vast main hall, a knight in armour, a slice of the original floor preserved under glass and the huge stone carved fireplace and if you look up you will see the circular suspended breakfast room. Here pretty flowery table cloths are complemented by Haiti paintings round the wall. Heidi, the present au pair, keeps an eye on your every need as do your hosts.

A salon on the first floor leads to a well-stocked library, open to guests. On the stone stairway one is likely to encounter almost life size Japanese figures, an ornate Chinese shoe cleaning apparatus, even an organ in an alcove off the landing overhangs the main hall. In the cellars is another vast chamber for banquets where the only windows are the old arrow slits.

Guest rooms are on the second floor. Four in each wing are furnished in different styles. Again space is the key-word with luxury bathrooms. I loved the corner rooms with dual aspect windows, *Oiseaux*, *Tulipe*, Bali has a fitting mural; but all have almost aerial views over the village to the countryside and the Jura mountains, 300/400f.

Parking is in the gravelled courtyard, where beds of roses soften the severity of the building.

Evening meals 140f with wine *compris*, if you book 24 hours in advance.

This reclaimed fortress is open to the public from Easter to June 15th at weekends; in the high season every day, except Tuesdays.

LANGUEDOC-ROUSSILLON

Départements: **Aude**
Gard
Hérault
Lozère
Pyrénées-Orientales

The Mediterranean coastline extends to about 175km of seashore stretching, from the Spanish border almost to the Camargue at the mouth of the Rhône. The name of the region signifies the north/south division of France in earlier times, when 'Yes' in the north was 'Oui' but in the South-West the word 'Oc' was used, hence 'langue d'Oc.' a language still understood today by about ten million people in the region.

In the **Pyrénées Orientales**, the most southerly *département*, the Catalan influence is very noticeable. Sovereignty passed from France to Spain and back again regularly for centuries, and although the southern part of the region is now firmly in France, most of the native inhabitants think of themselves as Catalan first and French second. Here at the eastern end of the chain of mountains which separates France and Spain was the escape route for many of our servicemen during the Second World War. The *Pic de Canigou* (2784 metres) dominates this area. The first bonfires to celebrate the feast of St John the Baptist (Midsummer's Day 24th June) are lit at the top, attended by notabilities from both sides of the frontier. Although the peak is covered in snow for most of the year, the flora and fauna are still magnificent in the gorges and pine forests on the lower slopes, and as early as March the hillsides are yellow with mimosa.

The *département*, whose main town is Perpignan, is mainly agricultural. The earliest cherries come from this area, and it is a great centre for tourism, with sandy beaches and camp sites stretching along the coast to the Spanish border.

Boulou is now bypassed by the autoroute to Spain. Two major valleys running westerly are interesting to explore: The Tech, along the N115, finishes up on the Spanish border; the other beside the river Tet is the N116, leading to Prades, and climbing to Font-Romeu. Close by, at Odeillo, reckoned to be the sunniest place in France, is the world's most powerful solar furnace, with concave mirrors collecting the sun's rays. Just south of Font-Romeu is the tiny Spanish enclave of Llivia, only about a kilometre from the Spanish border but totally surrounded by France. Close

LANGUEDOC-ROUSSILON

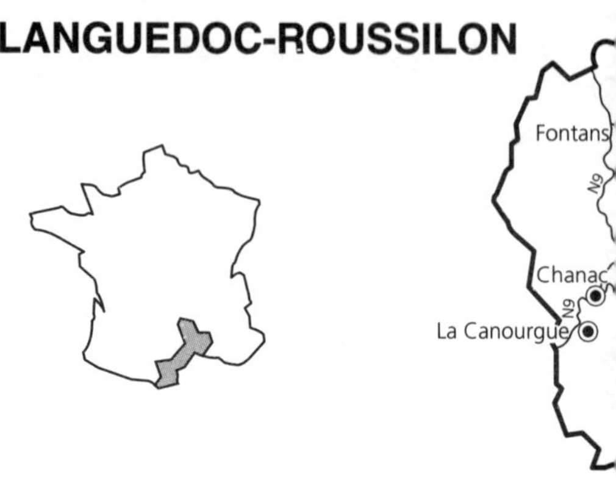

Chambre d'Hôtes

0 20km

by is the border town of Bourg-Madame where the road begins the long climb up into Andorra.

Aude, a *département* further north, contains the hot dry lands of the Corbières, whose wine, once despised as supermarket plonk, is vastly improved thanks to American and Australian technology and investment. This was the heart of the Cathar region. Further west you will find the pretty little town of Limoux, whose inhabitants insist that the famous sparkling *Blanquette-de-Limoux* is not a copy of champagne, as it was first made here in the 16th-century and so predates Dom Pérignon.

Carcassonne, the *préfecture*, in the north of Aude is two separate towns really, with the *Cité* a fairy-tale fort (albeit a clever 19th-century reconstruction) on top of a hill, overlooking the "new" town which itself dates from the Middle Ages. West of Carcassonne is Castelnaudary, famous for its *cassoulet*, a pork and bean casserole.

l'Hérault, to the north-east of the region, is pure wine country; there are no ordinary farmsteads, just vineyards. Names such as Minervois spring to mind. It is interesting that nearly all the b & b's in this *département* are in the middle of small towns and not way out in the country as in other parts. This is because nearly all the agriculture is devoted to the vine, and the *Viticulteurs* (vine growers) work out in the country but, as they do not own the land, live in town.

The *Canal du Midi* is a feature of this *département*. Starting at Toulouse, it runs for 240km to the *Bassin-de-Thau* at Sète, passing through 64 locks and over 55 aqueducts. The town of Agde, founded by the Greeks and given the name of "Agatha" is an impressive town, but the beaches near Cap d'Agde have become a boring conglomeration of characterless holiday flats and complexes, crowded in summer and deserted out of season. Montpellier, the *préfecture*, is a large and busy town, with a mixture of old and smart modern buildings, which has spread considerably in the last few years.

Yet further north is the department of **Gard,** rich in Roman history; the arena at Nîmes, the *préfecture*, is one of the best-preserved in Europe. Nîmes was colonised in about 40 BC as it lay on the "Via Domitia", the main route from Rome to Spain. 1480km of road used by merchants and the Roman legions, so of course it was fortified along its length. The name derives from the Roman god "Nemesus" (the god of rivers and fountains). Having been colonised and made a military fort and staging post, the city needed fresh drinking water, so an aqueduct 50km long was built between Uzès and Nîmes during the first decade BC The most spectacular part of this aqueduct is at the *Pont du Gard* (25km west of Avignon). Although it was built some 2000 years ago, the Pont has suffered little damage, and a thorough restoration programme is now in process. There is a "Pay and Display" car park on both sides of the bridge, but entry is free, even though this is the third most popular tourist spot in France.

In the 16th-century Nîmes was a Protestant stronghold, having come under the influence of the Huguenots who came down from the Cévennes. It was consequently right in the centre of the religious wars which followed the revocation of the Edict of Nantes by Louis XIV in 1685. The word "denim" originated here, as the material comes from the fabric *Serge-de-Nîmes*.

There are interesting geographical phenomena to visit in the north-west, such as the Grotte-des-Demoiselles, where a funicular train takes you into the mountain, and the curious Cirque-de-Navacelles, where the river winds so much that it leaves one bank high and dry, best seen from the hill top.

Further north in the region is the **Lozère,** a very different terrain, with the sweeping, massive hills better known as the Cévennes. Wave after wave of these chestnut-covered hills fade away into the sunset. It is the poorest department of France, but not in scenery. Robert Louis Stevenson tramped its hills and valleys with his donkey. In the south the Corniche des Cévennes runs from St. Jean du Gard to Florac, and the entrance of the famous Gorge du Tarn. Further north the N 106 winds its way between the *causses*, eventually reaching Mende, the adorable little *préfecture*, a case of small is beautiful. Sheltered by the Causse (high plain) on one side, the river Lot skirting it on the other, this compact little town is encircled by a charming boulevard, the cathedral and shopping area tucked in the middle. Even the industrial area, now an inevitable addition to all French towns, lies discreetly the other side of the river.

AUDE

MONTMAUR. 11320

42km SE of Toulouse. 50km NW of Carcassonne. A small village, with interesting local history, where the château cellars now store the Corbières wine of Château-la-Toque. From Montmaur drive down towards the D43 and La Castagne is signed on your left.

M. & Mme Martin. La Castagne (M)

(0)4.68.60.00.40.

You will be welcomed into this beautifully restored farmhouse, part of which was once a guard-house for the château. There is only one guest room, but others in the *gîte* if needed. The galleried landing looks down on a very comfortable salon with a large fireplace, where in complete luxury you may watch videos of the surrounding historic places, making your choice of what to visit much easier. A swimming pool is a big plus.

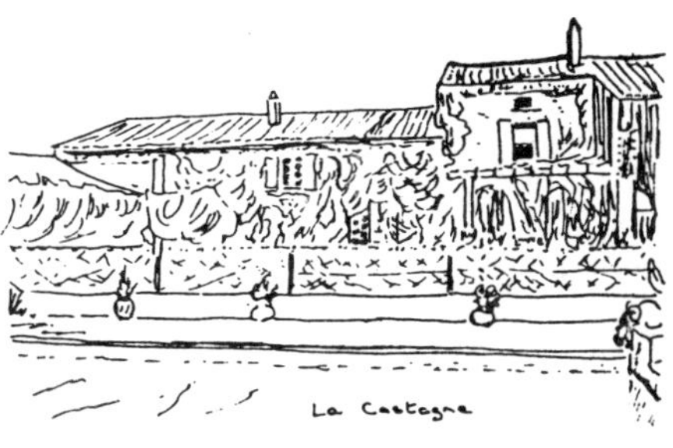

Madame Martin is a graduate in Law and Economics, who speaks fluent English, and runs weekly "Cordon Bleu" courses, using the gîtes to accommodate her guests. Chambres d'hôtes guests may join the cookery lesson each afternoon, gratis, the results of which will be appearing on the menu each evening. Evening meal 100/120f. All drinks from aperitif (*Muscat de Rives-Saltes*) and wine and coffee are *compris*. Not just *vin de pays* here; the right wine for the right course! Room 290f.

If you care to take the week's course, Madame takes great care to arrange it to suit her guests. The daily routine is a morning of walking, swimming or visiting such historic sites as Albi, with the Toulouse Lautrec museum and the cathedral, or Vielle-Carcassonne, churches and the Cathar Châteaux, antiques or food markets, followed by lunch in a *ferme auberge*. Afternoons are taken up with cookery classes and everyone relaxes in the evening over a superb dinner. I take it Madame makes sure no calamities reach the table!

A week of the course will set you back 7,000f, or 13,000f for two if you share a room, but all transport from picking up at Toulouse station or airport and *ferme auberge* lunches are included in the price.

PALAJA. 11570

5km S of Carcassonne. Close to the entrancing old city of Carcassonne. There is a delightful legend that Carcassonne owes its name to a foreign princess, Dame Carcas, who held the fortified city against the armies of Charlemagne. When the people had nothing left to eat but one solitary pig, she ordered the body of the pig to be thrown over the walls to show how well-off for food they were. Charlemagne fell for the bluff, lifted the siege and retreated. However history does not support this charming story as the *Cité*, one of the largest fortresses of Europe, was fortified by the Romans in the first century B.C. and given the name *Carcasso*. Situated as it is at a strategic cross-roads, it was taken by the Visigoths, then the Saracens, who were chased out by the Trencavel family in the eighth-century. This family also ruled over Albi, Nîmes and Béziers.

The Old City of Carcassonne is well worth a full day's visit. There is adequate parking outside the walls. A good way to start is to take a trip round the outer walls in a horse-drawn coach, complete with commentary from the driver. Then wander round the fascinating old streets, visit the ancient cathedral, sit in one of the many little shady squares and enjoy a cool drink and watch the world go by, and there's a lot of "world" in Carcassonne in the summer! After this, a visit to the modern city hardly seems worthwhile.

From the Autoroute-des-Deux-Mer exit 'Carcassonne West' turn right (SP. Limoux) and at the T junction in 1km turn left (SP La Cité) then first right on to a new wide road (SP. St.-Hilaire) carry straight on **NOT** taking the turning to Saint-Hilaire; but at the Charlemagne roundabout take the first right (SP Cazilhac-Palaja), bearing right to Cazhilac. Opposite the *mairie* turn left where the sign to the chambres d'hôtes is hidden in bushes behind the fountain. At the cemetery bear left and the *Ferme* is on your left in 1km.

NEW **Chris Gibson & Dianne Warr**
La Ferme de la Sauzette (M)
Route de Villefloure. (0)4.68.79.81.32. fax: (0)4.68.79.

Dianne and Chris will give you a very warm welcome in their newly built ranch-style home in the woods. They have five rooms, one especially designed for the handicapped. All have tiled floors, double and single beds, beamed sloping ceilings and modern bathrooms, one with a bath. 325/370f.

The well-lit corridor has many interesting baskets of goodies for guests, hair drier, hot water bottles, shoe cleaning materials, shampoos and a first aid kit.

The lounge and dining room open on to a terrace where meals are served in the summer, and there is a an open-sided summer kitchen for guests, but people with babies are welcome to use the main kitchen for feeds, etc. Dianne and Chris have tried to think of everything for your comfort in this quiet hideaway. Dianne loves cooking and you will be sure of a tasty and copious meal for 125f, all drinks *compris*.

A visit to viticulteurs can be arranged, including a lunch, to follow the production of wine from the grape to the tasting.

PECH-LUNA. 11420

18km. SW of Castelnaudary. From the A61 exit Castelnaudary. Take the D6 towards Mirepoix, in 10km turn right SP St. Amans and follow signs to Pech-Luna. 1km before Pech-Luna turn left to the Domaine-de Manso.

NEW **Mme Speyer. Domaine-de-Manso** (M)
Tel. & fax: (0)4.68.60.67.84.

Again not in the village, but signed off the D47, at Pech Luna. Mme Speyer breeds horses and offers very pleasant accommodation in her large *maison-de-maître* overlooking a grassy garden with swimming pool. The two spacious rooms on the first floor are light and airy and have excellent shower rooms for 260f. Two back rooms share a large bathroom and are only 200f.

Madame, who is German, offers evening meals for 90f each. A good dining/sitting room with toys for children adds to the amenities.

PENNAUTIER. 11610

6km NW of Carcassonne. If you feel like treating yourself to that little something extra, while visiting Carcassonne, this château is just the place. On the N113 2km west of Carcassonne, turn off on to the D203 SP Pennautier, follow the D203 through the village (one way system) SP Aragon and the château is on the right in 4km.

NEW ➤ M. & Mme Cassette-De-Stoop. Château-de-Liet (M)

(0)4.68.71.55.24. fax: (0)4.68.47.05.22.

This many-towered château suddenly appears at the end of a long tree-lined drive, where the resident peacock will give you a cautious welcome. The young owners have completely restored it over the last five years and it is now luxurious. Six modernised rooms with every comfort vary from 250f to 330f for the *Chambre Vert* which has a balcony and its own little tower room. This is real honeymoon stuff; a romantic dinner can be served in this room with breakfast for two for 600f. Not champagne, but Blanquette de Limoux. Cheaper still in the smaller double-bedded rooms, but not served in the single-bedded rooms! The rooms vary in size. On the first and second floors there is a choice of baths or showers.

A charming sitting-room opens on to the garden where meals are served in the summer, but breakfast, buffet-style and on separate round tables, is in a palatial dining room, where panels of red and white *Toile-de-Jouy* distract from the very high ceiling. Evening meals cooked by Madame taken together at one long table - 125f each - offer lobster and many specialities of the region. All drinks are *compris*, from *apéritifs* to *digestifs* including their own château wine.

There are 55 hectares of parkland to wander round, *dégustations* on the spot (or just laze by the pool in the garden). There are two *gîtes* in the grounds, whose occupants also use the pool.

This château has all the luxuries of a five-star hotel, but maintains the friendly atmosphere of a true chambres d'hôtes. So an arrow for good value.

GARD

BARJAC.

53km NW of Orange. 38km NE of Alès. A p
not far south of the Gorge de l'Ardèche,
found.
Outside the town the sign is past the 'Score'

NEW M. Divol. Le Mas Neuf (M)

(0)4.66.24.50.79.

Two sunny studio chambres d'hôtes, 50 yards from the farmhouse, both with terraces. Each one has a double bed, en suite shower, T.V. and a kitchen corner. Stairs lead up to a mezzanine with another double bed.

Madame had a hip replacement when I stayed, so Monsieur arrived with a breakfast tray, exactly on time. Steaming coffee, jam, fresh bread and croissants can be eaten on the terrace in summer.

Rooms 280f, 50f for an extra person.

BRAGASSARGUES. 30260

30km NW of Nîmes A tiny village with a handful of houses offering peace and quiet, but within sightseeing distance of many interesting places; the Arena at Nîmes, the Cévennes in the north, the Camargue to the south and the lovely fortified town of Aigues-Mortes.

NEW Mr. & Mrs. Chapman. La Maison des Rèves (M)

Le Village. (0)4.66.77.13.45. U.K. Tel: Nov-Mar 01273-514626.

This unusual house, right in the centre of the village with deep blue railings, is easy to find in a tiny lane between other buildings. You can't miss the steps to the flowery conservatory and small courtyard.

Your English host is an artist who has taught for many years and would be happy to instruct his guests. Pat, his wife, adores cooking and gardening. You will enjoy lazing in their multi-fruit orchard with a stream running through.

One room is prettily decorated with a white *ciel-de-lit*, and has stone walls, tiled

ouble bed and
room. A bath with
a separate shower
ent many a matrimonial
nps. Entry can be inde-
nt, from a raised terrace. The
er room is on the *rez-de-chaussée*
nd has a private courtyard. There are twin beds, and a fascinating large shower room, almost a cave, built into the cliff side of the house. There is a possible other room for children, sharing facilities.

A salon has lovely old tiles and a corner fireplace; but it is in the kitchen at a long table where you have breakfast and sample Pat's evening meals before an eye-level log fire that you will feel a real guest of the family.

Evening meals 100f all drinks *compris*.

Rooms 255f A very fair price for comfort and originality. This could be a winner.

CALVISSON. 30420

15km W of Nîmes The village of Calvisson is a pleasant working village in the wine-growing district of the Gard, **not** *touristique* at all but pleasantly populated by locals. There are small bars, cafés in the square, and a simple nicely-kept church.

From Nîmes take the D40 west and in 12km turn on to the D 409 to Calvisson. The b&b is through the village in a narrow street beside the covered market

NEW **M. & Mme Burckel de Tel** (M)

48,Grande rue. (0)4.66.01.23.91. fax: (0)4.66.01.42.19.

Situated on a narrow village street, this old house dates back to the 15th century and many of its old features are still intact. The spiral stone staircase leads to all the rooms, which have original stone slab floors or quarry tiles. Régis, an artist, and Corinne an art historian, have been careful to restore this house and furnish it in keeping with its age.

The small cosy sitting-room has a stone vaulted ceiling, as does the long dining room. Rooms have been kept rustic and simple and, apart from one, are surprisingly light, with views from the windows of the village, improving the higher you go.

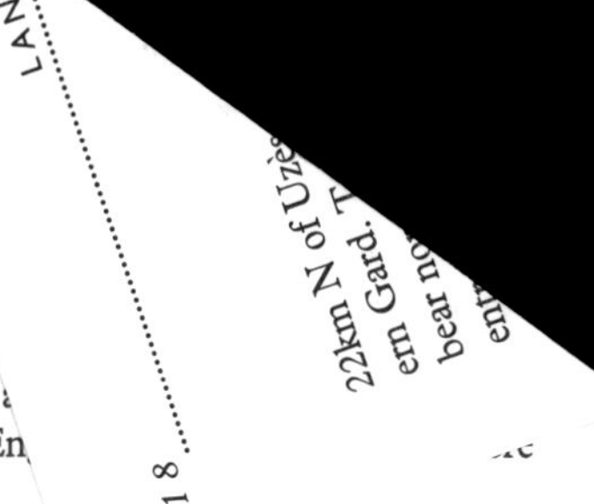

There is a terrace on the top floor as \ room, where meals are taken in summer anc ture of the old well. As it is a town house betw the good news is that they have a garage close t You have the advantage of being able to slip ou lage including a hairdresser. Rooms with great (wine *compris*, 75f.

Régis conducts weekly art courses for artists a French, though their name and Corinne's good En Dutch at first.

GENERARGUES. 30140

11km SW of Alès. 3.5k. N of Anduze. This small village is situated at the foothills of the Cévennes. There is a steam train from Anduze to Saint-Jean-du-Gard, which is the gateway to the Cévennes and the start of the Corniche-des-Cévennes, leading to Florac and the Gorges-du-Tarn. Small roads (not for caravans) drop down from the Corniche into the peaceful Vallée Française which runs a parallel course along a small river.

From Anduze take the D129, SP Générargues. In the village turn left on to the D50, SP Mialet. In 2km you will pass le Roucan on your right and the Hotel les Trois Barbus on your left. In 150 metres on the right is the entrance to the chambres d'hôtes between two low pink walls.

NEW The Hon. Mr. & Mrs. Vivian. Le Gamaos (M)

Vallée-de-Mialet. (0)4.66.61.93.79.

"*The chambre d'hôtes are well-appointed next to the main house, which nestles in a chestnut-covered slope with views across the valley through the trees. The Vivians give a warm welcome and provide an excellent evening meal and there is a splendid swimming pool - all excellent value in a beautiful area of France.*" John Tinehurst.

Mingled with acacia and wild cherry this comfortable home offers good accommodation. There are three guest rooms with showers and loos, a choice of double or single beds. One for a family with double and twin beds, 250f for two, 350f for three, 450f for four. Dinner on reservation 85f including wine is taken with your hosts.

LUSSAN. 30580

. 52km NW of Avignon. An old hill village in the *garrigue* of north-ake the D979 Nîmes to Barjac road and after the hill village of Lussan rth to La Lèque. The chambres d'hôtes is easy to find by the roadside at the ance to the village, surrounded by fields of horses.

NEW **Mme Dollfus. Mas des Garrigues** (M)

La Lèque. (0)4.66.72.91.18. fax: (0)4.66.72.97.91.

This 18th-century old farmhouse, 5km north of Lussan in a small hamlet, has a lot of character; the original old quarry tiled floors in the rooms and simple Provençal curtains and bed covers in different colours complement the white walls. There is a choice of double or single beds.

A pleasant salon has comfortable couches. This is a *Ferme Equestre* and the horses in the surrounding fields are for riding. Riding/picnic parties are arranged for people of differing capabilities (but do make sure your insurance covers you for riding accidents). Chatty evening meals round the long oak table in the dining room or on the terrace (every day except Thursdays) are 95f wine and coffee *compris*. Rooms are 290f but in July and August bookings must be for a week.

Though close to a road, you will be more likely to be woken by sheep bells; each animal wears a bell in this area and many a returning flock blocks the road. Madame owns a swimming pool in the village which she allows locals as well as guests to use, only a few paces from the farmhouse. There is a tiny covered market each Tuesday and Sunday next door.

L'HERAULT

SAUSSAN. 34570

10km SW of Montpellier. A quiet village not far from the Mediterranean beaches, and close to Montpellier.

Take the N113 from Montpellier to Fabrègues, then turn right on to the D27 to Saussan.

Mme Gine (M)

6, rue des Penitients. (0)4.67.47.81.01.

In the centre of the village a door on the roadside leads into a most spacious chambres d'hôtes. A large sitting room with patio doors opens into a walled garden. A kitchen is for self-catering. There are four well-furnished rooms, two on the ground floor. A sweeping staircase leads to a landing with a billiard table and the two other rooms - 250f. Mme Gine is a charming hostess who lives next door and there is space for parking in her drive. Central heating makes this a good winter stop. Freshly squeezed orange juice with your croissants for breakfast. A café/restaurant in the village; but there are more restaurants and shops in Pignan only 2km away.

LOZERE

CHANAC. 48230

14km SW of Mende. The ancient cheese of Roquefort comes from a small village of that name on the plain south of Millau where the limestone caves have just the right atmosphere for maturing it. Fable has it that a shepherd boy in the 12th century left some sheep's milk and bread in a cave where mushrooms grew while he went off to visit a girl friend. Three weeks later he returned to find the bread, milk and mushrooms had integrated into a mass of cheese. To this day the cheese is made in the same way, using the same caves to store it. A very special type of mushroom is used, grown only in this area, and the milk is collected from sheep farmers for miles around, one of whom is M. Pradeilles. Every day from January to July a lorry rushes the milk to the large *fromagerie* in the caves at Roquefort.
Turn off the D32 at Le-Cros-Bas, 4km south of Chanac.

Mme Pradeilles. Ferme Auberge Pradeilles (S)

Le Gazy. (0)4.66.48.21.91.

Hidden away in fields 2Km from the main road, you will be given a warm welcome from Madame and her son, who run the restaurant and b & b. Probably the best budget stop you will find in the area, judging by the number of cars here for Sunday lunch. A selection of five fairly basic rooms, with showers but some shared toilets. Try Great Grandma's matrimonial bed in the family room, now en suite 220f.

Chambres d'hôtes guests can opt for four courses at dinner for 60f, or best of all demi-pension for two is 300f. A good base for visiting the Gorge-du-Tarn only 25km away.

LA CANOURGUE. 48500

35km SW of Mende, 12km S of Chanac. From the N88 at Chanac turn into the town and take the D32 for 11.5km to the T junction with the D998 from La Canourgue to Sainte-Enimie. Turn left towards Ste-Enimie and in 100 yards you will see the sign to La Vialette opposite a roadside cross.

NEW **M. & Mme Fages. La Vialette** (M)
(0)4.66.32.83.00. fax: (0)4.66.32.94.62.

An excellent b & b close to the Gorges-du-Tarn but in open country. Rustic farm buildings surround the modernised *bergerie* where there are five varied rooms, smartly furnished with all mod. cons. including TV and telephones - 260f for two. Two rooms downstairs have access to a sunny terrace.

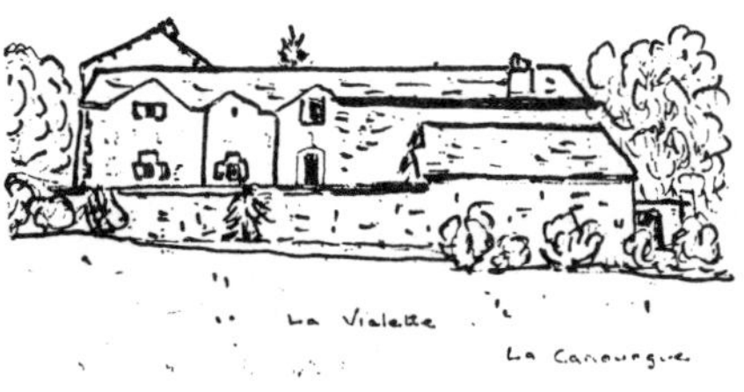

The large dining room adjoins Madame's kitchen where there is a fridge and washing machine guests may use. Demi-pension 200f each, with wine and coffee *compris*, makes this one of the best I found in the Lozère. Practical Mme Fages has everything running smoothly for your comfort. Just waiting for your reports.

FONTANS. 48700

36km W of Mende. In the northern part of the Lozère. Leave the Autoroute A75 at exit 34 and take the N106 SE towards Mende and in 8km turn left at the Pont d'Estrets on to the D7. Les Estrets is a little village, well before Fontans, where there is a small well-cared-for church completely in natural stone with beautiful polished wooden pews. The altar frontal is a fairly new carved picture of the Last

Supper. There are no shops in this village, everyone knows everyone else so you only have to ask the first person you meet where Mme Rousset lives..

➤ Mme Rousset. Les Estrets (S)

(0)4.66.31.27.74. Closed: 1/11 to 28/2.

Madame Rousset has a superb couple of rooms on the ground floor, one double and one family with the car parked right outside the window, for 230f. Lovely bunches of fresh wild flowers in your room. She serves excellent five course meals for 60f, vin *compris* in the modern cosy, dining room. Sit on the terrace in the setting sun or stroll round the tiny village before being called *à table.*

I can't recommend this place too highly, all comforts with simplicity and great kindness shown by your hostess.

PONT-DE-MONTVERT. 48220

60km SE of Mende. 21km E of Florac. Le Pont-de-Montvert is one of the prettiest little villages descended upon by Robert Louis Stevenson and his donkey. The river Tarn, fresh from its source, rushes through the main street. Nothing seems to have changed for years. The old bridge connects the two sides of the town, sunny cafés do a roaring trade on the main street beside the river.

Take the D998 from Florac to Pont-de-Montvert continue through the village and turn left at the sign to Le Merlet, which is two miles from the main road, bearing left.

NEW M. & Mme Galzin. Le Merlet (S)

(0)4.66.45.82.92.

At the end of a lane this cluster of typical Lozèrean buildings dating from the 17th-century has been restored and the rooms in a separate building are now modernised. Family and otherwise, all with showers, wood floors and central heating. One on the ground floor is designed for the handicapped. I have my doubts about a wheelchair bumping across the stony terrace, but the view of the Causse de Méjean from this south-facing rustic terrace is quite delightful.

Demi-pension obligatory here but, with wine *compris*, 225f per person is very acceptable.

LE ROZIER. 48150

21km NE of Millau. This interesting little hillside village lies at the confluence of the rivers Tarn and Jonte as they emerge from their respective gorges.

At the junction of the D907 and the D996 at Le Rozier cross the river Tarn and bear right on the one-way system until you see a small car park on the right. Turn immediately left and the Route de Capluc is first right, with the b & b a few houses up the hill on the left.

NEW **M. & Mme Espinasse** (S)
Route de Capluc. (0)5.65.62.63.06.

Wide steps sweep up to this modern house with a view over the river Jonte to the rocky cliffs of the Causse.

Four comfortably-carpeted rooms. Two at the front are brightest, and will cost you 230/260f including a very good breakfast. This friendly young couple don't offer evening meals because there are many restaurants within walking distance.

PYRENEES-ORIENTALES

ALENYA. 66200

10km SE of Perpignan. At Alenya take the D39 to the farm on your right.

M. & Mme Favier. Domaine du Mas Bazan (S)
(0)4.68.22.98.26. fax: (0)4 68. 22. 97.37.

This is a large isolated farmhouse, well off the road, with a swimming pool in the surrounding grounds. Four simple rustic rooms on the first floor with unpolished wood floors and natural stone walls are en suite with baths. All have pleasant views over flat terrain to the Pyrénées. 280f. Other rooms in the

barns are not recommended.

A large salon on the first floor takes care of the children in wet weather. There is a *ferme auberge* dining room on the ground floor, where during the season evening meals are on offer to house guests only, 100f, drinks included. Vineyards surround and M. Favier keeps pigs and chickens, and has ponies for children to ride.

ARGELES-SUR-MER. 66700

A very pleasant route along the eastern Mediterranean is the coast road turning off the A9 or N9 near Caves on to the N627 to Leucate. The road takes you south with the Mediterranean on your left and the calm waters of the Etang de Leucate on your right. At Port Leucate there is only a bridge dividing the two. Go on south, keeping to the coast past Perpignan to St. Cyprien-Plage, a purpose-built holiday complex, to Argelès-sur-Mer, a pleasant flat town with a small port and good beaches. From the N10 take the Route d'Elne, after the post office turn right at the Tricolores traffic lights, then under the railway bridge, then straight on, with the cemetery on the left. Follow the sign 'Maison de Retraite Les Capucines,' pass under the bridge of the RN114 and turn left, in 200 metres turn right in the direction La Montagne, in 2km take the right lane to the chambres d'hôtes.

NEW M. & Mme Romero. Mas Senyarich (M)

(0)4.68.95.93.63. fax: (0)4.68.81.17.27.

Here is an excellent choice for a week-long holiday, so near the coast, but away from the noise and bustle.

The typical rambling Catalan *mas* is approached up a narrow tarred track 4km from the sea but having sea views from all the rooms. Five rooms, all differently furnished in country styles, patchwork quilts, tiled and wood floors, heating for early visits, bathrooms and a definite Spanish touch. 295/300f.

A spacious comfortable lounge whose large fireplace has stone carvings depicting the various occupations of the area; the attached dining room has an enormous window looking over the swimming pool to the sea beyond. Your enthusiastic hosts serve evening meals *en famille*, for 125f each, all drinks included.

There is shady parking and a garage for two cars. Use of a washing machine for a small payment adds to one's comfort. Meals are not obligatory, so you have the option of trying the many Argelès restaurants.

CAIXAS. 66300

26km SW of Perpignan, 17km SW of Thuir. From Perpignan take the N9 towards Spain as far as Villemolaque then the D2 west to Caixas.

High in the Pyrénées Orientales, overlooked by the Pic-de-Canigou, this little village consists of scattered farmsteads and modern houses chequered over the hillside. The chambres d'hôtes is in an intriguing position, down a tiny lane leading to the Mairie which is situated on a spur of land with a circular lookout. Next door is a church (open once a year on feast day); but it is to the old house beside the church that you should head.

NEW ➤ Jane Richards & Ian Mayes. Mas Saint-Jacques (M)

Tel & fax: (0)4.68.38.87.83.

First impressions are not very exciting but you will soon change your mind. Three storeys tower up from the little patio outside this tall dwelling; further inspection will take you along the terraced garden to two summer rooms with expansive views, for two or three people. Hidden behind a wall is a sheltered swimming pool. In the main house the open-plan kitchen and dining room leads to a new covered conservatory, facing west, for breakfast on cooler days. Up the stone and wood spiral stairs, rooms are named after the ancient regions of Cerdanya. On the first floor there is a family suite of two rooms, double and two singles, sharing a bathroom. The top floor is taken up with a lounge and two more bedrooms, a treble with a balcony and one with two single beds, overlooking the pool and countryside, Capcir and Rosello. All rooms are light and airy, with good quality pine furniture, duvets and pristine white linen on the beds, luxury towels, and even hot water bottles for out-of-season travellers. 295f for two.

Plenty to do in this hidden mountain retreat where the air is so pure. Climb Mt. Hélèna for a breathtaking view of the mountains and coast, perhaps visit Céret where Picasso once lived, take a day trip on the Little Yellow Train round the mountains, or just relax by the pool. End the day with a convivial meal with your charming English hosts, Jane and Ian, who will have prepared you a feast of fresh local produce, all drinks included 95f.

Special courses in wine tasting can be arranged on a weekly basis.

ELNE. 66200

13km SE of Perpignan. Elne was the ancient capital of Roussillon. Established as a bishopric in the 6th-century, there is almost a Spanish atmosphere to the old town, now famous for the Cathedral of Ste Eulalie, consecrated in the 11th-century, and its cloister, which dates from the 12th. There is a good market in Elne on Monday, Wednesday and Friday, where you can buy fresh figs as well as peaches and other local fruit. Leave Elne by the D612 to Bages. The farm is on your right.

M. & Mme Tubert. Mas de la Couloumine (S)

Route de Bages. (0)4.68.22.36.07.

A swimming pool in the middle of a kiwi grove! M. & Mme Tubert have tastefully renovated an old house. Well insulated, it is warm in winter and cool in summer. There are six rooms to choose from, including a family suite. Some have views to the Pic du Canigou. M. Tubert grows his own salads all winter and Madame produces generous evening meals (if reserved), preceded by *apéritifs* in the lounge, for 80f, *vin compris*, reduced rates for children. Coffee *bols* for breakfast and kiwi fruits creep into all the jams.

Rooms 210f. You can have a third bed in the room for 50f extra, including breakfast.

Very busy here in the summer, so close to the beaches.

LIMOUSIN

Départements: **Corrèze**
Creuse
Haute-Vienne

An agricultural region, west of the Auvergne, frequent travellers to France have shot through it without ever knowing they have visited the area. At one time the Route Nationale 20 was the main road from Paris to Bourg-Madame, en route for Andorra and Spain. Now with all the new motorways it is much more peaceful and the lovely old villages, auberges, *Routiers* and small cafés lining its route can be enjoyed by travellers who have time to spare. Limoges, the *préfecture* of **Haute Vienne**, is a large town famous for the manufacture of porcelain. The city is large and busy, with rather attractive open squares. The cathedral of St. Etienne is mostly gothic, it has some colourful blue windows and a nice balcony with two spiral staircases under the organ. Occasionally on Sundays *Brocante* fairs are held in the forecourt. Walk behind the cathedral to find the Botanical Gardens tiered down to the river Vienne, where every plant has a name tag. However the most striking building in Limoges is the station, built in 1829, on a hill overlooking the city with its green domed roof and clock tower in which the Stationmaster dwells. The wide approach roads are lined with flower beds. The spacious entrance hall is where you can always find your English newspapers. A porcelain exhibition is held in Limoges from July to September, but there is no need to brave the traffic looking for your purchases. As you approach the city the roads have many small wayside shops with a choice of china, and the owners can direct you to the factory/shop in Limoges if you wish to place larger orders.

North-west of Limoges is the martyred village of Oradour-sur-Glane, well worth visiting, but be prepared for the sombre reminder of the horrors of Nazi occupation. The whole village was wiped out by fire on 10th June 1944. To this day they are not sure why. A completely new village has been built nearby and the original Oradour left in ruins, as a memorial to the 642 people who lost their lives.

In the east the **Creuse** *département* is purely agricultural, with the *préfecture* of Guéret hugging the hillside, overlooking orchards of apples and pears. On the whole the region is undulating farmland, especially in the north-east. In the south-east you will discover Aubusson, the Axminster of France, with a very fine Museum of Carpets and Tapestries.

LIMOUSIN

Haute-Vienne
Creuse
Corrèze
Bellac
Guéret
Limoges
Isle
Boisseul
Alleyrat
Aubusson
St-Pardoux-le-Neuf
Benayes
St-Julien-le-Vendômois
Égletons
Tulle
Brive-la-Gaillarde
Nespouls
N20
N14
N145
D951
N141
N147
N21
D941
N89
N120
Chambre d'Hôtes
0
20km

The southerly department of the Limousin is **Corrèze,** which is still very agricultural. To the east is the plateau of Millevaches where the river Vienne springs to life. As the name suggests it is the grazing land of many handsome brown Limousin cows. The N20 still ploughs relentlessly south, passing through Uzerche - the county town.

CORREZE

BENAYES. 19510

40km SSE of Limoges. Just off the N20 between Limoges and Brive turn at Masserat on to the D20 to Benayes; you will find Château Forsac signposted up a long winding drive on your left in 4km.

Mme Demontbron. Château Forsac (S)
(0)5.55.73.47.78.

If you feel like a night in a real château which has been in the family for over a hundred years and is steeped in history, then come to Forsac. Four plane trees in front of the house were brought from Marie Antoinette's garden at Le Petit Trianon by a captain of the king's guard, who was a regular visitor. When the château was first built in feudal times it had four towers; one of the original is still standing and is part of the house; the only other one has been rebuilt to preserve it. Situated in 200 hectares of wooded land it is a paradise for early morning walkers and children. In spring drifts of scillas and daffodils light up the lawn opposite the arched door, which has the family motto 'Moins Dire Que Faire' (Actions speak louder than words) above it.

Madame is a charming young Countess (de Cherade de Montbron) who speaks perfect English and will be delighted to give you a room. They are in the process of restoring the château internally and have a long way to go, so don't expect anything wonderful. The wide staircase leads to three large bedrooms, one with a crested bed-head! Two rooms can be inter-communicating for a family. Electric heating is not really suitable for cold winter weather, but the château is open all the year if you want to brave it. There is a sunny sitting room for guests adjoining the three rooms.

Breakfast is taken in the family salon, panelled with enormous rural paintings. No evening meals on a regular basis, but should you arrive tired and late Madame will take pity on you and knock up a light meal of omelette, salad and fruit.

So ignore the peeling walls and settle for the charming *accueil*, the tranquillity and improving your history. At 200f for bed and breakfast for two, it is a bargain. Feel you are contributing to the château's restoration!

NESPOULS. 19600

16km S of Brive-la-Gaillarde. A useful stop, just off the N20, for visiting Collonges-la-Rouge and Turenne, a small hill village with narrow, flower bedecked streets winding up to the old castle. Park by the church and you will be half way up! The Counts of Turenne often took their family holidays at the neighbouring village of Collonges-la-Rouge, so called because all the houses have been built in red brick. A very pretty little place to visit but unfortunately a popular stop for all the tour coaches. It becomes packed in the high season, but is well worth a detour at other times.

From the N20 travelling south at Nespouls take the D19 (SP Larche) and then immediately right SP Belveyre to the small hamlet where two chambres d'hôtes are signed.

NEW M. & Mme Lalle. Aux Sabots du Causse (S)

Belveyre. (0)5.55.85.84.47.

A typical towered Périgord house, this one has four rooms. One on the ground floor off the salon has garden access, and there is a similar room above. Entry to the two others is from an external staircase; one has a terrace, the other a family room for five (one double, one single bed and two beds in the mezzanine up a ladder), sharing a large shower room with two washbasins.

These compact rooms are carpeted, have natural stone walls and beds for three, dainty white *ciel-de-lit* or pretty flowered *tête-de-lits* and matching sheets, etc. There is a fridge in every room, with cold drinks for 5f each. Each shower room has a hair-drier and numerous extras such as razors - nothing forgotten here. 200f for two, 50f for an extra bed.

A copious breakfast. Evening meals served at a long table in the large salon 70f wine *compris*.

Regretfully Madame says she cannot speak English - just the place to brush up your French.

SAINT-JULIEN-LE-VENDOMOIS. 19210

24km WNW of Uzerche. Not far from Pompadour where the *haras*, a branch of the National Stud, is noted for breeding Anglo/Arab horses. There is a fine turreted castle here in this attractive little town, which is within easy reach of the N20. Although the castle was given to Mme Pompadour, she never visited it and Louis XV repossessed it on her death.

Take the D126 out of Arnac-Pompadour and follow the signs for about 5km.

Marquise de la Roche. Domaine de la Roche (S) (0)5.55.98.72.87.

A stay here at the Domaine, once the property of the King and Queen of Navarre, would enhance your visit to Pompadour. The young owners are farmers and have a delightful small restaurant in a 15th-century cottage. They make and tin all their own produce such as *confits* and *foie-gras*.

Madame does all the cooking and Monsieur waits at table as well as running the farm.

Bedrooms, in another building, are pleasantly rustic. One room can accommodate up to five people, with a double bed and bunks, and there are two doubles, for 220/250f. 70f each extra bed. Breakfast is served in your room. Bed and breakfast terms are available only out of season. In season you must stay on *demi-pension* terms, but this is no hardship at 265/295f, with dinner in the *ferme auberge*. If you stay for two weeks you get one night free.

CREUSE

ALLEYRAT. 23200

6km N of Aubusson.Take the Aubusson by-pass, then the D990 to Guéret and Montluçon. Branch left to Guéret on the D942 and turn left at the chambres d'hôtes sign to Ourdeaux on the D924A.

NEW **M. & Mme d'Hiver** (S)

Ourdeaux. (0)5.55.66.29.65.

A very relaxed homely place, off the beaten track. Your hosts are friendly young sheep farmers with a young family. who have made their stables into very pleasant rooms with beamed ceilings, tiled floors, good heating and family heirlooms. A south-facing terrace has views over fields; there are plenty of cats and kittens to entertain the young. Evening meal 80f if reserved. Otherwise the Café des Sports or a *Logis* just up the road on the D942.

Rooms 220f include fresh eggs for breakfast.

SAINT-PARDOUX-LE-NEUF. 23200

4km E of Aubusson on the D941 to Clermont-Ferrand turn right to Les Vergnes. Aubusson is the Axminster of France and has a fine carpet museum. Clermont-Ferrand is 60km east, in the Massif Central.

M. & Mme Dumontant Les Vergnes (M)

(0)5.55.66.23.74. Closed: 1/11 to Easter.

This really is a delightful spot for a restful holiday. Situated in open countryside, the rooms are in a restored farmhouse near the main house. Downstairs are a dining room and lounge for guests, and six well-furnished bedrooms, up and down, two adjoining, 280f. There are glorious views of the small private lake and wooded countryside from the lawns outside and a smart new swimming pool, solar heated, so you can swim sometimes as early as April or May.

Free fishing in the lake. When we were there, an Englishman had just caught twelve trout in one day; no prizes for guessing what was on the menu that night. Guests meet for a complimentary *apéritif* before an interesting evening meal served by your hosts, 95f. Wine extra works out at about 30/40 f a bottle.

HAUTE-VIENNE

BOISSEUIL. 87220

8km SE of Limoges.Take the A 20 south from Limoges direction Toulouse then exit (sortie)37 Boisseuil Zone Commerciales, then follow signs to chambres d'hôtes, past the school in Boisseuil.

Mme Brigitte Ziegler. Moulinard (S)

Tel & fax: (0)5.55.06.91.22. Open all year.

A useful place to stay for a visit to Limoges, only ten minutes from the centre of the town but a world away from all the noise and traffic. The farm is situated on a promontory between two valleys and guest rooms are in an old *maison-de-maître* nearby. Picnic or sit in the walled garden under the trees. You enter the house through the kitchen which has an amazing old floor tiled with moulds from the porcelain factories in Limoges.

Four large rooms, have polished wood floors and antique furniture - 220f. Good radiators for cold weather in the bedrooms.

Breakfast in Mme Ziegler's own farmhouse is beautifully served in her kitchen with sunny views of her garden where wild rabbits play. Fresh baguettes, home-made jams and the usual plentiful coffee, tea or chocolate with fresh flowers on the table make this a really enjoyable start to the day. There is no evening meal, but there are two *Logis* quite near at Solignac. Madame speaks a little English.

ISLE. 87170

8km W of Limoges. Leave Limoges on the N21 south and in about 3km, just after the turn to L'Aiguille there will be a chambres d'hôtes sign on the right and a fork right which will take you up a country lane to the Brunier's house on the right.

➤ Mme Brunier. Pic de L'Aiguille (S)

Verthamont. (0)5.55.36.12.89.

A real find. A beautiful, new, sprawling house on a hillside outside Limoges with lovely, peaceful views and a swimming pool. Two rooms are extremely pretty, carpeted, good wardrobes with patio doors to private terraces with tables and chairs. A

third room for a family is on the first floor under the eaves.

The Bruniers are a lovely family, with two teenage children, and receive one as a real friend of the family. Nothing is too much trouble. Drinks offered on arrival. Dinner on the terrace when fine. A typical menu is fish mayonnaise served attractively in lemon halves, followed by a boeuf daube with new potatoes, salad, cheese and fresh peaches in crème anglaise decorated with sprigs of cherries. Other specialities include *rôti de veau à la crème des champignons*, *tartes salées et sucrées*, and *gâteau au chocolat*. Vegetables are from the garden and vegetarian diets are available if wanted. Reserve your meal in advance and you won't be disappointed.

Evening meal 80f, wine *compris*. Room 220f. So an arrow. All round value here. Some English spoken.

Loire Valley

Départements:	**Cher**	**Indre-et-Loire**
	Eure-et-Loir	**Loir-et-Cher**
	Indre	**Loiret**

Companion guide to the area - 'French Entrée 8 - The Loire'

One of the most popular of all French tourist destinations. For many good reasons. With autoroutes and TGV linking the main cities, Parisians can, and do, nip down for the weekend. This means sophisticated hotels and restaurants and sophisticated prices. It's handy for the Brits too - a halfway stop on their way to the Med. and accessible after a fast three-four hour drive, making it ideal for the first or last night from and to the ferry.

The area offers great variety - wine production, university cities, cathedrals, abbeys and river attractions. But, of course, its unique attraction is the châteaux. There are legions of them, strategically sited to defend, enhance, and profit by the mighty river that used to be the main highway through the land. To come to this area and not visit some of them would be unthinkable, but do resist the temptation to tackle too many too quickly. Ration the daily allowance. One or two will do nicely. And be selective. Some, like gargantuan Chambord, lovely Chenonçeau and verdant Villandry, should be on every list. Others, like Loches and Valençay, are for connoisseurs. Thirty-one are described in FE8 with a (highly subjective) rating system. The Loire is the big name but some of its many tributaries are even more attractive than this shallow, sandbanked, often silted giant. Follow their courses, picnic by their willow-fringed banks and take a boat ride upon them, getting acquainted with areas other than the tourist-ridden Loire banks.

All this potential is good news for bed-providers. There are hundreds of chambres d'hôtes to choose from here and elimination was particularly hard. There are more in the 'L' bracket than in any other area for obvious reasons - the super-abundance of châteaux begging to be converted being one. Some were just too good to leave out, their standards being just as high as luxury hotels and, price for price, far superior. I did manage to find a few under 200f away from the main tourist areas. Those on a really tight budget should look elsewhere. In whatever category the availability of chambres d'hôtes, hosts for discussions scores highly here - they will advise on how best to allocate the time between so many fascinating diversions.

Here is a brief run along the river, from east to west:

Sancerre-Orléans: some of the finest scenery of the whole route. Sancerre is unique, with sizeable hills covered with vines contrasting with the general flatness of the region. The river here is fast-running and island dotted. The first important château is at Gien, famous for its porcelain, then Sully, where the river banks are sandy and the countryside somewhat dull. Châteauneuf is a pleasant, underestimated town and the river here is impressive. Further north the Forest of Orléans, peppered with lakes, is delightfully unspoiled.

Orléans-Blois: Orléans is the administrative capital of the region, mostly new but well laid out, with good shops.

South of Orléans lies the little-known region of the Sologne, wooded hunting country, spilling over into three departements, mostly Loir-et-Cher, Loiret in the north and the rest in Cher. Very pretty villages. Chambord and Cheverney are the principal châteaux.

Along the river the châteaux now come thick and fast and the roads along the banks can become uncomfortably busy at weekends. Meung and Beaugency are both worth a visit.

Blois-Tours: Blois is the first big château-town actually on the river and consequently congested. Amboise is best out of season; then it has much to offer. A diversion from Tours following the river Cher leads to the jewel in the crown, Chenonçeau. Montrichard is a narrow strip of a town between river and escarpment. St Aignan is infinitely more attractive.

Tours-Saumur: Tours is a lively university town, with some attractive restoration in its old quarters, good restaurants, outdoor cafés and markets. Cross to the southern bank and don't miss Villandry, Azay-le-Rideau and the fairy-tale Ussé. Chinon on the river Vienne has probably the most historically important château of them all.

CHER

AUBIGNY-SUR-NERE. 18700

48km N of Bourges. 67km S of Orléans. A small town with a large castle with strong Scottish connections, dating from the time of the Stuart kings. The museum in the town can supply much history of this period.

From the centre of the town take the D940 (SP Paris/Gien) and the chambres d'hôtes is 200 yds on the right.

NEW Mme Archard-Bouchez. 'Le Bien Dormir' (M)

12 Ave. de Paris. (0)2.48.81.04.04.

This 19th-century *maison-de-maître* stands behind locked gates where there is plenty

LOIRE (VALLEY)
Dreux
N23
A11
N10
Châteaudun
Danzé
Vendôme
A10
N152
Onzain
Rochecorbon
Fondettes
Tours
Lussault-sur-Loire
Bourré
Berthenay
Chouzé-sur-Loire
Savonnières
Cormery
Cinais
Chinon
Indre-et-Loire
Loches
Sepmes
Richelieu
N143
N151
Chambre d'Hôtes
0 20km

A10
N152
Montargis
N60
N60
Donnery
Orléans
Loiret
N7
N20
D952
La-Ferté-St-Aubin
Gien
Ménesteau-en-Villette
A71
Cher
Aubigny-sur-Néré
D940
N76
Montigny
Vierzon
A71
N151
Berry-Bouy
Bourges
Cher
N151
A71
N76
D934
N144

of gravelled parking. Newly opened in 1997 the owners, who have a restaurant 9km away, have redecorated the interior, partitioning large guest rooms to make equally large dressing rooms/bathrooms, most with modern corner baths. Tasteful decoration of walls and bedding in 'interesting' colours like turquoise and apricot revive the rooms considerably. All rooms have tea-making facilities. Two rooms in front share a private bathroom, making a family unit, two at the back have baths but share a WC on the landing. One on the ground floor with a shower has a private loo just outside the door. Heavy shutters reduce any traffic noise, 300f for two.

There is a small room with T.V. where breakfast is served at separate tables; but Madame is equally happy to serve it in your room, and offers many extra amenities such as baby sitting, washing lines and the possibility for families to picnic in her kitchen. No evening meals, but if you reserve well ahead Madame will arrange for a set four-course meal to be brought over from their restaurant (90f). Very useful if you arrive tired and hungry after a long journey and don't feel like walking into Aubigny, where there are other cafés and restaurants.

Mme Archard speaks very good English. There is a lawned garden behind the house with swings for children. As most guests are one-nighters en route from Paris/South there is little opportunity to get to know your fellow guests, making this chambres d'hôtes a bit like an hotel. However if you produce this guide you will get a 10% reduction and if you stay more than one night you will get an additional 10% reduction.

BERRY-BOUY. 18500

8km W of Bourges.What a pleasant drive it is down the N76 beside the Canal du Berry close to the river Cher, passing small villages overlooking the canal between Villefranche and Vierzon. The nearby A71 has exits at Vierzon (6) and Bourges (7), so this is a handy stop whichever way you are going.
From Mehun-sur-Yèvre south of Vierzon on the N76 take the D60 to Berry-Bouy. The farm is 1km on the right on the other side of the village.

Mme de la Farge. L'Ermitage (S)

(0)2.48.26.87.46. fax: (0)2.48.26.03.28.

An old manor house on a working farm. The spiral wood staircase in the tower leads to two very old rooms, tastefully modernised with every comfort. One, for a family with double and two single beds, with attached shower room, is really large.

Attention les pieds here, a beam runs right across the room at floor level to trip the unwary. The other room for a couple, with twin beds, has a bath. There are now three well-modernised en suite rooms in a separate building, which are exceptionally nice - 215/235f. In the equally old dining room an elegant breakfast (orange juice and croissants) is served by Madame who is equally elegant, a farmer's wife. We were offered Earl Grey tea on arrival, even at 6 p.m.

There are two restaurants within 3km. One upmarket, in the village, with menus from 140f, and the other at Marmagne only 2km further on, where, opposite the church at *Les Trois Amis*, Madame dispenses no choice evening meals of five courses, each left on the table to help yourself and a litre bottle of red wine, all of which will cost you 65f, including Madame's friendly chat between courses. Full of locals playing cards and eating.

MONTIGNY. 18250 HENRICHMONT

15km SW of Sancerre by D955 and D449 through Montigny. Signed after 5km. Still wine country, though now mixed with cereals; so near Sancerre, yet so rural.

➤ **Elisabeth and Jean-Louis Gressin. La Reculée** (M)
(0)2.48.69.59.18.

An absolute favourite, arrowed on all counts - welcome, comfort, position, good value and good food.

Jean-Louis is a farmer and his nice wife Elizabeth has turned some of the farm buildings into chambres d'hôtes with great style and imagination. The rooms are named after flowers and coloured accordingly - I like *Bleuet* best (forget-me-not) with twin beds, fresh blue and white covers and curtains and a blue bath - 260f. *Liseron* (bindweed) is pink and green, *Primevere* is naturally enough primrose and *Bouton d'Or* (buttercup) is a deeper yellow. *Cocquelicot* (poppy) is the most striking, all red and white with high ceiling and a shower, 260f a double.

Lots of blond wood has been used to give a Scandinavian feel and dispel the gloom that sometimes attaches to old buildings. The salon and kitchen (guests may use) follow the theme. Elisabeth cooks light, fresh evening meals for 90f exclusive of wine, using their own farm produce. A gem.

INDRE-ET-LOIRE

BERTHENAY 37510 JOUÉ LES TOURS

16km W of Tours. 5km SW of Villandry. Villandry, the last of the great of the great Renaissance châteaux built along the Loire valley, should be in the top half-dozen of essential visits. All that remains of its 14th-century origins is the keep and the interior does not match the interest of many others but of course it is for the gardens that one must make a detour. The finest in France they say. The formal French garden is designed on three levels: the water garden, the ornamental garden and the vegetable garden, all neatly encompassed by trimmed box hedges and yews. The vegetable garden is particularly fascinating, with its astonishingly vivid displays of purple cabbages, emerald leeks and lime green lettuces, all disciplined into intricate geometrical patterns.

The present owner has made an inspiring video of the garden in all its glory over the various seasons, shown of course to the accompaniment of Vivaldi. Whatever time of the year you happen to be in the district, you are assured of a special treat here. Allow plenty of time to enjoy it.

Berthenay is a small straggly village on a piece of land jutting into the confluence of the river Loire and Cher. From Villandry take the D7 to Savonnières. Turn immediately left across the bridge as you enter the village then right on to the D288 over the bridge and continue to a T junction. Turn left to Berthenay and you will pick up signs to the chambres d'hôtes.

Mme Millet. La Grange Aux Moines (M)

Berthenay. 37510. (0)2.47.50.06.91.

The house stands in a large garden with a swimming pool, tucked well away from main roads. There are six charming beamed rooms. All with showers or baths. One for a family on the ground floor, 320/370f. Evening meals are served at separate tables, 120f. (wine not included).

There is garage parking and bikes for hire.

CHOUZÉ-SUR-LOIRE. 37140 BOURGUEIL

5km S of Bourgueil, 16km N of Chinon. The countryside around is dull, but the situation is ideal for château-bashing, and Bourgueil is a delightful little wine town.

Mme Florence Goupil de Bouillé. Château des Réaux (L)

(0)2 47.95.14.40. fax: (0)2.47.95.18.34.

Wedding photos of Florence's great grandmother hang in the magnificent billiard room with its museum-piece table. It was she who bought the 15th-century château. Her daughter in her wedding finery and Florence in hers hang alongside and now that of a fourth generation, Angélique, daughter of Florence and Jean-Luc, who married Henri, owner of Villandry, so the two châteaux families are satisfactorily united.

The red-painted beams of the billiard room were discovered when the Goupils started renovating the castle, as were those next door in the salon, previously covered in plaster. It is here that the guests assemble for convivial apéritifs before dinner. In the last century this huge room was split up into several smaller ones that could be more easily heated, and the ceiling lowered, but now the original proportions can be appreciated again.

Nothing about Réaux is exactly petite. Our bedroom was the size of a ballroom, with a vast bed on a platform. Blue and yellow, Florence's favourite colours have been very successfully used for covers, curtains and chairs. In the superb bathroom even the loo seat is covered in the same fabric and if that sounds naff I apologise because the reality is not.

What could easily have been a grim fortress inside and out has had the Florence magic worked on it and become colourfully cheerful, like the hostess herself.
She was one of the pioneers of the château-b. and bs. For 14 years now she has been sharing her gorgeous home with multi-national visitors. She and Jean-Luc leave the guests to enjoy their four-course dinner, cooked by a *cuisinier*, in the dining room (blue and yellow stripes) and join them later for coffee back in the salon. At breakfast they are on hand again to answer the 'Where-do-we-go-today' queries.

The exterior of the château has recently been cleaned so that the pale stone gleams creamily again and the red chequered bricks of the tower stand out. There is a gravelled walk around the surrounding moat, willows and chestnut trees for birds to chirp in and plenty of rural serenity. Only the rush of a passing train jolts one back to the 20th-century.

Seventeen rooms with private bathrooms from 450-1150f. Breakfast 55f each. Dinner 250f.

CINAIS. 37500

4km from Chinon. This makes an excellent place to stay for visiting the charming little town of Chinon, strung out along the river Vienne, backed by the crumbling ruins of the many towered château, historically more interesting than many in the Loire. It was here that Joan of Arc started to persuade the reluctant Charles VII to regain his throne as King of France and be crowned eventually in Reims. Joan's tower is one of the many roofless ones to explore. Many happy hours can be spent wandering round the ruins and the views from the ramparts are splendid.

Just up the road is La Devinière, Rabelais' birthplace, where a huge *pigeonnier* dominates the small house. His statue is on the river bank at Chinon.

Vineyards surround the villages, many *dégustations* are in the area and further along the south bank on the D749 at Rivière is an intriguing little church where a special family pilgrimage is held once a year in May.

From the Chinon bypass - D751 (*direction* Saumur) at the roundabout 3km south of the river turn right (still on the D751). The mill is 100yds on the left, signed.

➤ Mme Daniele Cottereau. Le Moulin de la Voie (M)

(0)2.47.95.82.90. fax: (0)2.47.95.91.16.

A more than life-sized figure sculpted in metal greets the visitor to the heavily restored 17th-century mill. Don Quixote? Could have been, but it was raining so hard that I lacked the inclination to stop and work him out. His creator is M. Cotterau, who accepts commissions!

Even on such a foul day I could appreciate the setting - overlooking the river Negron, tables on the terrace and a pretty garden. The rooms are pretty too - one with yellow Provençal print fabrics, another with green painted furniture and a double bed covered in flowery cotton, and the smallest, all very light, bright and cheerful with good shower rooms. There's one more with bath and double bed which I particularly fancied. Rooms are from 270f to 350f. A pleasant sitting room with breakfast bar and a modern kitchenette is reserved for guests' use. Because it is near a busy road there must be some traffic noise I suppose, but it didn't worry me. Arrowed for *accueil* and so many amenities.

CORMERY. 37320

15km SE of Tours by the N143. A pleasant little town, famou roons and dominated by the ruins of the Benedictine abbey, fo tury.

➤ Mme Susanna McGrath. Le Logis du Sacri

3 rue Alcuin. (0)2.47.43.08.23. fax: (0)2.47.43.05.48.

I should never have found this one without some local advice; it is tucked away in a quiet street, sharing a small courtyard garden with the actual abbey. As her name might indicate, Susanna McGrath hails from Scotland - from Edinburgh to be precise - and decided to carry not only her own country's banner into foreign territory but those of Ireland and England, too, with bedrooms decorated in appropriate themes. The Scottish room is tartanised, the Irish is shamrock-green, the English green and white with English chinz. There is also an American room, I think, but I've forgotten the colour scheme. Anyway they are all quite delightful, furnished with pieces painted by the redoubtable Sue Hutton from Le Moulin (see p.146) and equipped with good modern bathrooms or shower-rooms; I particularly liked the one with four-poster, but the others at 290f and 330f are all to be recommended. The surprisingly large salon is particularly lovely, with comforting log fire burning away when I was there, warming the 15th-century stone walls; the kitchen, where breakfast is eaten, is pretty nice, too. Susanna serves dinner every night 130f, including wine, on reservation.

This is a very special b. and b., well situated for the culture bit, in a pleasant town centre but protected from traffic and with an English (sorry Scottish)-speaking, friendly and efficient hostess. An arrow for all these virtues.

FONDETTES. 37230 LUYNES

5km W of Tours on the north bank, N152. Look for the sign after the BP Bellerive petrol station (coming from Tours) or the Total station at Vallières from Langeais. It's a pleasant surprise to find village atmosphere so near the Tours agglomeration.

➤ M. et Mme Desmarais. Manoir du Grand Martigny (L)

(0)2.47.42.29.87. fax: (0)2.47.42.24.44. Closed: 1/11-1/4.

When I first stayed in le Grand Martigny in 1988 my feelings for the Desmarais were a mixture of admiration and pity. The admiration was for the improvements made to the erstwhile rambling 16th-century manor house and the pity for the enormity of the task still in hand. The blue and white *Toile de Jouy* bedroom I occupied then was so pretty, so comfortable that I had no doubt of the end result of the improvements, but the state of the salon and dining room - plasterwork in shreds, paint peeling, mirrors scarred, damp prevailing - gave cause for doubt as to just when M. Desmarais' dreams could all be achieved. They still haven't - on an estate this size there is always room for more and the aim is a new roof every twelve months. However, the two derelict rooms have indeed been restored, and more bedrooms transformed. I still like the blue and white one best, but it's now difficult to choose, since they are all so attractively decorated and equipped with super bathrooms. The four-acre grounds are lovely - a peaceful retreat and yet so near Tours. A walk round the lake works wonders after a busy day, though breakfast served on the terrace makes you never want to get up and go anywhere.

Best of all are the friendly, English-speaking hosts. They live in Mauritius in the winter and return each spring, revitalised, to start another stage of renovation and to welcome their guests. Five rooms, 690f; twin, 620f double-bed.

LUSSAULT-SUR-LOIRE. 37400

5km W of Amboise, 6km E of Tours by the south bank of the Loire on D751 through Montlouis. In Lussault, near the church, take the D283 (direction St Martin-Le-Beau) for 2km; château signed, via a potholed drive lined with plane trees. This is wine growing territory, and could not be more conveniently situated for visits to vineyards, châteaux and Tours.

M. et Mme Rault-Couturier. Château de Pintray (M)

(0)2.47.23.22.84. fax: (0)2.47.57.64.27.

The surrounding vineyards are Pintray property and Montlouis wine is produced on the estate. Samples available for purchase.

The château is neither large nor particularly grand, part 16th-century part 19th-century, with the distinctive blue shutters that are a common feature on the Isle de Ré, the owners' *pays*. The ground-floor blue and yellow suite with twin beds and independent entrance costs 520f for two and 620f for four, there is one room with double *bateau* bed and a good bathroom for 450f and another, rather grander version with wine-coloured *tissu* on the walls for 520f. The grounds immediately around the house are pleasantly shaded and feature a delightful little 17th-century chapel.

Breakfast is eaten outside whenever feasible or in one of the salons, and indoor exercise may be taken at the magnificent 19th-century billiard table.

ROCHECORBON. 37210

2km NE of Tours by N152 and D77. Virtually a suburb of Tours, but light years away in character.

Christine and Jacques Desvignes. Château de Montgouverne (L)

(0)2.47.52.84.59. fax: (0)2.47.52.84.61.

There could hardly be more aptly named chatelains since the château is surrounded by vines. Nor could there be a bigger contrast than its setting and that of the city just below the escarpment. You bowl along the D77 convinced that you have gone wrong somewhere when the château appears on the right, set in trees and quite removed from any other signs of construction. It's a magical place, 18th-century, wondrously converted by the present young incumbents, who took over in 1992 and did much of the conversion themselves.

I would find it difficult to choose between the lovely rooms - each one is so full of character. Perhaps the Lilac suite - two rooms, tiny dressing room in the tower and a marble bathroom, but then I love *Toile de Jouy*, and there is another room draped with red and white toile, coronet over Empire *bateau* bed, or yet the blue and white version, which has the biggest and best bathroom of all. Fleecy bathrobes hang on every bathroom door. This is luxury. All the rooms, including the stunning salons downstairs, are furnished with polished antiques and bright with flowers.

a sizeable swimming pool and expensive recliners. A ...n every possible asset - elegant château, perfect situation, ...ndly hosts. Four rooms, two suites, 590/790f for two, 750f or ...er 200f, including wine. Demi-pension, 2 days minimum 425-

145

ST JEAN-ST GERMAIN. LOCHES 37600

7km S of Loches on the N143. The village is signed on the left of the *nationale*. Follow the D992 over the first bridge and prepare to swing immediately left, continuing over the second narrow bridge. The Moulin is on an island in the river Indre.

➤ Sue Hutton & Andrew Page. Le Moulin (M)

(0)2.47.94.70.12. fax: (0)2.47.94.77.98.

Oh dear, I shall have to use that word. There is no other than 'idyllic' to describe the setting. The Indre is a lovely river - far prettier than its parent Loire - and here a wide curving weir tumbles and splashes in a chocolate-box kind of way. There's even a small, sandy beach from which to swim. English Sue Hutton, *patronne* of the Moulin, who thinks of everything, provides two fibreglass dinghies from which to explore the waterways, do some fishing and even whitewater down the weir. (Sue's done it!) It is all deliciously green and rural and peaceful; wonderful for picnicking.

Sue's territory occupies the whole boat-shaped island, mill amidships, prow in the form of terrace pointing to the weir and stern occupied by pretty flowery garden, leading down to launching jetty for fishing expeditions, organised by Sue's partner, chef, Jacques-of-all-trades, the youthful Andrew Page. It's a real home from home, where guests are pampered and mothered by kindly Sue. Too kind and too motherly sometimes, since she was born to be taken advantage of. An elderly couple stayed for three weeks and demanded two meals every day. During our visit, Parisians with four children turned up at 9.30 p.m. and expected dinner. 'No problem,' says Sue brightly. 'No problem,' says Andrew resignedly, retreating to his kitchen. So FE readers - don't let me down. This one is a winner. Don't kill the goose that lays a very golden egg. Be nice to Sue because she's certainly going to be nice to you.

She's been pretty nice to the mill too, transforming it from a wreck into an utterly charming home. The main room, where guests tend to gather at all hours, overlooks the water, and is full of artistic touches - lovely flower arrangements, paintings, drag-painted walls. Sue has stencilled the walls and painted much of the furniture herself (you can commission items if you like) and hung cheerful yellow and blue curtains. In summer the action moves to the terrace overlooking the river. Bedrooms are small but perfectly formed, mostly looking out over the millstream and the river beyond. Bathrooms are modern, two with showers, three with baths, and prettified again with Sue's stencils. 280f.

The evening meal is the highspot of the day, either in the cosy rough-walled, peach-curtained dining room on a long pine table, or on the terrace. Guests are offered an *apéritif* (not your usual small glass of wine but, in typically generous style, a gin, whisky, pastis - you name it). Conversation is flowing by the time Andrew brings in the first course. Having eaten one dinner there (110f inclusive and I mean inclusive), I broke my rule of one-night stands and booked a second night. Smoked haddock in cream/duck/salmon/trout/strawberry *sablé* all featured. When Sue asked us three couples what kind of wine we would like, one said white, one red and one rosé. She didn't turn a hair and repeat bottles of each colour followed on. A real treasure and arrowed of course.

SAVONNIERES. 37510

14km W of Tours. Autoroute exit 'Tours/St Avertin', then D7 to Savonnières, then direction Villandry.

Climb up the hill above Savonnières, looking down on the village on the banks of the Cher, and you are leagues removed from the fuss of Tours, just ten minutes drive away. An ideal situation in fact, especially as the lovely Villandry gardens are so near.

Mme Chaineau. La Martinière (S)

(0)2.47.50.04.46. fax: (0)2.47.50.11.57.

Signed on the right from the village. Check opening times. I did try to visit this one in the spring, but their guestrooms were not ready to receive visitors. By dint of much persuasion I did manage to see the rooms, in an ex-stable building of the old farmhouse, but when I found that this was also a *centre equestre* decided to give the whole operation a miss, since I generally find that where horses and humans are lodged under the same management, it is the humans who usually come off worse. Another minus factor was that here there are only two rooms with

private showers and the other four have to share a shower and loo. The price of 230-330f seemed a trifle high.

However, Sue has had firsthand experience and thinks differently; *'The guarantee that bedrooms are comfortable and dinner is excellent'.*

The riding aspect could prove a great attraction. Trails are organised and weekly packages available, with special tours for young riders from 12 to 20 years old during the school holidays. The evening meals, prepared by a cordon bleu cook, tend to be very jolly, convivial affairs, eaten al fresco whenever feasible. A chambres d'hôtes with speciality appeal.

SEPMES. 37800

27km S of Tours. 22km WSW of Loches. Take the D59 through Sepmes.

➤ Mme Vergnaud. La Ferme des Berthiers (M)

(0)2.47.65.50.61.

The large gates of the Ferme des Berthiers stand well back from the main road just outside the village of Sepmes on the road to Loches. Inside is a square courtyard surrounded by the tall farmhouse and other farm buildings. Our room was one of three on the first floor, very large and artistically decorated, using natural stone walls and warm floor tiles, with a new, pristine shower room to match the bedroom, yellow in our case. The other rooms are blue and red, with even loo seats co-ordinating. Our very pleasant room, with bowl of fresh flowers, had an extra bed and two comfortable armchairs by the sunny window, and there was still plenty of room to move about. We had arrived unexpectedly, and as Madame was out we could not sample an evening meal, but I am sure they are a real treat, judging by the breakfast we had next day. Mme Vergnaud, who speaks some English, is a perfectionist, and a stay in this lovely house, very handy for visiting the Loire châteaux (or a night stop on a route south) is not to be missed. Double room 240/270f. Evening meal on reservation only, 100f, wine *compris*. Another room on the ground floor, Gold and Blue with superb bathroom fittings (a reader tells me), since my last visit. The evening meal still excellent. The arrow firmly remains.

LOIR et CHER

BOURRÉ. 41400 MONTRICHARD

42km SE of Tours. 35km SW of Blois. I am always disappointed by Montrichard. It has everything going for it - a prime position on the north bank of the river Cher, some nice old timbered houses, two squares - and yet it remains without a heart and soul. There are few towns of this size in France without a centre full of lively cafés and brasseries, but Montrichard is one of them; its pedestrianisation hasn't worked - the main street is still traffic-ridden, and it certainly hasn't capitalised on the river aspect - not a single bar or restaurant apart from those of the hotels, in which to sit and sip and look out over the water. That said, you don't have to go very far to find more rewards - the forest of Montrichard lies immediately behind and the road that follows the river along its north bank in both directions is pleasant and not too busy. Bourée lies 2km E of the town.

M. et Mme Boussard. Manoir de la Salle du Roc (M-L)

79 route de Vierzon. (0)2.54.32.73.54. fax: (02).54.32.47.09

Pity about the railway line. which spoils so many views in the Loire valley, but there is enough distance and height between it and the Manoir to blur the blot on the landscape and any traffic noise. The gardens are lovingly cared for by M. Boussard and his gardener. 450 rose buses contribute to the colourful scene. Winding down the slope is an enticing path, with many a tucked-away corner shaded from public view where tables and benches have been. thoughtfully provided for shady repose. A water-course and fountains lend even more interest to the scene and there are galleries of chalk caves to explore and a tennis court on which to work off some residual steam. The grounds actually extend to the river, where there is a private island, reached by a little motorboat; a great spot for picnics.

The building is half 15th-century manoir, half 18th-century château, and, because of the slope, it is very hard to do justice to it in a photograph. Two families share the responsibilities of running it, Patricia and Patrick helping out Patrick's father and mother. There are guest rooms in both the tower and the main building, all furnished with antiques, including in one suite a 'sabot' bath (i.e. square). Others have more conventional sanitary ware, but boast canopies over the beds and family treasures like an 18th-century lady's pink shoe and lace baby clothes. Live fires in the rooms are the biggest possible treat.

Situated so near Chenonceaux (10km) and Amboise (20km) this would make an excellent, superbly comfortable base.

Four doubles, all with private baths 500-700f. Evening meal by arrangement.

DANZÉ. 41160

15km N of Vendôme by D36 to Danzé, then the D24 towards La Ville-aux Clercs. Lovely unspoiled rolling countryside. Vendôme itself is an enchanting little town, built over several branches of the river Loire.

➤ Madame Kamette. La Borde (M)

(0)2.54.80.68.42. fax: (0)2.54.80.63.68.

From Danzé take the second chambres d'hôtes sign, down a made-up road, rather than the first which leads very bumpily through the forest. This one is a real find, one of the best bargains in the book. It's a 1930s house set in ten hectares of green and pleasant land in pleasingly hilly countryside. The rooms are all large and well-furnished with modern bathrooms (shower or bath). One has its own terrace, two others (forming a suite) have floor length windows looking over the garden; all are miles away from traffic fret. All good news.

Even better and more unusual is that there is a new covered swimming pool in the garden. And there's nice Mme Kamette, who is an English teacher, so conversation will flow. But best of all are the prices; Mme knows that she cannot compete with accommodation along the Loire as far as site is concerned, but she certainly beats them hollow in value-for-money terms.

240/300f for two persons, 440f for four, or 450f for five in the suite. Reduced for 2nd night.

MER. 41500

16km N of Blois on the RN152. Follow signs to town centre.

Mer is one of those forgotten towns on the Loire that no-one (including *moi*) has ever heard of. No château, no great river views. It came as a pleasant surprise, with a quiet pedestrianised heart, on which stands:

➤ Chez Mormiche. Le Clos (M)

9 rue Dutems. (0)2.54.81.17.36. fax: (0)2.54.81.70.19

We had no trouble finding the house, which is well-signed: '*chambres d'hôtes centre ville*', once we had overcome our law-abiding English scruples about driving over a pedestrian area. But if this had not been France, I doubt if we would have proceeded further. The house, bang on the road, is grey and undistinguished from this aspect, with Claude's framing shop attached to it. It is not until you penetrate to the rear that all its 16th-century charms can be appreciated, especially the unexpected garden.

There are more pleasant surprises in store; the rooms are all light and airy, with good, white bathrooms. One is delicate pale blue and white, overlooking the garden - 280/350f - another with grey paint, has two white-covered beds, with the possibility of two more squeezed in - 400/550f for four - and there is a choice of baths or showers. The rooms that overlook the pedestrianised road have double glazing and cost 300f and all five rooms cost 50f less in winter.

Breakfast is taken in a nice beamed room or outside in the garden, which is a real bonus in the heart of a town, and there is covered parking space. Both Claude and her farmer husband Joelle, are exceptionally friendly and pleasant, but speak no English. However, 17-year-old daughter (Claude doesn't look old enough!) is around to help out.

I really like this one - atmosphere, situation, rooms and hosts, so an arrow comes with it.

MUIDES SUR LOIRE. 41500

15km NE of Blois on the south bank of the Loire. The château is set back from the main road, the D951, just before the town of Muides.

➤ Marie-France and Christian de Gélis. Château des Colliers (L)

(0)2.54.87.50.75. fax: (0)2.54.87.03.64.

Closed: 1/12-1/3

Most of the châteaux of the Loire lack any view of the wide shallow river that was their *raison d'être*. Many others, especially on the north bank, have offensive '*Nationales*' and main railway lines running between them and the water, ruining both the view and the night's repose. The Château de Colliers suffers from neither disadvantage and is probably the best-situated of any entry in this book. The floor-to-ceiling windows of every room look directly out over a grassy terrace to the fast flowing water and reedy islands, unimpeded on this quiet stretch by man-made views. There is a lovely walk along the river bank, which I thoroughly recommend after a day's car cramp, heading west directly into the evening sun duplicating its effect on the water.

Muides-sur-Loire 41 Loir-et-Cher

The 1750 château, bought in 1779 from the Chevalier de Beba, has been in Christian's family for eight generations. He was born and raised here. Portraits of his dignified ancestors look down from their gilt frames in reading room, salon, and dining room, where they have to compete with Sistine Chapel-esque murals and ceiling paintings. Over the main door is the family crest and motto in Basque, which, translated, reads. 'If you are happy here, stay awhile.' Advice that I wish I could follow, because I was certainly very happy indeed to be staying here.

In spite of the elegance of the building, with gravel courtyard raked every morning, the lovely panelling, antique furniture (I didn't see a single piece I did not covet) the atmosphere is far from intimidating. How could it be - this is after all a family home in which modest Marie-France has raised five children. Now they have fled their enviable nest, she cooks for even larger numbers - twelve guests often sit round her dining table and eat her delectable dinners.

The rooms, of course, are all different. Mine was ground floor, blue toile walls, flowery curtains and spread, magnificent Directoire beds, walnut chest and armoire and, best of all, a fire in the marble grate. The bathroom is unrepentantly luxurious. The room next door is the oldest, with gorgeous ceiling mouldings and double bed, another upstairs has a secret winding staircase leading to an unexpected large terrace where sun-worshippers can tan privately while taking in the view.

A lovely place to stay, stunning building, charming hosts, comfort and style. And very well-situated. Five rooms with private bathrooms 550-700f. Dinner 200f including wine.

ONZAIN. 41150

15km SW of Blois on N152, direction Tours. In Onzain take the road forMonteaux; after 3km look for a Citroen garage on the right and the house is opposite.

➤ **Mme Martine Langlais** (M)

46 rue de Meuves. Tel & fax: (0)2.54.20.78.82.
Closed: December to April.

I probably have more letters of commendation on this one than any other chambres d'hôtes in the Loire. Truth to tell, after all this praise, first impressions of the little house on the main road are somewhat disappointing and it is not until you push open the big iron gate that you begin to see what all the fuss is about. The rear aspect is entirely different, ivy-covered, cottagey, and the long garden does indeed extend to the river (but not the Loire, just a very minor tributary). M. Langlais proudly showed us his garden and pointed out the private parking slot in the front, off the road. Madame Langlais met us in her delightful salon, with yellow painted beams, matching chairs and curtains. Her good English makes conversation easy. Breakfast is taken in the garden or in the little sitting-room with french windows exclusively for the guests' use. The five rooms are all extremely pretty with attractive country fabrics, a green flowery version with twin beds for 340f and a pink Toile de Jouy fabric on the walls of another. Five altogether, all with excellent bathrooms.

A totally charming place, in which I am so certain that readers will be happy that an arrow follows.

LOIRET

DONNERY. 45450

18km E of Orléans Take N60 direction Montargis-Nevers. Leave N60 at FAY-aux-Loges. Go through the village, turn left at a flower shop. Cross the canal and turn left at the sign D709 DONNERY. 'Les Charmettes' is the first house on your left on the canal bank as you enter Donnery.

Mme Sicot. Les Charmettes (S-M)

(0)2.38.59.22.50. fax: (0)2.38.59.26.96.

Les Charmettes, on the fringe of Donnery on the Faye-aux-Loges road, is a large house situated between the canal and the main road. Steps sweep up to the house from the garden. On the other side there is a courtyard with ample room for parking. '*The evening meal and breakfast were excellent and beautifully served by Mme Sicot, a very charming and helpful hostess.*' A reader.

The bedroom on the second floor is en suite, but the other rooms share a wc on the first floor. Possible noise from traffic if you sleep with windows open. Rooms are now 250f for 2 persons. Evening meal on reservation 100f.

JOUY-LE-POTIER. 45370

20km S of Orléans. 10km from Bellefontaine. Exit 2 from the A71 continue south on the D15 for 11km and follow signs off the La Ferté-St. Aubin road.

M. & Mme Becchi (M)

778 rue de Chevenelle.
(0)2.38.45.83.07.

Just outside the neat village of Jouy-le-Potier is this immaculate modern chambres d'hôtes, well signed in a road with large houses in spacious grounds. A very restful stop after a fast drive from the Channel ports, and easy to find, but book ahead as there is virtually only one room here.

You will receive a warm welcome and be entertained to an excellent meal as real guests of the Becchis. The well-furnished main guest room is on the first floor and has two single beds, thick carpets and huge built-in wardrobe. It overlooks the back garden and fields beyond. There is a very spacious shower and wc adjoining it and on the landing a cosy sitting area with TV. Plenty of books are provided on the Loire region. There is another room on the ground floor which has an adjacent loo, but no washing facilities, suitable for an extra member of the family, sharing the upstairs shower room.

Mme Becchi speaks good English, and has decorated her house with some striking dried flower arrangements. An elegant stop in the Loire valley where your hosts will be delighted to give you any information about the area. 250f. Evening meal 90f each, *apéritif*, wine and coffee included.

MENESTREAU-EN-VILLETTE. 45

25km S of Orléans. 15km E of La Ferté St. Aubin. In the Solong Loire near to the more northern reaches of the river. From Marcilly-en the D64 (SP Sennely) and in 6km look for sign to Les Fourcault dow st track on the right, easy to miss.

NEW ➤ Mme Rosemary Beau. Ferme des Fourcault (M) (0)2.38.76.94.41.

Driving down this track penetrating into the forest you will think you are getting nowhere, but in one kilometre a house comes into view, and another a few yards to the right, and you have arrived.

This red brick farmstead, typical of the area, doesn't look particularly exciting and the rural grounds have outhouses yet to be converted. However, once through the front door the whole place is amazingly attractive.

American Rosemary Beau and her French husband bought the house ten years ago; they converted this ruin over the years, offering chambres d'hôtes for the last three. The spacious lounge, with interesting picture windows of forest views, is light and airy; a mixture of modern and ancient furniture extends to a dining area. One guest room on the ground floor has thick pile carpets, a private sitting room with a convertible for children and an en suite bathroom. Nothing stinted here. Upstairs is superb. An extensive white-walled bedroom, with thick pile carpet, stretches across the house past countless windows of all shapes and sizes. The mixture of old beams, modern queen-size bed, duvet and pretty fabrics is perfection. I wished I could be like their black cat who just strayed in from the forest, knew a good thing when he saw it and stayed firmly put!

Rosemary, whose easy American welcome is charming, does not cook evening meals; but if you reserve ahead she will give you a light salad snack on arrival. There are restaurants 15 mins. drive away.

I just loved everything about this place, particularly the utter quiet and the price - 280f, extra bed 70f including a copious breakfast. With only two rooms and 70% of her guests returning you will need to book well ahead to avoid disappointment.

Well worth an arrow.

Western Loire

Départements:	**Loire-Atlantique**	**Sarthe**
	Maine-et-Loire	**Vendée**
	Mayenne	

Companion guide: 'French Entrée 8 - The Loire' and 'French Entreé 12 - Brittany'.

It is a highly confusing piece of administrative bureaucracy that half the Loire valley should be in the region of 'Centre Val de Loire' and the other half 'Western Loire'; just to make matters worse the latter is sometimes referred to as 'Pays de la Loire'. Go to the tourist office in Chinon and they cannot help you with any information on neighbouring Saumur, and vice versa. The 'Centre' gets most tourists because of proximity to Paris and because many of the famous châteaux are here, but in many ways I prefer the Western Loire. The river here is more interesting. As if sensing that the end of its journey is near, it hurries along, rather than dawdling around sandbanks. There are islands, some inhabited, like charming Béhuard, and small fishing villages right up to the Nantes agglomeration. The pace is slower here, the crowds thin out, beds and meals cost significantly less. The roads following the river are quieter, with more space, better views, fewer lorries. Particularly attractive it the stretch between Saumur and Les Rosiers on the south bank, and so is the Corniche Angevin, high above the water, with lovely views down to the river and the vineyards.

If I had to pick just one base along the whole Loire it would be Saumur, if I had to pick just one city it would be Nantes, both in this region. The former has multiple interests - a fine château overlooking the river, famous sparkling wine, the prestigious Cadre Noir riding establishment and the mushroom caves, to name but a few. The pedestrianisation and restoration of the mediaeval section has been a great success, and Saumur is now a good town, of manageable size, to cover on foot. Nantes, again with a fine château and fascinating history, is elegant and underestimated.

The *département* of the **Loire-Atlantique** is still considered by many (myself included) as part of Brittany. Historically and culturally yes, administratively no.

Nantes certainly leans towards the Loire, but the rest is so distinctly Breton in character that I have included (the very few) chambres d'hôtes that I was able to find in the Brittany section.

The northernmost *département*, **Mayenne**, deserves to be better-known. It suffers from an identity problem - associated neither with Normandy nor the Loire Valley, so that many people have difficulty in placing it geographically. I was surprised to find how few guidebooks even bother to mention it. However it is a pity to consider it purely as a transit area since it encompasses some lovely green, unspoiled countryside and the river from which it takes its name flows swiftly through lush meadows. The two main towns, Laval and Château-Gontier, both on the Mayenne, are well worth a visit. The old part of Laval has some picturesque 16th-century houses clustered around a rather grim 12th-century château and Chateau-Gontier offers a fine Romanesque church and a pleasant walk through the old priory gardens (*le Bout du Monde*) to the narrow streets around the riverside.

Maine-et-Loire is the *département* most closely associated with the Loire, with most of the tourist attractions (and chambres d'hôtes) within its confines. The *préfecture*, Angers, is actually 8kms north of the Loire, on the banks of a very short river indeed, the Maine, formed by the confluence of the rivers Sarthe and Mayenne. From the château, one of the most interesting in the entire region thanks not only to its position and antiquity but to the miraculous Tapestry of the Apocalypse it houses, is a magnificent view of all the watery configuration below. There are good shops and restaurants to visit on gloomy days and as this is a university town, plenty of café-activity. Angers prides itself on being the cultural centre of the region, so you can also bank on a variety of concerts and exhibitions for further interest. Saumur comes within this *département* and the final resting place of the Plantagenets - Fontevraud - both of them top priorities on any tourist's list. North of Angers the tourists fade away and the prices tumble, but there is plenty of attraction still in the rivers that flow towards the Loire - this is the best area for a boating holiday.

Sarthe too has its share of tributaries; notably in the pleasant bustling country town of Sablé-sur-Sarthe, famous for its buttery biscuits - 'sablés' - where streams of the Sarthe, the Erve and the Vaige crop up all over the place. Neighbouring Solesmes is famous for the Gregorian chant that can be heard in its elephantine abbey, where many recordings of the newly-popular plainsong have been recorded. The main city of the *département*, Le Mans, is of course most famous for the 24-hour motor race which brings droves of enthusiasts into the area for one brief frenzy, filling the hotel beds for miles around. I wonder how many bother to explore the mediaeval city, let alone the cathedral where Geoffrey Plantagenet married Matilda of England, the granddaughter of William the Conqueror. Their son, Henry, later to become King, was born here.

LOIRE (WESTERN)

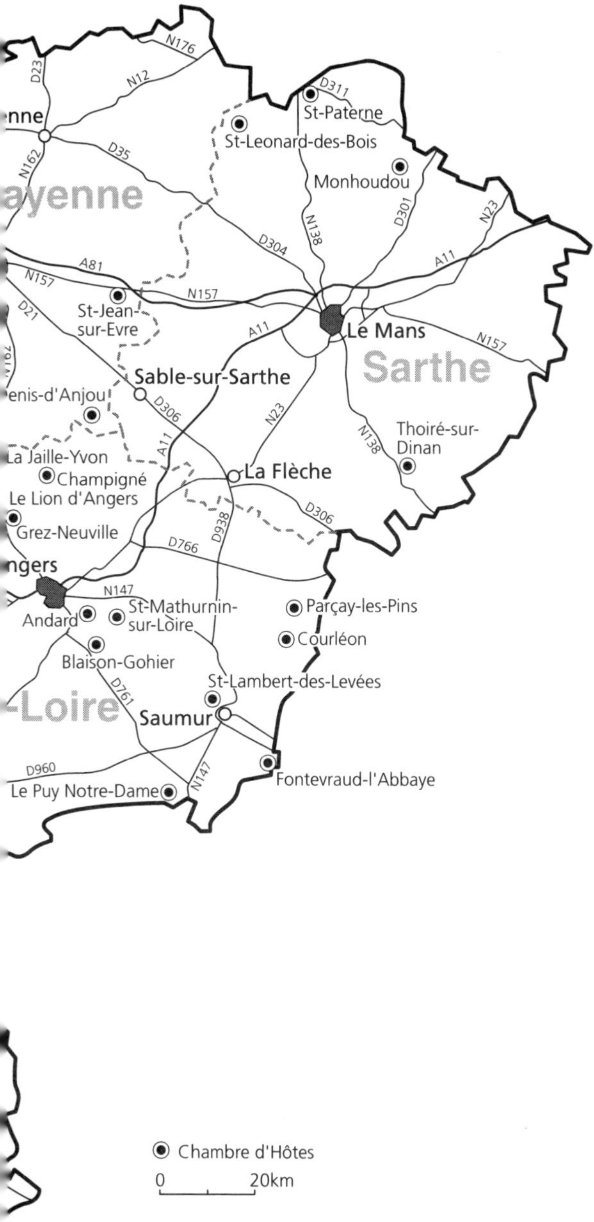

N176
D23
N12
D311
St-Paterne
St-Leonard-des-Bois
D35
Monhoudou
N162
ayenne
D301
N23
N138
D304
A81
A11
N157
N157
St-Jean-sur-Evre
D21
A11
Le Mans
N157
Sarthe
Sable-sur-Sarthe
enis-d'Anjou
D306
N23
Thoiré-sur-Dinan
N138
A11
La Jaille-Yvon
La Flèche
Champigné
Le Lion d'Angers
D306
D938
Grez-Neuville
D766
ngers
N147
St-Mathurnin-sur-Loire
Parçay-les-Pins
Andard
Courléon
Blaison-Gohier
St-Lambert-des-Levées
D761
-Loire
Saumur
D960
N147
Fontevraud-l'Abbaye
Le Puy Notre-Dame
Chambre d'Hôtes
0
20km

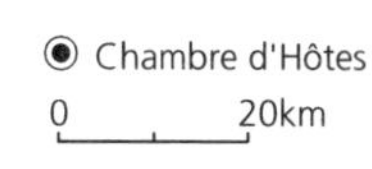

The **Vendée** is an area that often surprises those who believe they know all there is to know about France. Inland lies a unique watery network where the residents go about their daily business by flat-bottomed boat and the light filters eerily green through the overhanging leaves. The coast is one long sweeping sandbank, ideal for family holidays. It is a region more appreciated by the French than the British and tends to die outside their holiday periods. Consequently few chambres d'hôtes.

LOIRE-ATLANTIQUE

BLAIN. 44130

13km SW of Nozay. 32km N of Nantes. A nice little town on the Brest-Nantes canal, where boats tie up at the port by the bridge just south of the town. The Forêt-du-Gavre, noted for mushrooms, lies north of the town.

From the N137 take the Nozay exit (direction Blain) and in about 10.5km look for the chambres d'hôtes signs on the left, a few hundred yards down a small lane.

NEW **M. & Mme Pineau. 'La Mercerais'** (S)
(0)2.40.79.04.30.

Friendly Mme Pineau has won cups for her colourful garden and in her spare time makes attractive dried flower arrangements using musical scores. After retirement she and her farmer husband have kept the farmhouse and enclosed the garden.

There are three guest rooms. Two on the first floor for three, double and single beds (duck your head on the way up) are prettily decorated in pink or blue and have small shower rooms and windows overlooking the garden. A third room on the ground floor, for a family, has two double beds and a separate private bathroom with bath - 250f.

Mme produces a copious breakfast of cheese, served in many little baskets, but no evening meal, so take the opportunity to make for Le Port and watch the boats while you dine.

Excellent parking behind the house where there is external access to the two rooms upstairs. Relax in the garden or in inclement weather in the salon/dining room where Mme Pineau will regale you with local history.

CROSSAC. 44160

20km N of St. Nazaire. Only a short distance to the centre of the Marais, where you can take a boat trip, or hire bikes, the only form of transit in the middle of these waterways.

Take a turning off the D33, 7km north of Pontchâteau, turn left up a long lane, right at T junction, in 200 yards turn left at the Gîtes-de-France sign up a long tarmacked drive.

NEW Mme Houis. La Cossonais (S)

(0)2.40.01.05.21.

This modern house is very quietly situated in a cared-for garden surrounded by extensive lawns. Mme Houis has retired from a busy life in Paris and returned to her original roots - a keen gardener - her patio is edged with roses and herbaceous plants.

There are three guest rooms on the first floor, one for three with the bathroom and loo on the private landing, one with two single beds and a large luxury bathroom attached, and a third for three with shower can be reached from a staircase leading up from a guests' salon below, which opens on to a terrace.

Evening meal 70f sometimes possible.

Rooms 240f.

HERBIGNAC. 44410

23km N of Saint-Nazaire. 60km NW of Nantes. Herbignac is a small town in the region of the *Parc-Naturel-Régional-de-Brière*, the Camargue of the North. This château is situated between two golf courses, in 200 hectares of pastures and woods.

From Nantes take the N165 to Pontchâteau then the D33 to Herbignac. The château is on the D47 2km S of Herbignac, on the right.

NEW M. & Mme de la Monneraye. Château Coët-Caret (L)

(0)2.40.91.41.20. fax: (0)2.40.91.37.46.

There is large shady parking in the grounds of this quiet château built only about 100 years ago; the gîte in the grounds is 300 years older. Mme de la Monneraye is a natural flower-arranger and delicate fresh bouquets of her expertise appear in all the rooms.

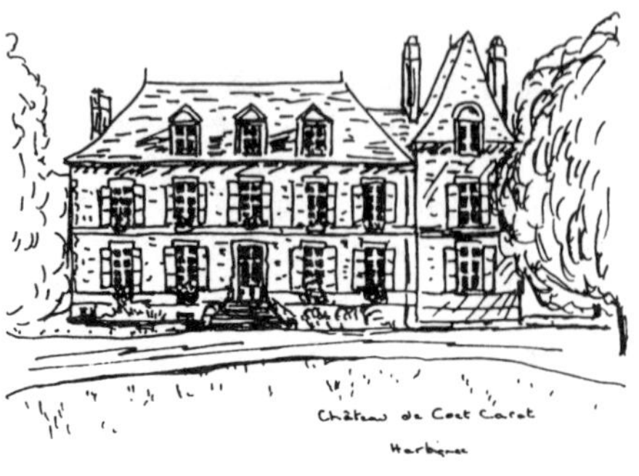

There are four guest rooms, all with a rural aspect over the grounds, well-polished antique furniture and tall true château windows and doors. Each is decorated in a different colour, with a choice of single or double beds. En-suite showers or bathrooms have many luxuries - hair-dryers, etc. Doré is a smaller but very pleasant yellow room - 450f. *Corail* sports a corner bath, for 500f. Emerald is the most luxurious, with a vestibule whose walls and ceiling are swathed with silky material, leads to a luxurious carpeted bathroom with two wash basins in darkest dark green - 600f.

On occasions it is possible to reserve dinner with your hosts, when Mme will cook and serve an elegant meal which is well worth changing for - 220f each. (Jeans and open-neck shirts are not appreciated on these occasions!) *Apéritifs* are served in the lounge where a large billiard table dominates the room.

Monsieur is a *forestier* who is very knowledgeable about this area. Horses are available for experienced riders. Peaceful boat trips on the Marais can be arranged.

MONNIÈRES. 44690

11km SE of Nantes.Close to the city of Nantes, in the centre of the wine-growing area of the Loire, famous for Muscadet and Gros Plant.

Take the N249 to Haie-Fouassière, then the N149 SP Clisson, then the D7 right to Monnières. The château is signed in the village. Take the D76 from the square, then left in about 1km.

NEW M. & Mme Calonne. Château Plessis-Brézot (L)

(0)2.40.54.63.24. fax: (0)2.40.54.66.07.

The Calonnes have moved from Calais and bought a charming 17th-century château, situated in two hectares of lawns and woodland surrounded by 30 hectares of their own vineyards.

The entrance to the château is through a gateway into a courtyard where there is a small chapel complete with bell tower opposite stable accommodation for horses and the all important *chai* where the Muscadet is made. *Dégustations* on the spot. They have renovated much in the two years they have lived here. Monsieur has a great penchant for antique shops and never visits one without buying something to add to the château. Attractive carved wooden friezes to put over the beds, tiny shelves and tables, choir stalls, panelling for the walls and antique wood doors all find their niche in the many rooms in the château. In the entrance hall is a magnificent stone carved archway at the foot of the tower stairway, uncovered by chance by Monsieur, it had been totally bricked up for years. The primrose panelling in the lounge is only a small part of the renovations. There is something particularly magical about waking in the early morning sunshine in a château and looking out at surrounding vineyards and feeling you are part of it, if only for a short time. There are five guest rooms in a wing of the château incorporating two of the towers, which have independent access from a newly panelled salon. One room on the ground floor, especially designed for the handicapped has a double bed and large shower room overlooking the rear lawns. Two rooms on the first floor are en suite with baths, heated towel rails, luxury white towels, soap, shampoo, etc. A twin-bedded room in front has a view over the vineyards and the swimming pool and the *Chai*. The smaller double-bedded room overlooks the peaceful rear woodland. On the second floor are two similar rooms; but, the higher you go the better the view, 460/660f for two.

A charming natural welcome from both Monsieur and Madame and their daughter. You will treasure the memories of a stay here.

SAINTE-PAZANNE. 44680

18km SW of Nantes. Not far from the coast and the magnificent bridge at St. Nazaire. The small neat town of Sainte-Pazanne has a large church and right beside it is this charming manor house in the centre of the town, two steps from the post office and chemist.

NEW Mme Mignen. La Plauderie (M)

1 rue de Verdelet. (0)2.40.02.45.08. Closed 31/10 to 1/5.

Though this manor house, rebuilt in the 19th century, is in the centre of the town it has a large walled garden and enclosed parking.

The entrance hall is enhanced by a charming circular staircase on one side with a leafy green wallpaper, overlooked by a stag's head. All salons are open for guests' use and the dining room opens on to the garden where breakfast is taken in fine weather. The church clock next door obligingly stays quiet until 7.30 a.m.

All rooms face the quiet back garden. Shower rooms have hair-dryers and there are tea/coffee making facilities which enables you to skip the copious breakfast, which is 35f extra per person, if you wish.

On the first floor a pretty flowery guest room with *ciel-de-lit* has a very large luxurious carpeted bathroom. 400f for two. There is an adjoining little room which is charmingly and practically furnished for small children - single bed, cot and a dainty frilly white cradle, changing mat on a table supplied right beside a wash basin, even a doll's cot. Mme Mignen certainly knows how to cater for children of all ages.

On the second floor are two light rooms with good views, up a steep staircase but worth the climb. Warmly carpeted with large shower rooms, one for three, double and single bed, and one with two singles has a cot. 270f for two, without breakfast. Central and electric heating makes this chambres d'hôtes really comfortable for year-round occupation.

A kindly hostess and the convenience of being in the centre of a town but with a large sheltered garden makes this a very attractive proposition.

VARADES. 44370

45km WSW of Angers. A little town on the north bank of the river Loire, pretty by the bridge but otherwise rather dull.

From Varades take the N23 in the direction of Ancenis. In about 2km you will see a chambres d'hôtes sign to the Château du Grand Patis on your left down a long drive.

M. & Mme Le Roy. Château du Grand Patis (M)

(0)2.40.83.42.28. or (0)2.40.96.09.21. Open weekends and school holidays.

The Le Roys have renovated this lovely old château and now have five large rooms with very good showers. Two adjoining rooms share facilities - which is ideal for children since it even has two school desks for them to scribble at. 220/260f for two, 400f for four, double and single beds available, some rooms on the second floor.

A very quiet night is assured, well away from traffic, and the extensive grounds are fun for small children to explore accompanied by the château chickens.

Breakfast is nicely served in the dining room or on the terrace. English spoken. Good value for the Loire. Reservation advisable.

MAINE-et-LOIRE

ANDARD. 49800 TRÉLAZE

7km E of Angers. The address is misleading. This is not in the village of Andard but on the other side of the N147. Heading east from Angers follow the U-turn directions signed Sarrigne; after the crossroads the house is signed on the left. There is very little of interest in the immediate region, since it is hemmed in by the main road, so it is not a good choice if walking is important, but excellent for Angers and other châteaux.

Mme Annie Guervilly. Le Grand Talon (M)
(0)2.41.80.42.85.

Light years away from the busy traffic, so near and yet so far in spirit; I cannot swear that you cannot hear it if you try, but it certainly didn't worry me, so soothing was the atmosphere of rural calm in Mme Guervilly's nice 18th-century creeper-covered house. She is a keen gardener and keeps the borders filled with brilliant geraniums and the lawns well mowed. Breakfast is served on the south-facing terrace whenever possible.

The three rooms are quite different - the two up a short staircase in a wing off the main building are small and dim but very cosy, attractively furnished with antiques (Mme G. used to be an antique dealer). They have a bath/shower apiece but share a loo. I would have been very happy in either, but because we had so much luggage with us we settled for the slightly more expensive ground floor room, with an abundance of space. It is light and airy, with big floor length windows, furnished very simply, mostly in white, with two double beds.

The breakfast room, with old beams, massive stone fireplace and tiled floor is similarly spacious.

A recommended stop with particularly friendly and helpful hostess (little English but lots of goodwill). 2 doubles at 290f to 300f. Dinner 110f excluding wine.

BLAISON GOHIER. 49320

15km SE of Angers. Cross the river, take the D791, turn left on to the D132 through St Sulpice and follow the signs to the village, which is only a kilometre or so from the river. It's a delightful rural ride through vineyards and sleepy hamlets.

Mme Antoine. Le Château de Chéman (M)
(0)2.41.57.17.60.

The approach to the 15th-century château is through a cobbled courtyard encircled with barns and enlivened with a few scratching hens. All round are the slopes of the vineyards from whose grapes is made the excellent and unique Cabernet d'Anjou wine named after the château. It's an extraordinary colour: a very pale golden rose is as near as I can get to describing it - *ambre gris*. Quite delicious, fresh and fruity. Take some home with you as a souvenir of a most unusual chambres d'hôtes.

Château is a bit of a misnomer; this is part farm, part country house, full of old beams, steps up, steps down, winding stone staircases, massive worm-eaten oak doors, crumbling stone facade, impossible to photograph, impossible to pigeonhole.

I wrote in FE8 that I found it hard to believe that Mme Antoine was 85 years old, and I now find it even harder to believe that she is older now. She is still so sprightly, climbing all those winding stairs, and enthusiastic about her rooms and knowledgeable about her wines.

She accomodates her guests in three spacious suites, with bedroom, sitting room and bathroom apiece; there are brass bedsteads and washstands, but modern bathrooms with efficient showers; there is a kitchen corner, too, so knocking up your own lunch would save a bit. Downstairs guests are welcome to make use of the salon, over-furnished perhaps in the old style, but with a wonderful old white porcelain stove throwing out lots of comforting warmth.

Certainly an intriguing stop for those who want absolute peace and quiet, with the interest of a working wine château, very near the tourist belt, with comfortable rooms, presided over by a kindly hostess.

3 apartments 450f each, with breakfasts, or 1500f a week without linen or breakfast. 1 double room with child's bed in alcove 400f.

CHAMPIGNÉ. 49330

32km N of Angers, by N162 and D768. Go through the village of Champigné and take the road for Sablé. The château is signed on left after approx 3.5km. This is

unspoiled farming country between the rivers Maye
undiscovered by tourists, with plenty of interest - boating, ch
Solesmes - all within easy reach.

➤ François and Hedwige de Valbray. Château des Briottière

(0)2.41.42.00.02. fax: (0)2.41.42.01.55.

Ask anyone in the château b. and b. business 'Do you know François de Valbray?' and the answer comes: 'Mais très bien, he is my friend'. François is everybody's friend, especially his guests'. A pioneer of the stately-home chambres d'hôtes he shares his acquired experience (some of it bitter, mostly lyrical) generously. His is a typical riches to rags story - the scion of an old family well endowed with châteaux, he now cheerfully carries suitcases, lays bricks, drives a tractor, pours out drinks, writes out bills, trouble-shoots. He inherited the stunningly beautiful 17th-century Les Briottières and took on the daunting task of restoring its fading beauty, subsidised by pigs. It's a never-ending mission. One year it's the stables that get the treatment, now used for wedding receptions, then the lovely *orangerie*, now converted into a charming villa, then the doll-sized chapel where the increasing brood of de Valbrays (six at the most recent count) get baptised, then the swimming pool, much appreciated by his guests in the long, hot summers. Some welcome extra income accumulated from letting out the whole château to the film crew making *Impromptu*, the story of Georges Sand and Chopin, who made two most attractive innovations - they painted the lovely glassed-in promenade panelling in Chinese yellow and added a trellis to the verandah.

I had Emma Thompson's bedroom, 'La Chambre de Ma Grandmère', decorated since my last visit in dusky pink and almond green, with chintz canopy and curtains, pink moiré walls and pink bathroom tiles. Lovely, and along with 'La Chambre de Mon Grandpère', the most expensive room, at 1100f. Another, with twin beds, decorated in pink Toile de Jouy, with marble bathroom costs 900f, as does 'La Petite Chambre Rose', where François has resurrected an old, green, claw-footed bath and lined the walls with old door panels, and there is another smaller but perfectly good version at 750f. Eight rooms altogether, all charming. Breakfast 50f extra.

It must be hard for Hedwige to spend her evenings alone, bathing and bedding their lively children, then cooking the guests' dinner, but it is certainly true that the success of these evening meals owes as much to François' ebullient presence as to her excellent cooking. He is a natural host, whose gusts of laughter soon break down the shyest guest's inhibitions. Fourteen frequently sit round the long *faux-*

…ne salon long after François retreats, …t. 300f includes copious alcohol. …an journalist commented on faded fabrics, …hich I certainly didn't detect, but in com… *privés*, it is no use going to Les Briottières in …ion. Go rather for appreciation of a charming …uilding, good company and the *joie de vivre* of 'I'm the King of the castles.'

…ZE-SUR-ARGOS. 49500

13km W of L… …ngers. Take the Candé road, the D770, and the turning is on the right 3km a… …ern d'Anjou, well marked.

This is fertile watery countryside, with several rivers speeding through to join the mighty Loire. Lots of opportunities to explore them by boats hired from Le Lion d'Angers and other pleasant bases.

Susan and Peter Scarboro. La Chaufournaie (M-S)

Tel & fax: (0)2.41.61.49.05.

The Scarboros (No, not Yorkshire but from Sevenoaks) first visited the region when their home village was twinned with Vern d'Anjou, and liked it so much that they resolved to buy something suitable for b. and b.s. Word of mouth from satisfied customers has ensured that even in their first year, without the assistance of any guidebooks, thank you very much, they welcomed many guests from England and elsewhere, and are enjoying their new lifestyle very much. The five rooms are well equipped with thoughtful extras like Teasmades, and although the windows are set in the roof, there is plenty of light and space. There is one larger one, at the end of the corridor, with twin beds plus a single, so I should bag that if you get in early enough. All cost 230f now, with 90f for additional beds.

A converted barn makes an excellent wet-weather retreat, with boardgames, books, a full-sized billiard table and an old English institution that must puzzle the natives - what is French for shove-h'apenny?. The English fry-up breakfast costs a mere 35f supplement, and nice, comfortable Susan Scarboro also provides a further taste of home cooking in the evenings. 'Nothing fancy', she modestly disclaims, at dinner-time - 85f for four courses including *apéritif* and wine. Susan looks forward to joining her guests at the table and sorting out their excursions for the next day.

COURLEON. 49390

36km N of Chinon. 24km NE of Saumur. A small village within the attractions along the Loire from Tours to Angers.

From the D749 30km N of Chinon at Gizeau take the D215 W to C

NEW **Mr. & Mrs. Briers. Le Bourg** (M)
(0)2.41.59.80.36. fax: (0)2.41.59.80.33.

"*We occupied a twin en-suite room in the Briers' tastefully renovated house in the village of Courléon in the Loire. The use of an excellent swimming pool was included - arrangements were made for us to dine locally at very reasonable prices and we were treated with extreme hospitality and integrated with their local friends*" - Paul and Deirdre Goodey.

Just one room, 250f for two includes breakfast, but from October to May there are a couple of self-catering studios let on a b. & b. basis - 300f for two. A four course evening meal is available on Saturday nights - 80f wine included.

FONTEVRAUD L'ABBAYE. 49590

16km SE of Saumur, 21km W of Chinon. A few introductory lines is no way to describe even a small part of the treasures of Fontevraud. Buy a guidebook (or even better *French Entrée 8* on the Loire!) and fill in the gaps on what should be an essential stop on every tourist's Loire itinerary. Particularly every British itinerary, since in the abbey here, dubbed the Westminster of the Plantagenets, lie four effigies that belong to our heritage - Henry II of England, his wife Eleanor of Aquitaine, their son Richard Coeur de Lion, and Isabelle of Angoulème, second wife of their son John Lackland. All most moving, especially if you get there early or late and can view them without the distraction of other tourists. Painted in faded blue and red, all individuals, Isabelle carved in wood and the others in tufa stone.

Their resting place is the largest and virtually complete ensemble of mediaeval monastic buildings in France. A whole village, in fact, within a village. Take a tour, but leave time to visit the Romanesque parish church of St Michel. The pleasant little town has plenty of comfort stops - a well-known family hotel, a Michelin-starred restaurant, several bars and a good *salon de thé*, so a visit here can be rewarding gastronomically as well as spiritually.

More comfort is at hand if you turn off the D947 some 3km before Fontevraud and follow the signs to:

➤ M. et Mme Dauge. Le Domaine de Mestré (M)
(0)2.41.51.75.87.

The monks of Fontevraud used the Domaine as an agricultural complex, and some of the weathered stone buildings round the courtyard date from the 12th century; traces of a Roman road indicate that there has been a settlement here since time immemorial. Good use has been put to the assorted outbuildings: one is now a shop selling tempting take-home souvenirs - fragrant soaps and toilet desiderata made from pure, natural ingredients, perfuming the whole room. In another building are four rooms, smaller than those in the main building and used in winter because they are easier to heat. A 12th-century chapel is now a lovely dining room, with dark, wormy beams straddling the lofty ceiling and a massive oak *armoire* presiding over all. This is where dinner is served, with lots of home-grown vegetables served as first course, along with meat or fowl, then cheese and home-made desserts. Rosine Dauge does all the cooking, farmer husband Dominique serves and daughter Marie-Amélie helps out here and in the shop. It is very much a family affair and always has been - the Domaine has been in the same family since the 18th-century.

The late Laura Ashley would have been delighted to see the good use that her fabrics have been put to here. I recognized my own yellow cabbage rose pattern in the dining room and our bedroom in the annexe exploited a familiar blue and beige bird design, but it is in the main building that Rosine has had most fun, using different colour schemes in every room (with co-ordinating bathrooms), every-one a winner, spacious and gracious, furnished with antiques.

There are extensive grounds attached to the Domaine and breakfast in summer is served on the terrace looking down to the green valley. All this is very good news indeed, at a reasonable price, with all the joys of Fontevraud thrown in; the bad news is that the word has got around and it is not easy to get a reservation in high season. So be sure to book early and don't miss out on this one whatever you do. Twelve rooms: from 325f for 2 and 510f for 3 plus a suite. Dinner: 140f, exclusive of wine. Breakfast 35f extra.

GREZ-NEUVILLE. 49220

16km NE of Château-Gontier by D28. 20km N of Angers. One of those time-warped villages, utterly delightful, with grey, sun-bleached stone houses, that one sometimes stumbles upon in France. In this case the big attraction is the river Mayenne that flows fast and wide here, over a weir. Boats are for hire, there are walks along the bank, the activity of a lock to contemplate, and a crêperie and bar make sitting, sipping, supping, watching the water, a leisurely delight. What an added bonus then to find next to the church:

➤ Mme Jacqueline Bahuaud. La Croix d'Etain (M)

(0)2.41.95.68.49.

An immaculate Directoire period house, very French, all grey and white and proving to be much bigger than one might guess from first sight. The yellow salon, embellished with an amazingly ornate grandfather clock, is huge, and a very pleasant place to sit if the weather does not suggest a seat in the garden (where breakfast is served in summer). The grounds too are surprisingly extensive - 1.5 hectares, much of it river frontage.

Bedrooms, each with individual character, are lovely, spacious, pleasantly furnished, and like the rest of the house, look as though they had just been painted. Two have splendid river views.

I rate this one very highly as an agreeable, comfortable place to stay, in a particularly attractive village. Four rooms - 380f. Dinner 130f by reservation, excluding wine. Officially closed Nov-Easter, but Mme Bahuard is in residence throughout the year and welcomes guests in winter if they phone ahead.

LA JAILLE-YVON. 49220

39km N of Angers. Turn off N162 to D189 and then D187 signed Chambellay. The château is well-signed.

An excellent location, not only for an *en route* stopover, but as a base from which to explore this gentle watery territory, where a river is never far away. At Le Lion d'Angers, 9km south, or at Chenille-Changé even nearer, you can take a soothing excursion on the meandering Mayenne. In total contrast, the urban attractions of Angers and many of the lesser-known châteaux are within easy reach.

➤ M. et Mme Benoist. Château Le Plessis (L)

(0)2.41.95.12.75. fax: (0)2.41.95.14.41. Closed: 1 Nov.-1 Mar.

M. Benoist is a pioneer in the aristocratic b. and b. business. The rule to join the illustrious Château Accuiel group to which he belongs is that the château must have been in the family for at least two generations. 16th-century Le Plessis certainly qualifies since it has been in Mme Benoist's family since well before the Revolution, when in 1793 all the furniture except one treasured table was burned by the rebels. However, to be able to say that the replacements date from the time of your great-great-great-grandfather is more then most of us can claim.

This continuity and the feeling that the furniture and house are there to serve the family, not to be regarded as 'antiques' permeates the atmosphere. This is a home that happens to be in a very beautiful and historic building; all is friendly and relaxed. Venerable trees and sweeping lawns, studded with primroses and daffodils whenever I've been there, surround the house and contribute to the calm. Tea on the lawn, *à l'anglais*, is a nice touch.

M. Benoist used to work for Mobil Oil, so his English is fluent and Mme Benoist is an unusually good cook, so that dinner round their large oval table, served with carefully-chosen Anjou wines is bound to be a rewarding experience. Eight rooms, all with bath, 600/770f. Dinner 270f.

LE LION D'ANGERS. 49220

25km NW of Angers. 5km NW of Le Lion d'Angers, a left turn k off the D863, signed on the left.

NEW M. & Mme Viviers. Domaine des Travaillières (S) (0)2.41.61.33.56.

This rustic farmhouse has been converted into a charming comfortable home. Well off the main road, quiet, with pretty gardens. Two family rooms have adjoining rooms for children, sharing the en-suite facilities, one on the ground floor has access to the garden. Another, just for a couple, has a double bed. The interesting *outeaux* windows in the roof actually open into the rooms and give a pleasant through breeze on a hot summer night.

Rooms are 200/230f and evening meals are occasionally possible if reserved but there are many restaurants in the vicinity.

Vivacious Madame is a superb cook and makes a lovely nut gâteau which often arrives on the breakfast table. Her daughter paints many of the pictures you find on the walls. Considering you are so near the Loire valley here the price is very good.

I think this one will prove very popular. English understood more than Mme professes.

PARCAY-LES-PINS. 49390

45km W of Tours. 22km NE of Saumur. 60km S of Le Mans the little village of Parçay-les-Pins lies north of the châteaux region of the Loire. Though small the village still has a *boulangerie, boucherie,* SPAR mini-market and a bar-restaurant, all within walking distance of the chambres d'hôtes.

From Arnage, S of Le Mans, take the D 307 to Le Lude and Noyant, then the D141 to Parçay. In the village turn on to the D53 (SP Vernoil) and the house is on the right.

Mr. & Mrs. M.J. Stockley and Mr. & Mrs. A.W. Grantham. La Croix Joreau (S-M)

(0)2.41.82.62.17. fax: (0)2.41.82.64.35.

Two English couples have converted this farmhouse and outbuildings into gîtes and chambres d'hôtes surrounding a large courtyard. The two single-bedded rooms, one on the ground floor and one above, have natural breeze-block walls and modern shower rooms, simple pine beds have flowery covers. The ground floor room is tiled and suitable for the handicapped, the room above is warmly carpeted. A cottage restored in '97 offers independent accommodation - with private patio. One twin-bedded room, kitchen and lounge make it a good idea for a family. Let by the week £200.

A friendly place to stay where you will be in close contact with your hosts and other guests. In the village the bar/restaurant cooks regional meals at very reasonable prices, much enjoyed by a reader on a previous visit.

Rooms, 225/270f according to season and reducing after three nights, include breakfast.

LE PUY-NOTRE-DAME. 49260

4km W of Montreuil Bellay, 20km S of Saumur. From Montreuil Bellay take the Thouars road, the D938, and after 4km turn right on to the D158, direction Passay; the mill is signed from here. The drive is through pleasant wine country.

M. et Mme Bergerolle. Le Moulin de Couche (M)

(0)2.41.38.87.11. fax: (0)2.41.38.86.99.

The river Thouet divides the *dèpartements* of Sèvres and that of Maine-et-Loire. The old flour mill stands on the banks of the latter. In 1993 Anny and Jean Bergerolle started the conversion into a comfortable chambres d'hôte in the actual mill and a restaurant in the old stables. The rooms have lovely views over the tranquil river, flowing to join the Loire near Saumur. The rooms are freshly decorated with flower themes like *Hortensia*, *Violettes* and *Bleuets*, with a mixture of old and new furniture, some with showers, some with old-fashioned baths, some with large, new ones, some adjoining to form suites.

The situation is perfect - especially for breakfast on the sunny terrace or under the willow tree - and there are relaxing walks along the river banks, far from any sound more disturbing than birdsong and bubbling water.

The restaurant, *La Ponote*, is very pretty indeed, decorated in lilac blue and white with a mezzanine floor looking down on the activity below, and a huge, raised fire, where grills are cooked in winter. Four doubles at 230f, suites at 390f and 400f. Breakfast 35f. The restaurant has menus from 90f-165f.

ST LAMBERT-DES-LEVÉES. 49400

3km W of Saumur on the north bank of the Loire. From Saumur cross the river, but don't turn immediately left on to the river road. Take the next turning, past the railway station, the D229. 3km further on look for the chambres d'hôtes sign on the right.

➤ Helga and Jean-Pierre Minder. La Croix de la Voulte (M)

(0)2.41.38.46.66. Closed: Nov-Easter.

Look no further if you seek a chambres d'hôtes with enthusiastic English-speaking hosts, stylish comfortable rooms, within easy reach of the Loire and Saumur, with a swimming pool thrown in, and all for a reasonable price.

German Helga, married for 30 years to French Jean-Pierre, opened the four rooms in the 15th-century wing of this mostly 17th-century house in 1990. Since then the Minders have continuously renovated and improved the property. Not only is the comfort exceptional but the taste is irreproachable - the character of the old manor house respected but with colourful touches to enliven the old stones. The rooms are all quite different and it is obvious that Helga has had great pleasure in choosing the decor for each one. The largest boasts a four-poster bed, massive stone fireplace and old *armoire*. Antique furniture throughout and low beamed fireplaces contribute to the atmosphere of times gone by (but with modern plumbing). The Minders like nothing better than to see their guests stretch out on smart recliners by their pool. They also like to see them mellow. So in each room is a *seau à champagne* - an ice-bucket, so that the guests can buy the local fizzy wine (who could resist?) and bring it chilled to drink by the poolside. Conviviality guaranteed. This is just one of the personal touches that make staying here such a pleasure. Jean-Pierre sees to it that the garden is full of flowers and a pleasant place to sit for breakfast. He is readily available to help plan the guests' day and advise on itineraries. Four rooms: 430f with bath, 330f with shower. Breakfast 35f. No dinner offered because there are so many restaurants in nearby Saumur or Les Rosiers to choose from.

ST MATHURIN-SUR-LOIRE. 49250

11km SE of Angers, 22km NW of Saumur, on the north bank of the Loire.

Claudine and Christian Pinier. Verger de la Bouquetterie (M)

118 rue du Roi René. (0)2.41.57.02.00. fax: (0)2.41.57.31.90.

1km from St Mathurin heading west.

There must be some initial doubts about traffic noise since the Pinier's pleasant 19th-century house is right on the road, but nice young Claudine assured me that there is little movement at night, definitely no lorries, and that the double glazing is most effective. That worry overcome, the advantages of actually overlooking the river prevail. There are surprisingly few establishments in this book that can actually claim to be within view of the mighty Loire.

The house is pristine, with pleasant, faded, old-fashioned furniture of the brown and beige persuasion, with several attractive original features, like the moulding on the salon ceiling and its marble fireplace. In spite of coping with two young children and having recently lost her husband, Christine runs an efficient operation and finds time for the extra touches like home-made jam and apple juice for her guests' breakfasts, and serving copious evening meals, supplemented by fresh veg. from a pleasant garden at the rear. Behind this again are extensive apple and pear orchards.

There are two new rooms since my first visit in an annexe, decorated in appropriate rustic style, complete with beams and dry stone walls; one is a suite suitable for a family. They are named after painters whose work hangs on the walls. In April, May and June Claudine organises special weekends - 2 nights b & b, two dinners, two light lunches all drinks and 7 excursions into the countryside to see flora and fauna and charming villages, a picnic at the waters edge, a visit to troglodyte caves, wine tasting and an evening dinner "spectacle" all for 1850f per person. All the bedrooms are spacious and light; You have the choice of overlooking the river or the guaranteed calm of one at the back. Six rooms, 285/325f. Dinner 115f including wine.

MAYENNE

ERNÉE. 53500

20km SE of Fougères. 24km W of Mayenne. A nice small town in the Haute-Maine with restaurants and two supermarkets for petrol and self catering, which all makes it a good place to stop and spend a night at this easy-to-find chambres d'hôtes. Signed on the N12 1km east of Ernée, on the right leaving the town.

M. et Mme Gendron. La Gasselinais (S)
(0)2.43.05.70.80.

Recommended by François de Valbray (see Les Briottières p.166), than whom there can be no greater expert on chambres d'hôtes.

Three rooms in a farmhouse each with private shower. François writes that the family room with mezzanine and kitchenette is ideal for families, spending a holiday on a working farm. He is quite right. We were cosseted by a log fire one cold September night in the large salon and invited to join our charming hosts and local friends who had just dropped in for a drink.

Rooms 150f for one, 190f for two, 240f for three. Highly recommended.

LAVAL. 53000

146kms S of Caen, 249kms SE of Le Havre.

An under-appreciated town, generally conceived as merely a staging post on the way between port and the Loire Valley. In fact there is much to value, particularly in the old town which clusters round the castle on the sloping west bank of the picturesque river Mayenne. The modern town centres on the huge square named after Marshal Foch, from which the main shopping streets radiate. Climb up to the courtyard of the Vieux Château, enclosed by ramparts from which there is a good view of the multi-coloured, multi-centred roofs of the old town. The bulk of the castle dates from the 13th and 15th centuries, but the windows, whose white tufa stone is carved with Italianiate scrolls, were added in the 16th century. The crypt and the keep are the oldest parts (12th and 13C). The most interesting feature of the keep is the extraordinary timber roof built in 1100 in an ingenious circular design, incorporating great beams radiating from the centre and projecting beyond the 6ft thick walls.

Take a walk along the quays on the east bank for the best overall views of Laval, across the now canalized waters of the river. The hump-backed Pont Vieux dating from the 13C also offers good views of the slate roofs, the narrow streets of half-timbered houses and the keep of the castle. Lovely walks in La Perrine Gardens, with rose garden, ponds and waterfalls.

➤ M. & Mme François Williot. Le Bas du Gast (L)

6 rue de la Halle aux Toiles. (0)2.43.49.22.79. fax: (0)2.43.56.44.71.
Closed: 1/2-30/11.

This one is special, on several counts. Although it is a rare city chambres d'hôtes, it is country-quiet by virtue of its setting in a sleepy square of dignified old grey houses and because of its surprising garden. The garden is typically 18C French, very formal and graced with no less than 85 box pyramids which the energetic M. Williot prunes himself every year. You can imagine yourself an elegantly dressed aristocrat as you play a gentle game of croquet, or settle for more plebian boules.

Hard to choose between the four lovely bedrooms, each decorated with style and excellent taste. I like the double-bedded Chambre Jaune (550f), but the Toile de Jouy version with twin beds, at 650f, is pretty nice too. Then there's the very imposing Chambre Napoléon with three beds (supplement 250f for third incumbent) or the suite of Chambres Bleu and Verte which can be opened up for one luxurious ensemble for 1100f, or booked separately. All have outstanding bathrooms with every conceivable freebie. M. Williot is the friendliest, most accommodating, English-speaking host, who will go to endless trouble to point you in all kinds of right directions. Arrowed for all-round excellence.

LOIRON. 53220

11km W of Laval. 23km SE of Vitré. A very handy night stop off the fast A81 which runs from Paris to South Brittany cutting through the northern part of the Loire region.

From exit 5 at La Gravelle take the N 157 back towards Laval for 9km. Don't take the right turn to Loiron but in 2km look for the signs to the chambres d'hôtes on the right at La Chappelle du Chêne.

NEW M. & Mme Rabourg. La Charbonnerie (M) (0)2.43.02.44.74.

A kilometre from the main road, surrounded by 40 hectares of fields where only the mooing of cows is heard. The house was once a *maison bourgeouise* with a small chapel in the grounds, demolished in the Revolution. Only the chapel remains, where the statue on the epistle side is of Saint Denis, patron saint of Paris, with head under one arm. Legend has it that when he was beheaded he picked up his head and walked away.

The present farmhouse, of typical stone and brick of the region, was built in the last century and has been in the same family since.

Two first-floor guest rooms are in a separate little cottage. The unadorned simplicity of the rooms is quite charming. A pretty pale-blue room for three has a giant double bed (which can convert to two singles) with a delicate *ciel-de-lit*, spotless white sheets and a vast *broderie anglais* duvet; there is plenty of room for a single bed under the eaves, little white pedestals support bedside lamps and the dual aspect low windows complement it all. The adjoining large bathroom has a bath with shower and a separate loo, good lights and hair-dryer. The second room for two is smaller and has a shower and yes, both are fully carpeted! 260f for two, extra bed 50f. A large farmhouse breakfast is included.

In the salon below is one of the largest bread ovens I have ever seen, now a feature fireplace. The dining room has a kitchen area. Mme Raborg joins you for satisfying evening meals - 85f wine *compris*. Her generous *tarte-aux-pommes* was the best I have tasted. Guests may opt for use of the kitchen and self-catering, but I would advise eating here at least once. Monsieur, busy on the farm, joins you occasionally. I think this chambres d'hôtes could prove very popular but there is not a lot of English spoken.

ST DENIS D'ANJOU. 53290

9km SW of Sablé by D27 direction Champigné. Just before the village, signed on the left. Lots of attractions in the area - Gregorian chants at Solesmes, boating on the river Sarthe, and the agreeable little town of Sablé. St Denis itself is a flowery mediaeval village with 16th-century market halls and ancient church.

Martine and Jacques Lefèbvre. Le Logis du Ray (M)

(0)2.43.70.64.10. fax: (0)2.43.70.65.53.

In the game of tracking down chambres d'hôtes there are some good days and some bad ones but I've never suffered one as totally frustrating as this. It was early November, the last tour before Delivery Day and the last chance to tidy up loose ends. I targeted seven likelies and set off in increasing drizzle and fog, buoyed up by the hope of adding seven amazingly exciting new finds to the book. It took all day and 170 miles and as darkness fell the tally was six visited and six blanks. What I had overlooked was that the November school holidays often overruled the landlady's assertion that she was *ouverte toute l'année*; and whereas some were just out - shopping with the kids, leaving aggressive dogs to do the accueil bit - others had packed up altogether and gone to see Grandmère for the week. Cynically I rang the doorbell of the seventh, Le Logis du Ray, wearily I asked if I might see a room, unbelievingly I heard nice plump Mme Lefèbvre offering me a cup of tea before showing me three rooms that I knew would rate very highly indeed. So if you detect a shade of prejudice here, please make allowances.

It's an old creeper-covered farmhouse, furnished with antiques (M. Lefèbvre is a man of many roles, among them that of *antiquaire* and *ebeniste*). Mme Lefèbvre has done her bit admirably, choosing cheerful stylish decorations. One room has blue and white mattress ticking fabric very successfully used on beds and sidetables, coordinating with blue paint. With good shower-room, it costs 385f for two or 480f for three. Another with four-poster and old *armoire* is decidedly Laura Ashley-esque, decorated in navy blue and white tiny flower pattern. Only the yellow shower-room is assertively modern. 385f again. The third, smaller but still recommendable, is blue again, with navy shower and suite, for 300f. Dinner 150f wine included.

I like this one very much, but is does have one shortcoming - no salon. However, there is a dining room and a garden and the Lefèbvre's smiles make up for a lot. Another house attraction is the horse and carriage rides that Monsieur organises to discover the area at an appropriate pace. Madame provides the picnic lunch.

SAINT-JEAN-SUR-ERVE. 53270

46km W of Le Mans. 30km E of Laval.This tiny village has a *boulangerie, charcuterie* and a restaurant.

Follow the N157 from Laval to Le Mans and turn off to the village 7km after Vaiges. The chambres d'hôtes is exactly opposite the Restaurant de l'Erve beside the bridge.

NEW M. & Mme Bigot. Clos de Launay (M)

Le Bourg. (0)2.43.90.26.19.

M. and Mme Bigot have spent four years restoring their house. Now the garden with green lawns extends right along the small river bank. The house is in the centre of the village but double glazing takes care of noise and there is little traffic. Mme does not serve evening meals, but as she says it gives them more time to enjoy their guests and there is a good restaurant literally on her doorstep.

Four immaculate rooms with separate en-suite loos have been thoughtfully designed - 280f for twin beds, 250f for a double. A rear room, with a charming view of the lake and river, has three beds. Warmly heated, with carpets, this would be a welcome winter stop. In summer lazing beside the river, picnicking in the garden would be ideal. A large parking space behind the house keeps your car safe. Your hosts really enjoy their guests and have much information of the area. An arrow very soon I feel.

SARTHE

MONHOUDOU. 72260

40km NE of Le Mans, 38km SE of Alençon by D311 to Mamers, then D300 to Courgains, then D32 to Monhoudou.

Vicomte de Monhoudou. Château de Monhoudou (M-L)

(0)2.43.97.40.05. fax: (0)2.43.33.11.58. Closed: 15/10 to 15/4.

An affordable luxury, well situated for a stop *en route* south. Rooms in this 1625 bijou château cost only 450/550f; we are not talking châteaux-belt here. It is set, reflected in its lake, in 20 hectares of grounds, with walking trails, outing by horse-drawn carriage and even hunting laid on for those suitably equipped.

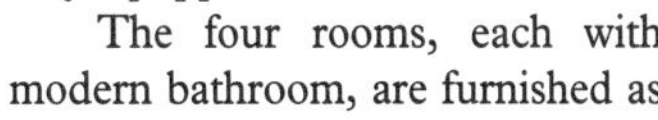

The four rooms, each with modern bathroom, are furnished as one might expect - with family antiques. Candlelit dinners can be booked ahead - 195f, with the chance to hobnob with a friendly Vicomte, who will be delighted to share his enthusiasm for the region.

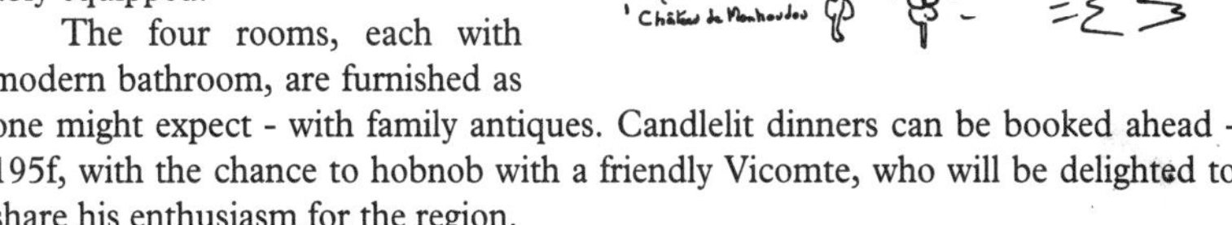

ST LÉONARD-DES-BOIS. 72590

19km SW of Alençon by D315, then at Moulins-le-Carbonel turn left to St Léonard. Drive through the village and the mill is signed on the right.

If for nothing else (and in fact there's a lot) I would be grateful to this entry for the chance to discover the gorgeous countryside in the area. I had never visited Les Alpes Mancelles before, and now I find it a region of, if not alps as we know them, sizeable hills, beech forests, deep valleys, rushing rivers, lush green vegetation. Yes, now I come to think of it, it is a bit like lowland Switzerland without the cuckoo clocks. What is more, it is a perfect *en route* stop from the ferry ports on the way south.

➤ Mme Claude Rollini. Le Moulin de l'Inthe (M)

(0)2.43.33.79.22.

Even if this were in a factory belt I would still give it an arrow. It was the very last chambres d'hôtes I checked out on my way home from the very last tour of the year and I think it is one of the best. The building and its site are, yes it's that word again, idyllic. The river rushes by, around and through the property, its gigantic old wooden wheel cleverly incorporated into a

glassed-in appendage to the lovely sitting room. Mesmerising. Hills slope down to water, picnic spots abound, there are walks galore, swimming in the river and riding nearby.

The old mill has been perfectly converted to retain its rusticity - rough brick walls, beams and tiles - while insisting on comfort - huge log fire burning (and it was morning and they didn't know I was coming), a piano, deep chintzy armchairs. Similarly the five bedrooms, with French windows opening on to the garden, have cheerful colours, and a mix of old and new furniture, with very modern bathrooms apiece. A bargain at 350f. Evening meal 90f wine complis.

Nice Madame Rollini who speaks English has only just started b. and b.ing, but I bet it won't be long before the word gets around about this one, so book soon and write and thank me. Arrowed of course.

ST PATERNE. 72610

3km SE of Alençon. On the Chartres road, the D311; since the new autoroute has been built, the village of St Paterne is now very well signed from all directions, and the château is in the centre.

➤ Charles-Henry de Valbray. Château de St Paterne (L)

(0)2.33.27.54.71. fax: (0)2.33.29.16.71. Closed: 1/1-1/3.

It is hard to believe that the experienced patron here, Charles-Henry de Valbray, is still not thirty. He runs his empire with enthusiasm, style and confidence, born of finding out the tough way what can and cannot be done on a small budget, a lot of unbelievably hard work and total dedication. He inherited the potentially lovely 15th-century château, crumbling and sad, from his grandmother, and, often with his own hands, has restored it to something of its former glory, helped by p.g. finance. The work goes on - there are many more rooms begging to have the magic wand waved over them.

FE3 readers loved what they found here, tentatively booking for one night first time and for a week subsequently.

Charles-Henry was able to pick up plenty of tips from his brother, François, who successfully runs Les Briottières (see p. 166) but the furnishing schemes are all his own. I love best the yellow room with pleated canopy over the bed, grey panelled doors, grey trompe l'oeil columns and antique furniture. I can sit at the table in the little tower to write up notes, looking out on to the daffodils in the park.

Down three steps is the bathroom with blue iron bath on claw feet, three steps down again to the loo (not advisable for the night-incontinent).

New since my last visit is the beginning of the restoration of the top floor, with one beamed room already functioning, decorated with oriental trophies collected from C.H's eastern travels. New, too, is a delightful conversion of the 12th-century *pigeonnier* into a comfortable suite of salon/kitchen and upstairs bedroom. Provençal style this time, all white tiles and simplicity, harking back to the de Valbray childhood in the South.

With the help of the admirable Marie-Louise - 'My creme brûlée went wrong so Marie-Louise has whipped up a tarte Tatin' - the tireless Charles-Henry cooks the evening meal, served by candlelight in the peach and green dining-room, warmed by a massive white porcelain stove. And very good it was too, with salmon trout and haddock on a bed of leeks sprinkled with red peppercorns, preceding roast pork and the tart.

Another new feature is the arrangement made with a band of Laotian refugees based in the town; in exchange for some land on which to cultivate their own delicacies and keep chickens, they keep the château totally provided with fresh veg. and flowers. So don't think you're going mad when you see the kitchen garden transformed into a slice of Asia, with coolies in cone-shaped hats tending their crops. Rooms 450-750f, breakfast 40f. Pigeonnier (four people) 450f or 1,800f a week.

Conveniently placed on the route south, this is a lovely place to stay with a charming host as a bonus. Arrowed as exceptional.

THOIRE-SUR-DINAN. 72500

40km SE of Le Mans. Right in the middle of the flat agricultural and wooded valley of the Pays de la Loire. (I was recommended this one by a reader, and decided to go and see for myself.)

Take the D304 from SE of Le Mans to Saint-Pierre-du-Lorouër then the D63 towards Flée, turning right to Thoiré, the house is first on the right.

NEW Mme Claudine Cissé. Le Saut-du-Loup (S)

(0)2.43.79.12.36.

The Cissés spent three years planning their chambres d'hôtes and visiting many others to make sure they had thought of everything.

The farm is now run by their son, who lives close by and he opens for cream teas in the summer; but if it is accommodation and an evening meal look no further than the long low farmhouse, sideways on to the road where you will be given a splendid welcome and shown to one of their three rooms, one of which is for a family with curtained-off adjoining room with two beds, sharing the shower room. Rooms are simply furnished but comfortably warm for all-year-round occupation, 240f.

The evening meal with Monsieur and Mme is great fun. Mme Cissé is an excellent cook and she and her husband really enjoy entertaining. All *compris* for 85f. A cosy log fire at one end of the room heats the whole house. Large lawns and a *pétanque* court border the house.

Le Saut du Loup
Thoiré sur Dinan
72

VENDEE

CHAILLE-LES-MARAIS. 85450

20km SW of Fontenay-le-Comte. 6.5km N of Marans.The Vendée is in the southern part of the Western Loire. Known as the Marais Poitevin it stretches from Maillezais in the north to Mauzé in the south and from Bessines near Niort in the east to Marans in the west. In the 11th-century the land was always being flooded in the winter from the rivers Sèvre-Niortaîse and Vendée. The monks got so fed up with their churches being under water they began to dig out canals to drain the land and the good work has been going on ever since. Now there are 12,000km of these linked canals. It really is a little-known area which the French keep to themselves.

A very pleasant way to spend a hot summer's day is lazing on a flat-bottomed boat with overhanging branches dipping into the water as you glide along. Cows and sheep marooned on islands step down to the banks to drink; no need for hedges to keep them on their grazing patch. Every house bordering a canal has its own boat tied to a pole. On a guided tour your guide will show you how pockets of methane gather under the canal bed by stirring up the mud and setting alight to the canal. Luckily you are in a metal boat!

Motor boats are allowed only on the rivers, so peace and quiet are assured in the backwaters. The lesser used canals tend to be overgrown with green weeds and algae. At Arçais there is one part that looks like an emerald green lawn.

Fontenay-le-Comte, in the north, is the largest town in the Marais. Visit the Abbey Church of Notre-Dame, which has attractive royal-blue stained-glass windows and an ornate pulpit. The town was always Royalist and suffered badly in the revolution. The ancient abbey at Maillezais is also worth a visit.

Chaillé-les-Marais is on the western fringe of the Vendée, a pleasant stop on the route to Bordeaux, and within easy reach of the waterways.

M. & Mme Pizon. Le Paradis (S)

Le Sableau. (0)2.51.56.72.15. fax: (0)2.51.56.73.39.

Not actually in the town of Chaillé-les-Marais; but in the village of Le Sableau 4km south on the N137. The long drive up to the house ensures that you are well away from the main road and there is no noise at night. Mme Pizon is a very accommodating hostess; not only does she have five rooms, but a kitchen especially for guests where they can cook their own meals or do their washing. All rooms have a small shower and loo. First floor, ground floor, double and family rooms to choose from. Ample parking and best of all a pristine clean swimming pool with plenty of plastic loungers - so in hot weather this is a reasonable respite from the hot sticky drive along the N137 to or from La Rochelle. Excellent breakfast included for 200/230f.

Evening meals on offer at 65f. Also there are two restaurants within five minutes walk, one a *Routier*. Good all-round value here.

MIDI-PYRENEES

Départements:	**Ariège**	**Hautes-Pyrénées**
	Aveyron	**Lot**
	Gers	**Tarn**
	Haute-Garonne	**Tarn-et-Garonne**

The Midi-Pyrénées stretches from the Lot in the north to the Pyrénées and is bounded by Aquitaine in the west and Languedoc-Roussillon in the east, incorporating eight *départements*, three of which lie along the Spanish border. Further north are the Gers, Tarn, Tarn-et-Garonne and Aveyron and, furthest north of all, the Lot. Altogether a very large slice of south-west France.

Tarbes, the *préfecture*, of the **Hautes-Pyrénées** is a rather ordinary industrial town with the main rail terminal from Paris and an airport with flights direct from Gatwick. The name most people associate with this department is Lourdes, a Mecca for the sick. There are hidden lakes high in the mountains, numerous cols to traverse for intrepid explorers and skiing in winter. The Cirque de Gavarnie forms a natural amphitheatre in the mountains on the Spanish border, south of Lourdes.

A small wedge of **Haute-Garonne** reaches down to the Spanish border, where the spa town of Bagnères-de-Luchon seems miles away from civilisation, a little Victorian-flavoured world of its own, a great favourite with the British both then and now. Twinned with Harrogate says it all!

The river Garoma rises in Spain and is joined by the river Pique to become the Garonne at Marignac, it then flows north to Toulouse, the fourth largest town in France, the *préfecture* of this *département* and the capital of the whole region. The N117 runs from the Atlantic to the Mediterranean almost parallel with the Pyrénées but well away from them, with smaller roads cutting up the valleys into the mountains, and arrives at Foix the *préfecture* of **Ariège,** the next *département.* The town, guarded by its old castle with three distinctive towers high above the main streets, is squashed between high mountains, a bottleneck for traffic, with the N20 trunk road rushing past to Andorra and Spain along the bank of the river Ariège. Help is on the way - there are signs of a new by-pass appearing.

Gers, sometimes known as Gascony, lies north of the Hautes-Pyrénées and life there can best be summed up by the old Gascon Prayer "Lord, give me good health, light work, fine meals frequently, a little love from time to time, but above all my daily ration of Armagnac"! The local brandy was already on sale in the 15th-century, two hundred years before Cognac (a dirty word in this area). Armagnac is distilled once, as opposed to the double distillation of its rival, and must age for at least two years in oak casks to be *Appellation.* Three stars indicates an Armagnac three years old, V.S.O.P. at least four, Napoléon at least five, and for *Vielle Armagnac* the age is indicated on the bottle. The rich local *apéritif* served in chambres d'hôtes is *Floc;* a mixture of Armagnac and grape juice, either white or red.

The Gers is a totally agricultural *département*, with rolling hills of sunflowers, corn and vineyards, beside the quiet roads. Ducks and geese are everywhere, heading for the *foie gras* market. Auch, the *préfécture*, sits regally on a hill in the middle, with all the roads converging on it. On one side is the magnificent *Escalier Monumental*, a great stone staircase sweeping up to the cathedral above. A statue of D'Artagnan stands majestically near the top. The 370 steps have shallow risers - it isn't the stiff climb it looks. The Tourist Office is housed in the *Maison Fedel*, a 15th-century building. The Cathedral of Ste. Marie has eighteen beautiful windows painted by Arnaud de Moles at the beginning of the 16th century. As he was a Gascon you will find other churches in the Gers with his handiwork. There is parking by the cathedral, but also in a large shady car park near the Place de la Libération.

The smallest *département* of the Midi-Pyrénées is *Tarn et Garonne*, but it certainly packs a lot into a small space. Montauban the *préfecture*, built in the red brick so typical of the Toulouse area, was originally built as a bastide. It suffered during the Albigensian crusade and is now strongly Protestant. Moissac, further west, is famous for the 11th-century cloisters at the Abbey. Close by the Tarn joins the Garonne and at Boulou, on a hill a few kilometres west, there is a lookout which gives a wonderful view of the converging rivers. The rest of the *département* is mostly agricultural with pleasant, small villages.

Tarn further east is north of Toulouse. Albi is the *préfecture*. Its dreary red brick cathedral, Ste. Cécile, is nothing to look at from outside, but inside the contrast is magical - one of the loveliest cathedrals in France. The red, blue and gold painted walls contrast with the white carved stonework, giving off such warmth it affects all who enter - not a miserable face in sight. There are 29 side chapels flanking the nave, all different, but in the same colours. Beautiful oak choir stalls lead to the high altar. The vaulted ceiling is superb. So much to see, impossible to describe, far better to go and look for yourself.

Behind the cathedral beside the river Tarn is the museum of Toulouse-Lautrec, open every day 10-12 and 2-5 p.m. (closed on Tuesdays). Many of his paintings are here, among those of other artists. It is an old bishop's palace, so the rooms are interesting in themselves. It is also possible to visit the house where he was born, in a corner of the rue de Toulouse-Lautrec. Good pedestrian shopping precincts fill the centre of the town, where an antiques fair is held on occasional Saturdays. Nicer views of the cathedral are to be had from the bridges over the Tarn, which flows through the centre of the *département.*

There are many other places to visit, such as the hill villages of Cordes to the north of Albi and Lautrec to the south. West are the vineyards of Gaillac, both red and white wines in the many *dégustations*. The *Appellation Contrôlée* is one of the

MIDI-PYRÉNÉES

Autoire
Mur-de-Barrez
La Croix-Barrez
D921
N140
D13
N122
Figeac
Entraygues
Estaing
N140
D988
St-Rémy
Onet-le-Château
N88
N9
Rodez
D911
Villefranche-de-Rouergue
D911
Aveyron
Millau
Cordes
N9
Albi
Loupiac
Tarn
N112
Castres
N126
N112
Chambre d'Hôtes
0 20km

oldest in France, dating from the 12th century.

Aveyron. First impressions of this *département* are of high barren *causses* grazed by cattle and sheep, with the rather commercial *préfecture* of Rodez up on the plain, but the delights are hidden in the valleys of the major rivers which cut through it, notably the Tarn, the Lot and the Aveyron itself.

Millau in a valley of the Tarn, is an attractive town famous for making gloves. But best by far in Aveyron is the valley of the river Lot, which runs along its northern border. Delightful, old villages like Entraygues, where the Lot is joined by the river Truyère, can be found on the banks of the river. The river flows north of Conques (which is almost a rival of Rocamadour in the popularity polls and not such an uphill walk from the car park), and wends its way to Cahors along the lush border valley of fruit trees, overlooked by Saint-Cirq-Lapopie

The **Lot** to most people means the river and Cahors, an area producing deep red wine, once used by the Tsars as communion wine. Cahors is the *préfecture* and is situated on a bend of the river. The southernmost part of the *département* is known as the Quercy, where many old bastide towns were built in the Hundred Years War, all well worth visiting. North of Cahors is Rocamadour, the hill village of all hill villages, which Henry 'Short Coat', the eldest son of Henry II, pillaged. He caught a fever and died later in Martel asking for his father's pardon. The whole area is full of history, you can spend many days visiting old fortified castles or taking it more leisurely along the river, whose banks are planted with orchards and vineyards, interspersed with rocky outcrops, when the road has to leave the river or take to a tunnel. A great tourist area next door to the Dordogne.

ARIEGE

SERRES-SUR-ARGET. 09000

9km W of Foix. Take the D17 from Foix and follow the signs through the village.

Foix is about six miles away down winding roads and after a day out there seeing castle and museum, visiting the large market on Friday and fighting your way through heavy traffic, you will be glad to speed back to your mountain retreat.

➤ M. & Mme Brogneaux. Le Poulsieu (S)
(0)5.61.02.77.72.

If you have always dreamt of a holiday in the mountains of the Pyrénées, this is just the place. You will think you are at the end of the world as you bump your way slowly up the last kilometre of the unmade track. Park your car out of sight and forget about it for a week.

Bob and Jenny Brogneaux (she is Dutch, so there is no language problem) will give you a splendid welcome and take you to one of their five rooms, with a choice of double or single beds, delightfully rustic, pretty windows giving glorious mountain views. There are four rooms in the main house and another family room for four in a small building across the courtyard, where young early risers can disturb only their own parents. This room has a double bed on the ground floor and a bathroom half way up to a mezzanine area with two beds for children.

Sunny tables for *apéritifs* in the courtyard but meals are taken at one long table on the large covered terrace adjoining the dining room, which has a splendid view of the wide valley and surrounding mountains. A refreshing swimming pool is on a raised terrace by the house; there are rumours of it being heated in future for the cooler months.

A delightful house-party atmosphere prevails. You eat with your hosts and no-one bothers about taking dinner elsewhere. It is too far to drive back and nowhere else will you find such an international menu. Four courses 70f including all drinks. Wine is offered as an *apéritif* and with the meal. Should you be desperate for something stronger you pay extra.

Rooms 220f. *Demi-pension* rates of 350f for two people apply after six nights.

I do realise this wouldn't be everyone's idea of an ideal holiday, so tucked away from towns and shops, but if you like mountain treks, beautiful scenery, swimming and good food and wine, make haste to book, and book you must - news is spreading fast.

VARILHES. 09120

10km N of Foix. Just a turn off the N20 north of Foix, well signed in the centre of the town take the road beside the *mairie* over the small bridge and turn immediately left. It will lead to the chambres d'hôtes in 1km.

NEW M. & Mme Baudeigne 'Les Rives' (M)

(0)5.61.60.73.42. fax: (0)5.61.60.78.76.

This stately home, well away from the main road, in a large beautiful garden, has a swimming pool and a tennis court. The atmosphere is of a small hotel rather than a chambres d'hôtes. Madame is not always there but a receptionist will show you round.

There are four pleasant large rooms, three with bathrooms furnished with good family furniture. An extra room shares facilities for a family. If you book well ahead and are staying for a week or more you may have the use of the kitchen for the family suite. 300f seems good value.

Two restaurants are recommended in Varilhes. 'Le Varhois' and the Auberge Marinette, both about 2km away. This would suit some people who prefer the anonymity of a hotel.

I should be interested to have some feedback from this one.

AVEYRON

LACROIX-BARREZ. 12600

45km SE of Aurillac. 22km NE of Entraygues-sur-Truyère. The small town of Lacroix-Barrez is high on the plain above the Truyère valley. Take the D904 north and in 3.5km turn right to Vilherols, a small hamlet signed from here.

NEW **M. & Mme Laurens. Vilherols** (M)
(0)5.65.66.08.24. fax: (0)5.65.66.19.98.

This exquisite cluster of buildings has belonged to the same family since the 12th century. Monsieur's parents live in the gracious manor house and he lives a few terraces below in a meandering old stone house with beautiful lauzes tiled roof. In between the two dwellings, charming guest rooms have been contrived out of unlikely material - one-time pig sties. Keeping the old stone walls and lauzes tiled roofs, two ground-floor rooms, identical in all but colours, have magnificent views over the fields around. Huge patio entrance doors lead to a sitting area with comfortable armchairs where, hidden behind doors, is a fully equipped kitchenette with a microwave oven. Up a raised step is a carpeted area with double bed and access to a luxurious shower room - 260f.

Approached by a paved slope, easily accessible, is a larger apartment with an extensive terrace, specially designed for the handicapped. This room has a double bed and a convertible couch for two people, shower room, washing machine, kitchenette and picture-windows, - 350f.

A family suite, consisting of a double room and bathroom, with tower room above, up a ladder, is in Madame's own house, where a copious breakfast is taken, served by English-speaking Mme Laurens.

Exceptionally good value, reduction out of season, if you stay three days.

There is a small restaurant/café in La Croix-Barrez or others at Mur-de-Barrez 3km away.

ESTAING. 12190

60km SE of Aurillac. 10km NW of Espalion. Situated on the river Lot, this old town has grown up round the château of the Estaing family, one of whose members was canonised. It is on the pilgrim route to Saint-Jacques-de-Compostelle. Even now true pilgrims can apply at an address in the village and they will be given a room and meal for the night. It is well worth a stroll round the cobbled alleyways to see the ancient bridges. The town seems very quiet nowadays. As one old man said to me, "All the young people have left." The château towering above is open daily except Tuesday but closed from 12 to 2 pm.

Take the D 920 from Estaing towards Espalion and turn left on to the D655, signed Vinnac, and the farm is well signed.

NEW **M. & Mme Alazard. Cervel** (M)

Route de Vinnac. Tel & fax: (0)5.65.44.09.89. Closed:10/11 to 1/4

Raised above the road on a bend, this well-maintained house on a goat farm has four bedrooms, furnished with good quality family heirlooms and luxurious new shower rooms. A family room has bunks for children, reached through the loo. Another room has a separate room for children, sharing facilities. Others are for two people - 260f, extra bed 75f.

Evening meals are 90f, all *compris*; but if you stay for more than three days you qualify for demi-pension at 200f each. You eat *en famille* and will learn a lot about the region from your affable hosts. Breakfast is taken in another room which doubles as a very pleasant sitting room for guests, complete with piano.

Bikes for hire at 30f a day. Some English spoken. Good value here.

ONET-LE-CHATEAU. 12850

4km N of Rodez. Rodez is the *préfecture* of the *département* of Aveyron, a large rather industrial town, it has a fine cathedral and good parking a short distance from the centre.

Take the D988 north from Rodez towards Sébazac. In 5km turn right on to the D224 and the chambres d'hôtes is signed from there, so close to Rodez yet totally in the country.

NEW M. & Mme David. Domaine de la Vialatelle (M)

Tel. & fax: (0)5.65.42.76.56.

This pile of old farm buildings in 10 hectares is in a superb position on a hillside. Already the Davids have created a home for themselves and charming chambres d'hôtes rooms above their dwelling. The old stone walls and vaulted ceilings of the original farm buildings have been restored intact, There is a separate entry to the six en suite rooms, which are all different. They have dainty wall paper and are light and airy in spite of small windows. Rooms for two three or four, having names like *Les Merveilleuses*, a large family room with bunk beds for the children 450f, *Le Directoire*, a smaller room 250f, *Messidor* and *Convention*, which have old brick fireplaces, are 300F. On the same floor is a delightful sunny breakfast/dining room. Two attic rooms *Germinal* and *Floréal* are 300f.

An evening meal is served, including a Merlot wine from Bordeaux for 80f, on reservation only. There is a small kitchen which can be used by guests. A magnificently restored stable in the grounds, has horses for riding, beginners welcome.

You will find your young hosts with a very young family quite charming. There are now rooms for seminars but this doesn't seem to interfere with the chambres d'hôtes rooms. Monsieur, who speaks good English, assures me that the British love this place and it does give good value for money, so I shall look forward to comments from readers.

Only one snag, one bath is very awkwardly situated in an alcove. Can't remember which, *Convention* or *Messidor*.

SAINT-REMY. 12200

7km N of Villefranche-de-Rouergue. Leave Villefranche-de-Rouergue by the D922 north, in 7km turn right just past the St. Rémy sign to Jouas, where the Mas is well signed.

The small hamlet of St. Rémy is below the main road, now more a dormitory village. A good base for visiting the nearby Lot valley.

NEW M. & Mme Salvage. Mas de Jouas (M)
(0)5.65.81.64.72. fax: (0)5.65.81.50.70.

Such a popular place you need to book for July and August by February. It is situated on a hillside overlooking a very nice swimming pool with three first-class rooms on each floor, for two, three or four, each with luxury bathroom and satellite TV. No evening meals. There is a large room on the swimming pool terrace, where a copious breakfast, including cereal, is served. It has a kitchen which guests may use for the rest of the day with washing machine, microwave, everything you could want.

Rooms 380f buys you a lot here and there is no charge for children under 3 yrs. 90f for an extra bed. English spoken.

HAUTE-GARONNE

CIADOUX. 31350

70km SW of Toulouse just north of St. Gaudens in the Pyrénées, this is a small village near the river Save. Leave Ciadoux on the D365 towards Boulogne-sur-Gesse, in 1.5km turn right down a small road.

NEW Mme Ingeborg Röhrig. Le Manoir de la Rivière (M)
(0)5.61.88.10.88.

"We had a most enjoyable stay in wonderful calm surroundings. We were made to feel so welcome and were so well looked after. The week was a really precious one which we will remember for a long time. When we need to escape from our busy lives in Paris we will think of the manor" - J & P Jenks.

There are three rooms in the manor; two have private bathrooms. Room three, for a family, has a bathroom and an additional room across the corridor. 260f/280f for two. 460f for four. Evening meals are 80f, wine not included.

Madame is a painter and offers painting lessons and also lessons in riding. French, English and German spoken. Sounds a nice place, but came in too late for a visit.

CINTEGABELLE. 31550

39km S of Toulouse. This would make a pleasant change for visiting Toulouse. From close-by Auterive station, where parking is free, a train runs regularly into the centre of the city. A hassle-free way of enjoying a day out. Cintegabelle lies just off the N20. 17km north of Pamiers, it is a small town whose church has a towered spire, and a selection of shops.

From the town take the D25 towards Nailloux for 3.5km and the chambres d'hôtes is well signed.

NEW ➤ M. & Mme Deschamps-Chevrel. Serres-d'en-Bas (S)

Route de Nailloux.Tel & fax: (0)5.61.08.41.11.

The old farmstead has been modernised. At one end is a completely new first floor with four simple, practical rooms with all modern amenities, doubles, singles, baths or showers, pretty matching decor. One room on the ground floor. All rooms 230f.

The view from upstairs is across the countryside overlooking the swimming pool and tennis court in the front garden.

Excellent evening meals are very jolly, beginning with an *apéritif* in front of a log fire, where a whole chicken may be turning on a spit, later to arrive on the table. Local specialities such as *cassoulet* are often on the menu. 85f, including wine. You dine with your hosts who take great delight in entertaining you.

Amenities for children include a tree house as well as the usual swings, and a new games-room in the making. A lot of 'chambres d'hôtes' for your money, adds up to real value and an arrow, I am sure you will agree. There is one *gîte* on the premises for four, but the chambres d'hôtes rooms are the best.

GERS

AUTERRIVE. 32550

On the D929 10km S of Auch.

Mme Gerda Wieggers. Poudos (S)

Tel & fax: (0)5.62.61.00.93.

Easy to find but not to be confused with the Auterive on the N20. Here are very fine chambres d'hôtes rooms, a caravan and camping site (6 tents only). Amenities are numerous with a large area of green lawn, a round swimming pool and good parking. Your hosts are Dutch and serve good *tables d'hôtes* in the sunny dining room.

There are four family rooms and one room for two, upstairs, downstairs, all en suite and very comfortable. Most of these rooms have tiled floors and independent entry from the garden, and face south. In a garage at the back are washing facilities for the campers and a washing machine for all. Pleasant views over the countryside.

Prices reasonable at 225/240f reduced for three nights. Evening meals 75f, but demi-pension is 155/175f. English, German and Dutch spoken. Might be a bit crowded in August.

CAUSSENS. 32100

5km E of Condom.Very handy for visiting the circular bastide of Fources and the delightful hamlet of Larressingle, which was built in the 13th century as a fortress for the Bishop of Condom; it now has a ruined church and castle and just a couple of restaurants. You approach by a bridge ov^r the moat.

Turn right about 2km east of Caussens and follow signs.

NEW Mme Courtes. Le Vieux-Pressoir (M)

(0)5.62.68.21.32.

This Ferme-Auberge, up a long winding lane (don't give up!), high on the Gers hillside offers a nice surprise when you arrive as it has vast views over a pleasant pool and Jacuzzi (for resident guests only).

The auberge salon is busy in the high season, but off-season the more cosy breakfast room is used for all meals. The blue room has twin beds and a bath, the green, with two large beds, has double aspect windows and is very nice. Another room which I couldn't see has an adjoining room, with shared facilities for a family. The large square house was once owned by a *viticulteur* and a pressoir is anchored on the front lawn.

Evening meals, offered even for late arrivals, are 90f, wine *compris*.

Rooms 290f. Demi-pension 230f each; reduction for over three nights. Cheerful young owners make this one of the nicest *ferme auberges* I've stayed in.

TOURNECOUPE. 32380

35km NE of Auch. A hill village situated close to St. Clar where in August there is a Garlic fair and everyone is treated to a plate of garlic soup! From Fleurance about 24km north of Auch take the D654 then almost immediately the D953 to St. Clar. In about 8km turn right on to the D8 to Tournecoupe, drive through the village and at the far end of the square bear right and immediately left.

M. & Mme Marqué. En Bigorre (M)
(0)5.62.66.42.47.

On a garlic farm (not a whiff of it!), the house is dominated by a large *château d'eau* (water tower).

One wing is allocated to guests. The five rooms are large and cool and well furnished. The garden, with green lawns and swimming pool, makes this an ideal place for children. Guests eat *en famille* outside on the covered terrace in good weather. Meals are of substantial local fare, with wine and Armagnac included. *Aperitifs* are set out by the swimming pool before dinner - very civilised. Guests may use the fridge, cooker and sink, etc. on the terrace to make their own lunch. M. & Mme Marqué are charming hosts who cannot do enough for their guests, and are very entertaining at dinner.

Rooms 260f. Evening meals 70f. Possible arrow. No feed back yet?

LOT

ALBAS. 46140

27km W of Cahors.The river Lot west of Cahors twists like a snake between high cliffs and flat vineyards. The main road (D911) to Puy-L'Évêque is fairly straight but if you follow the river bank, crossing the few bridges from time to time, you will become quite disorientated, especially at Luzech where the loop of the river necessitates two bridges. It is a lovely drive past tiny villages. When you reach Albas follow signs to a chambres d'hôtes way up in the hills, climbing bends for 2km, well signed.

NEW **M. & Mme Vos** (M)

La Meline. Tel & fax: (0)5.65.36.97.25.

Your Dutch hosts have lived in the Lot for 20 years. The house stands on a hillside, so high you will be able to have breakfast on the sunny terrace looking down on the white mists in the valley below.

Mme Vos was busy painting wood outside when we surprised her in March. Though open all year, rooms are by reservation only from October to April. However we were made most welcome, given tea and offered a bed for the night and a promise of a meal with the family. There are three guest rooms, one on the ground floor for the handicapped, en suite with a bath and separate shower. Two above with en suite showers. Bright white walls and dark beams, are small but well furnished - 275f.

In the compact lounge/dining room you will be treated as private guests, having *apéritifs* in front of a log fire before moving *à table* for a copious evening meal. 110f, all drinks included, and, of course, no language problems.

Their son is an estate agent working from home so this is just the place to stay if you are looking for property in the this *département!*

AUTOIRE. 46400

20km. NE of Rocamadour. What a lovely part of France this is, in the Lot department, but only a spitting distance from the banks of the Dordogne. Close by is Rocamadour, the famous hill village which Henry II's son pillaged. It clings precariously to the hillside, but there is a little train that will take the less energetic right into the heart of the village, and a lift to the castle with a wonderful view at the top. There are numerous restaurants and cafés to choose from, all with glimpses of the valley. Near at hand, too, is Padirac where there are large underground limestone caves through which a river flows. Carennac, along the road, is said to be where, in the striking old tower that stands isolated in a field, Fénélon wrote his novel *Télémaque*, in 1681, while he was Prior. The quiet little village of Autoire itself is well worth a stroll round as there are many interesting buildings.

From Rocamadour take the D673 (SP St. Céré) across the N140; in 14km turn left on to the D38 to Autoire.

Mme Gauzin. La Plantade (S)

(0)5.65.38.15.61.

This nice, old-fashioned farmhouse beside a stream is on a road leading to the village. You cross over a bridge to get to the house, which is rather fun for children. Modernised rooms, warm and comfortable, overlooking the garden have real linen monogrammed sheets, excellent spot lamps over the bed, and shower rooms apiece - 200f.

Widowed Mme Gauzin runs the chambres d'hôtes while her son looks after the farm; his school-teacher wife livened up the conversation at dinner and ticked off her husband for trying to smoke between courses. I am sure Monsieur would appreciate a fellow smoker here! Good value for rooms, plentiful farm fare and a friendly atmosphere. Evening meal 75f, all drinks *compris*.

GRAMAT. 46500

34kms NW of Figeac. 9km SE of Rocamadour.The pleasant small town of Gramat lies on the N140 south of Brive, close to Rocamadour, the Gouffre de Padirac, and the delights of the Lot and Dordogne valley.

Just 500 metres south of Gramat, turn off left down a small lane to the well-signed Moulin de Fresquet.

NEW ➤ M. & Mme Ramelot. Moulin de Fresquet (M)

(0)5.65.38.70.60. Closed 1/11 to 1/4.

A beautifully restored mill-house surrounded by three hectares of well-wooded land through which a small stream flows, passing under some of the rooms.

A delightful rustic dining room leads into an equally pleasant lounge where guests may relax among family portraits and many of Monsieur's charming etchings. The terrace for summer meals overlooks the mill stream, but the rooms are on a lower level, three having access to the garden. The smallest "*La Meunière*" (the Miller's Wife) is only 270f. The "*Bief*" lies right over the stream and has an appealing view along it. Altogether there are four double rooms and a family room with two double beds, all with cool tiled floors, stone walls and beams, rusticity combined with modern furnishing. 270/390f, including breakfast.

Five-course evening meals of regional and traditional Quercy and Périgord cooking are 110f, with wine *compris*. Excellent parking, as entrance gates are locked at night.

You will be made very welcome by the youthful owners who have spent the last nine years creating such perfection. In all the guides, so book well ahead to avoid disappointment.

SAINT-SOZY. 46200

10km SE of Souillac. As you approach the village on the D15 from Souillac, the house is on the right, well signed.

NEW Mr. & Mrs. Burch. Pech Grand (S)

(0)5.65.32.27.98.

A reader sent me the following: "*We arrived early; but were welcomed by Susan Burch with a cup of tea on the terrace. Susan and Ed have developed this chambres d'hôtes over the past three years offering comfortable accommodation. An enjoyable meal was consumed by voracious walkers in front of a glowing wood burning stove. Pech Grand provided everything we had come to expect from a good two-star French chambres d'hôtes.*" - H. Coe.

An extensive modern bungalow on a hill with views over the Rochers-de-Monges and village. Six en-suite rooms in an extended wing on the ground floor have a southern aspect. Ample parking provided. Rooms 210/230f. Evening meal 85f.

SARRAZAC. 46600

26km S of Brive. Hidden in the far north of the Lot department, the tiny village of Sarrazac has a Roman church where a hand, raised in a blessing, is carved in the stonework beside the door. The château was once a monastery and the village, now an unspoilt cluster of yellow houses with church, auberge and a school, was the seat of the Turenne parliament. Close by are the well-known villages of Turenne, Collanges-les-Rouges, Martel, and the river Dordogne at Beaulieu. In the other direction the caves at Montignac are well worth a visit.

From the N20, 20km S of Brive, turn off left at Cressensac on to the D87 to Hôpital-Saint-Jean. Continue on this road through the village until it meets the D100 and you will see the sign to the château on the right.

NEW Mr. & Mrs. MacConchie. Château Couzenac (M)

(0)5.65.37.78.32. Open all year.

An utterly irresistible château perched on the hillside overlooking the valley road to Sarrazac. The Scottish owners bought it many years ago as a bramble-ridden ruin abandoned for 50 years. In restoring it to its former glory, they uncovered a delightful flight of steps leading down to the front door. There is level parking by the old stables and a shady terrace under plane trees for summer breakfasts.

It is now a comfortable home, where you will be made most welcome by the helpful owners. Lone travellers would love it here. Courses can be arranged for watercolour painting, French language and even dry-stone-walling. Guest rooms in the four corners of the first floor all have bathrooms, dual aspect windows and natural golden stone walls - 250/300f. The stairs lead up to a large open library/sitting area, with windows overlooking the valley. A separate lounge and dining room downstairs is open to guests.

A large terrace room on a lower floor can be used for summer meals. Afternoon tea and cake is available each day at 10f each.

Evening meals (reserve) 100f, all drinks *compris*, but there is an excellent truly French auberge in Sarrazac, which is only ten minutes walk down the hill, one minute by car, where copious meals are served at excellent prices from 60/125f. So popular you won't be the only ones eating here in winter.

This is a château I would love to return to.

HAUTES-PYRENEES

CASTELNAU-RIVIERE-BASSE. 65700

40km N of Tarbes. 4km NNE of Madiran. A short distance from Madiran, renowned for its wine, this hill village overlooks the D935.

Drive up and through to the route de Goux and the château is a few 100m along this road, a turn up a long drive.

NEW M. & Mme Bolac. Le Château du Tail (M-L)

(0)5.62.31.93.75.

An attractive old château which has been totally rebuilt over the last few years; the stables have been converted into four very smart rooms overlooking a swimming pool.

On offer is a choice of double or twin beds, luxurious baths or showers, upstairs or downstairs, beds with *baldaquins*, you name it, it's all here. A salon too. Wonderful value for 300f, with a copious breakfast. Reserve an evening meal with your hosts for 85f, wine *compris*.

Another option:

In the tiny hamlet of Mazères on the other side of the D935 from Castelnau, drive round the church and you will discover the home of:

NEW M. & Mme Guyot. Flânerie (S)

Hameau de Mazères. (0)5.62.31.90.56. fax: (0)5.62.31.92.88.

Arriving unexpectedly one wet evening at the *Asinerie Pyrénéenne*, we received a warm welcome from M. Guyot who offered us an evening meal although he and his wife had arrived back from holiday only the night before, and Madame had returned to work. Fresh flowers were rushed into our room and appetising smells came from the kitchen, with Monsieur in charge.

This is no ordinary chambres d'hôtes. M. Guyot keeps Pyrénéan donkeys (a tall breed with no cross on their backs) for people who wish to take walking tours of the region. The donkeys carry picnics and small children, but not adults. You spend first and last night here, parking your car safely in their extensive courtyard. Rooms are booked ahead and luggage sent on.

The erstwhile ruined farmhouse now has four pleasant rooms, some for families, keeping their rusticity but now with en suite bathrooms. Salons on two floors have comfortable armchairs, and plenty of literature of the region to browse through. Tasty evening meals are usually cooked by Madame, who works part time as a tour guide in Lourdes and speaks English and German.

Don't expect anything palatial, but great hospitality from a lovely couple. Evening meals 90f, wine *compris*, children 5/12 yrs. 45f.

Rooms 250f. Open for non walkers too.

FONTRAILLES. 65220

32km from Tarbes. 40km from Auch. 3km from Trie-sur-Baîse The neighbouring Monastère-des-Carmes is being restored. Leave Trie by the D17 and in 2km turn right to Fontrailles. Signed from here.

NEW **Mme Casteret** (M)
(0)5.62.35.51.70.

On the corner of two small lanes this ivy-covered cereal and sheep farmhouse has just one luxury room for guests. On the first floor, a very comfortable guest room with double aspect windows overlooks the garden. It is reached by a private corridor, containing a large bathroom, separate loo and separate shower room. A lot of area for 300f. Another room is planned with similar facilities on the ground floor, suitable for the handicapped.

Downstairs is a library with a terrace for breakfast. Madame will gladly prepare you an evening meal, *en famille*. 100f, including wine.

The large garden in front has easy parking. A very pleasant quiet home to stay in where lone travellers would be made most welcome.

Another chambres d'hôtes just along the road from Mme Casteret is owned by an Englishman, whose wife is French.

NEW **Mr. & Mrs. Collinson. Jouandassou** (M)

(0)5.62.35.64.43. fax: (0)5.62.35.66.13.

This is a rustic old farmhouse where the restored stables, now house a variety of chambres d'hôtes rooms.

Country furnishing complements the beams and wood floors. There are practical mosquito nets, tea-making facilities and unexpectedly well-furnished shower rooms which are lushly carpeted and have smart repro-Victorian-style basins, etc. Two rooms can be adjoining for families, 320f.

The grounds have a very pleasant swimming pool and terraces where meals are taken in summer. 100f, drinks *compris*. In winter the family dining room is used. The Collinsons have a young family so children would enjoy it here.

LOUBAJAC. 65100

6km N of Lourdes on the D3. Lourdes, which lies on the Gave de Pau, owes its fame to the young peasant girl Bernadette Soubirous who, at the age of fourteen in 1858, claimed to have 14 visions of the Virgin Mary at a grotto. She was told by Our Lady that the waters of the well flowing from this grotto had healing powers. Once these powers were proved to the satisfaction of the Roman Catholic authorities the Church of the Rosary was built next to the grotto where the fountain runs and in whose waters the pilgrims are bathed. Bernadette became a nun at the age of 20, died 15 years later and was canonised in 1933. Over the central crypt is the Basilica of the Immaculate Conception with a bell tower, some 70 metres high. In front but on a lower level is the Basilica of the Rosary. Inside is a small chapel reserved for private prayer when there are no services taking place. There is also a large Basilica underground, named after Pius X, which can hold 25,000 people (completed in 1958 to mark the centenary of the visions) and unadorned except for the central altar.

The Castle rises above the town and contains a Pyrénnéan museum. Ste. Bernadette's birthplace can be seen at the foot of Castle Hill in the rue Bernadette Soubirous.

Lourdes is an international pilgrimage centre for the sick, and of course is crowded in the holiday months of July and August. Tourist souvenir shops abound in the town and I wouldn't recommend a visit then. Parking is almost impossible and the queues to visit the grotto horrendous in the heat. By September all has cleared and the weather is usually pleasant and sunny.

➤ **Mme Vives** (S)

Route de Bartres. (0)5.62.94.44.17.

There is a superb view of the Pyrénées from the Route de Bartres. Right beside the road is a small sheep farm where Mme Vives has created four delightfully beamed and warmly carpeted guest rooms on the first floor. Ask for one of the rooms which overlook the flowery garden and have views to the mountains. There is a small sitting area on the landing, and chairs in the garden for sunny days and facilities for washing clothes are thoughtfully provided. Rooms 200f.

Evening meals are 70f, wine *compris*. Guests eat together in the dining room but not with the family.

A really pleasant place to stay, the nearest and the best for Lourdes, and very reasonably priced. Arrowed accordingly.

PINAS. 65300

4.5km E of Lannemézan on the N117. About 20km to the south-east is St-Bertrand-de-Comminges, which must be one of the world's smallest cities with a population of about 217. An independent city, too, for when the present French departmental system was instituted in 1790 the Deputies of Comminges refused to amalgamate with the district of Couserans in Ariège, although they had artistic and economic links; so the border of Haute-Garonne was stretched southwards to include their city. The cathedral and old town are regarded as sights surpassed only by Mont-Saint-Michel. The city was founded by Pompey in the first century B.C. as Lugdunum Convenarum, from which the name Comminges evolved. In the nearby village of Valcabrère there is a very chic restaurant 'le Lugdunum' (menus from 150f). I have not yet had a chance to try this place but I am told that as well as regional dishes you can get genuine Roman cooking based on a cookery book by Apicius, who wrote some two thousand years ago.

Magnificent is the only way to describe St. Mary's Cathedral. It was originally built in 1100 in Romanesque style, but enlarged in the 14th century in Gothic. The Choir is completely enclosed, making it a church within a church, with 66 canons' stalls all intricately carved. However, in the cloister you will find the famous pillar of St. Bertrand, which consists of the four evangelists standing back to back. The Organ, again, seems to be in a church of its own, with the choir completely screened off and a wide open space in front. Fifteen metres high and ten metres wide with magnificent wood carving covering the whole facade, it is the centre of the music festivals which are held here every summer. (Information from the office at Mazères-sur-Salat, tel: (0)5.61.88.32.00.) The cathedral is open throughout the year, closing of course for lunch from noon till two, and at six in the evening in winter and seven in summer. It is open only to ticket holders when the festivals are on.

There are a few artisan's shops, good restaurants and cafés in the village, one with a delightful terrace overlooking the countryside.

Mme Colombier. Domaine de Jean-Pierre (M)

Route de Villeneuve. (0)5.62.98.15.08.

A really gracious mansion, covered with ivy, which has been in the family for many years and is well preserved. From the moment you enter the tiled hallway and climb the gently sloping stairs to the large airy rooms you will feel you could stay here for days. There are four interesting rooms with polished wood floors and large, well furnished bathrooms almost adjoining. One family room is for four, another for three people; others for couples. One room is warmly carpeted for winter use. All 250f for two.

A very comfortable lounge has one wall completely lined with books. Breakfast can be taken in summer on the extensive gravel terrace. Mme Colombier (a keen golfer) is a very charming hostess who speaks some English and will look after you well. This is a true chambres d'hôtes, where you really are private guests.

No evening meals, but at the 18 hole golf course only 3km away there are two excellent restaurants, Le Pré Vert and Le Swing, also the *gastronomique* L'Albatros.

SAINT-PE-DE-BIGORRE. 65270

7km from Lourdes. St. Pé is a small town with many useful shops, within easy reach of both Lourdes and the highest peaks of the Pyrénées. Take a drive across the Col du Tourmalet and follow the rougher road *(payant)* up to the Pic du Midi de Bigorre to the Observatory, founded in 1881, where there is the largest telescope in France, and on a clear day the finest panoramas of the Pyrénées; on other days you may wonder where you are, sitting on a damp cloud!

NEW M. & Mme Peters. Le Grand Cèdre (M)

6 rue du Barry. (0)5.62.41.82.04. fax: (0)5.62.41.85.89.

Not often do I recommend a chambres d'hôtes in a town; but on investigation this one has a large parking area locked at night and a very large tiered garden behind,

dominated by a huge cedar tree, nearly as old as the house, which dates back to 1604. Over the last three years the Peters have enjoyed restoring and decorating this mansion, furnishing each of the four guest rooms in a different period.

Two fountains play in the courtyard entrance, the rear garden has a small children's pool and is being designed in French *parterre* style; the *potager* already resembles a mini Villandry. Rooms are all entered from an outside canopied balcony overlooking the park. Room 1, in 1930s style, is for a family; a double bed and two singles leave ample room to move around and reach the matching en suite bathroom. A second room is authentic Henri II style; the free-standing bath, two wash basins and loo are hidden behind a dainty white *baldaquin*. The Louis XV room, with two large beds, can be used in conjunction with the Louis Philippe room to make a suite. Two of the rooms were originally salons with adjoining bedrooms and the coals were taken from the large fireplace at night to warm the smaller bedrooms. In each case the bedroom is now the bathroom area. There is a separate salon for TV, and a dining room furnished with many antiques opens on to the garden. Separate tables, with high-backed oak tapestry chairs, are prettily draped, and here elegant evening meals (cooked by Madame) are served by Monsieur, using the best crystal and silver. 130f, wine *compris*.

Rooms are now 320f. Extra beds 80f. Reasonable for such unusual rooms which offer every comfort.

TARN

CORDES. 81170

25km NW of Albi. One of the loveliest hill villages in France, sometimes known as Cordes-sur-Ciel, and often pictured floating in a mist above the valley, was built as a *bastide* by Raymond, Comte de Toulouse in the 13th century. It was involved in much fighting during the Cathar period. Now a peaceful Mecca for artisans, alive with tourists in summer, it has much to offer.

From the bottom of the village take the road left of the fountain (marked "Cité") up to the old village for .5km then fork left down a track to "Le Bouysset", in 200 metres, round a hairpin bend left, and the chambres d'hôtes is signed down a sharp bend to your right.

NEW ➤ **Mr. & Mrs. Thornley. Aurifat** (M)

(0)5.63.56.07.03.

In the 13th century part of this house was a watch-tower guarding the village. A farmhouse was added in the 17th-century and now an adjoining centrepiece in red Albi brick makes it into one complete home cunningly built into the hill-side - so most bedrooms on the upper floor are level with the parking.

Light, airy, south-facing rooms are simply furnished with modern beds, and have a sitting area as well as private balconies or terraces, where breakfast is usually served, taking advantage of the extensive views. Some rooms have carpets extending to the en-suite bathrooms and all are heated for winter use. The blue room is particularly nice, with a bath on legs but no shower. Two rooms share a bathroom with bath and shower for friends or family. On the second floor the 'Pigeonnier' room has a wood floor, beamed ceiling, and shower. 260f for two, 480f for four. The Thornton's sitting and dining rooms are on a floor below, where breakfast is served if preferred. Below again is a very large pool and terrace entrapping the sun, and a summer kitchen with fridge and barbecue for picnics beside the pool. Alternatively there are plenty of local restaurants.

A place where you can be private or chat to your English hosts, who are well used to entertaining guests. A winner here for such correct prices and character. I am sure an arrow soon. Booking ahead ensures your room and full directions.

LARROQUE. 81140

30km E of Montauban, 28km SE of Caussade.The Tarn east of the N20 reminds me of the Cévennes, with undulating countryside but spotted with hill villages. Puycelsi is especially interesting. Larroque is a little further on.

From Caussade on the N20 take the D964 to Montricoux then join the D115 to Bruniquel and turn on to the D964 again to Larroque. Carry on for 4km through quiet countryside until the D1 on the right SP Montclar. Uphill for 4km then look for the small sign to Meilhouret on the right, at the end of a tarred lane in 2km. Easier than it sounds!

NEW **M. & Mme Jouard. Meilhouret** (M)

Tel & fax: (0)5.63.33.11.18.

Retired farmers of 3,000 hectares of fields and woodland, their square ivy-covered mansion sits high on the hill, with sweeping lawns down to a large swimming pool overlooking a patchwork of fields.

The Greek room is very large and prettily decorated in blue and yellow, gloriously warm in winter with a view over the hills and valleys. The spacious private bathroom is just outside the door down a few tricky stone steps, but well lit. Decorated in green and white, it has a bath, bidet and many extras, including an old kitchen sink which makes a useful shelf. A second room is more traditional, having two bateau beds. The shower room is a few steps up, but attached to the room. 265f.

A large comfortable lounge/music room overlooks the garden with a piano and many classical tapes to play.

The Jouards welcome you warmly and Madame will offer very good evening meals, eaten with them, for 90f, wine *compris*, except during July and August when you have the use of a full summer kitchen for self catering, or the choice of restaurants in the local villages. You will want to stay far more than one night here; I was loath to tear myself away from the spacious Greek room, where only the birds wake you in the morning.

LOUPIAC. 81800

35km W of Albi. 31km NE of Toulouse. Just the place to stay for visiting Toulouse or Albi, practically halfway between the two, with easy access by motorway.

NEW **M. & Mme Crété. La Bonde** (M)
(0)5.63.33.82.83. fax: (0)5.63.57.46.54.

This long ivy-covered *maison-de-maître* surrounded by colourful gardens is elegantly furnished, a private sitting room with TV for guests is just one of the many comforts.

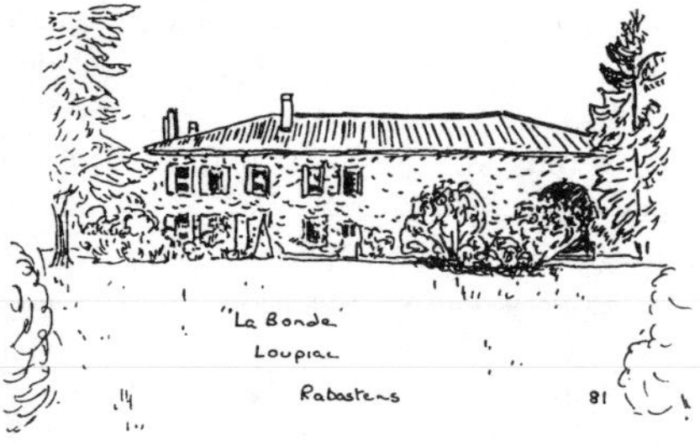

Madame Crété is a excellent cook and is noted for her cuisine in the area; you will dine in style.

The two rooms are large and richly furnished. One overlooking the back garden has a bathroom with ivy-covered wallpaper, bath, separate shower, bidet, every luxury you could wish for. The second room with double bed is charming, with two south-windows. This one has a small shower room adjoining, and private access from the floor below.

Charming hosts who think of your every comfort.

The price is excellent for such luxury - 260f, and 95f for an evening meal, which includes wine. Book well ahead.

MEZENS. 81800

30km NE of Toulouse. Just outside Mézens on D28 turn right.

M. & Mme Saulle-Bulteau. Le Cambou (S)
(0)5.63.41.82.66.

Mézens is right in the heart of the Gaillac vineyards in the Tarn valley; they are reputed to be the oldest in France.

Monsieur is a sculptor and Madame taught maths. Now they have converted rooms for guests in their old farmhouse on the outskirts of the village; some of the rooms still have *pisé* walls. The five rooms have varying en-suite facilities; something for everyone here. 210f.

You will enjoy sipping your *apéritif* on the long wisteria-covered terrace overlooking the countryside. Delicious evening meals, with all drinks *compris* at 70f taken with the your hosts.

Budget prices here.

TARN-ET-GARONNE

MONTPEZAT-DE-QUERCY. 82270

24km S of Cahors. Take the N20 south from Cahors; in 22km turn right on to the D20, signposted Montpézat-de-Quercy. A delightful *bastide* village unspoilt by modernisation. Go through the village and turn left about 50m after the post office. Signed on the left.

➤ M. Bankes & M. Jarros. Le Barry (M)

Faubourg Saint-Roch. (0)5.63.02.05.50. fax: (0)5.63.02.03.07.

On the ramparts of the village, this charming 17th-century terraced house is impeccably run, offering five spacious bedrooms, comfortably furnished but losing none of their old character. The sheltered garden, high above the road, with an inviting swimming pool, overlooks the Quercy countryside. Relax on the terrace and enjoy the green lawns and flower beds, a perfect setting for evening meals in fine weather, and alternative to the large lounge-dining room. Your English and German hosts really enjoy entertaining. Freshly squeezed orange juice for breakfast.

A great advantage here is being able to step right out into the old part of the town. The only snag is perhaps parking, which is under the wall of the garden on the roadside, but I have been assured that there has been no problem. Certainly worth a long stay here, to visit the lovely Quercy villages, or even Cahors and the Lot valley where the prehistoric grotto of Pech-Merle and the hillside village of St. Cirq-Lapopie are within easy reach. Evening meals are 110f, all drinks *compris*.

Rooms 325/350f according to season. A nice place. Arrowed for comfort and character.

NORD/PAS-DE-CALAIS

Départements: **Nord**
Pas de Calais

Companion guide to the area: 'French Entree 19 - The North of France'.

A much-maligned area. Anyone who still believes that the North of France is all featureless, flat, industrialised and boring, should be dragged to the Boulonais hills, the time-warped villages a few miles inland, the fascinating towns of Arras, Montreuil and St. Omer, the sophistication of Le Touquet, the glorious beaches, the unique canal network and the *hortillonages* (market gardens), and made to repent. Of course there is industrialisation and whole tracts of mining territory that do not contribute to the holiday scene, but even here the biggest city, Lille, is underestimated. It's a prosperous city and destined to become ever more important as the hub of a European multi-transport system. Its art galleries, restaurants and restored mediaeval heart rival those of many a better-loved town.

The autoroute system through this area is superb - fast, efficient and uncrowded. Pick it up at the Calais docks and Arras is just a short hop down the road. Don't always hurry on through. Devote a short break to the French region nearest to home, let FE 19 point out the best bits, and I guarantee you'll be pleasantly surprised.

This is not a great area for chambres d'hotes. Despised by the French holiday-makers who are even blinder to its merits than the Brits, it must rely largely on foreigners for trade. Things are looking up though and some welcome newcomers are opening up in time for Chunnel business.

NORD

COMINES. 59560

16km N of Lille. 18km NE of Armentières Comines is a border-town half in France and half in Belgium and very handy for visiting Ypres and the many ceme-

NORD / PAS-DE-CALAIS

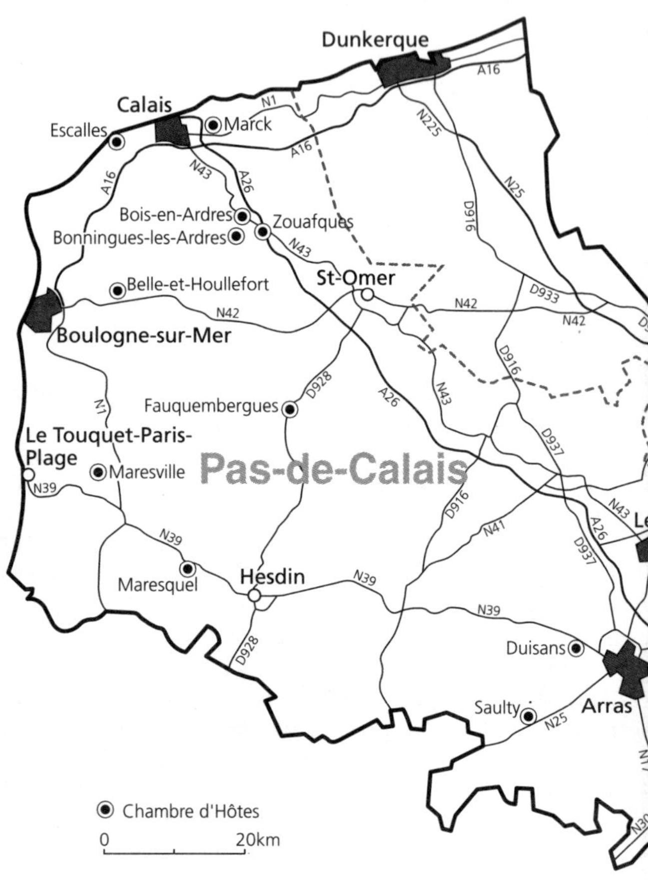

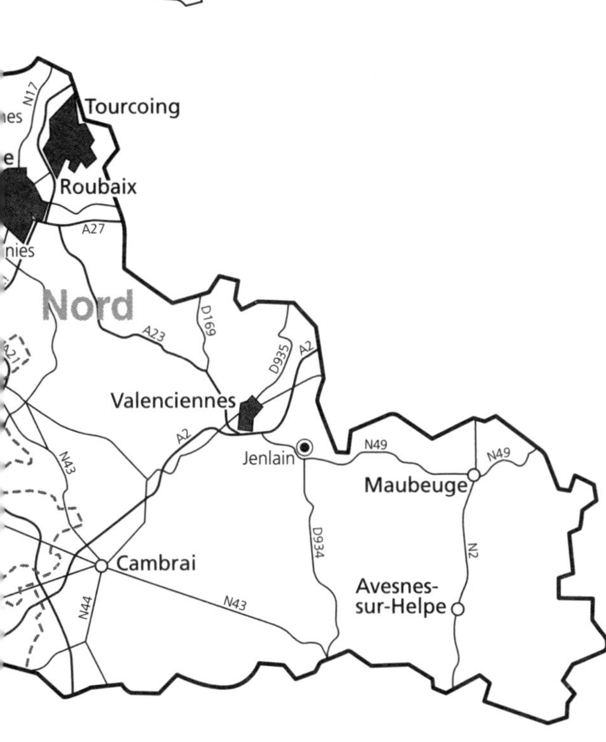
Tourcoing
Roubaix
A27
Nord
D169
A23
D935
A2
Valenciennes
A2
N43
Jenlain
N49
N49
Maubeuge
D934
N2
Cambrai
Avesnes-
sur-Helpe
N43
N44
N17

teries from the First World War.

By-pass Lille by the A 25 Autoroute leaving at exit 8 (Armentières) and take the D945 to Comines. Turn right just inside the town on the D 308 to Ste Marguerite. Just before the village turn right and the farm lies just under a kilometre down a very small road.

M. & Mme Vermès (S)

1221, Chemin du Petit Enfer. (0)3.20.39.21.28.

Looking for a chambres d'hôtes in the flat industrial land round Lille I was delighted to find a quiet farm just south of Comines, surrounded by fields.

Mme Vermès works in Lille all day and returns at 6pm with her three young daughters to cook the evening meal. Providing you phone ahead and book, Madame Vermes senior will come over from her farmhouse to welcome you with a refreshing cup of tea, if you arrive before 6 p.m.

The three rooms, which are spacious and attractively furnished, are warm and have very good en suite facilities. Double room 180f. There is one family room, with bunk beds in an alcove. Dinner, taken with the family, is excellent, with fresh produce from the garden and interesting dishes cooked by Madame - 60f, wine *compris*. Monsieur is a jolly, young host who speaks some English. Goodnight kisses from the young Vermes! Monsieur usually serves breakfast, with a variety of bread and home-made jams, as he is at home working on the farm all day.

JENLAIN. 59144

8km SE of Valenciennes by N49, direction Maubeuge. Industrialised suburbs, dominated by autoroutes, are not situations where one expects to come across stunning châteaux in lovely gardens. Don't despair when you turn off the *nationale*, following the signs to Jenlain (dreary). Before you turn right into the village you will see discreet gates straight ahead and a half-obscured chambres d'hôtes sign. This is it.

Mme Demarcq. Chateau d'En Haut (M-L)

Tel & fax: (0)3.27.49.71.80. Open all year.

Chambres d'hôtes don't come any more 'L' than this one. Your delighted eyes will alight, after a worrying drive up an overgrown drive, on a large and lovely château, set in well-kept and flowery grounds. Why the patronne, Mme Demarcq, should want to allow plebs like you and me loose amongst her valuable antiques and tread on her Persian carpets and sleep beneath her handworked quilts is beyond comprehension. Especially when she charges only 370f for a superb double room and breakfast.

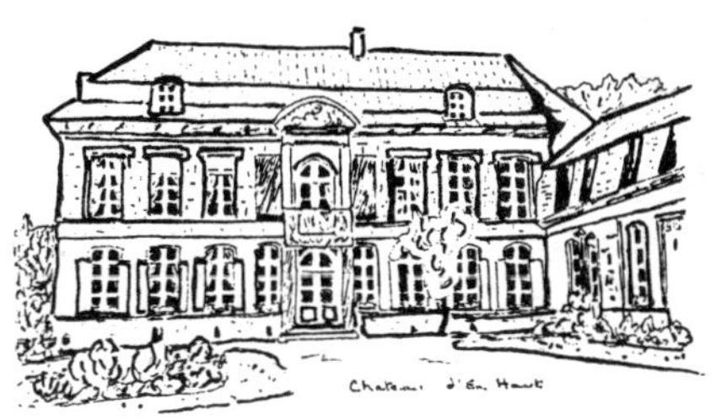

Breakfast, a good start to the day, is served in a stunning, yellow room with toile on the walls, at a yellow lacquered table. No evening meal but plenty of recommended nearby restaurants. All the rooms are different, all except one (cheaper at 270f) has its own bathroom, all are furnished not only with valuable antiques, but with great flair.

This is a most unusual b. and b., wonderful value, and would certainly brighten up the northern gloom or provide a sensational first night at the beginning of a holiday. Good, too, for a pampered, weekend break.

WATTIGNIES. 59139

3km S of Lille.This town is virtually a suburb of Lille and is next to the old part of the city. From the A25 take exit 4 and follow the signs for Wattignies. A good place to stay for visiting the city, when you can abandon the car and take to public transport. Close to many of the local battlefields and cemeteries.

NEW Mme Le Bot (S)

59 rue Faidherbe. (0)3.20.60.24.51.

This modern house is situated on a busy road but there is room to park two cars in front of the garages. A very peaceful rear garden compensates for any noise in front. There are two double and one single guest rooms, all with shower rooms, one en suite - 250f. The other shares a loo with the single room - 230f.

An evening meal if requested - 80f, but there are plenty of restaurants in the city. Your hosts speak excellent English. Mme Le Bot has taught English for 15 years. Bikes are available.

PAS-DE-CALAIS

ELLE-ET-HOULLEFORT. 62142

e. Now listen carefully - I shall say this only once - you take the N42 out o gne and after La Capelle turn left onto the D234 to Conteville and just past the turning to Wierre Effroy, look out for a sign to the left to Le Breucq. If you get to what the Michelin map marks as 'Belle' you've gone too far. Then bump for half a mile down a farm track. And the fact that I have to spell out such instructions is proof enough of the rural nature of the valley of the Wimereux - quite astonishingly near the *nationales* and port.

Mme de Montigny. Le Breucq (S)

Tel & fax: (0)3.21.83.31.99. Open year round, in winter by reservation.

If you crave for the Good Life and don't mind a bit of mud on your boots, this is the one. Such value! Such rusticity!

Mme Isabelle de Montigny has five spacious guest rooms in her large, rambling farmhouse. They are all furnished in a delicious time-warp of two generations ago, with the incomparable luxury of real fires in real fireplaces in every bedroom whenever the weather demands.

Belle-et-Houllefort

Fires we have, ensuite bathrooms we do not. Two shared bathrooms, painted in uncomfortably anachronistic bright paint, have showers and plenty of hot water, but as the general atmosphere would indicate heads-under-the-pump-in-the-yard plumbing, these must be considered very mod cons indeed.

The best room - grab it if you can - costs, wait for it - 185f, including two farmhouse breakfasts - and Madame makes all her own jams and brioches. For the truly impoverished, there are other rooms at 160f - extra bed 60f. Equally amazing value is the evening meal - 70f for four courses of home-grown produce. This would make a great base for a family of townees, wanting to experience the kind of country living which is fast disappearing. But forget the frills. I look forward to some reports on this one. Could be a star.

BOIS-EN-ARDRES. 62610

12km SW of Calais by RN43. House is at entrance to the village on the right.

Ardres, down the road, is an extremely pretty little town, long beloved by the English. It has two centres, a wide shady green square bordered by two little hotels, and the eccentric, triangular Grand' Place, cobbled, with houses aw... fine 15th-century Flamboyant Gothic church to admire and nearby a ... for fishing, sailing, pedaloing or just walking around. Cafés have terraces over... ing the water, and it's all ideal for kids, near the ports and peaceful.

M. et Mme Leturgie. La Chesnaie (S)

(0)3.21.35.43.98. fax: (0)3.21.36.48.70.

An attractive not-very-old house set in a large garden featuring swings and a sandpit. Nice youthful-looking Madame Leturgie has six children and, surprisingly, several grandchildren, so she is used to having a full house. She has obviously realised that children need space (for the adults' sakes as much as their own) and has allocated a large upstairs room as a playroom with dolls, darts, T.V. and lots of games. She proudly showed me the huge salon which is used for breakfasts in inclement weather. Its most striking feature is a full-sized French billiard table (different from ours in that there are no pockets).

She has four rooms, with lots of beige flowered wallpaper; they all have a private bathroom somewhere, opposite or adjoining, with choice of bath or shower. 220f. For children sharing the family bathroom - 100f for the first 60f for the second child.

BONNINGUES-LES-ARDRES. 62890 TOURNEHEM-SUR-LA-HEM

12km S of Ardres by N43, then right on to the D217 towards Licques. The house is in the village centre.

Mme Christiane Dupont. Le Manoir (S)

40 route de Licques. (0)3.21.82.69.05.

FE readers have approved of this nice, old, shuttered manor house, set back from the road in a lovely garden. At the rear is a terrace for breakfast and, surprising views of hills. Madame Dupont has furnished the six old-fashioned, high-ceilinged bedrooms as chambres d'hôtes. There are variations of twins, doubles, private bathroom, shared bathroom, bath/shower at prices from 200-220f.

DUISANS. 62161

pick one town in the North of France for a weekend stopover, it would be Arras. Big enough to offer good all enough to walk around, with easy parking. But that's acked with interest and history ancient and modern. the largest open square in Europe. The arcaded Flemish-style amental stepped gables, redbrick, old stone and heraldic signs, create ely satisfying total harmony; in fact few of them are the 17th- and 18th-century originals they would seem. The extent of the damage of four years' bombardment in the First World War can be seen in the photographs in the town hall (which forms one side of another glorious square, the Place des Héros). Almost incredibly the rubble was used to create the Grand'Place exactly as it was. Tours are available to view the underground tunnels and cellars that run like warrens underneath the town centre and were used for shelter during both world wars. See *French Entrée 19* for a fuller description of this beguiling town and its restaurants.

Try and arrange your visit for Saturday and Wednesday, when the best market in the North fills the accommodating squares.

Take the N38 direction Le Touquet; after 5km turn left on D56. The house is on the left.

Mme Annie Senlis. Le Cros Grincourt (S-M)

18 rue du Château. Tel & fax: (0)3.21.48.68.33.

An elegant and spacious manor house, grey stone walls, white painted shutters, floor-to-ceiling windows. Built originally in the 17th-century and added to over the intervening years, it was once an annexe to the next-door château.

Rooms are high-ceilinged, light and comfortable, furnished with family antiques and mementoes, so that the feeling is of a family home rather than intimidating grandeur. Readers have reported favourably of the welcome received from Mme Senlis (who has been incredibly patient over an error in the last edition).

She can offer one suite of two rooms and bathroom for 400f and one other room, also with bath, for 200f.

The combination of elegant house, lovely garden, locked parking, proximity to Arras and readers' confirmation that there is good value here leads to a new arrow.

ESCALLES. 62179

14km SW of Calais. From the ferry follow the signs to Le Port, bump over the level crossing into the town, turn right over the swing bridge and follow the coast road, the D940 all the way.

Once in Escalles turn left at the bottom of the hill and look for the signs a halfkm out of the village, on the right.

The coast road will immediately give the lie to the general theory that the Pas-de-Calais has to be flat and boring. The high chalk cliffs at Cap Blanc Nez are of considerable stature and the countryside is spectacularly rolling. There is a pebbly beach in Escalles and a very popular fish restaurant, Restaurant du Cap.

Jacqueline Boutroy. La Grand' Maison (S)

Tel & fax: (0)3.21.85.27.75.

This is one of the splendid old farm complexes that are such a pleasing feature of this part of France. Rustic buildings on three sides enclose a huge courtyard, big enough for small boys to be playing football where we visited, and an interesting square *pigeonnier* in the centre was soon pinpointed as the source of much contented cooing. The farm has been in Mme Boutroy's family for generations and is now getting the facelift it deserves, thanks to the pigs.

There was only one room left - the smallest - but it was pretty nice, all white with a blue frieze and garlanded curtains, bath and separate loo, for 220f. The larger rooms, termed 'studios', have less character but are good value for their size and comfort. *Accueil* and breakfast are both irreproachable. An excellent choice for port proximity, amongst many other considerations.

FAUQUEMBERGUES. 62560

22km SW of St. Omer. 40km SE of Boulogne. A26 from Calais, exit 4 to Thérouanne, then the D341 west to the D928.

A small town on the D928. Just off the town centre at traffic lights follow signs to La Poste. The chambres d'hôtes is exactly opposite across the square.

NEW M. & Mme Millamon. La Rêverie (M)

19 rue Jonnart. (0)3.21.12.12.38.

This 19th-century *maison-de-maître* right on the main road didn't have a lot to recommend it at first. When I got no answer from the front door I explored down a driveway beside the house and found it led to a beautiful garden, with parking. Young, vivacious Mme Millamon was delighted to see us, we were willingly shown all the rooms. A twin-bedded room, a ground floor extension, in sunny yellow overlooks the garden. In the huge white bathroom, the gold claw feet of the large bath match the taps and shower fitting. The other two rooms, filled with light, are on the first floor, overlooking the road. Difficult to choose between them, dark green set off by dainty white curtains and bed covers, with a polished wood floor, or pink and beige with a *ciel-de-lit* and thick carpet, which I fell for. Both have modern showers. Fresh flowers in all the rooms. Central heating.

The salon has a large wood fire and comfy armchairs, and breakfast is served in the dining room on Limoges china with silver cutlery, or sometimes taken in the conservatory overlooking the garden.

Finding a chambres d'hôtes like this makes my day, especially when I find rooms are 270f for two with a good breakfast. Open only a couple of months, I am sure this will be very popular. No evening meal but there are restaurants within walking distance. Excellent value for money. I feel an arrow on the way, someone please confirm.

MARCK. 62730

7km NE of Calais. From the A16 to Dunkerque take exit Marck or the D119. In the centre of the town take the D248 to Le Font Vert. The rear of this chambres d'hôtes overlooks the Calais aerodrome across fields.

NEW M. & Mme Houzet (M)

2528 Ave du General de Gaulle. Le Font Vert. Tel & fax: (0)3.21.85.74.34.

(Recommended to me by M. Calonne of Monnières.)

This long red-brick manor house was once a farmhouse owned by M. Houzet's uncle. Occupied by German generals during the war then looted by them on their retreat in 1944, it was left empty. Now a well-furnished manor house with prominent family antiques. Your caring hosts, who speak some English, offer three guest rooms in a ground floor wing. *Bluet* with a double bed and cot has a large bathroom with bath and all facilities for a baby. *Les Roses* with single beds in pretty green/pink, has a shower room. Both face the rear garden. *Coquelicot* is well named with striking red wallpaper, two single beds, well fitted with cupboards over the bed. Rooms have welcoming trays of biscuits, tea and coffee-making facilities and a

real kettle - 300f including a copious breakfast, baby cot free,

An Empire style salon for guests has stairs to another room above, with deep armchairs for watching TV. A well-furnished dining room,(high chairs and family portraits), leads to a rear terrace. Evening meals for 100f wine *compris*, if reserved when booking. Confirmation of bookings in writing please, preferably by fax.

MARESQUEL. 62990

10km SE of Montreuil by N39. There is a sign for the château but it faces the wrong way if you are coming from Montreuil, so look out for a *Depot Vente* sign just before the village of Maresquel and turn right here, past the church, up the hill, and the château is at the dead end.

Mme Pruvost. Château de Ricquebourg (S)
(0)3.21.90.30.96.

'Château' in French can mean anything from Versailles to a dilapidated large country house. Think in terms of the latter here. High on a hill overlooking the verdant valley of the Canche is this old manor house, potentially stunning, given a good deal more time and money than its owner, Madame Pruvost, has been able to apply. The stone is crumbling, the adjoining barns sag, the roof looks dodgy. So it was with some trepidation I included it in FE6 - one of the pioneer chambres d'hôtes. I did stress that it was atmosphere rather than luxury that counted here and to my delight it invoked nothing but praise from readers who had decided that the warm welcome, country peace and the simple life appealed more than a safe, hygienic, plastic cube.

...nges since then and all for the better. The nice old ...ns all have access to private bathrooms - 'Chambre ... with shower, as does 'Jaune' albeit next door. 230f. ...e, sloping garden, children are welcomed, and a special ...n the evening. Otherwise it's 100f including *apéritif* but with

MARESVILLE. 62630

8km NW of Montreuil. Alternative routes are north on the N1, turn left and follow any sign that says Maresville, or look for the sign on the N39 west of Montreuil, at Beutin, on the D146, and keep going. But whichever way you choose I guarantee astonishment that anything so rustic could lurk so near the coast, so near the Nationale.

➤ Mme Delianne. Ferme Auberge des Chartroux (M)

(0)3.21.86.70.68. fax: (0)3.21.86.70.38.

Restaurant closed Thursday and Sun. p.m. Rooms by reservation.

'Oh dear,' I said on a wet and windy, prematurely grey Wednesday evening. 'We shall be eating alone tonight,' Who, I thought, would want to drive through the dripping countryside to eat in a resolutely rustic *ferme auberge?* Fifty other diners, that's who. All of 'em French, all of 'em recognizing the value on offer at the Ferme des Chartroux is worth a muddy boot or two.

So near Le Touquet, so near Montreuil, the auberge typifies the diversity of the region. Leave the main road and you immediately come across hamlets and farmyards that look as though they have never heard of videos, so concerned are they with their cattle and ploughs and painting their cottages white and filling their window-boxes with geraniums.

The approach to Les Chartroux, which is M. Delianne's family home, is through an avenue of tall trees and already the clues are there - the verges are well-tended, the fences neat - this is not going to be a rough and ready experience. Assorted livestock raise their heads at the car's arrival. A plump white mare and her new foal, black-headed sheep, Charolais cows, a friendly donkey, chickens of course and some ornamental fowl.

The *auberge* is ridiculously picturesque - a typical 19th-century Picardy farmhouse, low, white walls, brown shutters. You step down into two surprisingly sophisticated dining rooms - Villeroy and Bosch china was not what I expected but the rusticity is happily preserved - rough walls, farm implements, open hearth. Plump and friendly Mme Delianne is there to welcome you. Her husband, daughter and son (very professional, doing a *stage* at La Réserve in Beaulieu) do the waiting while she cooks. And it soon becomes obvious why you have to book well in advance to get a table here.

The speciality is lamb - home-grown - which comes in the shape of leg, fillet or loin. Otherwise it's Charollais beef, so bad luck vegetarians. Before comes soup, *pâté de foie gras* or salmon; after comes salad, cheese and classy desserts, all for 140f. If your appetite is not up to it, pay 80f and skip the *foie gras* and cheese. Gloriously simple and good.

As are the rooms. Ours on the ground floor had pretty, green striped paper, green check curtains and covers on the twin beds, plenty of space and a very unrustic bathroom with shower. Upstairs three more rooms may have been carved out under the eves - all very pretty, but I like ours best (295f). They share a large sitting-room with a table big enough to spread out maps and books.

Hard to fault this one for charm and situation. Perhaps the breakfast was a little disappointing - I had hoped for home-made jam, fresh bread and perhaps a farm egg, but I can see that nice Mme Delianne and her team have more than enough on their hands.

A real winner, which I know will be top of the pops with FE readers.

SAULTY. 62158

20km SW of Arras. 17km NE of Doullens by N25. Conveniently placed for sorties into that most rewarding of northern towns, Arras. Follow signs from L'Arbret, on left coming from Doullens.

Pierre Dalle. 82 rue de la Gare (M)

(0)3.21.48.24.76. fax: (0)3.21.48.18.32.

The impression given by the address belies the reality. Not many imposing neo-clasical châteaux set in 15 hectares of grounds record their addresses as rue de la Gare. Montgomery chose it as a base in 1944, but he had to be installed in an armoured van outside for security reasons. We can be more fortunate. Inside the handsome building the atmosphere is equally unpretentious. No heavy drapes and

chandeliers - rather a casual modern decor, with each of the four rooms having its individual cheerful colour-scheme, and the dining room (breakfast especially recommended here) being particularly light and spacious.

Don't think either that château-grandeur is not compatible with children. They are warmly welcomed here, as indeed are all the guests.

260f for doubles, extra beds available at 70f.

ZOUAFQUES. 62890

7km SE of Ardres. Exit 2 on the A26, then the N43 towards Ardres. Well signed 1km before Berthem.

NEW M. & Mme Behaghel. La Ferme de Wolphus (S) (0)3.21.35.61.61.

This farmhouse has been built on the remains of the original Château Wolphus, burnt down by the Germans during the last war as Monsieur's grandfather wouldn't co-operate with them. Only the entrance gates remain. Still in the same family, it is a small farm with horses and sheep, etc. They now have *gîtes* and three chambres d'hôtes in the old stables. There is a small dining room with kitchen for guests where breakfast is served, sometimes joined by M. Behaghel, a most interesting host. Rooms are simple and unadorned. One room for four has a double bed and sturdy 3ft-wide bunk beds, tiled floor en suite with a shower, overlooking the rear fields. Don't be surprised if the resident peacock appears on your bedroom window sill. Upstairs are two more rooms for three, carpeted, Velux windows but quite light, shower and washbasin; they share a loo downstairs. Just a driveway from the main road it is very quiet here, even though the trains from the Channel Tunnel pass nearby.

Monsieur sells Bordeaux wines and was busy renovating the original *pigeonnier* as a *dégustation*. So quite a useful stay and taste on your way to the chunnel or ferry.

Rooms 210f for two. No evening meal but a restaurant about 1km away at Berthem.

NORMANDY

Départements: **Calvados** **Orne**
Eure **Seine-Maritime**
Manche

Companion guide to the area - 'FE 17 - Normandy'

Normandy has a special place in many British affections as their first experience of a real holiday in France. The toe may have been dipped briefly into the waters of Calais and the north on a day trip or in transit, but it is frequently Normandy that proves to be the base for further exploration, leading to long term addiction. Having no fewer than four ferry ports to choose from helps, of course.

Dieppe looks set to become a favourite, with a brand new ferry terminal, ever-decreasing crossing time and the short distance to Paris. Le Havre has excellent communications and frequent sailings. Ouistreham, right in the heart of the region, leads directly to some of its most appealing aspects of countryside and cultural heritage, and Cherbourg offers a shortish crossing, the calmer atmosphere of a smaller port and the laid-back atmosphere of the Manche.

The five *départements* that make up the region could not be more different: between them they offer an unsurpassed introduction to French scenery, history, coastline, customs, food, drink and people. There are more chambres d'hôtes here than in any other region, from picturesque Auge farmhouses to impressive châteaux.

The most northern *département*, **Seine-Maritime**, is dominated by the capital of Upper Normandy, the lovely city of Rouen, set in a bend of the Seine, protected by encircling hills. Recovery from its wartime horrors has been skilfully achieved and the city now offers a rewarding amalgam of mostly old, partly new, urban delights. It's an open-air city more light-hearted than its rival Caen, with plenty of incentives to linger at a café table in the historic and colourful market place or to drink in the atmosphere by the magnificent cathedral. There is an abundance of good restaurants to choose from.

Further north are the white cliffs familiar from Post-Impressionist paintings, fronting cobble beaches. Behind them are the chalky plateaux of the Caux area, dedicated mostly to cereal crops. It is a bit bleak sometimes, which makes the discovery of the occasional pretty village and rushing stream all the more pleasing. It is

HAUT-NORMANDY

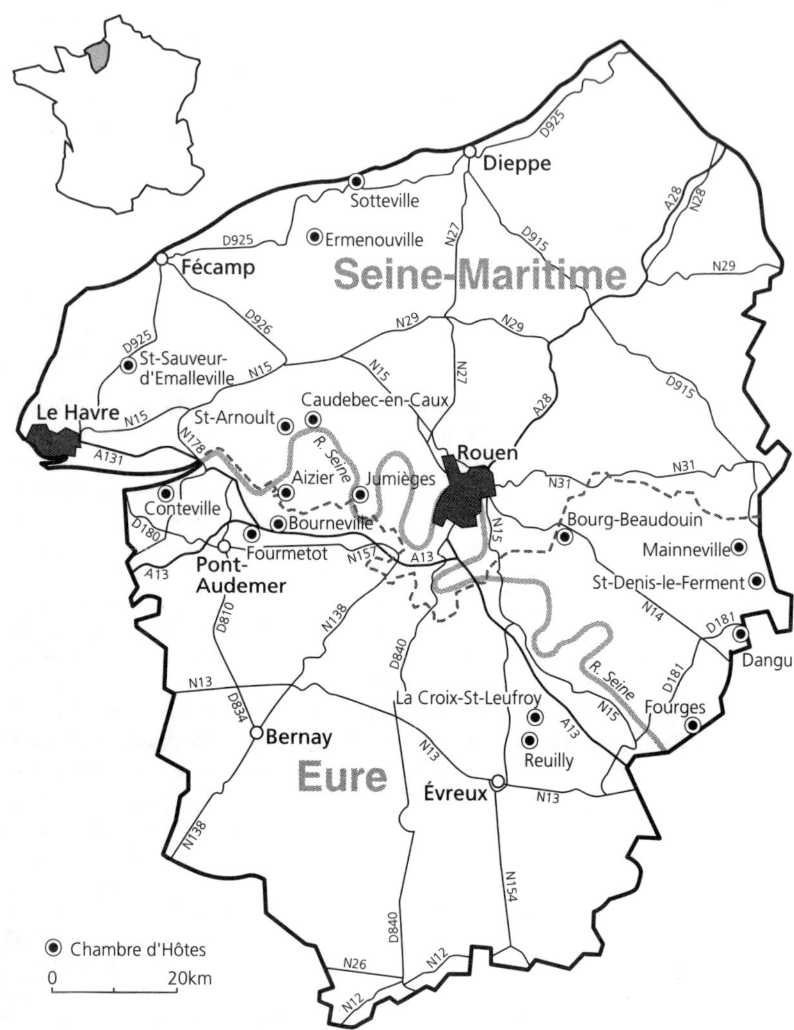

not generally tourist territory, which means more space to go round.

On the other side of the Seine we reach **Calvados** country, which is where the chambres d'hôtes cluster more thickly. This is Normandy at its most picture-book. The posters do not exaggerate. Guaranteed are half-timbered thatched cottages, hollyhocks round the door, gnarled apple trees, one dog, three sheep and six chickens. Take your pick of signed routes - *'fromage'*, *'cidre'*' and just *'touristique'* - it really doesn't matter. Wherever you leave the thunder of the autoroute you are bound to stumble upon hard-to-credit, stage-set rusticity.

The coastline will be no less familiar. Honfleur, the favourite of artists for many a generation, is still as picturesque but perhaps threatened by too many tourists, thanks to the new Pont de Normandie (go out of season). Deauville, a mere hop and a skip away from the deepest countryside, is posh Normandy. Expensive, well-groomed, elegant, humming during the August races, a conference centre for the rest of the year, it adds yet another dimension to the *département*. Next door Trouville is earthier and cheaper, with beaches just as fine. Good for families who are looking for sea and for the kids alongside plenty of grown-up activity

Three-quarters of Caen, the capital of Lower Normandy, was tragically destroyed in 1944, but it is still the home of two magnificent abbeys, built for William the Conqueror and his queen Matilda, an imposing castle in the city centre, some lovely churches and a thriving university. Linked by a canal to its port, Ouistreham, it makes a good winter base for shopping and eating. The *Mémorial*, a museum of peace, is one of the most moving and impressive museums I have ever visited. Don't miss it and do allocate half a day to its proper appreciation.

Bayeux is another must for any Calvados itinerary. Go early or late in the day to get the best value from the sensitively presented tapestry, and enjoy its ancient narrow streets and massive Gothic cathedral. The nearby Bessin countryside is gentle and pretty, with some attractive fishing ports along the coast, which, after the landing beaches, bends north at the dairy centre of Isigny.

Most of the popular Normandy cheeses - Pont l'Evêque, Camembert, Livarot - come from Calvados, where the black-and-white eye-patch cows are most prominent. Acres of apple orchards provide the raw material for Calvados cider.

The Cotentin peninsula forms most of the *département* of the **Manche**, which is, I suppose, my favourite. It is the least sophisticated, the friendliest, the easiest-to-handle. I recommend it for first-timers. Apart from Cherbourg there are no big towns and the pace is correspondingly slower. Inland some of the towns are boringly post-war, but a drive along the coast line is a good way to sample the scenic diversity that defied destruction.

West of Cherbourg one thinks of Cornwall - rugged cliffs, wild seas, granite cottages, fishing villages. The Nez de Joburg feels like the end of the world, not just France. Further south, and nature mellows considerably. Carteret is ideal for bucket-and-spade holidays, with lovely sands, rock pools, river estuary, trips to the Channel Islands and a Michelin-starred restaurant/hotel. Granville is a lively fishing port, looking across the bay to the fabled Mont St. Michel, rising like a floating mirage from the salt marshes.

BASSE-NORMANDY

Chambre d'Hôtes

0 20km

D513
D513
N175
aen
St-Hymer
Bures-sur-Dives
N13
N13
N13
Bretteville-sur-Laize
D579
Calvados
N158
Bernières-d'Ailly
D979
N138
Survie
L'Aigle
Argentan
N26
N26
D924
rolles
D916
N158
Orne
N12
N138
N12
D938
Alençon
D955
D955
Ceton

Drive east of Cherbourg to Barfleur and St. Vaast to find colourful, fishing harbours and marinas much favoured by British yachties. The seascape here is dotted with islands, the beaches sandy and undeveloped. Unless you are heading for the landing beaches, call it a day - the vast sandy Bessin bay is pretty featureless.

The **Orne** is an aristocratic *département*, rich in châteaux, manor houses and stud farms. Bagnoles-de-l'Orne, a dignified spa town, typifies the away-from-it-all, elegant relaxed atmosphere. The lovely river Orne flows through green, unspoiled countryside with attractive little towns like Mortagne, the cathedral at Sées and the stud farms in the Perche area to lend interest.

The mighty river Seine dominates the *département* of **Eure**. Exploring its looping course is a delightful exercise, revealing charming villages nestling in the escarpments, like Les Andelys. Giverny, the home of Monet, and its garden are a famous excursion. Approaching Paris it all gets busier and more developed, so swing westwards to explore some of the tributaries, like the meandering river from which the *département* gets its name - the Eure.

CALVADOS

AIGNERVILLE. 14710

15km. NW of Bayeux in deepest countryside. From Bayeux take the N13 for 16km direction Cherbourg. Look out for the D517 to Formigny on the right and then take the next turning left, signed Aignerville. At the first crossing turn left again and the entry is the second white gate on the right, all well signed.

Mme Yves Corpet. Manior de L'Hormette (L)

(0)2.31.22.51.79. fax: (0)2.31.22.75.99. Closed:31/12 to 15/3.

Madame Corpet has been a pioneer of the château chambres d'hôtes business from the very beginning, acting as secretary to the various groups of owners. She speaks fluent English and is an excellent source of local information of every kind. She is also a very good cook and has the unique distinction among b. and b. châtelaines of appearing in the discriminating Gault-et-Millau guide on the strength of her cuisine.

She charges 250f for dinner, eaten with the owners, but this includes wine before, during, and after, and coffee; reservations required.

Inside the immaculate 17th-century farmhouse she has three bedrooms with private bath or shower, one is split level to provide a sitting area, 450-550f for two, according to the season, and in the well-kept grounds is an independent cottage for four or five people for 700-750f. Breakfast is exceptionally good, with a selection of home-made jams, so perhaps you could skip lunch.

BERNIERES-D'AILLY. 14170

9km SW of St. Pierre-sur-Dives; 11km NE of Falaise on D 511 and then right on to D 242. The farm is 2km past the village.

M. & Mme Vermes. Ferme d'Ailly (S)

(0)2.31.90.73.58. fax: (0)2.31.40.89.39. Closed: 1/12 to Easter.

The Vermes have converted another room in their old stone farmhouse since my last visit. They now have five altogether in different styles. You can sleep *'Retro'* with *fin-de-siècle* lamps and beading, *'Romantique'* with a small draped four-poster, then *'Campagnard'* - very Laura Ashley or - oh dear, I forget. But you get the idea. Anyway they're all comfortable, with their own shower rooms and reasonably priced at 200f for two. Evening meal, as yet unsampled, costs 80f.

BRETTEVILLE-SUR-LAIZE. 14680

10km S of Caen by the N158 towards Falaise, then right on to the D23 at La Jalousie. Just before Bretteville turn right on to the D125, where the château is signed.

Anne Marie & Alain Cantel. Château des Riffets (M)

(0)2.31.23.53.21. fax: (0)2.31.23.75.14.

I am delighted with this success story. On my first encounter with the Cantel family I called on impulse at a terrible time - on January 1st, when every French family is cleaning up after the St. Sylvestre feast of the night before. The Cantels must have been horrified, but disguised their feelings magnificently, offering refreshment and welcome. They had just started their b. and b. operation and I recorded that the interior did not match up to the impressive first impressions of the approach up the drive, through extensive grounds, to the château. Many changes since then, as Anne Marie, who lived in England, and speaks and writes perfect English, tells me.

The bedrooms were always lovely high-wide and handsome and filled with light - but now they have their own shower rooms - two doubles for 500f and two suites for 600f. The public rooms have original period ceilings, but the furniture is modern.

Another new asset is the heated swimming pool - very popular with the Cantel's small daughter as well as the guests.

Dinner is served by a maid, but the family will join you if that is what you wish - 220f, all drinks included even old Calvados, and vegetarians catered for.

BURES-SUR-DIVES. 14670

15km E of Caen. 15km SE of Ouistreham. A visit to Pegasus Bridge is an absolute must. The original bridge has been dismantled and replaced by a new one, called Pegasus II. It was here that the first British troops of the Sixth Airborne Division landed on the morning of 6th June 1944. They took the vital bridge over the Caen canal and liberated the café right by the bridge, the first house in France to be freed by the invasion. M. & Mme Gondrée were in the café at the time and for three nights no sleep was had by anyone. Madame Arlette Gondrée, who was then four years old, has taken over from her parents and maintains the cafe just as it was; none of the decor has been changed, only enhanced by numerous gifts from visiting old soldiers, their friends and relatives. Open from March to November. With great charm she welcomes her many visitors, offering them drinks and sandwiches and her special Normandy omelettes at any time of the day. It is truly a living memorial to the most exciting day in French and British history this century. In summer you can sit outside on the terrace facing the canal or in winter sit at one of the café tables unchanged for fifty years.

To finish your exciting day book your room at Bures-sur-Dives. In the village of Troarn take the D95 to Bures, bear right to the church and the manor is down the lane alongside, well signed.

➤ M. & Mme Landon-Cassady. Manoir des Tourpes (M)

rue de l'Eglise. (0)2.31.23.63.47. fax: (0)2.31.23.86.10.

It was Arlette Gondrée who recommended this elegant 17th-century manor house. It stands beside the village church, with sweeping lawns to the banks of the river Dives, where the water rises with the tide. After persevering in French on the phone we discover that Monsieur is American, but Madame is French. We were given a very warm welcome, Madame switching easily from French to English and back

again as she showed us round, but generally the French atmosphere prevails throughout their home. Three bedrooms overlook the garden and river, all so different but each having a special allure, making a choice difficult. The largest almost a suite, is pure honeymoon material, with windows on three sides and the luxury of a real log fire. Thick carpets, fresh flowers by the bed, en suite bathroom in delicate peach and blue, thick towels and even a peach towelling gown. If the log fire isn't enough there's also an electric blanket. 360f for two. Next door, a smaller room with the most compelling view of all from the double bed, has a washbasin and a large private bathroom across the corridor with a deep old copper bath tub, but a shower too if you can't face the novelty; not many do, Madame tells me. The third bedroom is en suite with shower and toilet, and boasts a balcony. So charming are the rooms I shall not be satisfied until I've stayed in them all. There is now a fourth bedroom to consider. 280f.

Breakfast in the lounge/dining room, where a cheerful log fire blazes away, is laid on an attractive round table and is not to be hurried over. A wide choice of cereals, fruit juice, yoghurt, fresh fruit, jams, bread, brioche and all the usual drinks. You won't find such luxury in any hotel at these prices. No evening meals, but there is a Logis in Troarn, or your hosts will advise for further afield.

You will need to book ahead. Arrowed for situation and good value.

There is also a new *gîte* in the grounds, especially equipped for small children, with a fenced-in garden.

CAUMONT-L'EVENTE. 14240

38km SW of Caen on D9 towards Torigni. Turn right at Caumont on D28 towards Balleroy and the house is 300m on the right on the main road.

Balleroy is a unique little town, like a film set, with one wide main street of grey stone houses, all of a period, leading down to the focal point, the Château de Balleroy, built in the 17th century by Mansart. Nearby is the delightful forest of Cérisy and of course Bayeux is only a short distance away.

M. & Mme Boullot. le Relais (M)

19 rue Thiers. (0)2.31.77.47.85.

I can only find one fault with this attractive, well run, hospitable, good value establishment and that is I didn't find it first. It features in every known b. and b. guide and so, if you want a bed, you have to be quick off the mark.

Creepers clamber so abundantly up the walls of this old staging post that you can hardly see the building, apart from the glass conservatory built to overlook the lovely swimming pool. The exuberant hosts are horse breeders and *'equitation'* is one of the optional extras. Jeanne-Paule is a generous hostess and her breakfasts and dinners are all part of an enormous bargain on offer here. A typical meal might be a vegetable terrine, chicken Vallée d'Auge, cheeseboard, gooseberry fool, all for 140f, wine and cider included, on reservation.

Rather feminine, boudoir-ish rooms, furnished with some antiques and lots of personal touches, cost as follows: one double - 320f, one treble - 390f, one double suite - 390f, one treble suite - 470f, all with bath or shower.

ECRAMEVILLE. 14710

20km W of Bayeux. 85km SE of Cherbourg. Close to the landing beaches north of Bayeux. Leave the N13 at the Aignerville exit and follow the D30 right, signed to the chambres d'hôtes.

NEW M. & Mme Fauvel. Ferme de l'Abbaye (S)

(0)2.31.22.52.32.

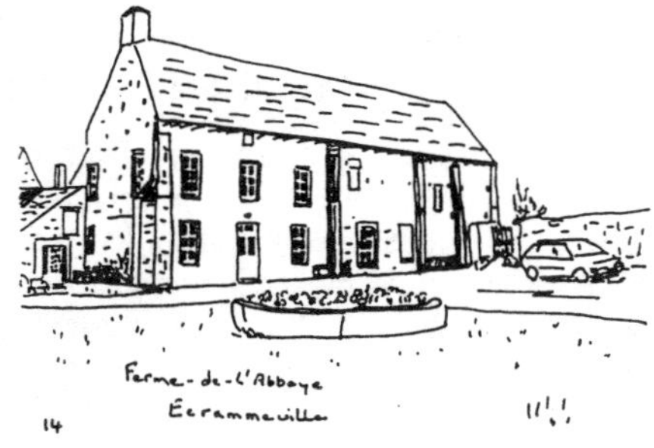

Whilst visiting the Marie family up the road I met Mme Fauvel, a sister-in-law, who lives 5km further east and also runs a chambres d'hôtes, next to the church at Ecrameville. This one is a 15th-century working farm but towerless and not at all austere, though the stairs to the first floor are still of the original old stone. The well-kept front garden is large and lawned, with colourful flower beds.

There is one family suite in a separate stone building across the garden - a very large room with double bed and sitting area and an adjoining room for children, with double access to the bathroom - a lovely spacious summer room for a family. 220f for two, 360f for four, includes breakfast.

Two more rooms in the main house: on the first floor a family room with two doubles is traditionally furnished, with modern shower room. Another on the ground floor is entered through an unused dining room; it has an adjoining area for a third bed and shower room but the loo has to be reached through the dining room. Evening meals are 85f cider *compris*, with demi-pension 165f per person. A stay of three days earns a good reduction. Your hosts entertain you in their own very pleasant *salon*, where meals are taken.

GEFOSSE-FONTENAY. 14230

65km SE of Cherbourg, 30km NW of Bayeux by N13 west, just past St Germain-du-Pert, then D514 towards Grandcamp-Maisy. Turn left on to the D199A to Géfosse-Fontenay. L'Hermerel is the second driveway on the right, but be sure you get the right chambres d'hôtes - there are several other signs around here.

What a fabulous position, set in the vast bay of Le Grand Vey, looking north all the way past the landing beach of Utah to St. Vaast. The light around here is unique - enough to tempt you to pack some water-colours. Vast sandy beaches to walk along, and Bayeux within easy reach. More practically - halfway between the two ferry ports, Cherbourg and Caen.

Agnes & François Lemarie. Ferme de l'Hermerel (S)

Tel & fax: (0)2.31.22.64.12.

Friendly and English-speaking Agnes Lemarie says that they are aware of their good fortune to live in such a house - a 17th-century fortified manor house, typical of the region. It's a working dairy farm - nearby Isigny is the centre of the dairy industry. The Lemaries have four children to look after as well as their guests and cows, but still manage to find plenty of time for friendly chat. They are justifiably proud of the gem of a Gothic chapel they have restored now used as a salon, and of the old *pigeonnier* in the courtyard where guests can enjoy picnics in a unique setting. The guest rooms are in the wing at right angles to the main building, where breakfast is taken in the stone-walled, chequered-floor kitchen with massive fire-place and copper utensils.

Furnishing in the four bedrooms, each with private shower, is simple and the stone can strike a little chilly at times, so perhaps this is a better choice for summer than on cold winter nights when the wind can howl across the bay. Pick fine weather and benefit from the proximity to the sea - only twenty minutes walk across the fields.

Accommodation is one twin-bedded room on the ground floor - 220f; one double on the first floor - 280f; two rooms forming a suite for two couples or a family - 280f, plus 70f per person extra; another on the second floor with a mezzanine, again for four or five people, again 280 plus 70f supplement.

MAISONS. 14400 BAYEUX

3km NW of Bayeux. Just a dot on the map, approached from the D100 between Tour-en-Bessin and Port-en Bessin.

In other words, the best of all worlds. No-one should miss this part of Normandy without a visit to Bayeux and its excellently presented tapestry - a year-round treat in an interesting and lively town, and no-one should miss Port-en-Bessin, the most attractive little fishing port on the Bessin coast, contrasting with the landing beaches on either side. The fishing fleet pull up along the quays of the deep inlet of the harbour, so you can stroll along the edge peering into the holds and checking the catch. Lots of head-clearing, ozone-packed walks here along the headlands.

➤ M. & Mme Jacques Aumond. Manoir du Carel (L)

(0)2.31.22.37.00. fax: (0)2.31.21.57.00.

The first time I wrote about the Manoir the Aumonds were still in the process of converting their superb mediaeval fortified manor-house, part of which is still a working farm, into a luxurious home with room for guests. This has now been achieved with a great sense of style and originality. A huge glass door has been let into the sitting room, allowing the natural light to illuminate the lovely galleried room and its grey and honey stone walls.

There are now three double rooms with a private bath or shower, from 350-600f and a small, independent house with lounge (sofa bed), one large bedroom, one small well-fitted kitchenette, and its own garden for four people for 650f.

Here is a chance to stay in great comfort with delightful, English-speaking hosts in a house steeped in history. FE readers have approved, so the arrow stays.

MONTS-EN-BESSIN. 14310

18km SW of Caen. 19km S of Bayeux. The Pré-Bocage area of Calvados, is renowned for its cider and dairy products. Take the D6 south-east of Bayeux direction Villers-Bocage and in about 18km turn left on to the D92 (if you reach Fains on the D6 you have just missed the turn) and follow the signs for about 1km. The house is on your left.

NEW **Mr. & Mrs. Edney. La Varinière** (M)
La Vallée. (0)2.31.77.44.73.

A warm and friendly welcome in one of the most compact manor-houses I have had the pleasure to visit. It has been gracefully restored over the last eight years and decorated to a high standard. You'll love the entrance hall in Wedgewood blue with white friezes and a charming fireplace with plaster figures. The comfortable salon in deep rose and white is just a taste of the pleasures in store. Across the hall is the yellow dining room (shades of Monet at Giverny?).

Five carpeted bedrooms all have en-suite facilities and typical long french windows giving views over the countryside. One features a bath on legs and Victorian wash basin, others are totally modernised. A charming sunny family unit with double bed and adjoining white room for children with a single bed and cot share a shower-room. On the second floor two rooms share a bathroom on the landing for a family of five or friends travelling together -280f for two, 350f for three. There is a small paddock where donkeys graze, and ample parking. No evening meals, but in Villers-Bocage, Les Trois Rois is one of the best restaurants in the *département.*

Don't miss this one, come back and tell me it deserves an arrow.

OSMANVILLE. 14230

12km E of Carentan. 30 WNW of Bayeux.Take the N113 from Carentan to Caen, in about 8km, at a large roundabout take the Osmanville road. The hotel 'Les Amies de la Route' will be on your left and right opposite is the turn into Champ Manlay; the main house is on the right past some chalets.

M. & Mme Manlay. Champ Manlay (S)
(0)2.31.22.02.91.

If you want to spend a few days in summer exploring the Normandy beaches this is a real find. Two rooms for families, in the main house, are now en suite with showers and kitchenettes, as are the two very practical rooms on the first floor of an annexe overlooking the swimming pool. 220f for two.

M. & Mme Manlay are natural and charming hosts. Breakfast is in their dining room. No evening meals but use the excellent cheap restaurant across the road, if you're not into self-catering. There are also five chalet-gîtes in the large grounds and a small flat on the ground floor of the annexe. All the occupants have access to the pool but this does not seem to make it at all crowded. Parking well away from the main road.

SAINT-GERMAIN-DU-PERT. 14230

28km W of Bayeux 80km SE of Cherbourg. Take the N13 to the Osmanville exit and follow signs to Saint-Germain-du-Pert. The farm is well signed on the right.

NEW **M. & Mme Marie. Ferme de la Rivière** (S)
(0)2.31.22.72.92.

In the Bessin area of Calvados are many fortified farmhouses like this one dating back to the 15th century.

Drive up the lane to the rather sombre looking dwelling almost surrounded by farm buildings. No active signs of farming - the owners have now retired and have more time to entertain their guests. You will be offered a choice of three rooms on different levels approached by the old stone steps of the original tower. A large wood-floored family suite occupies a whole corridor. Two high-ceilinged rooms have beds for five, a bathroom with a carpet and a separate loo at the end of the corridor. They have central heating and views over the countryside. Trot up a few more steps to a smaller room with two beds and up again to a small room - cosy but facing north. 200f for two.

Kindly hosts make you welcome in their large *salon* and they will provide an evening meal for 85f, cider *compris*. Demi-pension at 170f each for three days or more is good value.

SAINT-HYMER. 14130

3km S of Pont-l'Evêque. 40km E of Caen. Leave the A13 at sortie Pont L'Evêque and take the N175 direction Caen. In about 1km take the D48 direction Lisieux then the D 285 and the mill is on the right.

NEW Mme Françoise Vallé. Le Moulin de Saint-Hymer (M)

(0)2.31.64.23.51. fax: (0)2.31.64.39.72.

Situated in the lovely hilly *Pays d'Auge*, this mill was built in the 13th century and was working until 40 years ago.

The huge picture window of thc dining room incorporates the large mill wheel, now silent; but out on the terrace you may eat beside the gentle noise of the waterfall which never dries up. Fields surround the property and goats, ducks and horses add to the country atmosphere. Up the polished wood stairs are two rooms with choice of bath or shower. The large bathroom for one room is just next door. The smaller room has a shower room. On the second floor are two rooms sharing a bathroom for a family.

Evening meals with your hosts are 100f, wine not *compris*; and optional *foie-gras* is extra.

320/350f for two is fair considering the rarity of such an old mill house and your hosts look after you well.

EURE

AIZIER. 27500

45km E of Le Havre. 45km W of Rouen. From the A131 take exit 27 to Bourneville, drive through the village, following the D139 to Aizier. In the village turn left on to the D2 and the chambres d'hôtes is on the right opposite the *mairie*.

NEW M. & Mme Laurent. Les Sources Bleus (M)

(0)2.32.57.26.68.

This ivy-covered *maison-de-maître* of the tall slim variety makes an idyllic chambres d'hôtes, where every room from dining room and lounge to the topmost bedroom has a glorious view of the Seine flowing past the garden.

Ideal for families, as two first floor rooms each with bathrooms, have a tiny single room attatched, where you can still sit up in bed and see the river.

On the second floor are two heavily beamed rooms under the eaves, each with double bed and two singles. A spare single room on the top landing can belong to either - 250f for two. A working chair lift for the handicapped means they can enjoy the first floor rooms.

Mme Laurent, who lives in a house across the garden, is very sweet; she serves breakfast in the dining room, where there is a kitchen bar, or in the garden under a canopy in summer. Make haste to book, I think this one will prove very popular.

No evening meals but there is a restaurant close by.

BOURG-BEAUDOUIN. 27380

35km. NW of Giverny. 20km E of Rouen. From Rouen take the N14 east for 18km. Just before the village turn right, SP Radepont, and follow the signs past the church.

NEW M. & Mme Delavoye. Ferme de Coquetot (S)

46 rue de Coq. (0)2.32.49.09.91.

On a busy dairy and cereal farm. Young Mme Delavoye, even with three small children, is following in the footsteps of her mother, Mme Marc at Mainneville, and has converted the granary of this brick and stone farmhouse into four very nice freshly-decorated guest rooms, with a private entry. On the ground floor is a cosy salon with fireplace and an adjoining small kitchen for guests. Above a compact blue double room is warmly carpeted, and on the second floor a family room and two others, with sloping beams and tiled floors; all have central heating. 210f.

Breakfast is served in the attractive apricot-coloured salon, decorated with lampshades painted by artistic Mme Delavoye.

Evening meals (only if firmly reserved) 80f, *cidre compris* and a glass of wine with the cheese. Well off the main road, next to a château, with so many amenities, this makes a very good budget stop for a family.

BOURNEVILLE. 27500

40km E of Le Havre via the Pont-de-Tancarville. Exit from the A 13 at Bourneville, turn left in the village when you reach the *mairie* and the house is on the left, well signed.

NEW **Mr. & Mrs. Brown. La Grange** (S)
Route d'Aizier. (0)2.32.57.11.43.

Such a handy stop for the Le Havre ferry, just off the *autoroute* for arrivals or departures, within walking distance of many amenities in the village - restaurant, *boulangerie*, hairdresser, etc. A typical Normandy house, long and narrow, tastefully converted from a barn, keeping the old beams, it has a lounge/dining room with windows on both sides and comfortable sofas by a log fire.

Two guest rooms opening on to a terrace, looking on to a pleasant garden, have modern showers and loos and are prettily furnished with fresh pine and pretty wallpaper.

Mr Brown is a teacher of French, and Madame is a true *Normande*. The welcome here is really warm and you have the advantage of speaking either language.

Rooms at 230f for two with an excellent breakfast. Extra beds not available.

CONTEVILLE. 27210

9km SW of Pont de Tancarville, by the N178, or a 16km drive eastwards from Honfleur on the coast road, D312. It's a pleasant route all the way, very rural with glimpses of the Seine estuary. From here you can rest assured that Le Havre is only 45 minutes away, or even less over the new Pont de Normandie, so a convenient last stop before catching the ferry might be in the village of Conteville.

Mme Anfrey. Le Clos Potier (M)
(0)2.32.57.60.79.

There are several chambres d'hôtes in the region, but only one Ferme du Pressoir, so make sure you follow the signs to Le Clos Potier. You will find it tucked away in a lane behind a white fence, a half-timbered archetypal Normandy farmhouse, festooned with geraniums from tubs, pots, window boxes and wheelbarrows. It takes its name from the massive grape press dating from the 17th century which is still in working order; but, says Mme Anfrey sadly, "We no longer have the horses to pull the crushing stone round the trough."

The 250-year-old farm has been in the family for three generations and nowadays the energetic Mme Anfrey and her husband concentrate on the raising of cows and chickens; this does not hinder her making guests feel pampered and welcome. Furnishing is family antiques, copper pans, dried flowers, lace cloths, resulting in a pleasantly cluttered homely atmosphere. There are three smallish rooms in the house, with private bath or shower, and one family room with two double beds and bathroom in an annexe. 260f for two.

The evening meal is an excellent 120f worth, with all drinks included, and breakfast is charmingly laid out with white Limoges china on a pink tablecloth.

LA CROIX-SAINT-LEUFROY. 27490

100km SE of Le Havre. 40km S of Rouen. Much to see in the area: Les Andelys, Monet's garden and the Seine are all close by. Don't miss Les Andelys. Le Petit-Andelys is tucked in by the river under the hill on which the ruined Castle Gaillard stands, a fortress built by Richard the Lionheart to prevent the French king Phillipe-Auguste from reaching Rouen in 1196. For the energetic there is a lane up to it behind the Tourist Office; otherwise drive three kilometres through Le Grand-Andelys and follow the signs. Once high on the car park the view is fabulous, the Seine below like a silver ribbon winds in and out of view, protected by sharp white cliffs on the north-east bank. Barges steadily make their way to Rouen. A glorious place for a picnic. The farm is deep in the country on the plain above the small village of La Croix-Saint-Leufroy, just off the D10 but only 3km from the A13.

➤ M. & Mme Senecal. Ferme de la Boissière (M)

Hameau de La Boissaye. (0)2.32.67.70.85. fax: (0)2.32.67.03.18.

When we arrived on a bitterly cold winter's day Madame showed us to a huge ground-floor room with a dark, red tiled floor. Ugh! Not another cold, carpetless trip to the loo. Mysteriously the room was quite warm and I looked in vain for the central heating. The equally large salon next door was just as comfortable. Puzzled I asked Mme Senecal, whilst she was making us a cup of tea, how the house was

heated. "Underfloor heating," came the answer. By water pipes, masses of them. We were shown all the pictures of the reconstruction of this old stable about eight years ago. Every inch of the bathroom floor was warm too. What joy! The old house dates back many hundreds of years when it was once used as a home for the monks at La Croix-Saint-Leufroy. Nothing has been spoilt in the reconstruction. The old beams and windows, now double glazed, remain. The large light salon adjoins their own house.

Three other bedrooms, beautifully furnished and electrically heated, overlook the enormous front garden where ducks of all varieties were walking on the icy pond, and we even saw black swans and a peacock.

Madame is happy to give you an evening meal even if you arrive late. We had booked only half an hour before and were lucky to get a room and an excellent meal for 70f, drinks *compris*, which we ate by a log fire - *Oeufs-en-cocotte au jambon, escalope de veau à la Normande* laced with cream, cheeses of the region and a delicious apple crêpe. The aperitif Pommeau (Calvados and apple juice) is to be taken cautiously. Madame shared an aperitif with us and served the meal but Monsieur is too busy on his cereal farm to eat with guests each night. There are usually other guests to join one for dinner. You will want to stay far longer than one night here at this recommended year-round stop.

Rooms 250f.

DANGU. 27720

8km SW of Gisors, preferably by the pleasantly green little D10 (D181 if in a hurry). This is the Vexin region, far enough away from Paris (60km) and the ports to be untouristy, near to very pleasant countryside, the river Epte that Monet loved to paint, the valley of the Seine and Giverny.

➤ **Mme de-St. Père** (M)

4 rue de Gué. (0)2.32.55.04.95. fax: (0)2.32.55.59.87. Closed:16/12 to 15/3.

A firm favourite, well deserving an arrow on the strength of many readers' commendation.

The 18th-century restored house is in the village, close to the bridge. Look for the distinctive green shutters. They are green at the rear, too, opening out on to a large paved courtyard with a luxurious tent arrangement for shielding guests from the sun during their repose. The flowery garden slopes down to the banks of the

river Epte. It's all so pretty, with petunias and geraniums contributing to the colourful scene. It's pretty nice inside too, with a clever mixture of family antiques, paintings and cheerful colour schemes. When it is not garden weather, it is in the cosy salon, before the fire, that *apéritifs* are taken before the evening meal. Don't miss it. Invariably it turns out to be a very jolly affair, with plenty of liquid laughter. One guest arrived without a booking and was immediately invited to join the family for a beef barbecue.

The two pretty double rooms, above average size, are reached by independent staircase; one with shower en suite looks out on to the village and the other overlooking the garden has a bathroom and loo next door. Nicole writes that 1998 fees will be 290f for 'friend's room' and 315f for 'Granny's room' (for two people).

Nicole was at school in England, and trained as a translator, so there will be no language problems. She volunteers the information that she has brought up five children and is now divorced. A very popular lady. 24 hours notice for dinner (130f for the gastronomic menu, 90f for Granny's dinner).

FOURGES. 27630

10km E of Giverny. 50km SW of Beauvais. 65km SE of Rouen. From the A13 SE of Rouen take exit 16, the D181 to Vernon then the D5 past Giverny and through Gasny to Fourges.

NEW ➤ **M. & Mme Stékélorum** (S)

24 rue du Moulin. (0)2.32.52.12.51. fax: (0)2.32.52.13.12.

This 17th-century farmhouse on the roadside is the oldest in the village. It faces into a small garden hidden by high locked gates. Delphiniums blue, geraniums red and climbing roses grow rampantly. Lie beside the little pond and listen to the gentle trickle of water, where a lively frog hops among the lily leaves but the ducks stay firmly asleep!

The Stékélorums are charming people who love entertaining guests and offer a warm welcome. The original inhabitable part of the old farmhouse incorporating the old bread oven and many other rustic features has been made into a salon for guests. Furnished with antique furniture which came with the house, a property which has long been in Madame's family. It is here round an oval table that a copious breakfast is served on pretty china, on cold days in front of a blazing log fire.

The granary is now the owner's private residence. Between the two is a charming double-bedded guest room with stable door opening on to a small terrace. Across the garden are two rooms (one for three people) on the first floor of the original stable, both charmingly furnished with pretty fabric.

No evening meals but recommended restaurants close-by the beautifully situated Moulin de Fourges (see *FE Normandy*) just a few paces away, or the Auberge '*Au Vieux Donjon*' at La Roche Guyon.

Down the road the owners also have a small *gîte* which is sometimes used for chambres d'hôtes guests staying for a few days. This has the advantage of a kitchen with washing machine.

Rooms 180f for one, 210/230f for two with double bed, 250f with single beds, 280f for three. Locked parking for three or four cars, and a well deserved arrow.

FOURMETOT. 27500

4km NE of Pont Audemer by the D139. There is such a tangle of autoroutes and nationales, such a hurrying to be in Paris or Honfleur or Rouen, that this corner of Normandy, only a 40 minute drive from Le Havre, often gets neglected. Pont Audemer is an attractive little town, once you penetrate behind the railway sidings and dusty concrete outskirts and discover its ancient heart. Here rivulets from the river Risle thread their way beneath old bridges and beamy old houses overhang the water. The best market in the district takes place here on Mondays and Fridays, when the rue de la République is closed to traffic - priorities correct!

Turn right at the church past the turning on the right to La Croisée, and l'Aufragère is on the left.

➤ Régis & Nicole Dussartre. L'Aufragère (M)

La Croisée. (0)2.32.56.91.92. fax: (0)2.32.57.75.34.

An 18th-century half-timbered house, recently restored by the Dussartres to provide five guest rooms, with attractive different characters but all with private bathroom - 280f for two, 340f for three.

The big attraction here, apart from the friendly welcome from the hosts, is English-born Nicole's culinary skill. She is a professional cordon bleu cook, making good use of the wonderful range of local produce in the market to produce a superb evening meal for 120f, all drinks included. If you want to cook like her, sign up for one of the long weekend or five-day gourmet cookery courses she organises at l'Aufragère. Régis too is involved in matters gastronomic. He is a cheese specialist and will share his expertise in advising which of the tempting display on he market stalls should be purchased to take home. He also makes his own cider in large wooden casks in one of the barns on the premises, so you can sample that, along with the local Calvados, of which he always has a good stock.

A lovely place to stay, arrowed for good value, good company and goodwill.

MAINNEVILLE. 27150

10km. NE of Etrepagny. 23km E of Rouen. From the D915, halfway between Gisors and Gournay-en-Bray, turn west to the village of Mainneville. The church is very large for such a small village, serving a lot of the hamlets in the rolling countryside around. It houses the only authentic and lifelike statue of St. Louis (Louis IX) who was canonised by popular demand in 1297, very soon after his death. The statue dates from the early 14th century.

In the southern part of the village take the road signed Le Timbre and the farm is immediately on your left, next to a *maison-de-maître* once owned by the grandson of Victor Hugo. This makes an economical stop for Giverny, only 40km south.

➤ M. & Mme Marc. Ferme Sainte-Geneviève (M)

(0)2.32.55.51.26.

A ewe on the front lawn keeps an eye on all approaching visitors to this lovely old farmhouse whose central heating is fuelled by straw! A warm welcome awaits from Mme Marc. The back garden is enclosed by the main house and converted barns.

Two large rooms are on the first floor of the main house and there is a cosy room on the ground floor. Two others on the first floor of the building opposite share a kitchen, ideal for a family or friends. 220f. Two salons for guests.

"*With advance notice Mme Marc will provide dinner of excellent quality and more than adequate quantity. Four courses with a different selection of cheeses each evening, plus all the coffee one can drink and a bottle of wine for each couple, and all for only 80f.*" - Michael Turner. Evening meals a pleasure to look forward to are now alas served only occasionally.

Mme Marc is such a sweet person who thinks of your comfort all the time. Here is the true spirit of a chambres d'hôtes, an economical stop for Giverny 40km away, and arrowed accordingly.

Mme Marc's sister (Mme Vrel) keeps a chambres d'hôtes in Ygrande, Allier (see section on Auvergne).

REUILLY. 27930

8km N of Evreux. A useful base for Monet's garden at Giverny. The gardens are small and laid out in straight lines. The co-ordinated colours are magnificent, wallflowers, tulips, polyanthus from cream to dark red in great drifts, with lilac and cherry trees shedding their petals in the wind. The water garden, with the renowned bridge, is across the main road, now reached by a subterranean passage-way. It is a complete contrast to the rest of the place, and Monet painted here frequently. The house, open to the public (not from 12 to 2 p.m.), is long and narrow and the rather uncomfortable rooms are redeemed by the cheerful yellow dining room. Not a stick of furniture has escaped the yellow paint, but how I enjoyed this room; ancient kitchen in blue and white.

Take the D155 from Evreux north through Gravigny and branch right on to the D316 to Reuilly, turning left at the silo on your right. The Ferme de Reuilly is on your left in the middle of the village.

M. & Mme Nuttens. Ferme de Reuilly (S)

20 rue de l'Eglise. (0)2.32.34.70.65.

We were so early that Mme Nuttens was still out shopping, but her son who speaks some English had been briefed about our arrival and showed us to our room. There are three warm, comfortable, homely rooms at one end of the house, with a small guest kitchen downstairs - 230f. The dining room with armchairs and TV links the guests' part of the house to the Nuttens, all immaculate. We relaxed over an excellent evening meal with the family. 80f, cider *compris*, served every day except Sundays. The Nuttens are very pleasant hosts and keep up a lively conversation over dinner.

SAINT-DENIS-LE-FERMENT. 27140

8km NW of Gisors. 26km NE of Les Andelys.Well away from main roads, one long narrow road runs through the village bordered by immaculately kept old and new houses, not an un-painted shutter in sight - an estate agents' dream village. In the centre of the village the rue des Gruchets climbs a small hill and the chambres d'hôtes is signed on the right.

NEW Mme Rousseau. Le Four au Pain (M)

8 rue des Gruchets. (0)2.32.55.14.45.

Behind locked gates this adorable rustic cottage is sideways on to the road, parking inside the gates. The garden is terraced down the hillside.

Mme Rousseau, a retired business lady, has one guest room for three, double and single bed, under her own roof. Beautifully furnished, complemented by rustic beams and warm carpets and a quality en-suite shower and loo. A possibility of putting a fourth bed for a child on the landing. Windows overlooking the garden, it is the perfect cottage bedroom. 240f for two, 300f for three includes breakfast in her large dining room/salon, furnished with antiques and knick-knacks collected over the years, guests are welcome to use this room. The second room for two is in a small stone house in the garden, where the original *four-au-pain* takes pride of place, lit up inside, enhanced by an attractive display of fresh flowers. There is a double bed, and a small kitchenette with all facilities for self catering. The en-suite ultra-modern shower has temperature settings. The floor is tiled: but this one has the advantage of a private lawned terrace. 300f. No evening meals but a restaurant in the village. An arrow just waiting to be confirmed.

MANCHE

CARANTILLY. 50570

88km S of Cherbourg. 9km W of Saint-Lô. 15km E of Coutances. Signed on the D972 between Saint-Lô and Coutances. From Saint-Lô it is on the left just before the hamlet of Le Poteau, opposite a factory making smoked ham.

NEW M. & Mme Delabarre. Haras-de-la-Jourdanière (S)

(0)2.33.55.60.03.

Well off the main road up a long private lane the Delabarres breed steeplechasers. There are many horses grazing in the surrounding fields and a few in spotlessly kept boxes near the house, often with a captivating young foal.

Two nicely decorated new rooms, at one end of their long house, have independent entry up an external flight of steps. They have large windows, parquet floors and are en suite with baths/showers and separate loos, and ample wardrobe space for longer stays. Central heating willingly put on for cooler nights even in May. 200f for two, only 250f for three.

Nice Mme Delabarre serves you a generous breakfast in her large modern kitchen, the hub of the house. No evening meals; but you are welcome to use the barbecue and picnic on the terrace in summer. Or take this as an excuse to visit the restaurant 'Auberge des Tisserands' 6km away at Cametours, which is popular with locals, and you'll rarely meet a car on the way back.

I liked this chambres d'hôtes very much - real value.

ISIGNY-LE-BUAT. 50540

30km from le Mont-Saint-Michel. A turning off the N176 between Ducey and Saint-Hilaire-du-Harcouët. 9km from Ducey turn left on to the D85 (SP Isigny-le-Buat). At a T junction by a factory turn left and the chambres d'hôtes is the fifth house on the left, 200yds from the *auberge* on the D47.

NEW M. & Mme Heurtaut. Le Grand Chemin (S)

(0)2.33.60.40.14.

This smart modern house has three spotless, light and airy, warm rooms, all carpeted. Two, including a family room with two double beds, have modern shower-rooms, a third has a larger private shower room just alongside on the corridor. 180f for two, 300f for four.

There is a large glassed-in veranda for guests, overlooking the small garden, where there is parking beside the house. Perhaps some traffic noise may be heard from the front room but this isn't a busy road.

No evening meals; but there is an *auberge* within walking distance serving regional dishes from 80 to 100f. Madame is equally happy to warm up a meal in her microwave if you wish to bring in a picnic and eat in the conservatory. So a good budget stop for families.

MONTFARVILLE. 50760

27km. E of Cherbourg. 2km S of Barfleur. Barfleur is a neat little port full of bobbing boats. The light from one of the tallest lighthouses in France at the Raz de Barfleur sweeps the port at night. This chambres d'hôtes is easy to find, just off the coast road from Barfleur to St Vaast. Leave Barfleur on the D9 and take the second turning right after the town exit sign, it is the next turn left. If you turn earlier you will be in the mess we were, circling the village of Montfarville. Matilda (wife of William the Conqueror) commissioned his ship here for the invasion of 1066 and all that!

M. & Mme Gabroy. Le Manoir (M)
(0)2.33.23.14.21.

Fresh flowers even in December greet you in your room in this tall, granite manor house, overlooking fields of thriving vegetables and sea views of the English Channel. There are two rooms in the Manoir, large, warm and comfortable, one up a spiral staircase, the other, easy for off-loading, on the ground floor. 280f. These large rooms take some heating in winter but Madame had everything on full blast for us after we had booked ahead by phone.

Le Manoir

No evening meal, but there is an excellent restaurant in Barfleur - the Moderne (see *FE Normandy*). Breakfast is served in a dining room/sitting room for guests, all attractively set on a flowery tablecloth.

NICORPS. 50200

4km SE of Coutances. 40km from Mont-Saint-Michel. 80km S of Cherbourg. A hamlet just outside the cathedral town of Coutances, amid narrow lanes with high hedges.

From Coutances take the D7 towards Gavray (Villedieu-les-Poêles), turn left to Nicorps on the D27, then it is well signed. Don't confuse it with another chambres d'hôtes further up the road in the same hamlet.

NEW M. & Mme Posloux. Les Hauts Champs (S)

La Moinerie-de-Haut. (0)2.33.45.30.56.

The stone built 17th-century farmhouse is flanked by a large old stone well.

Whilst the restoration was going on old papers were found hidden in the beams, dating the house. The original slate floors are still intact in the salon.

There are two rooms on the first floor, both comfortably furnished, with a sunny south outlook. One with red moquette walls is en suite, the other has a private bathroom along the carpeted corridor. There is a further attic room for children with climbing ability up a steep staircase, when they share facilities with the parents below.

Rooms are only 180f and you can have an evening meal cooked by Madame for 85f, wine and cider *compris*. A charming hostess and the house has a very pleasant garden. This chambres d'hôtes may well interest readers who are into show jumping as M. Posloux is a professional show jumper and breeds his own horses.

PERCY. 50410

100km S of Cherbourg. 25km SSW of St. Lô. Halfway between the Landing Beaches and Mont St. Michel, in the centre of the Cotentin peninsula in lovely unspoilt countryside.

Leave Percy by the D58 (direction Hambye) and almost immediately turn left on to the D98 towards Sourdeval-les-Bois. La Voisinière is on the right.

Mme Duchemin. La Voisinière (M)

(0)2.33.61.18.47. fax: (0)2.33.61.43.47.

This is a delightful sunny house and garden for a long holiday or for just passing through the Manche area of Normandy. Trips to the Channel Islands from Granville, Portbail and Carteret. Gardeners will love it - nearly as colourful as Monet's garden. On arrival you will probably find Madame deep in the lilies.

An outside staircase leads you to a pretty blue room; its double bed has cherry wood ends and a third bed is slotted into an alcove behind a dainty blue curtain. The low window overlooks the large peaceful garden massed with bushes and flowers for all seasons. Above is a room with twin beds; but the stairs could be rather tricky for the elderly. Three other rooms are in a separate cottage, where there is a shared kitchen for guests. 210/250f. Mme Duchemin offers light meals out of season, but self catering would be a real pleasure here and there are some very good restaurants close by - notably F.E.3's hotel of the year, the *Auberge de l'Abbaye* at Hambye, just by the ruined Abbey.

A charming hostess, a possible arrow. Reports please.

SAINT-GERMAIN-SUR-SEVES. 50190

16km W of Carentan. 20km N of Coutances. In a central position on the Cotentin peninsula, within easy reach of beaches on the east and west coasts (I would recommend this place highly for a delightfully comfortable farmhouse holiday.)

Coming from Périers on the D971 take the third road left, the CD301.

M. & Mme Vautier. Les Tilleuls (S)

rue de Remeurgues. Tel & fax: (0)2.33.46.64.34.

An old favourite, outside the village, this old Normandy house is excellently maintained and has five well-furnished rooms, four on the first floor. There is one family room, a suite of two rooms for five, with a fridge. All have either baths or showers. The ground-floor room sleeps three, has a kitchenette and with independent entry is suitable for the handicapped.

A very warm welcome from M. and Mme Vautier, but sadly they no longer produce evening meals, due to pressure from local restaurants. However Mme Vautier will allow you to use her own kitchen to prepare a light meal on occasions. Rooms still very reasonable at 195f for two.

SAINT-JAMES. 50240

21km SE of Mont-Saint-Michel. A small town with central market square, all very French and un-touristy. Surprisingly spelt the English way, a relic of the Hundred Years War. Easy to find this on the D12 just west of St-James.

Mme Tiffaine. La Gautrais (S)

(0)2.33.48.31.86. fax: (0)2.33.48.58.17.

A dairy farm with a modern house overlooking the valley and a lovely terrace.

Rooms have polished wood floors, exceptionally good storage space and baths or showers. One also has a kitchenette, and now a self-contained studio has been added. There is central heating for winter and the *accueil* to go with it. 195f. Excellent evening meal for 85f, and the best Calvados I have tasted, made on the farm.

VERGONCEY. 50240

12km. 5km S of Pontaubault by D 998, then right on to D308. Pleasant countryside only 18km from Mont-St-Michel.

Mme Gavard. Ferme de l'Etang. Boucéel (S)

(0)2.33.48.34.68. fax: (0)2.33.48.48.53.

The creeper-covered farmhouse overlooks the large lake from which it gets its name. The welcome and helpfulness of dairy-farm owners, who speak good English, has been particularly applauded, as has the evening meal featuring produce from their farm, served in winter by a huge fireplace, at 80f.

The rooms all have private facilities, but not always adjoining; ones facing the lake do have a preferred view. 200/220f for two, 300f for four with two double beds.

ORNE

CETON. 61260

8km NE of La Ferté-Bernard. 56km SE of Alençon. Just in Orne, a small town with a lake.

Approaching from the north, drive straight through the town on the D107. At the "end of town" sign fork right following the chambres d'hôtes sign. A long lane bearing right past a couple of houses will end in an attractive garden encircled by well-kept stone houses.

NEW M. & Mme Pinoche. L'Aitre (M)

(0)2.37.29.78.02.

Kindly hosts cater strictly for vegetarians here. Even the wine is produced from organically grown grapes.

In a separate building is a large high-beamed salon/dining-room, with natural stone walls. Meals are normally served here but on occasions taken with the family. Central heating does its best in winter and Monsieur complements it with a log fire on chilly nights. Above is a family suite, and a room for two, both with private facilities, firm beds and many thoughtful extras. A further two rooms for a family, in the main house, share a bathroom. The price of 280/320f, extra bed, 50f, reflects the specialised amenities.

The evening meals are both interesting and nourishing for 90f, wine *compris*.

Behind the house are lawns, a view of the lake and a parking area.

FAVEROLLES. 61600

13km S of Putanges. 10km N of Bagnoles. Bagnoles-de-l'Orne is an unique little town, centred round its lake, spa and casino. For six months of the year it relapses into somnolence, hotels and shops shuttered, but come Easter and it comes most attractively to life again, a cool green oasis animated with Parisian style.

Coming south on the D19 to Bagnoles before the village of Faverolles look for the chambres d'hôtes signs on your right.

M. & Mme Fortin. Le Mont Rôti (S)

(0)2.33.37.34.72.

Not far off the D19 to La-Ferté-Macé, this farmhouse on a dairy and cereal farm has been completely rebuilt in a modern style using much natural wood in ceilings and furnishings. There are three rooms, immaculately kept, with plenty of well-fitted cupboard space, centrally heated and warmly carpeted. Rooms are for two, three or four, reached by a staircase from the very large conservatory in the main house. The third room has private access from an outside wooden staircase. Excellent meals, taken with the family, are unbeatable value, all drinks *compris* at 75f.

Rooms 200f for two, 275f for four.

SAINT-PIERRE-DU-REGARD. 61790

50km S of Caen. 12km N of Flers. In the undulating Suisse-Normande countryside.

From the D562 100 metres south of Condé-sur-Noireau end of village sign, take a little lane on the left. The drive leading to the manor is then on the left.

NEW **Mme Prévot Manoir de Moissy** (L)

(0)2.31.69.01.49. Closed 1/10 to 30/3.

What a delightful elegant little manor house this is, tucked away off the main road and surrounded by trees and green lawns.

The cosy library with floor-to-ceiling books is where Madame will greet you with tea or an *apéritif* on arrival. There are two centrally-heated rooms on the first floor, beautifully furnished with many antiques. One, with panelled walls, has a double wrought-iron four-poster, with white *broderie anglaise* duvet, complemented by polished wood floors. An attached large bathroom has a Victorian washbasin and free-standing bath. This is not a room for people who have to pad to the loo at night as the w.c. is down-ne dining room. 400f for two. Children up to two years decorated to the hilt in pale pinky-mauve *Toile-de-Jouy*. , you name it, all covered in a very old design of Sir Walter *e*. The design continues through the vestibule and bathroom, red, and surrounds a large built-in bath. This room has the completely en suite, 500f.

g room has a large fireplace and a sturdy oak table for breakfast; but in summ… you will opt for the gravelled terrace overlooking the peaceful garden behind the house. No evening meals, but on return from a local restaurant, Madame, will be waiting to share a Calvados with you.

SURVIE. 61310 EXMES.

120km from Le Havre, 176km from Cherbourg, 56km from Caen. In the *Pays d'Auge* just below the Falaise gap where the last battle in Normandy was fought. The small hamlet of Survie is on the D26 between Vimontiers and Exmes.

NEW **Mr. & Mrs. Wordsworth. Les Gains** (M)

Tel & fax: (0)2.33.36.05.56.

Having arrived here only three years ago, complete with sheep and household goods, the Wordsworths have converted an old *fromagerie*, where Camembert was once made, into rustic guest rooms furnished with a mixture of modern beds and family heirlooms. There are three rooms for two or three. Two rooms overlooking the garden and *pigeonnier*. 220f for two, extra bed 50f, children especially welcome.

There is a comfortably furnished salon/dining room for guests where breakfast and evening meals are served in winter, from which a door leads to the garden and terrace for summer meals beside the stream inhabited by tame ducks. Alas the fox had been round while I was there.

A friendly welcome from Diana, a true farmer's wife, busy with the lambing when we called but not too busy to cope with guests.

Not often the English are brave enough to take over a large farm as well as a chambres d'hôtes, but Kit Wordsworth, a descendant of William, was an established farmer before he came to France. Diana is a keen gardener and you will find many rare plants in her borders. If you are a lone guest you may well be invited to eat in the family kitchen, the real hub of the house. Evening meals 120f include *apéritif* and wine.

SEINE-MARITIME

CAUDEBEC-EN-CAUX. 76490

51km E of Le Havre. 36km W of Rouen.There are several routes from the ferry to Caudebec. Leave the port by the autoroute and turn off on to the D982; or turn off to Norville on the D81, surprisingly high above the Seine, for a pleasant drive along the river.

Not much of the town survived the fire in 1940. Only three medieval houses and the very fine 15th-century flamboyant Gothic church, described by Henry IV as 'the most beautiful chapel in the kingdom', remain to drop a hint of how attractive it must once have been. Sad though its concrete reincarnation may be, the setting remains attractive, a good base from which to explore the Seine valley and Rouen. It also has a good Saturday market. From a small roundabout near the quay take the Yvetot road (D131) and the rue de la République is on the right just after the end of town sign. The chambres d'hôtes at no.68 is well signed on the corner.

Mme Villamaux (S-M)

68 rue de la République. Cavée Saint-Leger. (0)2.35.96.10.15. fax: (0)2.35.96.75.25.

"*Television, refrigerator and microwave for use in both rooms. Off-street parking available on site. Nice breakfast with selection of delicious home-made jams. Open all year. Mme Villamaux solicitous and most pleasant.*" - John Procter.

Easy-going Madame Villamaux now offers a choice of five rooms, all totally different in size, shape and decor, with heating and TV. Three larger rooms have fridge and microwave, others share them in the main salon. No evening meals, small-scale self-catering expected, china supplied. Best of all - no washing up, dishes left on a tray are whisked away by Madame. Pleasant upward sloping garden and terrace behind the house. One locked garage now available and Madame will pick you up from bus or train. Many Brits love this place and it improves all the time.

Rooms 245/265f. Exceptionally good value for so many amenities.

ERMENOUVILLE. 76740

7km S of St. Valéry-en-Caux. 70km N of Le Havre. 30km NE of Fécamp. From the A13 direction Rouen take exit 25 (Pont-de-Brotonne/Yvetot). At Yvetot take the D20 towards Saint-Valéry-en-Caux. At Sainte Colombe 2km after the village take direction Houdetot and the château is about 2km on the left.

NEW Dr. & Mme Kayali. Château du Mesnil Geoffroy (L)

(0)2.35.57.12.77. fax: (0)2.35.57.10.24.

The ancient trees touch overhead in the drive up to this red-brick château, which has changed little since it was built in 1748 (look for the date scratched onto a pane of glass in the entrance salon). It is now a historical monument furnished entirely in 18th-century style. You will have a great welcome from charming hosts. The entrance salon with black-and-white chequered tiles spans the mansion and has a beautiful reproduction of a penny-farthing bicycle. People arrive for *réunions* with their own penny-farthings. There are marble fireplaces in all the rooms, where authentic Louis XV furniture is freshly upholstered to match the delicately-painted panelled walls. There are two other salons, one with TV for guests, and a pleasant dining room where brunch-type breakfasts are served. Dinner (reservations necessary) with your hosts is cooked by Mme Kayali, using 18th-century recipes and her own foie gras.

The park and original garden, designed by Le Nôtre, has an aviary and a maze. Extensive beautifully manicured lawns are dotted with cone-shaped bushes, topiary *Buis* (the latter is used on Palm Sunday in France, instead of palms). Red-brick walls were built round the main garden as protection from the salt winds. A statue of Neptune and one of Venus stand alone on the lawn.

Six surprisingly compact guest rooms of various shapes and sizes are named after previous owners. All have their original bathrooms, and oak floors. Although one still has the copper *'chauffe-bain'* in situ, modern plumbing has taken over and extra luxuries like hair dryers, towelling gowns and tea-making facilities now blend in with the original design.

One ground floor room has the bed slept in by Prince Montmorency, brother of Louis XVI, who was the original owner. Family portraits blend with scattered antiques like a *directoire poêle*; but nothing is overdone.

Five rooms up the oak staircase are all different. The Marquis de Cany's room (the most expensive at 650f) has a *baldaquin* and a bathroom hidden behind panelling down a few steps. Most rooms face the rear garden but a very small room in a front tower (the Ecuyer de Mainneville's room), delightfully light with two windows and white *ciel-de-lit*, would be my choice. Consellier Belgard has a double bed. Chevalier d'Accainvillier is yellow and blue.

Your hosts were born to château life, their original homes were either sold or destroyed by war, so they decided to buy Le Mesnil du Geoffroy five years ago, furnish it in 18th-century style and offer guests a taste of château life. As it is an historic monument, it is open to the public on most days, but still remains a private home.

Rooms 380/650f for two according to size. Breakfast 50f extra. Evening meal 200f each, *apéritif*, wine and coffee *compris*. 250f with champagne.

JUMIEGES. 76480

28km W of Rouen. Famous for the Benedictine Abbey (rebuilt then consecrated in 1067 in the presence of William the Conqueror) now in romantic ruins. Its two imposing towers dominate the village.

M. & Mme Douillet. La Mare au Coq (S)

3093 Route de Mesnil. (0)2.35.37.43.57.

Very popular with locals, this newly built *ferme auberge* is opposite the Abbey towers on ground surrounded by trees and fields. Ducks, geese and chickens wander around and a ferocious turkey guards the door. Three large, modern, comfortable rooms for two, three or four people cost 220f for two. Extra bed 50f includes breakfast.

It is truly a charming family who look after their resident guests superbly and eat with them on rare quiet nights. Ferme auberge meals 120f/145f, wine and coffee *compris*. Opt for a special resident's meal of four courses, excellent pâtés, large helpings, *apéritif* to coffee all included at 90f.

Sound-proof floors take care of the restaurant noises, but double-glazing loses the battle with nearby quarry lorries on weekday mornings. Aim for Saturday nights here unless you want an early start!

SAINT-ARNOULT. 76490

30km E of Le Havre. A useful place to stay to or from the Le Havre ferry.

From the A15 at the roundabout just before the Pont-de-Tancarville take the D982 (SP Lillebonne). Just before Lillebonne turn right on to the D484 for about

12km to Saint-Arnoult. The road to the ferme auberge is first left on the other side of the village.

NEW **M. & Mme Lefrançais. La Bergerie** (S)
Route de la Bergerie. Tel & fax: (0)2.35.56.75.84.

Aptly named, this sheep farm is well away from main roads. The tall house has ample parking and luxurious arum lilies fill the front border. The *ferme auberge* dining room operates at week ends, high days and holidays, when resident guests may eat there *(gastronomique)*. During the week, evening meals are shared with the family in the homely farmhouse dining room - 80f all drinks *compris* - an opportunity to improve your French.

Two guest rooms, furnished with family hand-downs and antiques, have double beds and sofa-beds for two children. A first floor room has a large shower room with two pretty flowered wash-basins, a shower and a bidet, but the loo is on the ground floor. The other on the second floor has a private shower and loo.

Rooms 220f. One person *soirée-étape* 250f.

SAINT-SAUVEUR D'EMALLEVILLE. 76110

12km N of Le Havre.Take the N925 north from le Havre to Goderville. Turn right at the road after the sign to St Sauveur and the chambres d'hôtes is signed on your right.

➤ M. & Mme Debreuille (M)

Route de la Ferme Chevallier. (0)2.35.29.50.01. fax: (0)2.35.28.39.90.

At last I have found an ideal night stop near Le Havre so good that it is worth spending far longer. Totally peaceful here yet only twenty minutes from Auchun and Mammouth supermarkets and the ferries.

The picture-book, half timbered thatched house stands in a country lane, surrounded by large hedges. Madame who speaks some

English has three very pleasant beamed first floor rooms with independent entry up an outside staircase, each with good-sized shower rooms. One extra room for two in the main house has private facilities on the landing. All have quality carpets and pretty matching decor. A large log fire heats a 'Marmite' central-heating system. Monsieur keeps a few sheep and poultry and has a very large garden.

Evening meals, mostly home produced, taken *en famille*, are very convivial - four or five courses, all drinks *compris* for 85f.

Rooms at 220f include a good breakfast, but demi-pension is only 350f for two if you stay three days.

SOTTEVILLE-SUR-MER. 76740

24km. SW of Dieppe. Close to the enchanting Veules-les-Roses (see *FE Normandy*). Sotteville is a small village 200 yards back from the cliffs, where at low tide a tiny beach can be reached by wooden steps. Church, restaurant, *boulangerie* and two *épiceries* are all near the village square and a small road from there beside the telephone box, leading to the D925, will take you to the farmhouse home of

M. & Mme Lefèbvre. Le Bout du Haut (S)
(0)2.35.97.61.05.

Situated in a pretty orchard garden sideways on to the road, the house is of colombage construction. Next door in her mother's modern house, Mme Lefèbvre has three guest rooms; there are private facilities for each but not all adjoining. One particularly nice room with a balcony is en suite. All have good furniture and are warm and comfortable year round - 210f. You trot next door to the farmhouse for meals; dinner with your hosts is good value at 80f, all drinks *compris*. You'll love it here, so friendly, the real spirit of a chambres d'hôtes

PARIS (ILE DE FRANCE)

Départements:	**Seine-et-Marne**	**Essone**
	Yvelines	**Val-d'Oise**

Companion guide on Paris – 'French Entrée 10 – Paris

Understandably dominated by its illustrious capital city, Paris, the Île-de-France tends to be a nonentity in most tourists' consciousness. Chambres d'Hôtes suggestions here are primarily intended as bases for visiting the city or EuroDisney, letting the train take the strain. This is not the place to extol Paris's many virtues or list the attractions. Suffice to say that everyone should see for themselves where the magic lies. And then come back and back (clutching FE 11 of course!).

Seine-et-Marne, the largest *département* of the region. lies on the eastern border of Paris, extending from just north of Charles-de-Gaulle airport to south of Fontainebleau, watered by the rivers Marne in the north, and Seine in the south. The Seine turns north at Fontainebleau and heads for the centre of Paris. The closer to Paris the more thickly populated and modern, with ugly flats springing up, but most of the area is flat countryside, interspersed with small towns, villages and farm land. It is here on the fringe of Paris that you will find **Parc Euro Disneyland,** easily reached by skirting Paris by the north or south motorways.

Essonne is in the south-west of Paris, on the borders of the lovely forest of Fontainebleau, a much smaller *département* and more rural, with many farms among the small villages. Forests round Paris are of the huntin' shootin' fishin' variety, not just green belt woods.

Yvelines. The *département* west of Paris, extends north to include part of the river Seine as it flows westwards and sea-wards from Paris. The beautiful palace of Versailles, built by Louis XIV, is the main attraction in this area. The forest of Rambouillet covers a vast area. **Val-d'Oise** is a small narrow *département* in the valley of the river Oise, north of Paris, bordering lower Picardy

SEINE-ET-MARNE

CHÂTILLON-LA-BORDE. 77820

12km E of Melun. 16km NE of Fontainebleau. From the Autoroute A5 take Sortie Châtillon-La-Borde, then signs to La Borde.

M. et Mme Guerif 'Labordière' (S)

16 Grande Rue, Hameau de La Borde. (0)1.60.66.60.54.

A quiet little hamlet just a few km from the Seine and Fontainebleau. The road by the Seine is quite pretty between Chartrettes and Fontaine-le-Port. (Fontainebleau Château is open 9.30 to 12.30 and 2.30 to 5 p.m.) Parking at Bois-le-Roi station is free and the train to Paris takes one hour. Come back to an evening meal prepared by Monsieur, who has retired from his charcuterie in Paris and enjoys cooking. He is now the mayor of La Borde. Madame still commutes daily to Paris. No 16 is next to the *mairie*, where you park; it's a pleasant old house, restored by the owner four years ago and has west facing sunny bedrooms, one with a shower room as big as the bedroom, featuring two arched entrances. You could put a family through in record time in one way and out the other. There is also a central dual vanitory unit, no ablutionary fights in the morning here! 240f. Two other rooms, united by a sitting area, make a good family unit, sharing one shower room, 210f for two. A nice sitting room downstairs opens on to a shady enclosed back garden. Evening meal 110f each with *aperitif* and Red Burgundy wine *compris*, reserve ahead. Worth it but, alternatively, there is a small restaurant a few doors away.

CRISENOY. 77390

8km NE of Mélun. 30km from Eurodisney. On the eastern outskirts of Paris, this small quiet village has a *boulangerie*, *boucherie* and a restaurant. A turning off the D36, just across the road from the church, is the home of:

NEW

M. & Mme Valery (S)

6, rue de l'Église. (0)1.64.38.83.20.

The old house is on the roadside, with rooms over the large entrance gates. Excellent locked parking would suit people going south with camping gear with no need to off-load.

Mme Valery has two simply-furnished rooms with windows overlooking the garden, one has a shower and wash basin (but the loo is downstairs), the other has a private shower and loo on the landing.

PARIS (ILE de FRANCE)

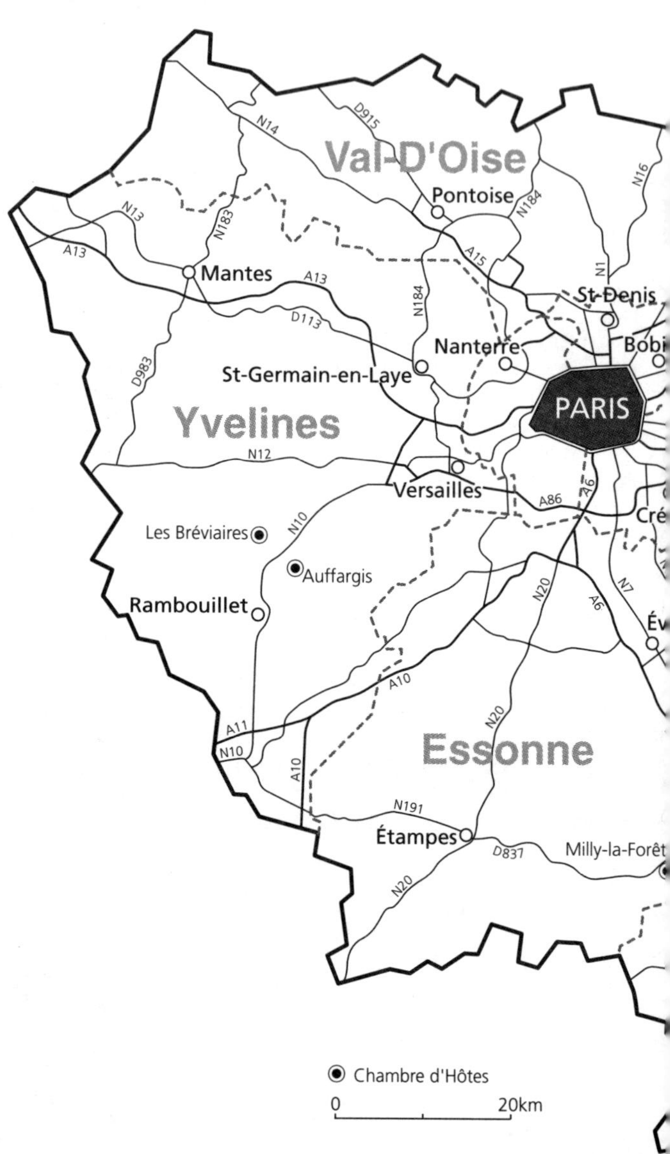

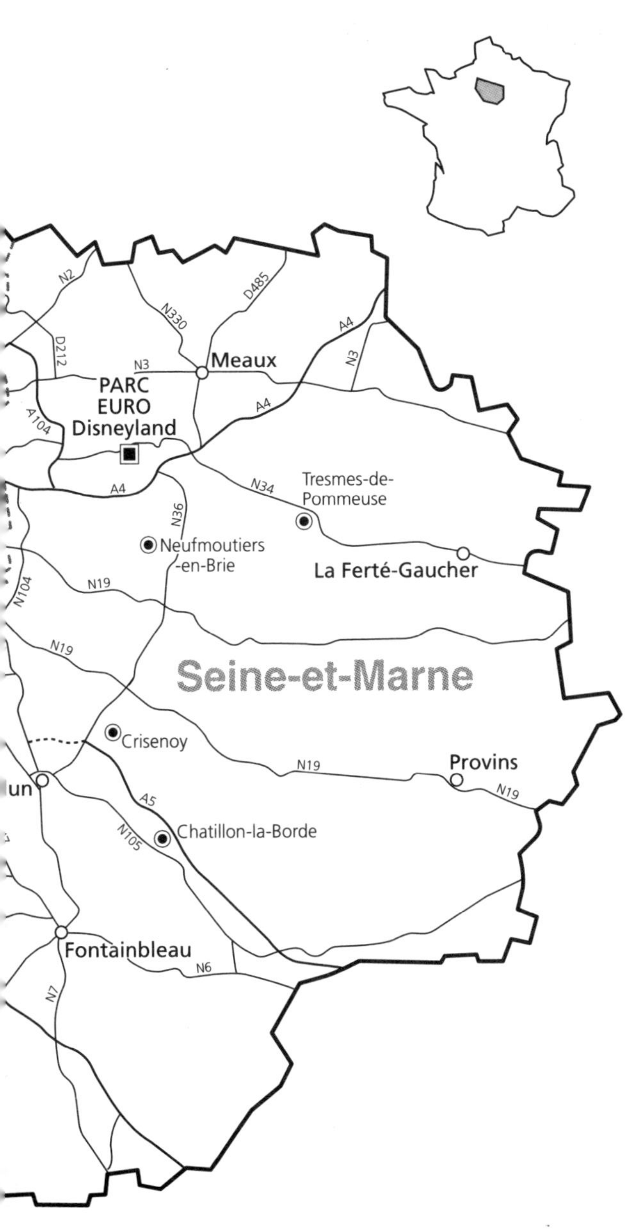
N2
D485
N330
A4
D212
N3
Meaux
N3
PARC
EURO
Disneyland
A104
A4
A4
N34
Tresmes-de-
Pommeuse
N36
Neufmoutiers
-en-Brie
La Ferté-Gaucher
N104
N19
N19
Seine-et-Marne
Crisenoy
N19
Provins
N19
un
A5
N105
Chatillon-la-Borde
Fontainbleau
N6
N7

230f. A third suite of rooms across the garden has a sunny terrace with access to a large lawn. There are two bedrooms, single beds or double, sharing a shower room and a salon where there is a possibility of an extra double bed - 460f for four, reducing to 400f for more than three nights.

Friendly young Madame Valery will give you a good breakfast in her dining room, or bring it to the salon for those in the suite. A good choice for visiting Disneyland or overnighting near Paris.

No evening meals but a restaurant is within easy walking distance.

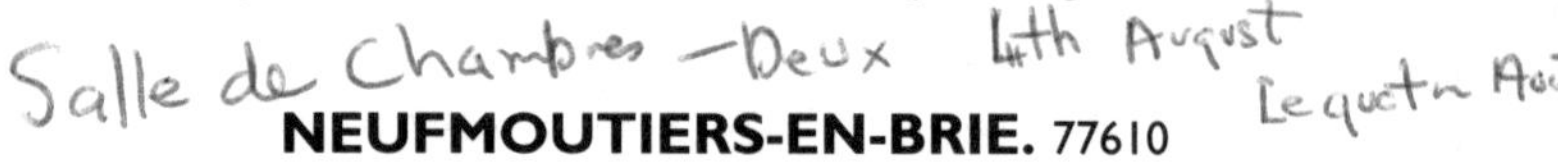

NEUFMOUTIERS-EN-BRIE. 77610

30km N of Mélun. Only 12km south of EuroDisney, an easy drive along country roads. From Mélun take the N36 north for approx 29km, then turn left at the sign to Neufmoutiers-en-Brie, or from the A4 take exit 13 to Villeneuve-le-Comte, in Villeneuve take the D96 to Neufmoutiers and follow chambres d'hôtes signs in the village.

NEW M. & Mme Galpin. Ferme-de-Bellevue (S)

01.64.07.11.05. fax: 01.64.07.19.27.

Once an isolated *Briarde maison-de-maître*, this 19th-century mansion has unfortunately been crept up on from the rear by an expanding new village. However the house still overlooks a large garden and surrounding fields, so you can pretend the village isn't there.

When I visited the whole place appeared to be taken over by a large christening party which looked like lasting until the sun went down. With difficulty I located M. Galpin in his own house and he was *désolé* he couldn't show me the rooms, so reports would be particularly welcome. I'm assured there are five comfortable rooms in a separate wing, particularly suitable for families as, four of the five have a double and two single beds and the other has four singles - all with modern shower rooms and TV - 245f for two, 90f for an extra bed.

It is one of the few chambres d'hôtes in the region offering evening meals - 95f, drinks not included.

There is a sitting room, a play area for children and bikes may be hired, useful in this flat countryside. Your hosts, on request, will guide and even chauffeur you to all the well known sites in the area - Versailles, Fontainebleau etc. A booking deposit of 25% of the price is requested in Euro-Cheque or travellers' cheques.

TRESMES-DE-POMME

50km E of Paris. 19km SE of Meaux. 15km SE o seven hamlets in the Commune de Pommeuse, an are of Brie cheese. From the N4 south of Meaux take the 10km turn right on to the D25 nearly opposite an air Tresmes. Opposite the school at a flashing white light tu street and the last house on the right belongs to:

NEW **➤ M. Jacky & Mme Annie Thomas**
Le Cottage du Martin Pècheur (M)
1, rue des Iris. Tel & fax: (0)1.64.20.00.98.

Charmingly situated, this renovated old house has lawns down to the bank of the river Grand-Morin. Ample gravelled parking with gates locked at night.

Though right in the centre of the village, with two guest rooms overlooking the road, it is still very quiet at night. Thick carpets help. Two other rooms, one for a family of five, face the garden. All are prettily and comfortably decorated, have TV and varying sizes of en suite shower rooms - 250f for two.

Vivacious Mme Thomas goes out of her way to accommodate her guests. She speaks little English although she has acquired two English sons-in-law and her small grandchildren are bilingual. Drinks on arrival, and loungers in the garden by the river are just right to complement a hard day's sightseeing.

A copious breakfast will set you up for a day at Disneyland or a trip to Paris. Leave the car and walk over to the station across the bridge and take the train. M. Thomas, who works in Paris for the railway, will readily advise.

No evening meal, but a café/restaurant in the village and many more in Coulommiers. Arrowed for situation, comfort and *accueil.*

YVELINES

AUFFARGIS. 78610

10km NE of Rambouillet.West of Paris, handy for visiting Versailles. From the N10 (Rambouillet-Versailles) take the exit to Le Perray-en-Yvelines, then the D61 to Saint-Benoist, a quiet dormitory village. The chambres d'hôtes is on the right as you enter the village.

Mme Lorber (S)

, rue de la Croix Picard. (0)1.34.85.80.99. fax: (0)1.34.94.98.14.

modern house has locked arking and a large garden at the back which guests are welcome to use. Friendly Mme Lorber has two comfortable guest rooms, a double with bathroom - 280f - another with a shower - 260f which can be linked as a suite of two rooms sharing facilities - 400f. Breakfast is in the garden in summer or in her kitchen if too many for the little alcove outside the rooms.

No evening meals but plenty of restaurants in Le Perray-en-Yvelines, mentioned above.

A pleasant quiet stop for visiting Versailles or the Abbaye-de-Cernay at Auffargis.

LES BREVIAIRES. 78610

40km W of Paris. Only about 20km SW of Versailles, where the most famous palace of the French Kings was built by Louis XIV.

From the N10 take the Auffargis/Les Mesnuls exit and head northwards on the N191 towards Les Mesnuls. In about 2km you will see the D60 to Les Bréviaires left. Ignore this and take the next turn right in about 300m just after a residence.

NEW Mme Cornelius. Domaine de la Grange du Bois (L)

(0)1.34.86.15.66.

On this estate, well away from main roads, where horses are bred for trotting, the old stone house has been restored with great taste, and now accommodates guests in two very pleasant rooms. One on the ground floor with twin beds with shower and dressing room has a lawned terrace - 480f.

On the first floor a sunny room overlooks the swimming pool from a pleasant private terrace. An L shaped salon has a king-sized bed with all the trimmings, press buttons to raise either end, a telephone which can also communicate with the other room (often used for older children), delicately embroidered sheets and a vast duvet. There is a marble fireplace with log fire (extra logs outside the door) and generous central heating. Sink into the thick carpets throughout. Pale green walls lined with soft velvet material contrast with the darker leather couch. A wood-panelled dressing room and large shower room adjoin, with a pretty mosaic shower and wash basin, and all the little extras from towelling gowns to razors supplied - 580f for two includes breakfast, worth the price, though bath lovers might not think so.

Mme Cornelius trots up with a very good breakfast whatever time you wish. No evening meals but a bar/restaurant nearby (La Venerie) or more up-market in Les Bréviaires.

A luxury place for honeymoons or to complement a visit to Versailles.

ESSONE

MILLY-LA-FORÊT. 91490

19km W of Fontainebleau.This small town proves to be more interesting than appears when first visiting it. Roman remains have been found, and the covered market in the centre dates back to the 15th-century. The town has been noted for the production of medicinal herbs, grown in the surrounding forests, since the 12th-century.

From Milly-la-Forêt take the D837 and turn off on the D1, Route de Gironville. The farm is on your right in 3km.

NEW M. & Mme Desforges. Ferme de la Grange Rouge (M)
(0)1.64.98.94.21. fax: (0)1.64.98.99.91. Closed 15/12 to 30/1.

This lone cereal farm beside the main road is easy to find. It has a large couryard surrounded by buildings. The neatly furnished guest rooms are on the first floor of a separate building. There is a dining salon and five bedroom with smart new shower rooms. Beds vary from family carved bed-heads to wrought iron or modern divans, with a choice of singles and doubles - 250f - extra bed 60f. A nice straightforward sort of place but no great family contact. It is a busy farm and Mme Desforges has young children, but this is a reasonable price for this area south of Paris. No evening meals - restaurants in Milly-la-Forêt.

PICARDY

Départements: **Aisne**
Oise
Somme

Companion guide to the area - 'French Entrée 19 - The North of France'.

The battlefield of Europe bears many scars and memorials as lasting witness to its tribulations. Its rich and inoffensive farming land is where yeomen archers lined up, where horses were caparisoned for battle, where trenches were cut, where marching boots churned up the mud, where tanks rumbled, where treaties were signed, and where the victims of conflicts fell, body upon body. It's such a short drive and such a long time between Crecy and the Somme. But Picardy is not all negative sadness and monotonous plains.

There is no other region that can rival the Gothic churches and châteaux of the region. In villages, cities, crossroads throughout the *département* you can trace the development of Gothic art, from the very first pointed arch at Morienval to the final expression of the Flamboyant. The cathedrals of Senlis, Amiens, Beauvais, the abbeys of St Germer-der-Fly and St. Riquier are individual history lessons of the conception of religious architecture of the times. Some, like Amiens, are constructed with such industry that a young craftsman might live to see its completion; some, like St. Riquier, whose building was interrupted by war, and St. Germer, delayed by additions and reconstructions, explain, as no schoolteacher could, how fashions changed in the intervals.

The little-known area of Aisne receives few tourists, apart from those visiting the miracles of Laon and Soissons cathedrals. St. Quentin is a typical big provincial city, with attractive central square and unusual art galley. Vervins is completely different - ancient, fortified, self-contained, and hinting at the Ardennes next door.

In the south, less than 50km from Paris in the departement of Oise, lies the incomparable Chantilly, whose château and stables, together with the neighbouring Senlis, alone would merit an excursion to this region.

For those who have already explored the Pas-de-Calais and are looking for a worthwhile extension to their experience of the accessible North of France, I would suggest a drive down to the Somme. The capital, Amiens, well repays a visit; look beyond its wartime devastion to the remarkable restoration in the St. Leu area, take a cruise on the waterways and allow plenty of time for the stunning cathedral. The battlefields of course are an abiding interest and sobering jolt. The lively port of St Valery, with good market, superb walks and lots of fishing activity, would make a good cheerful contrast.

AISNE

BERZY-LE-SEC. 02200

5km S of Soissons. The house is 2km S of Berzy, so head for Léchelle, via N2, and turn left on D172, and left again on D177. House is signed at entrance to village.

Mme Nicole Maurice. Ferme de Léchelle (M)

(0)3.23.74.83.29. In winter by reservation only.

A pretty country house, white shuttered, creeper-clad, courtyard-fronted. The furniture is family antiques; the floors are polished wood. Bedrooms are mostly decorated with pretty Laura Ashley designs, but there is one more modern with sloping pine ceiling and dormer window. Some have private shower rooms, three share one between them in a suite, and there is a single room at 180f with no private facilities. Otherwise they cost 230/250f.

Breakfasts are especially good, served on pretty pink china and including extras like cereals and yoghurt. They are served on a big pine table by the open fire in winter. Chic Mme Maurice (who talks so volubly that I can only catch half of what she says) will sometimes provide an evening meal (on reservation) for 100f, but I sensed that this is offered somewhat reluctantly.

CHIGNY. 02120 GUISE

12km W of Etréaupont by the D31 and D26. Surrounded by fields and approached by narrow winding lanes, there is an atmosphere of deep, deep repose about Chigny. Presumably there are births, marriages and deaths in the village, but it is hard to imagine its somnolence disturbed by any great passion. Its red-brick flower-

PICARDY

Le Crotoy
St-Riquier
Abbeville
Vauchelles-les-Quesnoy
Erondelle
Somme
Amiens
Creuse
Oise
Beauvais
Compièg
Chantilly
Senlis
Po
N1
D924
N25
D925
A28
N28
D1015
D901
N29
D929
D934
D915B
D916
N17
A1
N31
D981
N16
D200
D915
N330
Chambre d'Hôtes
0
20km

Saint-Quentin
Chigny
Aisne
Laon
Vic-sur-Aisne
Soissons
Berzy-le-Sec
Villers-Agron
N43
N2
N29
N44
A26
D1
D337
D966
N31
A4
N3

bestrewn cottages are typical of the Thiérache; some of them date from past centuries, many of them were built just after the First World War.

➤ **Mlle Françoise Piette** (M)

6/7 Place des Marronniers. (0)3.23.60.22.04.

One of the most successful recommendations in FE7. The file is full of letters approving. This is a small red-brick 1765 Thiérache farmhouse, white doors and shutters, near the village hall, in a chestnut-shaded square - les Marronniers. The sisters Piette live in the modern white-washed house next door. They have converted the upstairs of the old farmhouse, once a granary, still with exposed beams and rafters and steps up and down, into five bedrooms, all beautifully decorated and furnished with antiques. One of the beds has a lovely old white bed-cover, a family hand-me-down.

The garden is obviously the subject of tender loving care. It positively burgeons with healthy plants, and the revelation that the Mesdemoiselles are vegetarians comes as no surprise, having seen the size and content of their *potager*.

The price for two people is 270f; dinner is 90f and requires prior warning. Specialities include *galette végétarienne*, *chou farci*, *flamiche poireau* and *terrine de céreales*, all according to the season naturally.

Arrowed for comfort, good food (especially for the usually deprived vegetarians) and good value.

VIC-SUR-AISNE. 02290

16km W of Soissons by N31. A pretty village, well situated for visits to the forest of Laigue, picnics on the river Aisne and the A1 autoroute.

M. et Mme Martner. Domaine des Jeannes (M)

rue Dubarrie. Tel & fax: (0)3.23.55.57.33.

Not easy to find, but in fact it is tucked away a few minutes from the centre. Follow the narrow rue Dubarrie off the main square beside a greengrocer and the gates of the Domaine are on the right.

It's an imposing 17th-century house, built on a prime site high above the river, with lawns rolling down to the water's edge.

The most impressive room in this unpretentious establishment, well run by M. and Mme Martner, is the dining room, with massive carved fireplace and tall windows making the most of the view. Mme Martner enjoys cooking and her evening meals are served at well laid tables, with high quality linen and glass (good value at 95f).

All the five bedrooms have views of the river and grounds, and although simple in decor and furnishings, they do all have private bathrooms - 320/370f, depending on season. Added bonuses are a swimming pool and tennis court. Credit cards accepted.

Another opportunity when you enter the village over the river Aisne from the N31 you will find this house on the left.

NEW **M. & Mme Henry. L'Orchidée** (S)
2bis. Avenue de la Gare. (0)3.23.55.32.76.

First impressions of this house behind railings are not impressive, as the rather dilapidated red-brick house adjoining it detracts from it; but inside the locked gates on the gravelled parking the prospects are much better. Once probably the stables of the large house alongside, two wings at right angles have been converted by the Henrys. The colourful salon and dining room with pretty flower friezes leads to five rooms on the first floor. All nicely beamed in one wing are two family rooms accommodating up to five, with double bed and bunks overlooking the courtyard. Double glazing takes care of the main road's proximity. The other three rooms for two, with velux windows, overlook the quiet back garden. All have excellent modern showers and loos en suite and are carpeted and well furnished. There is a small kitchen for picnics and snacks. The evening meal is 75f, a carafe of wine included. Rooms only 210f, 60f for an extra bed.

Lively Madame speaks fluent English and there is a library of books in English and French. Altogether a much nicer chambres d'hôtes than I expected from looking at the outside. A very warm terrace at the back overlooks a lawned garden, albeit with a factory building on the skyline.

You can book ahead with confidence here. If you are the only guests having an evening meal, your hosts will join you.

VILLERS-AGRON. 02130

18km SE of Fère-en-Tardenois on the D2. Just north of the A4 autoroute and only 23km SW of Reims but light years away in character. This is deep, deep farming country.

➤ Ferme du Château (M)

(0)3.23.71.60.67. fax: (0)3.23.69.36.54.

If Xavier Ferry were not still an active *agriculteur* and his wife Christine an even more active mother of three hyperactive children, one would be tempted to call this an hotel, so well equipped are the rooms, so well organised the comfort of the guests. But the sandpit on the terrace (among lots of expensive chairs and recliners), the child's desk, the homework on the piano, the board games on the table, all make it a home not a hotel and this is what chambres d'hôtes are all about.

That said, this is a quite exceptional representative of the genre. The old farmhouse starts off with two enormous advantages - a lovely stone building, a slope down to the river, a delightful setting - and Christine and Xavier have skilfully capitalised. Their four spacious rooms are furnished with style; all have colourful chintzes, and luxury bathrooms with fittings probably more refined than yours or mine back home. The salon is huge - raftered, log fire, piano - the dining room extremely elegant.

Christine's cooking is way above average for a farmer's wife. 165f is well spent on her evening meal. As is 240/300f for any one of the rooms, all of which have delightful rural aspects. There is even a golf course for the pampered guests.

There is one snag. After a visit *chez* Ferry you will be spoilt for any other b. and b. Arrowed for excellence.

OISE

CHANTILLY. 60500

40km N of Paris. 10km SW of Senlis. Make for the railway station and the rue Victor Hugo runs parallel behind the station. If arriving by train there is an exit on this side, across the road from the chambres d'hôtes.

NEW **M. & Mme Lokmer** (M)

30c rue Victor Hugo. Tel & fax: (0)3.44.57.63.91.

This little studio in a peaceful garden is superbly situated for visiting Paris. Park your car safely behind locked gates and take the train. Half an hour to the Gard du Nord, and 1hour 20min. to Eurodisney.

Just one cosy room, twin beds, television, a neat little kitchen corner with a microwave and a shower room, all so compact with a small terrace and garden. Entry is independent from the main house. Electric heating ensures all year round occupation. Your hosts set you up for the day with a copious breakfast in their own dining room across the garden, or you can have it delivered to your room. Both the Lokmers speak English and French and can be a great help to you planning a trip to Paris, or around Chantilly. Supermarkets are a few steps away or there are plenty of restaurants in the vicinity.

Active Mme Lokmer is English and works part-time at Charles de Gaulle airport, but Monsieur, also bilingual, is always there to welcome you and give advice. Studio 350f for two, 280f for one includes breakfast and all electricity. Extra bed possible for short-stays, 80f but not a lot of room for it.

PONTPOINT. 60700

14km N of Senlis by N17, then right at St. Maxence on to D123. The neat little village of Pontpoint is hidden away, heavily disguised behind the main road. Turn left after the sign to the Stade into rue du Gaudin and the house is on the right.

An area with too many attractions to pack into a single twenty-four hours. Stay several days to visit the enchanting old town of Senlis, to see the château, gardens and stables at Chantilly, the abbey of Chaalis, the forests of Compiègne, Halatte and Chantilly. In the village itself are numerous lakes, with the possibility of sailing, fishing, windsurfing and canoeing. Good picnicking. Restaurants, gastronomic and simple, abound. And Paris is a mere 30 minutes away by train, so leave the car safely parked for a day and hit the capital the easy way. It will be a pleasure to return to:

➤ Chez Flochmoan (M)

rue du Gaudin. (0)3.44.70.03.98. and (0)3.44.72.52.03.

Despondently we learned from Madame in a chambres d'hôtes south of Senlis that, although it was a Monday night and we had arrived early, all her rooms were taken. Sceptically we listened to her suggestion that a friend of hers might be able to accommodate us, and wearily we drove back into Senlis and up to Pontpoint.

One look at the charming cottage that was to be our home for the night (we stayed longer) was enough for the spirits to rise. The welcome from the lovely Flochmoans completed the restoration of *joie de vivre*. The *joie* here is a completely independent cottage, which the hosts have converted over a period of seven hard years from an old barn. We didn't even cotton on that this was all for us - a huge living room, luxury kitchen (sauna leading off) two spacious double bedrooms, two large bathrooms, (showers, alas, but good ones) our own garden, two terraces. For 290f.

There were even our own cherry tomato plants from which M. Flochmoan encouraged us to pick the little red globes to eat with our much-needed *apéritif*, which was a welcoming bottle of wine left in the fridge. 'Can I write that you do this for all your guests?' I asked as the Flochmoans invited us to drink on their terrace, catching the last of the evening sun. 'Only the sympathetic ones, but the wine is there for everyone.' So you will know how you are rated.

Their 300-year-old cottage is almost a mirror image of the restored barn. In term-time both the Flochmoans work at the college in Senlis, he as a P.E. instructor, she in administration, but of course their long holidays correspond with the busiest tourist seasons and at other times they are home early enough to welcome their guests. He is a mine of information about the region and endlessly helpful and she is a quiet, supportive back-up. They are justifiably proud of what they have achieved, much by their own labour - three separate houses (one for their grown up children).

Prices will be kept at this level for another year to encourage new customers and then - who knows? Better book that ferry now.

SAINT JEAN AUX BOIS. 60350

9km S of Compiègne. Quite close to the ridiculously pretty château at Pierrefonds, right in the middle of the Forêt-de-Compiègne, this little village has the quiet opulence of commuter villages near Paris, where beautifully restored old houses hide behind high walls.

NEW **Mme Langevin** (M)

2 rue du Parquet. (0)3.44.42.84.48.

On a corner of the road at the entrance to the village this rambling old house has a lovely walled garden, terraced down to a small round swimming pool. There is parking for two cars behind locked gates.

The guest rooms are well modernised in a restored barn across the garden. Two for a couple on the ground floor have independent entry with smart new shower rooms, simply furnished - 300f. Up an independent flight of stairs are two rooms for a family, one with double bed has a wash basin, the loo is shared on the landing; the other with three singles has shower and wash basin. Usually let together for a family - 500f; but they can be let individually for 300f. Breakfast is in a room in the main house where the fireplace has a barbecue for guests who may also use the kitchen area.

No evening meals but a choice of two restaurants within easy walking distance, or the option of self catering.

Madame is away working in Paris most of the time; but a charming young lady stands in for her.

VARANVAL. 60880 JAUX

6km W of Compiègne. This peaceful little hamlet is hidden in the country, but within easy reach of the Wagon-des-Lits the other side of Compiègne where the Armistice was signed in 1918. A reconstruction of the carriage is now on the same spot in the Bois-de-Compiègne. The original was burnt by the Germans during the last war.

Leave the A1 at sortie 10 (Beauvais/Compiègne) and take the N31 towards Compiègne for 4km. Turn right on to an un-numbered road signed Varanval, bearing right at the first junction and you will come to La Gaxottière on your right in about 2km.

NEW Mlle Gaxotte. La Gaxottière (M)

363 rue du Champ du Mont. Tel & fax: (0)3.44.83.22.41.

Huge barns surround this old farmhouse, hiding it from the road. Locked parking behind giant wooden doors lead to a delightful small garden completely walled in by the two houses. The guest rooms, which have a sunny terrace, and a *gîte* are in one and Françoise Gaxotte (a semi-retired pharmacist who real enjoys her guests) lives in the other. Staying here is like returning to an old friend's house, as you share a cup of tea on arrival and she quietly continues with her petit-point. Two friendly dogs who guard the garden will accept you just as easily. A most relaxed place to stay.

The two guest rooms have huge fireplaces, with fires when required, and old

family furniture, which includes comfortable armchairs, and curiosities collected on Françoise's many travels. A double-bedded room, which has a large bathroom with bath and bidet, shares a loo with the twin-bedded room between their respective bathrooms. The latter, with a shower - 300f.

The *gîte* alongside, often used as a chambres d'hôtes when rooms are full, has the added advantage of a kitchen and salon for the same price as the other rooms.

Françoise prefers you to book ahead, so don't turn up on spec. No evening meals; but 'La Maison du Gourmet' in Meux is well worth the short drive.

SOMME

CREUSE. 80480

13km SW of Amiens. The village of Creuse is well placed for visiting Amiens, the ancient and historic capital of Picardy, home of the largest, most magnificent Gothic cathedral in France. Set in a unique water landscape, it must be on every Northern France itinerary. It does have its traffic problems and a maze of one way streets, so obey the Fenn No 1 city rule which is to head for the spire of the cathedral and dump the car as soon as possible. From here everything of interest is within walking distance. The newly restored area of St. Leu is now a delightful enclave of bars, restaurants and old houses, just behind the canal and always within sight of the glorious spire. Another good reason for a visit is to take a trip around the watery wonderland of the *hortillonges*, an hour's meander in a high-prowed punt that will give you a duck's eye view of the squares of gardens criss-crossed with mini-canals, all irrigated by the rivers Somme and Avre. Allow plenty of time to visit the magical cathedral, if possible early or late when the tourist crowds have gone. Good shopping and restaurants are a cheer up for a wet day.

Leave Amiens by the N29 then left on to D162. Signposted from Creuse.

➤ **Chez Mme Lemaître** (M)

26 rue Principale (0)3.22.38.91.50.

As you turn in from the road under the archway you are likely to be greeted by a selection of residents. Two geese were being very protective about their territory, decorative bantams were pecking about and a shaggy dog lay soaking up the sun. More decorative fowl strutted on the lawns of the delightful garden, but although the 200-year-old building, whitewashed, dark beamed and brown shuttered, was indeed once a working *fermette* it has now been converted into an elegant and highly attractive home, with the stable block serving as chambres d'hôtes accommodation.

Doors lie open, white, wrought-iron chairs dot the lawn and there is a charming feeling of outdoor living, under the shady trees, on the well-kept grass. Chic, blonde Mme Lemaître has decorated the four rooms with style, but always kept the rustic character. She loves white so a light and airy atmosphere predominates, helped by long french windows and in one room by a white canopy over the bed - 300/350f with bath, same price for another room with shower and a small kitchenette.

I was not surprised to learn that Mme Lemaître is a painter - her clever sense of decoration is evident again in her own house, where breakfast is served in winter by a huge log fire. A lovely place to stay, highly recommended.

LE CROTOY. 80550

19km NW of Abbeville. On the Baie-de-Somme opposite Saint-Valéry-sur-Somme On the north bank of the magnificent Somme estuary, but claiming to have the only south-facing beach in the north of France. This may well be and it's a very fine beach too, especially when the tide recedes, but the decidedly bracing air that always seems to be whipping up the waves makes one think of Skegness rather than the Mediterranean. The town comes to life at weekends, when the tourists come to walk along the harbour, enjoy the beach and consume bowlfuls of mussels from the range of restaurants that specialise in sea food.

NEW M. & Mme Weyl. Villa la Mouclade (M)

Quai Jules Noiret. (0)3.22.27.09.44.

You will be assured of sea breezes here as this one is right on the promenade, a few steps away from the beach. Exuberant Mme Weyl has decorated rooms vibrantly. Black matt paint and mirrors predominate. The lounge on the ground floor has views over the bay but also an alcove which opens on to a tiny courtyard behind. Above is the dining room, where mirrors reflect the sea whichever side of the table you sit. The five guest rooms up various staircases are all differently decorated, each with a sea view. There is a family room on the top floor, another, which has a large garden mural, makes you feel you are literally sleeping in the garden, a third has an extra single room for a child, plentifully furnished with dolls. All have shower rooms and most have baths, *ciel-de-lits*, family heirlooms, knick-knacks collected over the years - they are all there. Rooms 350f for two.

The cellar has been adapted as a music room with white grand piano and vast leather couches, where you can enjoy an *apéritif* listening to music. Evening meals had been temporarily abandoned when I visited, as Madame had broken her leg; but I am assured of Mme Weyl's reputation as a cook, and meals will be resumed as soon as she is fit in 1998. A new kitchen off the dining room will help. Meanwhile no problem as there are restaurants in the town, most specialising in sea food. Nice M. Weyl quietly and efficiently serves breakfast whenever guests require it. No fixed time for breakfast here. They like their guests to feel relaxed.

Parking is allowed on the road just outside the house.

ERONDELLE. 80580 PONT-RÉMY

12km SE of Abbeville. Not easy to locate on a dark and dirty night and not in Erondelle at all, so play safe and head for Pont-Rémy (on the D12 from Abbeville), cross the river towards Liercourt, then take the D13 towards Huppy, from which the Manoir is signed. The countryside around is truly lovely - deeply forested, hilly enough for good views down the valley of the Somme

➤ **Mme Helene Thaon d'Arnold. Manoir de la Renardière** (M-L)

(0)3.22.27.13.00. fax: (0)3.22.27.13.12. Closed: mid Jan-mid Feb.

The quirky Gothic house set at the end of a long lime alley has come a long way (ever onwards and upwards) since I wrote about it some eleven years ago. What was a somewhat ramshackle eccentricity has now become a romantic folly of enormous charm. Its turrets, towers, balconies in the fashion dubbed by the French *le style Anglais* are newly painted and scrubbed, the garden slopes have been cleared to reveal a stunning view of the Somme lakes, and expensive white tables and chairs are set out on terrace and grass for summer relaxation in perfect serenity. 400/500f for two persons

Mme Thaon, who speaks near-perfect English, is a very unusual, exceptionally hard-working hostess. She has decorated the interior with light bright colours, banishing Victorian gloom. The dining room is particularly charming - white and green, with high-backed chairs covered, unusually but successfully, in striped mattress ticking.

Our bedroom - the Garden Room - was the smallest (you have to book early to get the best) decidedly *bijou*, but with every necessity in its place - plenty of towels, good lights, midget bath and shower, Sanderson wallpaper, 400f. Bigger rooms with larger bathrooms, open fire, white monogrammed pillow-cases and balconies cost 450-

500f (350f midweek). A two nights' stay is the minimum is high season.

But it is the atmosphere that makes La Renardière so special. There is absolutely no feeling of this being a purely commercial enterprise. Mme Thaon gives freely of her time and experience, relishing her guests' company. She was a literature teacher until recently and knows the area, its inhabitants and attractions inside out. Her formal candlelit dinners on Saturdays (other days on request) are much in demand. She specialises in generous seafood platters, but her cooking is way more sophisticated then that normally encountered in chambres d'hôtes - 250f for four courses inclusive of *apéritif* and plenty of good wine and conversation. Elegance may be the word that springs to mind about the whole enterprise, but not so elegant that guests are disinclined to march into the kitchen and help carry out the croissants or chat there with Madame. With an English painter friend and Jack-of-all-trades, John, she also runs her 'pub' in a cottage in the grounds, where simpler meals are available at 100f. And if, as would be a very good idea, you stay for several days, there would be a superb alternative - the little restaurant at the bottom of the hill, *Le Temps Jadis*, which I consider to be one of the best discoveries of this particular tour.

Classical music lovers should arrange to be there on the third Saturday in the month, when Madame arranges a concert in the elegant salon; tours of *antiquaires* and especially interesting churches are also organised. In fact - you name it and the lovely Mme Thaon will make sure your wish comes true.

ST. RIQUIER. 80135

9km E of Abbeville by D925. Just a square full of plane trees, dominated by the abbey, impressive and strikingly beautiful - the centre of what is now a small town, but was once, eleven centuries ago, one of the most formidable strongholds in Picardy. Razed, rebuilt, razed, rebuilt, it never regained its former importance. Today's abbey is mostly 17th-century, with only traces of its 13th-century origins. The local white stone has been delicately wrought into icicles of flowers and leaves and animals. Inside, don't miss the statues and glorious staircase. The *Centre Culturel*, in the monk's refectory and upstairs in their cells, is one of the best of regional museums.

Chez Mme Decayeux (M)

7 rue du Beffroi. (0)3.22.28.93.08. fax: (0)3.22.28.93.10

Once a *Relais de Poste*, now a cereal/dairy farm of 40 hectares, deceptively hidden behind the house. Couldn't be more central, near the belfry, opposite the abbey, a nice old 18th-century house, now offering five bedrooms, colour coded, with bathroom apiece, *Jonquille* has a double bed, *Marguerite* is smaller again with a double bed, *Rose* has twins, *Lavande* is a single and *La Primavère* has one double and two singles - 300/350f, plus 70f for each extra bed.

Evening meal 100f including wine and *apéritif*, is good value, and so is the excellent breakfast included in the price.

There is a pleasant *salle de séjour* with big, open fire, and TV everywhere - in the salon and in each bedroom. You can park the car in the locked, central courtyard at night so there is no need to off-load.

VAUCHELLES-LES-QUESNOY. 80132

3km E of Abbeville. From Abbeville take the D925 (SP. St. Riquier). In 1km turn right on the D153. In the village, this chambres d'hôtes beside the church is well-signed, behind locked gates; your car is very safe.

NEW **Mme Crépelle** (M)

Place de l'Église. Tel & fax: (0)3.22.24.18.17.

This attractive long white house with dark-green shutters dates back to the 17th century. Madame is a sculptor and a painter. She professes not to be, but her charming paintings of birds on cupboard doors rather belies this. The garden could be an English country garden, with paths leading to wooded areas which would delight children.

Steep stairs from the kitchen lead up to well furnished rooms, with many family heirlooms. A double room has a single room attached - 250f for two, 350f for three; another suite of three adjoining rooms share a bathroom and separate shower room, but have plentiful wash-basins. This would accommodate a family party of six or seven, doubles, singles, doubles, singles - I lost count, 250f for two, extra beds 100f. One room off the ground floor has separate shower and two wash-basins. 300f. Breakfast is in a pleasant *jardin d'hiver*. No evening meal, but a restaurant 1km away.

Poitou-Charentes

Départements: **Charente** **Charente-Maritime**
Deux-Sèvres **Vienne**

South of the Loire, north of Bordeaux, this western region of France stretches from the Atlantic to the Limousin. Poitou-Charentes is divided into four *départements*; in the north Deux-Sèvres and Vienne lie side-by-side, as do Charente and Charente Maritime further south, the latter on the Atlantic coast.

Deux-Sèvres is so called because there are two river Sèvres flowing through the department, the Sèvre Nantaise heading for the Loire at Nantes on its way to the Atlantic at St. Nazaire in the north, and the Sèvre Niortaise in the south, which has given birth to the delightful little canals of the Marais Poitevin west of Niort. This area is usually attributed to the Vendée, but some of the prettiest parts actually lie in Deux Sèvres. Do visit these quiet waterways and small villages; you will be amazed at what you have been missing. Niort, the *préfecture*, has a large central parking area in the Place de la Brèche, and a colourful indoor market. Only on Saturdays when the large market takes up the main square is parking a problem.

Vienne again takes its name from the river, one of the prettiest in France. The large town of Poitiers is the *préfecture*, once the home of the English King Henry II and his wife, Eleanor of Aquitaine. Steeped in history and historic buildings, the town is well worth visiting. A few kilometres north to Jaunay Clan (exit 18 off the A10) is the *Futuroscope*, a large theme park, which is a must for all visitors passing this way. It comprises a wonderful exhibition of cinemas and commerce of the future with ample entertainment for children (see Avanton-Martigny p.301)

Travel down to **Charente,** named after another river, a lovely, tranquil, country area where the old town of Angoulême rules the *département* - but the really famous name here is Cognac, where all the grapes grown in the warm countryside are turned into brandy. Such names as Hine, Courvoisier and Rémy Martin flash by as you drive along (see Lignières-Sonneville). Make sure you taste the *aperitif* of the region, *Pineau*, made from grape juice and brandy.

La Rochelle is the busy port of the **Charente-Maritime** where the river Charente finally finds its way to the sea. A very attractive town with the fortress and the harbour always coming into view as you wander through the main streets. This is a strong Protestant region and many Huguenot churches are still here. A wonderful indoor market every day sells the fruit and vegetables of the countryside as well

POITOU-CHARENTES
N149
Deux-
Sèvre
Parthen
D949
Champdeniers
Germond-
Rouvres
Niort
Coulon
Ile de Ré
N137
N11
Vallans
La Rochelle
Surgères
N137
D939
A10
N150
D939
Fouras
D911
Charente-
Maritime
Rochefort
Ile d'Oléron
N137
St-Sornin
St-Savinien-sur-Charent
D728
Saintes
D733
N150
Royan
D730
A10
N137
Mirambeau
Chambre d'Hôtes
0
20km
Pouill

Mouterre-Silly
N147
N10
A10
Vouneuil-
sur-Vienne
Bonneuil-Matours
Avanton
N149
Poitiers
N151
A10
N11
N147
La Trimouille
Vienne
teuil
N10
D948
D948
-Vaussais
D951
D951
D948
Fontenille
Luxé
Charente
N141
N10
N141
D939
41
Angoulême
ères-
eville
N10
Aignes-et-Puypéroux
D939
bezieux

as the *produits de la mer.*

From here you take the toll bridge to the attractive island of Ile de Ré where the tiny ports are bursting with small craft in season and the tall lighthouse towers over the island.

Further south visit the old Roman town of *Saintes* where the large Arc de Triomphe still stands by the river side and remains of old Roman baths are just outside the town. Visit the pottery at La Chapelle-des-Pots, just north of Saintes, where you will find many old French designs on reproduction pottery, the only place that makes the two-handled Charentais serving dish used in the farms in the last century.

CHARENTE

AIGNES-ET-PUYPEROUX. 16190

24km S of Angoulême. A very useful stop on the way to the Dordogne. About 20km south is the interesting little village of Aubeterre, where a subterranean church has been discovered.

The village is on the D674. 3km north of Montmoreau, the chambres d'hôtes is signed on the left.

NEW **Mme Le Roy. Chez Jambon** (S)
(0)5.45.60.20.32.

Right in the country with extensive views, three rooms have entrances from the sunny covered terrace, each having private facilities. 200f, extra folding beds available 50f. There is also a kitchenette with fridge for guests. Evening meals are offered for 70f, wine *compris*.

English guests staying here have recommended this one, I have yet to visit, as it came in too late, but think I might be missing something good. Let me know if I am, if you get there first.

FONTENILLE. 16230

27kms N of Angoulême. Handy for Cognac, Angoulême and Saintes. Leave the N10, going south, by the Mansle exit and before Mansle turn right on to the D61 to Goué and you will find signs to the chambres d'hôtes in the tiny hamlet of Les Morices. Not marked on the Michelin. Ask if you get lost.

NEW **Mr. & Mrs. Jolley. Les Dès** (S)

Les Morices, Fontenille, Mansle. (0)5.45.20.39.72.

This pleasantly modernised dwelling has a corner situation facing south, overlooking a lawned shady garden and fields beyond, with the added attraction of a small swimming pool tucked away beside the house.

When you walk in the door Brenda's collection of thimbles explains the name of the house. Two rooms have showers but share a loo, a family room, which sleeps four, also has a shower, but shared toilet. On the ground floor a double room is en suite. All rooms have excellent open views, are light and airy and prettily decorated. A bargain at 205/230f for two, 280f for four, if sharing a loo doesn't worry you. A warm welcome from both Brenda and Kit and excellent evening meals with good English desserts and wine included, are 65f if reserved. Ideal for those who don't enjoy struggling in French during their evening meal.

LIGNIERES-SONNEVILLE. 16130

21km S of Cognac. From Cognac take the D24 to Ségonzac, then the D1 to the cross-roads with the D699. Turn left here and the house is on your left.

M. Matignon has vast vineyards all around growing Ugny Blanc grapes and sells all his produce to Rémy Martin, just up the road. First the grapes are pressed on the premises then left to ferment for one month before being collected by the Remy Martin tanker as Grande Champagne wine for distillation. Most distilleries charge for visits but Mme Matignon will give you free vouchers for a visit to Remy Martin.

M. & Mme Matignon. Les Collinauds (S)

(0)5.45.80.51.23.

This huge three-storey house in the heart of the Grande Champagne region of Cognac is in very large walled gardens. Perhaps it is now a shadow of its former glory but still has plenty of charm, overlooking an extensive view of hilly vineyards and offering a peaceful retreat. The house, built in 1825, has housed fifteen generations of this family. Now the young owners are restoring it slowly. There is a super sunny grass terrace the length of the house with steps down to the lawns.

Three rooms for two, three or four, all have private bath/shower rooms but not all en suite. One has a *bâteau* bed, polished wooden floor, an old fireplace laid with logs and a marble washstand with basin and jug - which give it an authentic touch. The other two are carpeted. 210f for two, 240f for three and 300f for four. Evening meals are now on offer if reserved ahead, 60f. The dining room has an enormous Charentaise sideboard dwarfing the small round breakfast table. Look out to the garden and the hills beyond as you enjoy an excellent breakfast with orange juice, fresh croissants and baguettes.

In a converted coach-house is a nicely equipped kitchen for self catering. The Matignons have small children and welcome others, and there is an extensive enclosed garden to play in.

LUXÉ. 16230

28km N of Angoulême. Angoulême is near and well worth a visit, Cognac is a little further south-west and has a good shopping precinct; but if you like French pottery do visit the tiny village of La Chapelle-des-Pots just north-east of Saintes, where there is a factory and large showroom with an enormous range of products. English spoken.

From Mansle on the N10, south of Poitiers, take the D739 to Luxé Gare. Turn right to Luxé and you will find the Ferme des Vignauds the other side of the village.

➤ M. & Mme Richard. Les Vignauds (M)

Luxé-Bourg. (0)5.45.39.01.47.

One of the first chambres d'hôtes I ever stayed in and still going strong. Four luxurious rooms occupy the first floor of this beautifully restored farmhouse. There is a terrace and large swimming pool, with pool-side barbecue and kitchen facilities. Mme Richard is an excellent cook and really copious meals are taken with the family in her well-furnished dining room.

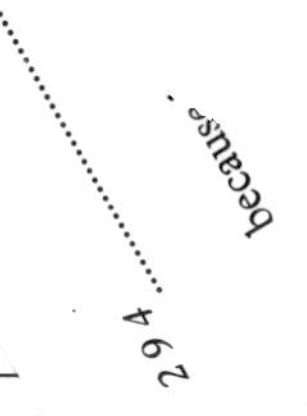

Double room 275f. Treble 310f. Evening meal 80f, sion 210f each.

An arrow for continued high standards.

CHARENTE-MARITIME

FOURAS. 17450

22km S of La Rochelle. Right on the coast, the peninsula at Fouras extends like a nose into the sea. I was pleasantly surprised with this select little seaside resort. No crowds in September. A wide tree-lined promenade leads to Fort Vauban, housing the tourist office. It was at the tiny harbour of Port Sud that on the 8th July 1815 Napoleon last stepped on French soil on his way to exile in St. Helena. No huge hotels on the front here but mostly three-storey apartments overlooking the sea, with the usual selection of cafés, restaurants and pizzerias.

From the N137 16km south of La Rochelle turn on to the D937 to Fouras, branch right at next junction on to the Route des Valines, straight on along the Avenue Pierre Loti. At the next large intersection the rue des Courtineurs is on the right.

➤ Mme Lefèbvre (M)

4 ter. rue des Courtineurs. (0)5.46.84.02.87. Closed: 1/10 to 30/4.

The rue des Courtineurs, a cul-de-sac on the fringe of the town, leads straight on to the beach, only 150 metres away so there is no traffic noise. This particular stretch of beach has many wooden fishing piers, where the fishermen hang their nets to be filled by the incoming tide.

This modern house has a wing on the ground floor with superb carpeted rooms, each with brand new facilities; every convenience thought of. Double bed 300f, single beds 320f.

The excellent breakfast, outside in fine weather or brought to your room, is elegantly served. No evening meal, so take a trip out to the Pointe-de-la-Fumée where there are fish restaurants and you have views in all directions, or make for the front where the choice is wider. We ate at the Chianti, with views of the setting sun, and *moules marinières* at 40f on the menu. We must have made a good choice by 9 p.m. the tables were all full while other places were almost empty.

M. Lefèbvre is an architect; parking is in the garden with gate locked at midnight, so all is very safe.

MIRAMBEAU. 17150

70km N of Bordeaux. 45km S of Royan. From the A10 (exit Mirambeau) head straight for the town centre and the château is on the right soon after the tourist office on the left.

NEW M. Ventola. La Parc Casamène (M)

95 Ave. de la République. (0)5.46.49.74.38.

What an easy place to find, just off the busy autoroute to Bordeaux. A very handy night stop for weary travellers. Shady parking and gates shut at night.

This neat château, built in 1877, has a park of five hectares containing some very interesting old trees. One cedar predates the château. The present owner and his partner have completely restored the building over the last five years and have newly opened as a chambres d'hôtes, furnishing all the rooms in uncluttered 19th-century style.

The salon, which guests may use, overlooks the park behind, as does the dining room where warm pink flowery walls are a backdrop for two identical polished sideboards, acquired with the château. Evening meals are prepared and served by your hosts who join you at table. 150f, all drinks included.

On arrival appropriate refreshment is always offered and I can vouch for the very nice fruit cake.

One guest room on the ground floor has a fireplace, is pleasantly decorated in blue with matching Louis XV bed and wardrobe and has a large pale green bathroom adjoining. Luxury aubergine-coloured carpets are in all the guest rooms. Three rooms all overlook the garden, each one entered by a vestibule dressing room, with space for suitcases. One, known as the cedar room, has dual aspect windows. Two more rooms will be ready by 1998. There is a choice of single or double beds, well equipped bathrooms, bidets, duel washbasins and separate toilets all en suite. 300/400f. Extra bed 80f includes breakfast.

Far too good for just a night stop.

POUILLAC. 17210

57km S of Cognac and approx 47km NE of Bordeaux on the N10. A most convenient stop on the way south to Bordeaux. Coming from the north turn right off the N10 at the chambres d'hôtes sign in Pouillac.

NEW M. & Mme Billat. Le Thébaide (M)

La Galaze. (0)5.46.04.65.17. fax: (0)5.46.04.85.38

A very warm welcome from Madame if you are lucky enough to stay here. I tried, but it is so popular that an early reservation is essential. The old house is full of character, set in a small flowery garden in the tiny hamlet of La Galaze.

Two rooms for three on the ground floor have external entrance and are beautifully decorated. Upstairs is a little landing decorated with dolls and toy cots "The dolls' chambres d'hôtes", Madame called it. The rooms overlook the garden, and have prettily panelled doors to match the decor. One has the loo on the landing, another a large private bathroom also outside the room. A nice garden salon leads to a large dining room, once the *cave* of the house.

Evening meals 100f are good value, wine *compris.*

Rooms 270f. Extra bed 60f, includes breakfast.

You would be assured of a very relaxing stay here, but heed the early booking. Just waiting for confirmation for an arrow.

SAINT-SAVINIEN. 17350

19km N of Saintes. 15km SW of St. Jean-d'Angely. From Saint-Savinien take the D145, SP Bord, to Pontreau and turn left at the sign to the chambres d'hôtes 200 metres up a lane. The house is on the right.

NEW Mr. & Mrs. Elmes. Le Moulin de la Quine (M)

Le Pontreau. (0)5.46.90.19.31.

Everyone's dream cottage; white with green shutters, edible grapes cascading down one wall, hidden in 4 to 5 acres of fields and trees, not a house in sight. Only an English woman could have designed this peaceful garden, with well-kept lawns and interesting island beds.

Facing south, all rooms overlook the terrace, a veritable sun trap. Jeni and John have been here five years and have two large rooms for two or four guests, both with bathrooms. The tiled downstairs room has its own terrace, but upstairs is

fully carpeted and has delightful small windows and extensive views. Tea-making facilities and hair dryers add to the many extras in the room. Many guests have come for a night and stayed a week.

Evening meals with your hosts are most congenial and include all drinks for 75f each. You won't be looking for restaurants here. Rooms 250f for two, 380f for four, are excellent value and I feel a well-deserved arrow on the way. Someone please confirm.

The lovely old mill tower in the garden is now an unobtrusive *gîte*.

Parking is in the shade of a large linden tree.

SAINT-SORNIN. 17600

27km W of Saintes. 12km E of Marennes. A neat little village, with a *boulangerie* opposite the church. The countryside is flat here on the edge of the salt-pans. Within easy reach of the bridge to the Ile d'Oléron, one of the largest islands lying off the west coast of France. Also close to the unexpected isolated village of Brouage, known to many Canadians, as it was the birthplace (in about 1567) of Samuel de Champlain, the founder of Quebec. The small village is totally surrounded by a star-shaped wall. You can walk round the high ramparts and have an excellent view of the flat salt-pans stretching along the Havre de Brouage to the sea. As the salt-pans have declined, they are now used for storing shell-fish. Enter the village by the old stone archway on the north side and wander round the quiet streets with just a few restaurants serving really fresh fish menus, and the odd shop. The church has a reredos looking like a piece of fine Wedgewood blue-and-white china, but it actually is wooden and was restored by the Canadians who have also put up the memorial to Samuel de Champlain. The most striking view of the village is from the air, so buy a card from the tourist office and see what I mean.

From Saintes take the D782 (SP Marennes) for 27km and turn right at the sign to the village. Turn left by the church and the entrance to the chambres d'hôtes is on the right.

NEW ➤ M. & Mme Pinel-Peschardière. La Caussolière (M)

10 rue du Petit Moulin. (0)5.46.85.44.62.

It is not often I give an arrow after a one night stay; but this one is exceptionally nice. Monsieur is the local mayor, and Madame modestly says she is a bit of an artist. Her work enhances all the rooms. Doors, lampshades, bathroom tiles and pictures are all tastefully painted to match the colour of the rooms. It doesn't stop there - the bed covers, table clothes and even mats are exquisitely made in matching patchwork.

One double-bedded room, in the main house, with luxury bathroom, has access to the garden; two much larger rooms are in the granary on the other side of the swimming pool. Sunflower-yellow on the ground has a double bed recessed behind dainty curtains and a settee which doubles for children in the salon area. The room with bath is very large and well furnished, including tea-making facilities and electric heating. Above, up an external stairway, the rose room, with double and single beds, warmly decorated with appropriate flowery walls and bathroom in deep pink, has all the same excellent facilities. Rooms 350f.

There is a lounge in the main house, plus a restful garden where you can watch the fish and frogs in the pond, but in summer it is the terrace beside the swimming pool which will attract most.

Convivial evening meals with your hosts 120f each, include all drinks, but there are restaurants at Pont L'Abbé 8km, or Marennes 12km. Breakfast, early in the year on the sheltered terrace, is copious. Madame has a workshop where guests may learn to paint on silk and where much of her unique work is on show.

As in all Charente-Maritime chambres d'hôtes, there is a 2f *taxe de séjour.*

DEUX-SEVRES

CHAMPDENIERS. 79220

18km N of Niort. 20km S of Parthenay. Only 20km from the Marais Poitevin, the eastern part of the Vendée waterways. An excellent place to stay a night on the route south, but I think you will want to stay longer here. From Champdeniers on the D748 take the D6 (SP: St. Maixent) and in 2km just after the sign 'St. Denis' turn left up a lane. Well signed.

NEW **M. & Mme Renaud. La Grolerie** (S)
(0)5.49.25.66.11.

"*Delphine Renaud's evening meals were excellent and I strongly feel she should be recommended.*" Val White. A reader's comments, so I hastened to visit.

The long farmhouse stands well back from the main road overlooking a large pond. There is spacious parking under cover in the huge ex-stables. The Renauds have themselves renovated the whole house, keeping its original stone flagged floors downstairs and the wide wooden staircase. There are three very large centrally-heated south-facing freshly decorated rooms, in blue, green or yellow, for three or four people, each with a well-designed shower room and separate loo. Shelves for vanity bags much appreciated. Comfortable beds have sheets embroidered by Madame's grandmother and duvets when needed. Two are on the ground floor, one with a separate entry from the garden. The third is on the first floor, with a high beamed ceiling, a modern divan bed and a *bateau* bed.

The salon/dining room is very pleasant with a large log fire where guests can relax before a meal with the family for 80f. Wine in litre carafes 20f.

Rooms at 220f for two, extra bed 50f, make this a very good place for families with a hectare of wild garden for the children to roam around. Madame does all the cooking with produce from her parents' farm close by.

COULON. 79510

11km W of Niort. Situated on the banks of the Sèvre-Niortaise in the Marais Verte at the eastern part of the Vendée. With all its tourist attractions and plentiful restaurants, it remains unspoilt.

Leave Coulon on the Vanneau road beside the river and turn right in 1km at the sign to La Rigole.

➤ Mme Fabien. La Rigole. (S)
(0)5.49.35.97.90.

On the edge of one of the prettiest villages in the Marais Poitevin, this lovely modernised cottage, well off the main road and right beside the canal, would be my choice for a holiday exploring the hidden waterways. Boats for hire at Coulon, or take a ride on the little train round the canals or even a river trip with inclusive lunch or dinner down the Sèvre Niortaise.

Mme Fabien has three delightful beamed rooms, for four (two double beds), for three and for two with even a *ciel-de-lit*, 200/210f. She will give you a very large breakfast, but no evening meal; plenty of options in Coulon. Bikes for hire. Arrowed as the best introduction to an under-appreciated area.

GERMOND-ROUVRE. 79220

23km SW of Parthenay. 2km west of the D743 between Parthenay and Niort. Just off the route to La Rochelle and only 20km from the *Marais Poitevin.*

➤ M. & Mme Blanchard. Breilbon (S)

(0)5.49.04.05.01.

This is one of those lovely little places I would like to keep quiet about, but fear it is already well known. The owners have diligently restored the lovely old house at the end of a hamlet near Germond-Rouvre. Peace and quiet is assured.

A reader thought so too; '*This was the highlight of our holiday. The house and garden beautiful, the hospitality second to none. Squeezing fresh oranges in the early morning sun for 'le petit déjeuner', eating superb dinners under a starlit sky, course after course was a speciality of the region, all using the produce from the garden, and cooked supremely well by M. Blanchard. We loved everything about Breilbon. It was unforgettable and we long to go back. It really does deserve an arrow*' - Wendy Stagg; and an arrow it shall have, Mrs Stagg - you were not the only one to sing its praises!

There are two rooms bordering on luxury class. One on the ground floor has a separate private toilet, the upstairs one is totally en suite.

There are two bikes for guests too. Rooms at 200f, and meals 65f with all drinks *compris*, make this exceptionally good value.

NANTEUIL. 79400

28km S of Parthenay. Turn off the N11 at St. Maixent on to the D737; in 1km signed to La Berlière on your left.

➤ M. & Mme Memeteau (S)

2, Impasse de la Berlière. (0)5.49.05.60.71.

Tucked away on a quiet hillside this ancient farmhouse is only 6km from the A10, with views over the valley and stream below. One pretty blue room with warm carpeting, fluffy white towels and good reading lamps is very comfortable. The suite is totally independent, and very prettily decorated with beds for four and kitchen area. A bargain stop for a family of four at 320/340f according to season, including breakfast.

A five-course dinner, all drinks *compris*, included *farcie-en-pot*, a local speciality of lettuce, spinach, onion and ham all puréed together and cooked in cabbage leaves, and finished with strawberries and cream and liqueur chocolates. At 60/80f it was excellent. Such a pleasant family - M. Memeteau used to be in the French Air Force and his son still is.

Rooms for two 200/220f, even less for a three-night stay, deserve an arrow.

SAUZE-VAUSSAIS. 79190

50km SE of Niort. 54km S of Poitiers.

NEW M. & Mme Ragot. Le Puy d'Anché (S)

(0)5.49.07.90.69. fax: (0)5.49.07.72.09.

A true ferme-auberge where the family are kept busy bottling the produce of the farm; foie-gras, various patés, jams, etc. A large dining room has interesting fire irons in the great fireplace. All meals are taken here and it is open to the public.

Rooms in a newly converted barn a few steps away are pristine, with high beams and plenty of room for extra beds; plainly furnished, but with much appreciated underfloor heating in the well-appointed shower room. Spot-light bedside lamps and fitted wardrobe. Lovely white linen but the all-too-common one bath, two small towels. Ask for another if staying more than one night. A salon downstairs for guests.

Madame is young and most obliging and although you eat at separate tables guests are relaxed and friendly. A good off-season stop where you will find regional food; the dining room might be rather busy in season. Meals 90f, wine *compris* but *apéritifs* charged. Breakfast: apple juice, baguettes, jams and a cake *à la maison*.

Rooms 250f, reduced after the 3rd night.

VALLANS. 79270

4km SW of Niort.Take Sortie 33 from the A10 or from the N11 Epannes exit. Drive through Epannes and take the D1 to Vallans. Well signed in the village.

NEW Francis & Patric Guillot. Le Logis d'Antan (M)
140 rue Saint Louis. (0)5.49.04.91.50. fax: (0)5.49.04.86.75.

Close to the Venise Verte in the Vendée. Visiting this one first on my list augured well for the rest of the tour. This rustic *maison-de-maitre* has been converted into a first-rate chambres d'hôtes. All rooms have independent entry from outside, plus fridges, hair dryers, TV, phones and tea-making facilities, and are furnished with taste, combining modern amenities with interesting antiques. Upstairs two are carpeted. 'La Salicorne' has a double bed and an attached room with bunks for three children. 'L'Engelique' for two with a double bed has a charming *ciel-de-lit*. On the ground floor, for three, is 'La Piballe' - large, with parquet floor and many windows plus a log fire in the winter. Another room overlooking the front garden has a tiled floor and ornamental fireplace.

Evening meals served in the dining room, or pleasant sun lounge, cooked by Patric, offering local specialities, should not be missed. 109f all drinks *compris*.

Rooms at 290-330f (extra person 100f). Highly recommended. I am sure an arrow in the offing.

VIENNE

AVANTON-MARTIGNY. 86170

12km N of Poitiers. 5km west from exit 18 on the A10. Avanton-Martigny is an excellent place to stay for those wishing to visit the Futuroscope, which is a very large theme park just outside Poitiers with entertainment for all the family. The large futuristic buildings can be seen for miles around. You need stamina to spend a whole day looking at all the cinemas and the exhibitions. The inclusive entry fee is 120f for adults and 90f for children (5-16); entrance is free for the under fives. This fee covers one day but there is a two-day option at 200f (adults) and 150f (children). Just inside the entrance at the Vienne tourist office you can obtain free headsets which can be set to translate the French commentaries into English. You have to leave something like a driving licence as a deposit.

There are plenty of activities for children. 76 separate entertainments, of which only six carry an extra charge.

Take a picnic. Food in the numerous cafés and restaurants can be expensive for a family, and there are long queues at peak times. The grounds are ideal for al fresco eating with lovely lawns and lakes. A change of clothing or a swimsuit is useful for children; they won't be able to resist trying the water maze, tempting on a hot day. Don't miss the Magic Carpet cinema, it is superb. Nor the 3D cinema, nor even the 360° one. Avoid the Simulator unless you adore the horrors of a roller coaster. Funnily enough it attracted the largest queue of the day, parties of school children and the *troisième age*. I can't believe they knew what they were letting themselves in for, seven minutes of shuddering big dipper type film with the floor and your seat moving, synchronised with it. Afterwards calm yourself by taking a peaceful boat ride through the mural landscapes of Europe, or take the lift up the revolving tower for an aerial view of the whole of the park. There were some very weary people making their way to their cars and coaches after a full and happy day, so perhaps one should take advantage of the two-day option.

➤ Mme Arrondeau. Ferme du Château (M)

Martigny. (0)5.49.51.04.57. Closed: 1/12 to 14/3.

In a main street of the village you will find this delightful old house in a walled garden, once part of the château, where the stables have been modernised for comfort but keep all their old character. Two rooms on the first floor can each take an extra bed. On the ground floor is a family suite with double bed and two singles on a mezzanine.

There is a really comfortable sitting-room with dining alcove, a smart kitchen area and all facilities, even a microwave. Coffee, tea and cold drinks all provided free and there's a nice patio in fine weather. Definitely my choice near the Futuroscope, but book; always busy in holidays and at weekends. Locked parking in the garden beside the house. I couldn't fault this one; excellent *accueil*, and the addition of a swimming pool since my last visit, keeps the arrow firmly in place.

Rooms 260/280f. 10% discount for three nights

BONNEUIL-MATOURS. 86210

16km S of Châtellerault. Handy for a night stop, off the D749 in the valley of the river Vienne, and 19km east of the Futuroscope. Just on the fringe of the town and well signed in the centre of the town.

NEW M. & Mme Gallais-Pradal (M)

Chemin des Pierres Blanches. (0)5.49.85.24.75.

The three rooms in this modern house are most attractive. Year round comfort, electric heating and carpets everywhere, even in the bathrooms. A summer kitchen available for guests by the pool.

Louisiane upstairs has bath and separate shower cubicle. Here the blue carpet creeps up the walls and on to shelves - enough to satisfy even me! The cosy if slightly dark room has the benefit of a large south-facing private terrace, a great asset in fine weather. There is another smaller room with pretty painted furniture, and shower-room which can be let in conjuction for a family. If let separately, the loo is downstairs. On the ground floor *Primevère* has a charming *ciel-de-lit*, a study area and a terrace leading to the pool. The large bathroom here is just outside the room. Smaller Granny's room next door has shower and wash basin, loo across the hall. Rooms 240/260f.

A very friendly welcome here, a comfortable salon and dining room open on to the terrace.

Evening meals on request - 80f, drinks included - are good value.

MOUTERRE-SILLY. 86200

36km SSE of Saumur. From the D759 west of Loudon turn left to Mouterre-Silly. Silly is 1km further on.

➤ M. & Mme Pouit (S)

rue de la Fontaine. (0)5.49.22.46.41.

The tiny hamlet of Silly has neither commerce nor church; the Pouit's large farmhouse, once visited by Cardinal Richelieu, dominates the village with its two towers and extensive gardens of lawns and vegetables. Antique cart-wheels decorate the large enclosed courtyard, outbuildings on all sides; a collection of fossils found in a neighbouring field is displayed on one wall.

If you have been château-bashing all day you will think you are still at it as you climb the stone staircase in the tower to one of the rooms here, and even more so as you open the very old door with a latch and an enormous 8-inch key. Two tall *armoires* and a huge fireplace dwarf the double bed and small single in the corner of the warm carpeted room. There are excellent modern shower and loo facilities in the adjoining round tower. A second room, for three, has been created since our last guide, and very pretty it is too, with flowery wallpaper and blue predominating, both 220f for two, 270f for three.

Having been given the menu for dinner on arrival we were invited to *apéritifs* with the grandparents in their adjoining house. Soup, asparagus soufflé, roast duck, cheese and fresh strawberries, everything but the cheese from the garden. "Is that all right?" asked Madame. At 75f it was a feast with *apéritifs*, wine and coffee all *compris*, especially as we had booked the room by phone only half an hour before we arrived! Their youngest daughter speaks quite good English, and Mme Pouit understands more than she admits.

Breakfast included fresh strawberries. A *gîte* for 4/5 people also next door.

LA-TRIMOUILLE. 86290

44km SE of Poitiers.Take ʟ e D975 south from Le Blanc to La Trimouille (24km). The road number changes to D675 just north of La Trimouille. Leave La Trimouille on the D675 and in about half a mile take the first fork right and follow the signs to Toël, which will be on your left.

The little village of Trimouille now boasts a snake museum, and is on a very pretty alternative route from Blois on the Loire to Limoges down the D675, where the roadside is lined with poppies in spring.

➤ M. & Mme Vouhé. Toël (S)

(0)5.49.91.67.59. Closed: 31/10 to 30/4.

As we drove down a small country lane just off the main road from Trimouille we soon found Toël, a long low farmhouse well back from the road, surrounded by fields and outbuildings. Toël is another superb upmarket farmhouse chambres d'hôtes, a goat farm this time. It was a Sunday afternoon when we broke in on this peaceful scene of a small child riding a pony, with grandparents in attendance. As we hadn't booked a room we were delighted with our reception. Madame had one room left, and yes, we could dine there. So after stowing our gear we came down and joined both M. and Mme Vouhé for tea.

Three comfortable bedrooms are on the first floor; with shower - 200f, with bath - 220f.

Never miss dinner here. Madame is a true French cook and the meals are excellent and delightfully served on Limoges china. There is a real dinner party atmosphere with many laughs and the conversation never flags. *Aperitifs*, wine and *digestifs* are all *compris* for 80f.

Leave time for a tour of the goat farm after breakfast with the Vouhé's small grandson, who is a budding French guide. A perfect example of a chambres d'hôtes, with Monsieur and Madame both participating in the pleasure of entertaining guests.

VOUNEUIL-SUR-VIENNE. 86210

16km S of Châtellerault. This quiet village is only 15km from Futuroscope.

From the D749 south of Châtellerault turn right on to the D15 to the village of Vouneuil, left by the post office near the church and follow the signs. Ignore the first sign on the left and continue 50 yds to the chambres d'hôtes sign on the right.

NEW M. & Mme Penot. Les Hauts de Chabonne (M)

(0)5.49.85.28.25. fax: (0)5.49.85.55.17.

A gravelled drive leads you to a large parking area in front of this well-restored farmhouse. The five guest rooms are in a separate building, three on the ground floor, two above, all with baths. Not all are carpeted but large mats help. They are pleasantly furnished and most have extra beds. Outside a large wooden staircase leads to the first-floor rooms. 270f. Special rates for families and for longer stays. Evening meals 95f *vin compris*. There are vast country views all round and sunny lawned terraces to sit on, or guests are welcome to use the family lounge in inclement weather.

Les Hauts de Chabon
Vouneuil-sur-Vienne

A second choice in this village:

On the D749 turn left 16km S of Châtellerault at Ribes at the chambres d'hôtes sign, and follow the sign uphill and left again, the house is the last on the left.

NEW **M. & Mme Poussard. La Pocterie** (M)

(0)5.49.85.11.96. or (0)5.49.49.59.11.

This beautifully-restored old house at the end of a tiny lane overlooks the valley of the Vienne. A useful quiet place to stay away from the main road. There is a pool in the garden, and two luxurious guest rooms "Les Violettes", on the ground floor with access to the garden, and "Jonquilles" on the first floor. There is an extra large room available in summer, with the bathroom on the corridor. Good value at 260f. Madame is at work most of the day, so do book ahead so that she can be there to receive you. Unfortunately the rooms are not accessible from midday to 5pm, when Madame is out. You will be given an excellent and un-hurried breakfast. Unfortunately this isn't a place for lounging by the pool all afternoon, but the rooms are extremely nice, and it is in a lovely position.

PROVENCE

Départements:	**Alpes-de-Haute-Provence**	**Haute-Alpes**
	Alpes-Maritimes	**Var**
	Bouches-du-Rhône	**Vaucluse**

Companion guide to the area: 'French Entrée 11 - Provence' by Peter King.

Situated in the south-east corner of France, Provence since 600 BC has been colonised by Greeks, Celts and Romans, all leaving their imprint, mostly noticeable in names of towns. After the fall of the Roman Empire in the 4th-century, Franks, Burgundians and Visigoths all descended on the area. It was a kingdom in its own right in the 9th-century, became part of France in 1481, then came under the domination of the Italian kingdoms, and was eventually ceded to France by Sardinia in 1860. The modern autoroutes A8 and A9 follow the route of the old Roman roads from Italy through Nice, Aix and Arles then onwards to Narbonne and Spain.

The climate is hot in summer, mild in winter, except when the Mistral, the cold fierce northerly wind, is suddenly funnelled down the Rhône valley from the Alps.

In the north the **Hautes-Alpes** extend to Savoie and the Italian border in the east. The *préfecture* is Gap, a small town on the Route Napoleon N85. The enormous Parc de National Des Ecrins takes up a good part of this mountainous area, where Briançon is the highest town in Europe. Major roads like the N94 follow the river valleys. The river Durance was dammed 30 years ago to make the Lac de Serre Ponçon, now a popular holiday resort.

South-east the **Alpes-de-Haute-Provence** *département* is sandwiched between the Vaucluse and the Alpes Maritimes, with a small Italian border in the East. The *préfecture* of Digne-les-Bains lies in the west of the *département*, also on the Route Napoleon. Due of course to the mountainous terrain, roads again skirt where they can, avoiding the mountains. Covered with snow in the winter, it is a wild terrain with no famous ski resorts as in the Alps.

Descending into the **Alpes Maritimes** the mountains are even more precipitous, reaching to the coastline in places, with many roads running through tunnels. Between Menton and Nice are three corniches tiering up from the Mediterranean coast, with pretty perched villages like Eze on the *Moyenne Corniche*. On the upper road are the striking remains of the Trophée des Alpes at La Turbie, built in the 6th-century BC, to commemorate the final submission of the 44 tribes in the area to

PROVENCE

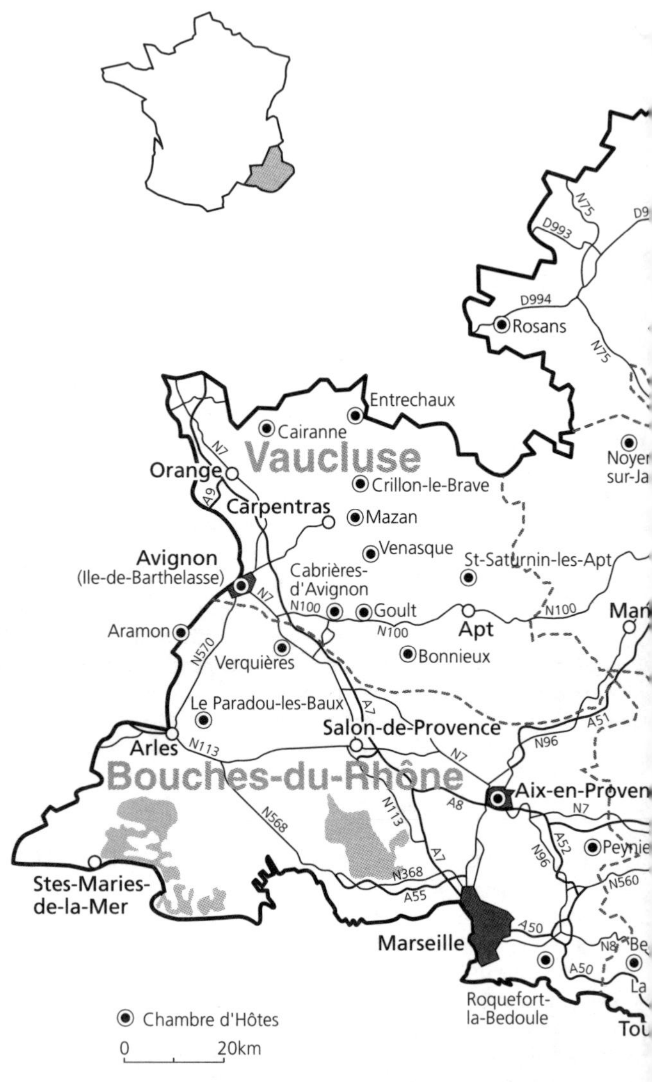

Rosans
Entrechaux
Cairanne
Vaucluse
Orange
Crillon-le-Brave
Carpentras
Mazan
Venasque
Avignon
(Ile-de-Barthelasse)
Cabrières-
d'Avignon
St-Saturnin-les-Apt
Goult
Apt
Aramon
Bonnieux
Verquières
Le Paradou-les-Baux
Salon-de-Provence
Arles
Bouches-du-Rhône
Stes-Maries-
de-la-Mer
Marseille
Roquefort-
la-Bedoule
N75
D993
D994
N7
A9
N100
N570
A7
N113
N568
N368
A55
A8
N96
A51
A52
N560
A50
Chambre d'Hôtes
0 20km

N91
Briançon
N94
Hautes-Alpes
N94
D900
Barcelonnette
Alpes-de-Haute-Provence
Digne
Alpes-Maritimes
N204
N202
N202
N85
La colle-sur-Loup
Courmes
A8
N7
D2085
Grasse
Valbonne
Nice
N7
Draguignan
A8
Cannes
Var
Lorgues
N7
A8
A8
N98
N97
A57
St-Tropez
N98

obedience to Rome. There is a panoramic view over Monaco from the surrounding gardens. Now there is a higher motorway all the way from Nice to Italy, easier by far but lacking the excitement and the views of the three Corniches.

Nice, the *préfecture*, is right on the coast with the Promenade des Anglais overlooking the stony beach. Away from the coast the old town is still very interesting and the port is just round a corner where the ferries leave for Corsica. This narrow coastline was once the loveliest in France, but it has been over-exposed and in summer is jam-packed, the beaches strewn with people like sardines in a tin of Ambre Solaire! But venture up into the hills and you will find peace and quiet and delightful hidden villages like Courmes near the waterfall in the Valley du Loup. Higher behind the coast is Grasse, the perfume capital of France. Busy with its own concerns it seems detached from the tourist excesses of the coastal towns. A daily market and the added attraction of the perfume factories might make this town worth a visit. Vence and St. Paul de Vence are a bit too popular but you will regret it if you miss seeing them too.

Napoleon landed at Golfe-Juan and marched up through France along what is now known as the Route Napoléon (N 85) through Grasse and on to Grenoble.

Further west the *département* of **Var** occupies a coastal position and stretches back into the hills as far as the Gorge du Verdon. Toulon, the *préfecture* is the largest naval port in France. Near the coast the lesser hills of the Massif Des Maures keep the north winds away from the beaches from Toulon to Fréjus, and the Massif de l'Esterel protrudes into the sea making many lovely coves. Inland the Var is more penetrable than the Alpes Maritime; more roads straddle the plains, leading to the Lac de Ste. Croix, a large man-made lake at one end of the Gorge du Verdon. The Gorge is a massive canyon made by the river cutting a winding course through the limestone rock, 21km. long from Aiguines to Rougon and varying in depth from 250 to 700 metres. There are good roads on both sides, with viewing points (*belvédères*) at the best parts.

The most westerly *département* of **Bouches-du-Rhône** has the great Mediterranean port of Marseille as its *préfecture*. The flat salt marshy lands of the Camargue lie west of Marseille, cut by the delta of the river Rhône, where the white horses roam and the flamingoes add their brilliance to the wildlife of the many lagoons. The infamous hill village of les Baux is on a peak of the Alpilles mountains, now with its past well behind it, is a most attractive village.

Aix-en-Provence, north of Marseille, is an attractive and dignified university town, with a cool shaded heart - the Cours Mirabeau, a tree-lined boulevard running through the centre of the town. The **Vaucluse** seems to be the most populated and most popular of the *départements*. Here the chambres d'hôtes come thick and fast. Small mountain ranges intersperse with valleys all producing the sunkissed Rhône valley wines, particularly from the slopes of Mont Ventoux. The Lubéron is the most southerly range, a great favourite with climbers.

Avignon, the *préfecture*, on the river Rhône, is firmly tucked away in the northwest. The Popes made their home there in the 14th century when lawlessness broke out in Rome. Their old palace is open to the public. Of course don't forget to dance under the St. Bénézet bridge which is only half a bridge since a flood washed part away in the 17th century. The dancing was never **Sur le Pont d'Avignon** but on an island underneath.

In the plains the perfume of the large lavender fields wafts through the air on a warm day. There are many old Roman towns in the department. Orange with its well preserved theatre and glorious Arc-de-Triomphe dating back to 6 BC, simply mustn't be missed.

ALPES-DE-HAUTE-PROVENCE

LES MEES. 04190

16km S of Sisteron. An ideal place for an easy night stop off the Autoroute 51. Les Mées itself is far from exciting but the spectacular *rochers* (Les Penitents) overhanging the town are. The story is that they are monks turned to stone. Rimbaud, Seigneur de Mées, took seven beautiful Moorish ladies into his château. The Prior of the monastery at Les Mées decided this was scandalous and threatened him with excommunication if he did not release them. He did, and whilst everyone was watching them emerge from the château Saint Donat, a hermit who lived at Lurs on the other side of the Durance thought the flock of monks watching were in moral danger so he petrified them on the spot. More realistically the weather has worn the rocks down to this shape, resembling a column of monks.

Some of the purest olive oil is produced in this valley - visit the co-operative for tastings.

From the A 51 exit Les Mées, head for the town over the river Durance past the Intermarché supermarket, a useful place for refuelling both the car and picnic supplies. After you cross the river branch right, SP Oraison D4, and the chambres d'hôtes is on the left at Bourelles, well signed.

NEW M. & Mme Verger. Le Mas des Oliviers (S)

Les Bourelles. (0)4.92.34.36.99.

Open all year. A modern house, well designed to catch the sun, on the hillside just below the Canal-de-Durance.

There are four rooms: *La Lavande* upstairs has a bath and a private terrace. On the ground floor three others with shower rooms but two have their loos on the corridor. *Les Eglantines* has a private terrace. Parking off the road in the hillside garden. Rooms are cosy in winter, with lots of small extras supplied - tissues, soap, sewing kit, etc. Evening meals, willingly offered, are simple and adequate and the welcome is warm and very friendly. Rooms at 230f and evening meal 70f, wine *compris*.

NOYERS-SUR-JABRON. 04200

12km SW of Sisteron. 48km W of Digne.Take the N85 (Route Napoléon) south from Sisteron, and in 4km turn right on to the D946. Noyers is 11km along this road. Take the first right on leaving the village and follow the signs.

NEW M. & Mme Morel. Le Jas de la Caroline (M)

Chênebotte. (0)4.92.62.03.48.

A wonderfully peaceful retreat where you will be given a warm welcome by the owners, now retired, who bought his charming rustic house, once a sheep farm, about four years ago. The matured stone walls and vaulted ceilings are an interesting feature of the house.

There are two rooms on the ground floor with baths; they share a terrace and a south-facing salon, which is pleasantly decorated with some lovely antique furniture. 260f.

A charming sunny suite is designed particularly for the handicapped, with two single beds and a very pleasant salon opening on to a terrace. The shower room is kitted out with rails in all the right places and floor gently slopes to facilitate the use of a wheelchair. It also has a little kitchen with a vaulted roof built on to the foundations of the house. I found the little suite utterly charming and well worth 400f, including breakfast.

Madame Morel will produce an evening meal for you for 100f, including wine, but only 80f if you stay more than one night. All well worth a detour.

HAUTES-ALPES

ROSANS. 05150

25km W of Serres. 75km from Bollène.The ancient little hill village of Rosans in the Haute-Alpes, 700m high, is between Serres and Nyons on the D994, an alternative route to Provence.

It was once a fortified village, Celts, Saracens, Gallo-Romans have all played their part in its development, bequeathing a rich history. The narrow streets and remains of fortifications make it an interesting setting. Take the D994 Nyons to Serres and in 1km after Rosans you will find L'Ensoleillée just off the road on your right.

NEW **M. & Mme Pacaud. L'Ensoleillée** (M)

Le Béal Noir. (0)4.92.66.62.72. fax: (0)4.92.66.62.87.

Easy to find this purpose-built chambres d'hôtes. You may think this is like a motel; but the friendly reception belies this (Travellers Cheques are accepted).

The young owners have been running it for seven years and it still looks new. The six rooms are in a separate building. All have good quality en suite facilities. A very large family room on the *rez-de-chaussée* is divided into three sections, with two single beds in each, for six people. There is a large bathroom.

Above are five rooms accessible from the parking level, two for three people have two wash basins in each, others are for two. They are all prettily furnished in different colours with showers and loos and private sunny terraces overlooking the mountains. Evening meals are served in the main building where the dining room has yellow Provençal decor. 85f, wine *compris*.

Rooms 230/260f, extra beds 80f, includes breakfast.

An ideal spot for a night stop but book ahead and arrive early to enjoy the scenery, visit the old village and swim in the new pool hopefully in situ by 1998.

ALPES-MARITIMES

LA COLLE-SUR-LOUP. 06480

15km from Nice. A busy town at the foot of Saint-Paul-de-Vence. St. Paul is probably the best known hill village in the Alpes Maritimes, a haunt for artists for many years. The ramparts are still intact and the cobbled streets and stairways are charming. The church built in the 12/13th century contains many fine works of art. There are museums, boutiques and of course art galleries galore. It attracts so many visitors there is now a vast underground car park just outside the village and entry is only on foot.

The b. & b. is tricky to find, so listen carefully. From the Autoroute A8 exit Villeneuve-Loubet, follow the signs Saint-Paul-de-Vence via La Colle-sur-Loup. In La Colle-sur-Loup after the Leclerc supermarket on the left, at the traffic lights by the church, turn right down a narrow road, rue M. de Lattac de Tassigny, straight on into Bld. J.B.Layet which leads into the Chemin du Pré du Bar, and the Chemin des Rouguière is about the 5th road on the right, the house is 20 metres on the left.

NEW Mme Béatrice Ronin-Pillet. Le Clos de St. Paul (M)
71 Chemin de la Rouguière.Tel & fax: (0)4.93.32.56.81.

Looking for the Ronin-Pillet's home nearer Grasse, I found they had moved to another house close to St. Paul, and their chambres d'hôtes there was up and running.

A tasty *apéritif à la maison* on arrival was most welcoming. There are three attractive rooms - *Les Blés*, with appropriate yellow and green designs, has a black iron bedstead and *ciel-de-lit*, with spring-like yellow and green towels to match the yellow bedding. *Les Olives* has single beds and french windows to the garden, as has *Les Pivoines* with a double bed. I liked the little touches, like the beds being turned down at night and a chocolate left on the pillow, Fragonard soap and a sample scent in the shower room. The attention to detail all adds to the enjoyment of staying here, and Madame Ronin-Pillet speaks good English.

No evening meals but Saint-Paul-de-Vence is only 2km up the road, with a wide choice. Try the 'Quatre Coins', with a jolly patron.

Breakfast with a selection of breads including *fougasse* from Grasse is served in a glassed-in veranda - if not warm enough for the garden.

Room with shower 300f, 320f with bath. In July and August 350f and 400f. Extra beds 90f.

COURMES. 06620

23km NE of Grasse.Turn off at Pré-du-Lac, east of Grasse. and follow the road to Pont-du-Loup and just after the bridge fork back left on the D6. Follow this road past the cascade, which has a viewing bridge and is part of the river Loup. Turn right at SP Courmes, onto a narrow road for 4km. Go through the village nestling against a hill (you'll be lucky if you see a soul) and turn right down a private road to the stone-built farmhouse, home of the Baracco's, on a wooded hillside where they grow vegetables.

M. & Mme Baracco. La Cascade (M)

(0)4.93.09.65.85.

There are six very pleasant new rooms on the ground floor, all with baths, three for two people and three family rooms with double bed and bunks. Plenty of freedom for children in this isolated place, with mountain walks from the door. Not far from Grasse or Gourdon. Madame does her shopping up at Cipières, a village well worth visiting with a château and a couple of restaurants and the ever necessary *boulangerie*.

Evening meals 80f. Wine about 35f a bottle.

Rooms 270/290f, according to season.

VALBONNE. 06560

10km from Antibes. 20km from Nice airport. Situated 4km from the popular village of Valbonne which is an attractive place, large enough to boast an excellent choice of bistro-type restaurants and boutiques, and a large parking space to keep cars from choking the main roads, small enough to keep an intimate friendly character. Streets are narrow, winding, dripping with flowers, houses are old, photogenic. Altogether well worth an excursion or even better a longer stay.

This chambres d'hôtes is in an ideal position for visiting the coast, the mountains or the lovely old town of Grasse - the centre of the world's perfume manufacturers.

From Valbonne take the D3 towards Antibes and at a roundabout in 2km take the third exit onto the D103, SP Antibes (Route du Parc). Near a yellow bus stop on the left called 'La Petite Ferme', turn left up a little lane and the house is the one on the left.

NEW M. & Mme Ringenbach. Le Cheneau (M-L)

205 Route d'Antibes. (0)4.93.12.13.94. fax: (0)4.93.12.91.85. Open all year.

Reservations only here please, so don't just turn up or you will be disappointed. The beautifully appointed villa, in a large park with plenty of shade, has three large, well-furnished guest rooms in different colours, blue, noisette, etc. - one on the ground floor and two on the first floor in a separate wing of the house, all with baths.

There is a very nice salon opening on to the garden (with a double-bed settee) and a smart modern kitchen which can be let together with any of the other rooms, as a suite, for 220f extra. The suite then will not include breakfast. Good value for a family of four who wish to self-cater. Other guests have the use of salon where breakfast is served.

Price varies from 320f for Blue, the smallest, to 420f for Noisette, a lovely spacious room. 10% reduction for stays over three days.

Parking is excellent behind the house in the shade. Rumours of a swimming pool in the future. Highly recommended.

BOUCHES-DU-RHONE

AIX-EN-PROVENCE. 13852

16km N of Marseille. A university town, home of Cézanne, perhaps best known for the majestic Cours Mirabeau, the wide tree-lined boulevard where the restaurants and brasseries remind one of Paris. The Cathedral of St. Sauveur has a famous Triptych of the Burning Bush, viewing at certain times. Leave Aix by the A51 SP Marseille, take exit 3 SP 'Bouc Bel Air'; then the D59 on the right. The Domaine du Frère is signed in 3 to 4km on this road on the right. Easier to book ahead and receive a clear map of directions, as this one is definitely not in the town but 6km to the south.

NEW M. & Mme Bouvant. Domaine du Frère (M)
495 rue Ampère, Pôle d'Activités des Milles. (0)4.42.24.24.62. fax: (0)4.42.24.37.89.

It is quite extraordinary to find such a pleasant house in a suburb, virtually surrounded by large office blocks. Built in 1735, it stands marooned in a large park. There is a sheltered garden, a swimming pool, tennis court and a huge parking area.

The house still has the original stairs and floors and is a maze of passages and short steps to various rooms. The delightful mellowness will take you back years. Bathrooms, a mixture of modern and antiquated, are not all en suite but usually private, even if on a different level. The rooms are homely and comfortable. Madame will cook you an evening meal, if reserved, for 100f, wine and coffee *compris*.

Rooms 280/340f. The vibes seemed right here.

ARAMON. 30390

11km SW of Avignon. As this chambres d'hôtes is so close to Provence, I have agreed to list it under our Provence region, though the official postal address is still in the Gard, Languedoc. I just hope Napoleon, who created the French *départements* isn't turning over in his grave!

From the D2 Avignon to Aramon road turn right on to the D126 to Saze. In about 2km fork left at sign to "Le Rocher Pointu". Coming from Avignon the D126 is just before the Pont de Barbentane over the Rhône. Aramon is a quaint old town almost on the banks of the Rhône, partly walled, with tiny passageways and a rampart on one side.

M. & Mme Malek. "Le Rocher Pointu" (M)

Plan de Deve. (0)4.66.57.41.87. fax: (0)4.66.57.01.77.

'Heavenly, we hope to return' - Jill Silversides.

If you are looking for a true old Provençale atmosphere the rooms in this large meandering house nestling under the Rocher Pointu are just the thing. Four cosy rooms, every one different, one with a mezzanine for one to two children. 370/430f.

Le Rocher Pointu (Aramon)

Rocky paths round the house leading to the swimming pool are not for the handicapped. A high terrace extends past the pool with magnificent views to Mont Ventoux and all around. No picture does it justice. The pool is ready for use in March for the stalwarts! No shortage of plastic loungers here. Beside the pool a covered sitting area (with fridge) traps the sun.

No evening meals but a nice little kitchen and barbecue for guests to cook their own meals faces a terraced corner leading from a large comfortable sitting room. The 'Trudaine', a restaurant/pizzeria as you enter Aramon, is recommended, only 3km away.

There are a few studios for 2-4 which are equally well furnished down to the last serviette. 460/590f.

LES BAUX-DE-PROVENCE. 13520

15km NE of Arles. Les Baux village (900m by 200m in area) is on a spur of rock detached from the Alpilles, with ravines on both sides. It gave its name to bauxite, a mineral discovered on its land in 1822. In the middle ages the lords of Les Baux were all warriors, who warred with their neighbours continuously.

The Turenne family controlled Les Baux at one time when Viscount Raymond de Turenne became guardian of his niece, Alix, the last Princess of Baux, in 1372. He was known as the 'scourge of Provence', and delighted in throwing his unransomed prisoners over the rock face. The King of France joined Raymond's enemies and defeated him in 1399. When Alix died in 1426 the Domaine was incorporated into Provence and became a Barony.

In the 17th century Les Baux became a Marquisate under the Grimaldi family of Monaco, who still patronise the village. There is only one approach road. In the summer when the car parks are full vehicles overflow down the hill. The village is most attractive now, so compact, full of historical interest, flowers cascading from the many delightful bijou boutiques, cafés and restaurants. It is a 'must' on everyone's itinerary.

NEW M. & Mme Fajardo-de-Livry. La Burlande (L)

Le Paradou. (0)4.90.54.32.32.

Tucked away off the road from Paradou to Les Baux in the middle of the Alpilles mountains this pleasant modern villa has three elegant bedrooms in a separate wing on the ground floor, furnished with antiques, with baths or showers, carpets and central heating for all-year-round occupancy. Two rooms can be adjoining for a family. All rooms have access through patio doors to the garden and pool. 470f for Blue and Green to 670f for the suite for two. Evening meals offered at 140f, but wine is not *compris*.

Your hosts enjoy musical evenings round a grand piano or are equally happy to play bridge.

PEYNIER. 13790

23km SE of Aix-en-Provence. A quiet little town which is easily reached from the Autoroute A8, peacefully away from busy roads, south of the Mont-Ste-Victoire which Cézanne loved to paint.

From the D6 outside Trets, take the D908 to Peynier through the town.

NEW Mme Lambert. Mas Sainte-Anne (M)

3 rue d'Auriol. (0)4.42.53.05.32. fax: (0)4.42.53.04.28. Closed: August.

This house is at the west end of the village close to the post office, just up a lane from the main road.

The 200-year-old farmhouse, standing in a lovely green enclosed garden with a refreshing pool, has a most inviting old terrace. The salon, on a different level, is a delight and the original tiled and brick floors still survive. Rooms upstairs are full of character; a very nice one on the first floor has a bathroom along a sloping corridor with an enormous ornate bath, shower, bidet and washbasins (resembling sinks) all in the same rather bizarre green tiles. Unusual to say the least! Another attic-like room on the top floor (hold on to the rope on the way up!) is less formal, with adjoining shower and wc overlooking the garden.

The house is full of character and the *accueil* is charming. Rooms 295/330f.

ROQUEFORT-LA-BEDOULE. 13830

20km E of Marseille. A small village in the hilly regions behind the coast at Cassis, a small fishing port, now packed in summer with tourists, but delightful out of season, when the many excellent fish restaurants can be best enjoyed.

From Roquefort-la-Bédoule take the D1 towards Roquefort village for 3.5km and the chambres d'hôtes is on the right.

NEW M. & Mme Ulivi. L'Acampadou (M)

Quartier des Nouvelles. (0)4.42.73.13.17.

Good walks into the *garrigue* from here.

A Provençal villa situated well off the road with good views. One simple room for guests on the first floor faces south overlooking the garden and pool. A private bathroom/wc is on the landing. 290f. Locked parking and an evening meal if requested approx 90f, depending on what you order (but there is a promising auberge further up the road). Your pleasant hosts have a beauty salon in the town.

VERQUIERES. 13670

10km W of Cavaillon. 8km NE of Saint-Rémy-de-Provence. A neat village north of the Chaine-des-Apilles, which is central to many well-known towns. Avignon a few miles north, Cavaillon in the east where the largest fruit market in France is held daily, and St. Rémy-de-Provence a few miles south-west where the painter Van Gogh once lived.

From the telephone box in the centre follow signs to this chambres d'hôtes past orchards for 3km.

NEW M. Pinet. Mas-de-Castellan (M)

(0)4.90.95.08.22. fax: (0)4.90.95.44.23.

Hospitable M. Pinet is a semi-retired antique dealer who enjoys having guests. His lovely old house, dating from the 18th century, is full of interesting furniture collected on his travels. You will be welcome to use the large comfortable salon with log fire. Breakfast is served in the conservatory, full of greenery, overlooking the garden, which has a pool.

One of the five very comfortable rooms opens on to the garden; all are charming in different colours and furnished with taste, with baths or showers. I loved the blue one with the baldaquin and large windows.

No evening meals but restaurants nearby, many in Eyragues.

Rooms 400f, reduced after four nights.

VAR

LE BEAUSSET. 83330

15km NW of Toulon. An attractive small town. From the N8 opposite the Casino supermarket take the Chemin de la Fontaine de Cinq Sous by the boulangerie and in 1.5km turn right for 100m, then first left.

NEW **M. & Mme Zerbib. Les Cancades** (M)

(0)4.94.98.76.93. fax: (0)4.94.90.24.63.

One kilometre from the village, high on the hills above. The beautiful Provençal-style villa, built about 25 years ago, overlooks a lovely garden and pool where there is an attractive summer kitchen.

A charming green room faces south with a balcony, but the loo is shared on the landing. One on the ground floor at the back is rather darker but has a luxury bathroom and independent entry. Another upstairs is en suite. A difficult choice here, since all are so pretty. 350/400f.

I haven't met the owners, only the son. You may picnic in the garden, or use the owners' kitchen for evening meals, or use one of the many restaurants in the village. A *gîte* for four in the grounds shares the pool.

LA FARLEDE. 83210

15km NE of Toulon. Close to the Autoroute A57 to Nice. At Exit 6 take direction Crau, straight on at roundabout under a railway bridge. In 300 m. turn left and the chambres d'hôtes is signed on the right.

NEW **M. & Mme Lallier. Villa Arcadie** (M)

1417 rue de la Gare.Tel & fax: (0)4.94.33.01.79

This modern villa, in a small garden, makes a good stop from the Autoroute Nice-Toulon. A refreshing pool in the front garden is overlooked by two bedrooms which have terraces. Two other rooms again open on to terraces behind the house. They are prettily decorated, with painted rattan furniture in different colours. A family room is available upstairs. 260/320f.

A young goat, rabbit and cat plus swings will entertain the children, and there is a fridge for guests.

The real spirit of a chambres d'hôtes here. Your hosts join you for dinner - 88f wine included - in their dining room or by the pool in summer.

LORGUES. 83510

60km E of Toulon. 15 SW of Draguignan. In a part of the Var better known for expensive *gîtes* than chambres d'hôtes, but only 43km from the sea at St. Maxime.

From the N7 at Vidauban take the D10 to Lorgues and the chambres d'hôtes is 3km before Lorgues on the left.

NEW **Mme Kerbarch. La Boisseraie** (M)

2762 Route des Arcs. (0)4.94.73.99.42. fax: (0)4.94.68.69.84.

Turn up the small lane and you will find this pleasant hillside villa with a pretty rural garden, where anemones peep out of the grass in spring and violets creep among the stone steps. Parking is well off the main road. You will have a very friendly welcome from both your hosts, now retired.

The guest rooms are on the ground floor of the villa beside the swimming pool. One for three is very large, with the extra single bed in the entrance hall by a shower room, with good quality fitments, generous towels and lovely white embroidered bed linen. Central heating and duvets for winter, when large mats cover the tiled floors. A second room, for two, is smaller but has a covered patio. A summer kitchen and fridges in both the rooms make this a perfect spot for a long holiday, where you have the choice of picnicking by the pool, or trying the local restaurants. Visit nearby villages the Gorge de Verdun and the sea, or just relax on the loungers by the pool and chat to your congenial hosts.

Rooms 280f, with a good breakfast in a sun room overlooking the garden, or on the terrace in summer. All excellent value, just waiting for someone to confirm an arrow.

VAUCLUSE

ILE-DE-LA-BARTHELASSE. 84000 AVIGNON.

Right opposite the Saint-Bénézet bridge at Avignon is a long island in the middle of the river Rhône, approached only from the Edouard Daladier bridge. This small island is a complete contrast to the busy roads on either side of the river. The sudden peace and quiet is extraordinary. From the A7 take the Avignon exit, then take the road to *Pont Edouard Daladier.* Halfway across the bridge take the small road to the right. There is only one main road through the island. Follow the signs to Ferme Jamet for 3km.

NEW **M. Etienne Jamet. Ferme Jamet** (L)

(0)4.90.86.88.35. fax: (0)4.90.86.17.72.

Standing in a very large park with tennis court, swimming pool and a small gymnasium, this ivy-covered *maison-de-maître* has much to offer, far from the madding crowd. In the dining room a long table is elegantly laid for breakfast. No evening meals, as there are plenty of restaurants in the vicinity, to which your hosts will direct you.

Five rooms in the main house for guests are furnished in different periods and named after French artists, with every mod. con. including choice of bath/shower. Only one has a bathroom on the landing; it has a decorative 100-year-old-wash basin in the room. Matisse, the largest, has a double bed and two singles behind a curtain, Louis XV style. The smallest has a smart shower room but overlooks a lane at the back. 490/800f, according to size.

In the grounds are some small cottages let for two or more days - they have kitchen facilities. There are also larger self-catering apartments. Book ahead and discuss your requirements with your hostess who speaks very good English.

BONNIEUX. 84480

46km E of Avignon. A busy little hill village in the Lubéron at the meeting of many roads. The neighbouring village of Lacoste, where the Marquis de Sade once lived, is now a favourite tourist haunt - in the tiny narrow streets are plenty of cafés and restaurants. Ménerbes, made famous by Peter Mayle, is on another hill close by.

From the A7 exit Avignon Sud, follow signs to Apt via the N100, and 14km after Coustellet take the D 149 SP Bonnieux to Pont Julien, over the old Roman bridge. In 2km the house name is on the right, easy to miss as there are no Gîte de France signs.

M. & Mme Kozlowski. Jas des Eydins (L)

Route de Pont Julien. (0)4.90.75.84.99. fax: (0)4.90.75.96.71. Closed: 1/11 to Easter.

The house and garden are quite delightful and the 360° view over lavender fields and olive groves extends to snowy Mont Ventoux, Lacoste and Bonnieux on their respective hills. Four double rooms, decorated with country antiques and designer fabrics in detached buildings close to the house and large pool, are all slightly different but in keeping with the Provençal design of the main house. 480/600f. No evening meals. There is a summer kitchen for guests, and *apéritifs* are often offered by your Polish and English hosts on the terrace or in front of a log fire, before you go out to dinner.

CABRIERES-D'AVIGNON. 84220

34km east of Avignon via the N100. A small village south of Gordes. There is a large market at Coustellet nearby, every Sunday.

Madame Truc. 'La Lubéron' (M)

04.90.76.97.03. fax: 04.90.76.74.67.

On the edge of the village. Busy Mme Truc has five rooms in all. Some open on to a balcony, others to a small sitting area in the corridor. Two rear rooms overlook the road behind, so ask for the sunny rooms overlooking the swimming pool. Parking in the small garden is a bit tight. No evening meals but there is a good choice of restaurants within walking distance. A copious breakfast takes care of lunch.

Rooms now 280f or 320f for single beds. Reductions to 260/300f after three nights and 240f after eight nights.

A well organised chambres d'hôtes and absolutely no smoking.

CAIRANNE. 84290

18km SE of Bollène, a well preserved little town with the *vieux village* high on the hill above. It is noted for especially good wine from the surrounding vineyards.

Entering by the D8 from Sainte-Cécile-les-Vignes turn left (SP *Chapelle*) just after the *Cave Co-operative* and follow the signs to the chambres d'hôtes, bearing left.

NEW **Mme Molla. Le Moulin Agapé** (M)
(0)4.90.30.77.04.

Once an old flour mill, this old house has been completely restored and now has five bedrooms with well-modernised shower rooms (hair dryers, etc.) All but one are on the first floor, reached from an external staircase. The tiled floors will keep you cool in summer, but there are electric heaters and duvets for other seasons. There is a family suite with a garden entrance, and another room on the ground floor. Sunny terraces, a swimming pool and a friendly young hostess, who produces a copious breakfast of cereal, cheese, eggs as well as the normal baguettes, makes this a good place to stay and you can reserve an evening meal for 100f, all drinks *compris*; Rooms 270f with shower, 290f with bath. The price is right - could be a winner.

CRILLON-LE-BRAVE 84410

15km NE of Carpentras. A tiny hill village on the south side of Mt. Ventoux. The statue of Crillon stands supreme by the *mairie*. He was a captain of Henry IV, and the village, which dates back to Grecian times, was in his wife's dowry. His descendants founded the famous Hotel Crillon in Paris.

NEW **M. & Mme Ricquart. Moulin d'Antelon** (M)
(0)4.90.62.44.89. fax: (0)4.90.62.44.90.

Down the hill in the valley (3km S of Bedoin on the D974) with a fine view of Mont Ventoux in 8 hectares, with a stream running through and a very large swimming pool (25m x 12m), cleverly heated by the sun.

This ancient flour mill has been sympathetically restored with the mill wheel incorporated in the decor of the salon/dining room. Three rooms overlook a sheltered courtyard where breakfast is served in summer; two others in the main house have baths and one has an extra room for a family, with views to the pool. Charming hosts. Monsieur is a retired French Air Force officer, who speaks good English.

There is a restaurant just a few yards along the road, the only other building near, but evening meals *en famille* are sometimes possible. You'll enjoy the quiet luxury here and bask in the attention and welcome of your hosts.

Rooms 320f reduction to 280f out of season.

ENTRECHAUX. 84340

6km SE of Vaison-la-Romaine.You are spoilt for choice with places of interest in this part of the Vaucluse. There are two routes round Mont Ventoux, one taking you over the top by the observatory. Along the way are *dégustations*, especially near Bédoin, and Roman theatre remains at Vaison-la-Romaine.

Leave Vaison-la-Romaine by the D 938 bypass. Take the first left, D75, to St. Marcellin then bear right (SP Entrechaux) and you will pass the Auberge d'Anais on your left, and soon afterwards the chambres d'hôtes is on your left, opposite the hill village of Entrechaux.

M. & Mme Gallo. L'Esclériade (M)

Route de St. Marcellin. (0)4.90.46.01.32. fax: (0)4.90.46.03.71.

The modern rooms are quite superb, with choice of bath or shower, walk-in wardrobes, private patios, every convenience. It would be difficult to find a chambres d'hôtes in a nicer position, on the side of the hill, southerly views over Mont Ventoux and a swimming pool nestling below the terrace. All quite perfect, designed by M. Gallo, who is Italian; Madame is French.

Separate tables rather curtail the comradeship. Madame cooks expertly while M. Gallo serves at table in a very professional manner; but they find time to chat to their guests over coffee - 100f. Rooms 320/360f.

GOULT. 84220

38km SE of Avignon. A good place to stay for visiting many of the historical and interesting villages in this area west of Apt. Most renowned of all, the hill village of Gordes, where artists flocked in the 1930s. Partially destroyed by the Germans in the last war, it has been rebuilt. Now a Mecca for artisans, whose shops line the hilly, narrow streets. The château dominates the village, where in the square coach-loads of tourists arrive constantly; the most prevalent accent is American. On a hot day take refuge in the simple cool church. Nearby is a small village of *bories* - old circular stone huts looking like giant beehives; once lived in by shepherds, now restored - a great attraction. The tourist trade has driven prices sky-high so you will be glad to find a less costly resting place on the fringe of a nearby hamlet.

From the N100 at Lumières take the D106 right (SP Lacoste) over the bridge then take the D218 (SP Ménerbes) and the house is 500m on the left.

NEW ➤ M. & Mme Chabaud. Mas Marican (S)

(0)4.90.72.28.09.

Easy to find this old Provençal farmhouse which Peter Mayle used for his guests; it is on a large agricultural estate of maize and vegetables and has an enormous courtyard for parking outside the house. You will receive a very warm welcome from Madame if you book ahead and let her know when to expect you; she works in the local Cave Co-operative during the afternoon, but the above phone number will always find her.

There are five neat rooms with sunny aspects, tiled floors, en suite loos and showers, good lighting and central heating - four on the first floor, including a very nice family room, and one on the ground floor suitable for the handicapped. 250f.

You will be offered aperitifs before a generous evening meal with the family. 70f, all drinks *compris*. Lively Madame keeps the conversation flowing and everyone feels at home immediately.

An arrow for welcome, food and all-round comfort and the price is right.

MAZAN. 84380

7km E of Carpentras (D942). 30km NE of Avignon.The little town of Mazan makes a good central place to stay for visiting all the interesting places round Mt. Ventoux, where snow glistens on the top as late as March.

From Mazan take the D70 (SP Caromb). The chambres d'hôtes is on the right in about 700m.

NEW Mr. & Mrs. Dunn. Le Mas de Cante-Perdrix (M)

690 Route de Caromb. Tel & fax: (0)4.90.69.78.69.

Once an early 19th-century silkworm farmhouse, this spacious tall house, sideways on to the road, stands in a large flat garden right in the middle of the wine growing area, with views of Mont Ventoux. Built of honey-coloured stone it now has green shutters and has been beautifully modernised inside. All floors have the new pink

Provençale tiles; but the old beams have remained exposed. A comfortable lounge/ dining room with English-style furniture is for hosts and guests alike.

In front there are two rooms on the first floor, one very chic in black-and-white check with matching shower room, the other with deep pink walls and bathroom. Four more rooms are being converted out of the adjoining barns. 320f. The comfort here merits the price. Evening meals at 130f, drinks included, are not obligatory but I am sure you will enjoy them. Cooked by Laraine using local produce.

Central heating makes this chambres d'hôtes comfortable for year-round occupation and with the friendly welcome and flexibility of meals it is an ideal place for lone travellers to stay - if they are the only guests, they will be welcome to join the Dunns for meals in their cosy new kitchen. Possible future plans for the garden may include a swimming pool.

A very new chambres d'hôtes run with enthusiasm; I wish them every success.

SAINT-SATURNIN-LES-APT. 84490

8km N of Apt. A small village on the hillside north of Apt. Take the D101 from the N100 just west of Apt to the little hamlet of Les Bassacs. Turn left on to the D2 (direction Tulière) and at the brow of a hill you will see a small turn to Les Bassacs, easy to miss. The chambres d'hôtes is 100 metres up the lane. Look carefully for a large double gate with the letters **M.G.** on it.

NEW M. & Mme Bennett. Maison Garance (L)

Hameau des Bassacs. (0)4.90.05.74.61. fax: (0)4.90.05.75.68.

This ancient *maison-de-maître* rambles besides a long narrow garden, whose fresh green lawns lead to a swimming pool, with magnificent views of the Lubéron. Something particularly attractive about the setting.

There are at least three small salons where you can relax bedside log fires in winter. The rustic Provençale style has been well maintained in the meandering rooms full of character.

I liked the strong contrast between the room with bright orange walls and its Mediterranean blue bathroom. The design of both rooms and bathrooms is unique; but all five have en suite facilities and telephones. The smallest has the bathroom on the ground floor and the bed above on a mezzanine.

Rooms are from 450 to 600f, but sadly breakfast is an extra 50f each. Madame, a celebrated cook, will produce an evening meal twice a week for 150f when reserved. Restaurants in Apt and nearby villages. Parking is in the lane of this small hamlet.

VENASQUE. 84210

12km SE of Carpentras. 32km N of Cavaillon.Venasque is a perched village, rare in the Vaucluse, which is well preserved but has lost none of its interesting origins. Bishops from Carpentras used to move here in time of trouble in the 5th to 10th centuries. A delightful village to wander round and if you feel like a bit of luxury stay with:

M. & Mme Maret. 'La Maison Aux Volets Bleus' (M-L)

Place des Bouviers, le Village. (0)4.90.66.03.04. fax: (0)4.90.66.16.14. Closed: 12/11 to 14/3.

As Peter King says: '*It is a very rare occasion when it is possible to recommend a chambres d'hôtes as being in the same quality and value category as a 700f-a-night hotel, but this is the case with the aptly-named Maison aux Volets Bleus. La Maison is right in the heart of the old town and was once just another house. It has been transformed by Martine Maret and her husband and now Martine runs it with efficiency, style and careful attention to her guests' needs. There are six rooms and all are different and beautifully furnished. All have en suite bathrooms. Evening meals at 8 p.m. are 120f. each, and well worth it. The produce and the cooking are Provençal. Lamb and trout are two of the carefully prepared and extremely tasty specialities of the region. Martine speaks English. Parking is not immediate but there are several spots in the village only a couple of minutes away.*'

La Maison aux Volets Bleus

I tried hard to fault this place. It is quite charming, the cosy family atmosphere enjoyed by four cats, combined with the fabulous views, from all but the family suite, really does seduce one. Long may it continue. One forgives the lack of parking; off-loading at the door helps.

Rooms 350/420f for two includes breakfast.

RHONE-ALPES

Départements: **Haute-Savoie**
Isère
Savoie

Bordering on Switzerland in the East of France, this is the region with the highest mountains of France, the Alps, towered over by Mont Blanc (4807 metres).

There are two seasons of tourism here; the longest is the winter ski season followed by a short spring in May, leading to the summer season.

The **Haute-Savoie** lies along the southern bank of Lac Léman and extends southwards into the mountains. Geneva in Switzerland takes nearly all the air traffic for this region.

Drive down to Anneçy and take the road to such places as Thônes and La Clusaz, then over the Col des Aravis to Megève, one of the oldest and most unspoilt ski resorts. There is a delightful little chapel at the top of the Col, and many tourist shops. When you post your card, as undoubtedly you will, one foot will be in Haute Savoie and the other in Savoie. Further east is Chamonix, the most famous name of all, a ski resort at the foot of Mont Blanc, - pretty, crowded and expensive. In this direction further south are many purpose-built ski resorts such as La Plagne, packed and practical in winter but utterly lacking in beauty in summer. Stay a while in Anneçy; nothing ever spoils this lovely old town situated on probably the most attractive lake in France - a chocolate-box picture at all times of the year.

Continue south to **Savoie,** still mountainous; these two *départements* merge into each other. Visit the old Roman town of Aix-les-Bains on the longest lake in France, the Lac du Bourget. Further south, Chambéry is the *préfecture.*

South again is **Isère,** another mountainous *département* with skiing on high ground. Chartreuse, the liqueur, is produced in the mountains above Grenoble, which lies in a wide valley. This large university city, the *préfecture* of Isère, is bursting with commerce and traffic. Not easy to avoid if you wish to drive south, as the mountains are so high round it, but you can skirt the town and take the Route Napoléon N85 which takes you all the way to the Côte d'Azur - small villages and friendly chambres d'hôtes en route. West through the town for Lyon.

ISERE

LES ABRETS. 38490

30km W of Chambéry. From the A43 "Les Abrets" exit follow the signs to the town and to the chambres d'hôtes for 2km.

NEW M. & Mme Chavalle-Revenu. La Bruyère (M-L)

(0)4.76.32.01.66. fax: (0)4.76.32.06.66.

Situated among fields and woods in a large garden, this old farmhouse, originally built in 1820, has had an unusual face-lift. Marble stairs now lead to six neat but luxuriously furnished rooms in beautiful subtle colours; curtains and king size beds are in matching materials. Separate bathrooms adjoin each room, some with smart corner baths, all with hair dryers. Luxurious thick carpets to step on and telephones by the bed. Views from all windows. Two family rooms which extend across the second floor have convertible couches for children. 350/470f. Stay a few days and qualify for a bathrobe for your jaunt to the swimming pool.

A salon and dining room take up most of the ground floor with doors to the patio. Vivacious Mme Chavalle-Revenu cooks evening meals for 150f, all drinks *compris*, 75f for children 5 to 12 years, but it is not compulsory to eat here. Monsieur speaks some English. Breakfasts are copious. Do book ahead; such upmarket rooms attract the Parisians at all times of the year.

CHASSELAY. 38470

2km N of Varacieux. 38km W of Grenoble. 38km NE of Romans-sur-Isère. Within easy distance of the *Palais-Ideal* garden at Hauterives. Not far from the Pont-en-Royans where the houses cling to the rocks overlooking the river Isère at the entrance to the Gorges de la Bourne which leads to Villars-de-Lans, a high ski resort SE of Grenoble.

Take the D518 from St. Etienne-de-St. Geoirs to St. Marcellin and just over the Col du Cogne the road descends to Chasselay.

NEW Mme Jullin et Fils. Auberge La Bourrelière (M)

(0).4.76.64.21.03. fax: (0)4.76.64.25.97.

This smart auberge with a tower suddenly comes into view above the main road. It has six rooms, with a choice of double or twin beds, carpeted, all with baths and a

RHÔNE-ALPES / RHÔNE VALLEY

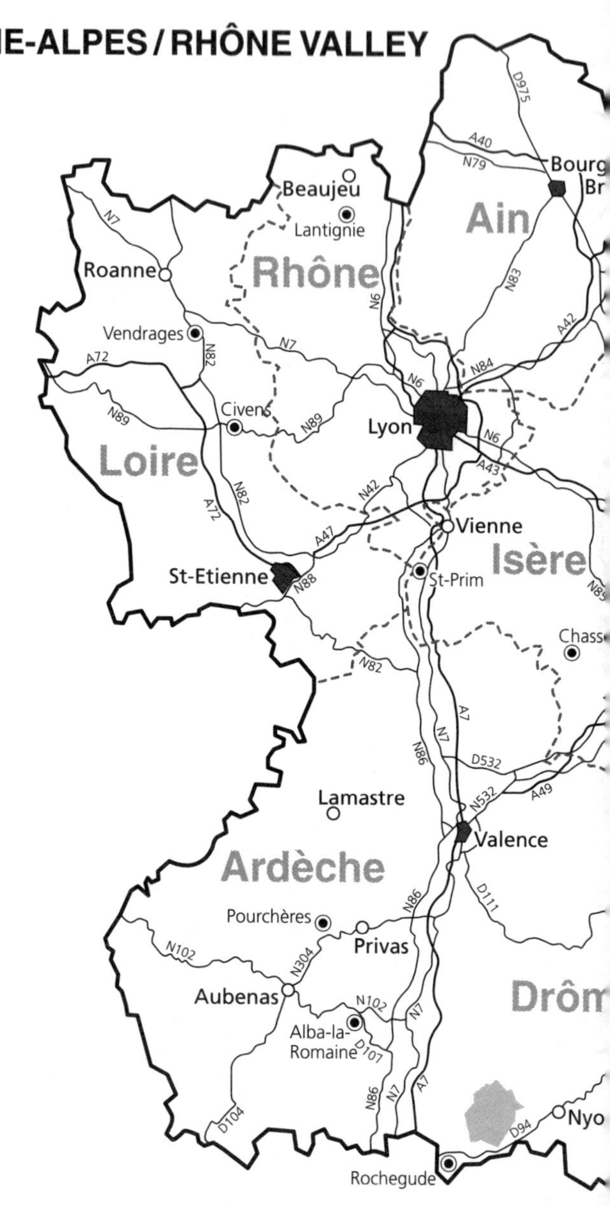

Chambre d'Hôtes
0 20km

third bed, sometimes a mezzanine. The room in front is very nice but the others at the side opening on to a terrace are equally good. Mme Jullin will give you a great welcome, and if you stay three nights D/P is only 210f. For one night it's 240f, but wine is *compris*.

Someone taste the food and tell me this is a winner. I wish I had found this at 6 p.m. instead of 11 a.m. en route for somewhere else.

Rooms 190f. Breakfast 35f extra, optional. B & B, 260f.

ST. PRIM. 38370

40km S of Lyon. Just across the bridge from Condrieu on the opposite side of the Rhône is St. Prim. Over the bridge turn immediately left and halfway up the hill is Pré Margot.

M. & Mme Briot. Le Pré Margot (S)

Les Roches de Condrieu. (0)4.74.56.44.27. fax: (0)4.74.56.30.93.

The situation is lovely on the hillside overlooking the river. At the closed gates we obeyed the sign to *sonnez la cloche* and miraculously the gates slowly opened; we drove into the short driveway and Monsieur was there to marshal us into a parking space. Only then when he had got us where he wanted did introductions begin and we asked if he had a room for the night. Not only one but five! So we had a conducted tour. All the rooms, are very modern, with TV, parquet floors and air conditioning. Pristine-clean, sanitised to suit the most fanatical. Flannels in sealed packets, to say nothing of plastic loo seat covers that move on at the touch of a button, always great fun for children!

Strictly no smoking here. To emphasise this there is a large ash tray fixed to the outside wall at the entrance. Had I been a smoker I should have felt compelled to empty all my packets of cigarettes in it!

The *pièce de resistance* was the enormous glassed-in veranda (very pleasant and full of tropical plants and gentle muzak), which enveloped two sides of the house, all 80 feet of it, with a busy view of the river.

The evening meal was perfectly served and cooked, but we ate alone. The food could not be faulted. Everything, even the bread, as Madame expressly told us, was made by her. Many people from all over the world stay here and clients come back regularly for their summer holidays. Good value for money at 85f which includes *apéritif*, but no wine.

Perhaps this one is more like an English guest house than a true chambres d'hôtes, with M. and Mme Briot as very pleasant patrons. Rooms 240f.

HAUTE-SAVOIE

COPPONEX. 74350

25km S of Geneva. 20km N of Annecy. Very handy for visiting Geneva or Annecy, half way between the two. Take the N201 from Annecy north to Cruseilles. In 2km after the village take the D27 to Coppenex. Follow the signs to Châtillon after the cemetery.

NEW **M. & Mme Gal. La Becassière** (M)
Châtillon. (0)4.50.44.08.94.

A warm welcome here from jolly M. Gal and his wife. The old farmhouse is in the country and simple modern rooms have views, smart shower rooms with separate loos, and a choice of double or single beds. 260f. All very good value and you'll be assured of a convivial evening, eating with your hosts - 80f, wine *compris*.

La Becassière is often used as an example for putative proprietors at the chambres d'hôtes course at Autrans in the Isère.

SAINT FELIX. 74540

A small village 12km S of Anneçy on the N201, renowned for its cheese, notably "La Vache qui Rit". Just a kilometre out of the village in the hamlet of Mercy is the home of:

NEW **M. & Mme Betts. "Les Bruyères"** (L)
Mercy. (0)4.50.60.96.53. fax: (0)4.50.60.94.65.

Bernard and Denyse just retired from Canada had always adored Anneçy and after much searching in the area discovered this partly-converted farmhouse, once part of a large estate belonging to a "*pied-noir*" family (French returning from Algeria after independence). Situated on top of a hill it looks down to a wooded bird sanctuary and has views both to the Jura and the Alps.

On the top floor the original hay-loft with machinery remains, but at one end of the house Bernard and Denyse have rebuilt the first floor turning four small rooms into two luxurious suites for guests. Reached by a private external flight of steps, a colourful corridor leads first to *L'Albanaise*, a light and airy room freshly decorated in blue and white. Deep recessed windows hiding radiators overlook the front garden and tennis court. Sink into comfortable primrose armchairs while you look around at the elegantly-covered twin beds with matching *tête de lits*, all made by Denyse. Ponder on the two doors, one a cupboard discreetly hiding a T.V. the other leading to a cute little "powder room" with loo and wash basin, which complements a much larger modern shower room. Soft lights, restful prints and interesting pieces of carved furniture delight the eye. The *L'Aixoise* suite at the rear of the house has warm red walls and matching decor, with a *tête-de-lit* and pretty floral bed cover. Thick carpets on polished wood floors, ample cupboard space, fresh flowers and plentiful reading material all distract you from the fact that the windows are of frosted glass to avoid looking into the original old house behind. Compensated by a large, brilliantly-lit bathroom, complete with bath and shower. Copious towels and toiletries are dotted around.

In winter, breakfast with freshly-pressed orange juice, croissants and local breads just collected by Bernard is elegantly served beside Napoleon's bust in the Bett's salon, partitioned from the dining room by a huge fireplace. In summer months, the piggery, a more rustic room with a log fire and terrace, is used for meals. Denyse, who writes cookery books, presents delicious dinners at 150f, including drinks.

Parking is under cover, or if necessary a garage is available. Their full-time gardener keeps the *potager* and grounds in perfect order and fresh fruit and veg are delivered daily to the kitchen.

Your hosts, who are English and Canadian, will advise on places to visit in and around Anneçy, produce picnics and even accompany you on occasions.

Rooms 550f.

RHONE-VALLEY

Départements: **Ain** **Loire** **Ardèche** **Rhône** **Drôme**

To most people the Rhône Valley just seems one giant passageway from Lyon to Marseille, carrying roads and railways and dominated by the large river Rhône, but there is more to it. The river rises in the Rhône Glacier in the mountains of Switzerland; it flows through Lac Léman and out again. Bolstered by the river Arve, it continues through the department of Ain in a south-westerly direction.

Though the region is called the Rhône Valley after the river, there are five very different *départements*: the Ain, Rhône and the Loire in the north, the Drôme and the Ardèche in the south.

Ain is in the north of the Rhône valley on the Swiss border, close to Geneva, and is separated from the Rhône *département* by the river Saône. The sudden change of landscape over the border of the river is remarkable, the one side tremendously hilly, sheltering the Beaujolais vineyards, the other in Ain suddenly flat as a pancake with masses of tiny lakes in all directions. Not a decent grape to be seen! In summer the villages are bedecked with flowers, mostly geraniums, tier upon tier almost burying the cottages. Bourg-en-Bresse, the *préfecture*, which gives its name to the cheese *bresse bleu* and the succulent dish *poulet bresse*, has a compact shopping centre, but is especially noted for a famous monastery at Brou on the edge of the town In the middle of the *département* the Gorge-de-l'Ain leads to higher ground where there is skiing in winter.

Continuing west, the river Rhône passes through Lyon, the second largest town in France, and flows on through the **Rhône** *département*. The whole of this *département* is given over to the wine trade, notably the Beaujolais in the north and the Côtes-du-Rhône in the south.

The '*Autoroute du Soleil*', the main route south from Paris to Marseille, comes through this valley with vineyards on every available slope. At Condrieu the Rhône is a magnificent sight viewed from the top of the hill - a wide navigable river where the pleasure boats and barges ply their trade. The climate is mild in winter except when the *Mistral* funnels down the valley, but in summer it can be very hot. It is here that the river forms the boundary between the departments of Isère and Rhône.

RHÔNE-ALPES / RHÔNE VALLEY

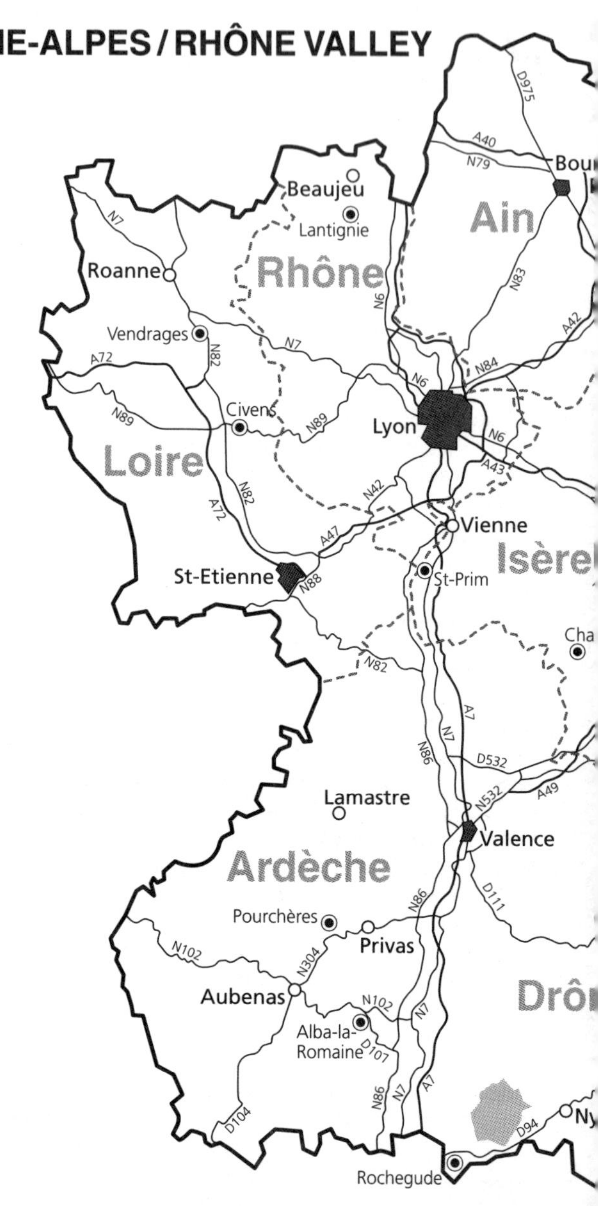

Thonon-
les-Bains
Haute-
Savoie
Sergy
Copponex
Chamonix
Annecy
St-Felix
Albertville
Chambéry
Savoie
St-Jean-de-
Maurienne
Grenoble
N5
N206
N205
N203
A40
N84
D984
A41
N508
N212
N90
A43
N6
D520
N75
N91
N85
Chambre d'Hôtes
0
20km

West again is the department of **Loire,** taking its name from the river flowing north. Attractive hilly farming countryside. Use this alternative route for that long journey south, not so busy as the A6/A7 round Lyon and a much more pleasant run from Nevers round Roanne to St. Etienne on the N82, until further south the road joins the river Rhône, where railways run parallel on both banks.

The southerly *départements* of this region are totally different. The **Drôme** in the east, still fairly high from the descending Alps, has lovely mountain roads occasionally running into small, hidden villages in the valleys. One interesting part is at Valréas where a small area belongs to the Vaucluse. In 1317 the Papacy was at Avignon in the Vaucluse and Pope John XXII bought the land round Valréas to extend his territory. Later he bought Richerenches (now a big truffle market) and Grillons; but at the end of the 18th century when all new boundaries were established the people of Valréas were offered the choice of living in the Drôme or staying with the Vaucluse. They opted for the latter and to this day a small piece of land surrounded by the Drôme still belongs to the Vaucluse.

On the right bank of the Rhône is the **Ardèche.** Turn up into the high rugged cliffs into a different world - probably the wildest area of France. Isolated farmsteads crop up in most unexpected places: no town planners have been round here! The main roads are good, but the smaller ones can be very narrow. Occasionally you run into high, flat areas in the south with rather pleasant little villages, giving strong reminders of the Roman occupation. The small hilly town of Privas is in the centre and a road runs across the *département* from here, the D102 on a high ridge; marvellous views on both sides and many small lanes lead off to hidden hamlets where there is often a chambres d'hôtes with very rustic rooms, but modern amenities. A lovely place for getting away from it all. Gorges and rivers, plenty of scope for canoeists and many holiday camp-sites round the little town of Thueyts, which also has an excellent market on Fridays.

Right on top of the Ardèche, on the D102, is the watershed for the Atlantic and the Mediterranean, and close by the source of the Loire. Wild flowers abound; in May the *genêt* (broom) covers all the hillsides, interspersed with tiny daffodils and narcissi. A walker's paradise. If you like it rough, rugged and rural choose the Ardèche; it has it all.

AIN

SERGY. 01630

10km W of Geneva. Just west of Geneva under the Mont Jura is the peaceful little backwater of Sergy, one of the many tiny villages which dot the D89. It's a straggly village with old and new houses and farms all mixed up. Little vegetable gardens come right up to the roadside. A bus or train ferry service runs directly from Sergy to Geneva, saving one all the hassle of driving and parking in that city.

Mme Moine (S)

Chemin de la Charrière. (0)4.50.42.18.03.

No shops, just a little *logis* opposite the *mairie* and a few yards further on the modern houses where Mme Moine has her b. & b. Make for the Chemin de la Charrière just behind the *logis* and beware of running over ducks; it is more of a farmyard than a through road, Mme Moine's house is the second on the right. If you have booked ahead she will be looking out for you and rather than explain where your rooms are she hops on a bike and leads you round the corner to them.

Now six guest rooms with central heating are in two different houses, having twin beds, and room for a third. In Le Verger, two rooms have the most compact kitchen corner I have ever seen. Automatic washing machine and ironing facilities in the garage. Garden at the back to sit in and views up to the Jura mountains behind. In La Forge, the new house, there are four similar rooms and a salon.

Mme Moine, though a busy farmer's wife, is so obliging and friendly. There is now a possibility of an evening meal 70f, 1/4 *vin compris*. Excellent value, close to one of the busiest cities in Europe.

ARDECHE

ALBA-LA-ROMAINE. 07400

15km W of Montélimar.Turn off the N86 at Le Teil near Montélimar on to the N102. Climbing up into the Ardèche mountains the scene changes dramatically; the old houses made of small round stones are dotted sporadically around the country-side. Good, fast, winding roads bring you to Alba-la-Romaine just off the N102. An attractive little village, surprisingly lively and sporting many old Roman ruins, including a well-preserved little theatre only 1km from the village. No turnstiles here; you can park beside it and even picnic on the theatre seats. The village has shops, restaurants and is not far from the much-photographed Gorges de l'Ardèche.

M. & Mme Arlaud. Le Jeu du Mail (M)

Tel & fax: (0)4.75.52.41.59.

Down a cul de sac leading to the cemetery only 100 yds from the village centre is a large old house which has three rooms for two and a couple of adjoining rooms for a family. 280-340f. No evening meal, a kitchen for guests' use in summer.

Ex air-hostess Mme Arlaud speaks perfect English and knows how to pamper her guests. With a swimming pool in the garden, you will want to stay here more than one night; so many places to visit.

M. Arlaud makes his own wine, calling it "Le Jeu du Mail", like their house, after a ball game played in the Middle Ages.

POURCHÈRES. 07000

16km W of Privas. If you like it rough and rugged and hardly a car in sight, north-west of Privas in the Ardèche is the place to make for. A twisting N304 west of Privas will take you to the Roc de Gourdon where you turn on to the D122, a smaller road which winds up and down dale across the region. 2km along this road turn right on to the D260 to Pourchères - not a chance of passing or being passed by another car so narrow is this road. The beautiful scenery will not be appreciated by the driver, as the bends are continuous. After 5km you will reach the village of Pourchères - just a few houses and a very squat church in local stone.

M. & Mme Goetz (M)

(0)4.75.66.81.99. Closed 1/1-31/3.

Past the church, and well signed. Six rooms, family and otherwise, are all extremely rustic, with beams, stone walls, niches and windows of all shapes and sizes. Rugged scenery all round and flowery terraces and small lawns to laze on. An attractive old dining room has kitchen attached, where you can see your meals being prepared.

Plenty of good bracing walks with wonderful views straight from the door make this a delightful place to stay a week or so; but it is too out-of-the-way for just one night.

Demi-pension 450/520f, for two, includes wine.

DROME

ROCHEGUDE. 26790

16km N of Orange. In the flat wine-growing area of the Rhône Valley, within easy distance of Orange. Take the Bollène exit from the A7 and follow signs round Bollène on the D8 to Rochegude. At the wine co-operative turn left and follow signs to the chambres d'hôtes up a lane on the left in about 1km.

NEW M. & Mme Lurault. Le Mas des Vignes (M)
Route-de-Bollène. (0)4.75.98.26.60. Open all year.

A very friendly chambres d'hôtes where one dines with the family. Spacious, tiled, and decorated with Provençal curtains and covers, all the rooms on the first floor have independent entry from a balcony. Some have baths and a couple boast tiny kitchenettes. Central heating in all for year-round occupancy. *Aperitifs* are dispensed in front of a log fire and a jolly meal of interesting fare is enjoyed each night - 85f wine *compris*. Exceptionally good value, with a swimming pool for the summer and good parking under the shade of a hundred-year-old plane tree.

There are good views over vineyards, looking south to the floodlit castle of Rochegude.

I enjoyed my visit here and feel it could be heading for an arrow. Rooms 250f.

LOIRE

CIVENS. 42110

34km N of Saint-Etienne.Turn at Feurs on to the D113. Confusingly this is called the Loire *département*, where the young river flows through from south to north. A good alternative route south via St. Etienne takes you past Feurs; if you are looking for a night stop try the following farm:

M. & Mme Palais. Les Rivières (S)

(0)4.77.26.11.93.

Mme Palais will welcome you with a drink. She has two comfortable en suite rooms, one with a balcony, for 200f, and is happy to give you an exceptionally good meal with very little notice for 60f, wine included. Eating with the family, the conversation is relaxed and entertaining.

VENDRANGES. 42590

14km S of Roanne. The Loire department, not to be confused with the Loire Valley region, is part of the Rhône Valley. It lies as a narrow wedge south of Burgundy and east of the Auvergne, so-called because the river Loire flows north right through the middle, wending its way from its source in the Ardèche. As soon as you enter this *département*, skirting the large town of Roanne in the north, the landscape changes: really high hills and pitched valleys make it quite picturesque. Vineyards on the more southern slopes produce the well-known Vin-du-Forez. This part of the Loire has its own elegant Château-de-la-Roche, almost an island, dating from the 13th century; it has passed through many hands and was finally restored at the beginning of this century - a great tourist attraction. Wonderful sightseeing tours and walks, ancient villages and churches, without having to drive too far each day. It is such an attractive area it really needs a week or more to get to know it well.

From the N82, south of Roanne, turn right at Vendranges on to the D42 to Saint-Priest-la-Roche and in 1km you will see a delightful farmhouse on the right in a dip with its own lakes. (There is another chambres d'hôtes in the vicinity, so make sure it is the 'Ferme de Montissut'.)

➤ M. & Mme Deloire. Ferme de Montissut (S)

(0)4.77.64.90.96.

A charming welcome from Madame, a busy farmer's wife, to this dairy farm. Two rooms each have an adjoining room for two children, cosy and prettily furnished with duvets and fresh flowery wallpaper for 190f for two. The whole house has warm central heating in winter and is immacu-

lately kept.

Evening meal not obligatory but is well presented country-fare with all drinks *compris* for 65f. You may picnic in the garden in summer if you have a family and need to budget more tightly.

A really delightful place. Even at the end of November I found this a most comfortable refuge. Children will enjoy watching the milking in the pristine parlour beside the house. Arrowed for all round comfort.

RHONE

LANTIGNIE. 69430

25km SW of Macon. Driving south from Macon through Beaujolais country on the N6, one passes signs to villages whose names are more common on dining tables in England, such as Pouilly Fuissé and Fleurie. Visit Beaujeu, a small town steeped in the wine trade, then climb the hill to Lantignie, with vineyards on either side cropped tight in March. Hard to miss as there is an enormous sign BEAUJOLAIS LANTIGNIE written across one of the fields in straw, clearly visible from the other side of the valley, or was the last time I was there.

M. & Mme Nesmie. Domaine des Quarante Ecus (S)

Les Vergers. (0)4.74.04.85.80. fax: (0)4.74.69.27.79. Closed during the *vendage* (September).

A typical *viticulteur's* old house. If Beaujolais is your tipple, learn all about it here watch the grapes grow, drink it and even sleep on it, as the rooms here are on the second floor above the *caves*, where all the wine is stored, old and new. Reached by what must once have been the servants' oak staircase, there are four rooms in all, two en suite and two sharing a shower and toilet on the landing. All rooms are carpeted, basically furnished, but spacious - 250f. Behind the house is a garden with a swimming pool which would be a pleasant respite from a hot drive. The *caves* under the house are well worth visiting even if you don't stay. The wine is in huge oak vats; tasting all day, but avoid 12 to 2 p.m.

No frills here but peaceful, safe parking and good views over the hills.

No evening meal but plenty of choice in Beaujeu, 3km down the hill.

STOP PRESS - LATE ENTRY - AUVERGNE REGION

HAUTE-LOIRE

LE-BOUCHET-SAINT-NICOLAS. 43510

29km SW of Le Puy. This was one of the first villages that Robert Louis Stevenson stayed in on his "Travels with a donkey". The old Auberge is now a private house. The Lac-du-Bouchet is a mile further north. Take the N88 south from Le Puy and in 19km at Coastaros turn right on to the D311, bear left through the village and the chambre d'hôtes is on the right. Beware there is another chambres d'hôtes in the village.

M. & Mme Reynaude (S)
(0)4.71.57.31.91. fax: (0)4.71.57.31.13.

The guest rooms are over a large garage beside the farmhouse on the main road. A sunny dining/sitting room opens on to a wooden balcony facing south. Three new pine furnished bedrooms, one for a family are all en suite with showers.

Evening meal 60f wine compris. Rooms 210f. A pleasant budget stop in an isolated village, popular with walkers. The only traffic I encountered was a herd of cows returning at eventide one Sunday; but I have since heard that passing traffic mid-week is more noticeable, though all is quiet at night.

Wines and spirits by John Doxat

AN INTRODUCTION TO FRENCH WINES

Bonne cuisine et bons vins, c'est le paradis sur terre. (Good cooking and good wines, that is earthly paradise.)

King Henri IV

French food positively invites accompaniment by wine, albeit only a couple of glasses because one is driving on after lunch. At dinner one can usually be self-indulgent. Then wine becomes more than a sensory pleasure: with some rich regional meals it is almost imperative digestively. Civilised drinking of wine inhibits the speedy eating that is the cause of much Anglo-Saxon dyspepsia.

The most basic French wine generically is *vin ordinaire*, and very ordinary indeed it can be. The term is seldom used nowadays: *vin de table* is a fancier description – simple blended wine of no particular provenance. *Vins de table* often come under brand-names, such as those of the ubiquitous Nicolas stores (Vieux Ceps, etc.) – and highly reliable they are. Only personal experience can lead you to your preference: in a take-away situation I would never buy the absolute cheapest just to save a franc or so.

Nearly every restaurant has its house wines. Many an owner, even of a chain of establishments, takes pride in those he has chosen to signify as *vins de la maison*, *vin du patron* or similar listing. In a wine-rich area, house wines (in carafe or bottle) are likely to be *vins de pays*, one step up from *vins de table*, since this label indicated that they come from a distinct certificated area and only that area, though they may be a blend (thus sometimes an improvement) of several wines.

Ever since they invented the useful, if frequently confusing, *Appellation d'Origine Contrôlée* (AC) the French have created qualitative sub-divisions. An AC wine, whose label will give you a good deal of information, will usually be costlier – but not necessarily better – than one that is a VDQS. To avoid excessive use of French, I translate that as 'designated (regional) wine of superior quality'. A newer, marginally lesser category is VQPRD: 'quality wine from a specified district'.

Hundreds of wines bear AC descriptions: you require knowledge and/or a wine guide to find your way around. The intention of the AC laws was to protect consumers and ensure wine was not falsely labelled – and also to prevent over-production, without noticeable reduction of the 'EEC wine lake'. Only wines of reasonable standards should achieve AC status: new ones are being regularly admitted to the list, and the hand of politics as much as the expertise of the taster can be suspected in some instances. Thus AC covers some unimportant wines as well as the rarest, vastly expensive vintages.

Advice? In wine regions, drink local wines. Do not hesitate to ask the opinion of patron or wine-waiter: they are not all venal, and most folk are flattered by being consulted. By all means refer to a vintage chart, when considering top class wines, but it cannot be an infallible guide: it has no bearing on blended wines.

Bordeaux

Divided into a score of districts, and sub-divided into very many *communes* (parishes). The big district names are Médoc, St. Emilion, Pomerol, Graves and Sauternes. Prices for the great reds (châteaux Pérus, Mouton-Rothschild, etc.) or the finest sweet whites (especially the miraculous Yquem) have become stratospheric. Yet château in itself means little and the classification of various rankings of châteaux is not easily understood. Some tiny vineyards are entitled to be called château, which has led to disputes about what have been dubbed 'phantom châteaux'. Visitors are advised, unless wine-wise, to stick to the simpler designations.

Bourgogne (Burgundy)

Topographically a large region, stretching from Chablis (on the east end of the Loire), noted for its steely dry whites, to Lyons. It is particularly associated with fairly powerful red wines and very dry whites, which tend to acidity except for the costlier styles. Almost to Bordeaux excesses, the prices for really top Burgundies have gone through the roof. For value, stick to simpler local wines.

Technically Burgundies, but often separately listed, are the Beaujolais wines. The young red Beaujolais (not necessarily the over-publicised *nouveau*) are delicious, mildly chilled. There are several rather neglected Beaujolais wines (Moulin-à-Vent, Morgon, St. Amour, for instance) that improve for several years: they represent good value as a rule. The Maçonnais and Chalonnais also produce sound Burgundies (red and white) that are usually priced within reason.

Rhône

Continuation south of Burgundy. The Rhône is particularly associated with very robust reds, notably Châteauneuf-du-Pape; also Tavel, to my mind the finest of all still *rosé* wines. Lirac *rosé* is nearly as good. Hermitage and Gigondas are names to respect for reds, whites and *rosés.* Rhône has well earned its modern reputation – no longer Burgundy's poorer brother. From the extreme south comes the newly 'smart' dessert *vin doux naturel*, ultra-sweet Muscat des Beaumes-de-Venise, once despised by British wine-drinkers. There are fashions in wine just like anything else.

Alsace

Producer of attractive, light white wines, mostly medium-dry, widely used as carafe wines in middle-range French restaurants. Alsace wines are not greatly appreciated overseas and thus remain comparatively inexpensive for their quality; they are well placed to compete with popular German varieties. Alsace wines are designated by grape – principally Sylvaner for lightest styles and, the widespread and reliable Riesling for a large part of the total, and Gerwürtztraminer for slightly fruitier wines.

Loire

Prolific producer of very reliable, if rarely great, white wines, notably Muscadet, Sancerre, Anjou (its *rosé* is famous), Vouvray (sparkling and semi-sparkling), and Saumur (particularly its 'champagne styles'). Touraine makes excellent whites and also reds of some distinction – Bourgueil and Chinon. It used to be widely believed – a rumour put out by rivals? – that Loire wines 'did not travel'; nonsense. They are a successful export.

Champagne

So important is Champagne that, alone of French wines, it carries no AC: its name is sufficient guarantee. (It shares this distinction with the brandies Cognac and Armagnac.) Vintage Champagnes from the *grandes marques* – a limited number of 'great brands' – tend to be as expensive in France as in Britain. You can find unknown brands of high quality (often off-shoots of *grandes marques*) at attractive prices, especially in the Champagne country itself. However, you need information to discover these, and there are true Champagnes for the home market that are *doux* (sweet) or *demi-sec* (medium sweet) that are pleasing to few non-French tastes. Champagne is very closely controlled as to region, quantities, grape types, and is made only by secondary fermentation in the bottle. From 1993, it is prohibited (under EEC law) to state that other wines are made by the 'champagne method' – even if they are.

Minor regions, very briefly

Jura – Virtually known outside France. Try local speciality wines such as *vin jaune* if in the region.

Jurançon – Remote area; sound, unimportant white wines, sweet styles being the better.

Cahors – Noted for its powerful *vin de pays* 'black wine', darkest red made.

Gaillac – Little known; once celebrated for dessert wines.

Savoy – Good enough table wines for local consumption. Best product of the region is delicious Chambéry vermouth: as an aperitif, do try the well distributed Chambéryzette, a unique vermouth with a hint of wild strawberries.

Bergerac – Attractive basic reds; also sweet Monbazillac, relished in France but not easily obtained outside: aged examples can be superb.

Provence – Large wine region of immense antiquity. Many and varied *vins de pays* of little distinction, usually on the sweet side, inexpensive and totally drinkable.

Midi – Stretches from Marseilles to the Spanish border. Outstandingly prolific contributor to the 'EEC wine lake' and producer of some 80 per cent of French *vins de table*, white and red. Sweet whites dominate, and there is major production of *vins doux naturels* (fortified sugary wines).

Corsica – Roughish wines of more antiquity than breeding, but by all means drink local reds – and try the wine-based aperitif Cap Corse – if visiting this remarkable island.

Paris – Yes, there is a vineyard – in Montmartre! Don't ask for a bottle: the tiny production is sold by auction, for charity, to rich collectors of curiosities.

HINTS ON SPIRITS

The great French spirit is brandy. Cognac, commercially the leader, must come from the closely controlled region of that name. Of various quality designations, the commonest is VSOP (very special old pale): it will be a cognac worth drinking neat. Remember, *champagne* in a cognac connotation has absolutely no connection with the wine. It is a topographical term, *grande champagne* being the most prestigious cognac area: *fine champagne* is a blend of brandy from the two top cognac sub-divisions.

Armagnac has become better known lately outside France, and rightly so. As a brandy it has a much longer history than cognac: some connoisseurs rate old armagnac (the quality designations are roughly similar) above cognac.

Be cautious of French brandy without a cognac or armagnac title, regardless of how many meaningless 'stars' the label carries or even the magic word 'Napoléon' (which has no legal significance).

Little appreciated in Britain is the splendid 'apple brandy', Calvados, mainly associated with Normandy but also made in Brittany and the Marne. The best is *Calvados du Pays d'Auge*. Do take well-aged Calvados, but avoid any suspiciously cheap.

Contrary to popular belief, true Calvados is not distilled from cider – but an inferior imitation is: French cider (*cidre*) is excellent.

Though most French proprietary aperitifs, like Dubonnet, are fairly low in alcohol, the extremely popular Pernod/Ricard *pastis*-style brands are highly spirituous. *Eau-de-vie* is the generic term for all spirits, but colloquially tends to refer to local, often rough, distillates. Exceptions are the better *alcohols blancs* (white spirits), which are not inexpensive, made from fresh fruits and not sweetened as *crèmes* are.

Liqueurs

Numerous travellers deem it worth allocating their allowance to bring back some of the famous French liqueurs (Bénédictine, Chartreuse, Cointreau, and so on) which are so costly in Britain. Compare 'duty free' prices with those in stores, which can vary markedly. There is a plethora of regional liqueurs, and numerous sickly *crèmes*, interesting to taste locally. The only *crème* generally meriting serious consideration as a liqueur is *crème de menthe* (preferably Cusenier), though the newish *crème de Grand Marnier* has been successful. *Crème de cassis* has a special function: see *Kir* in alphabetical list.

THE LOIRE THROUGH A WINEGLASS

The most peaceful holidays I have enjoyed in France have been spent ambling (if one can amble by car) through the tranquil Loire valley, just before or after the summer holidays. We always avoided the large towns and showed minimal interest in tourist attractions, staying at random in secluded and very comfortable country hotels, lingering over delicious meals, and quaffing much pleasing wine.

Ignoring the glamour of the fabulous châteaux – one can easily understand why they were built there – I find the great virtue of the Loire to be its understated beauty. This gentle, civilised unpretentiousness is reflected in the variety of its copious reservoir of wines. The Loire does not boast of vintage rarities about which connoisseurs rave, for which huge prices are paid, nor does it attract writers to pen those fancifully adjectival descriptions of numbing inconsequence to the generality of drinkers. It is for the wine-lover of modest experience, intelligent but not over-demanding, that the Loire offers many delights and, unlike some wine regions, it produces no utterly bad wines.

Let us briefly examine the most important.

Muscadet

This is not the most splendid Loire wine but it is the most widely known. It comes from the westerly Pays Nantais: the great city of Nantes is the regional capital. Yet until comparatively recently, Muscadet – a grape, not a place – was little drunk outside its own principal locality, Sèvre-et-Maine, which is now almost synonymous with Muscadet.

The Muscadet grape originated long ago as the 'Burgundy melon'. It made a wine renowned as a sauce base: it is still in minor cultivation in Burgundy for a handful of gourmets. Around two and a half centuries ago, the vine was planted in the Loire region and did well. It is only in the last thirty years, or less, that production has rocketed to meet demand.

Muscadet is unique amongst French wines in that, for reasons I do not know, it is the only one to have a legal maximum strength – a perfectly adequate 12.3°. Muscadet is best drunk young: if more than one vintage appears on a list, choose the most recent. All but the simplest Muscadet AC is now described – or most are – as *sur lie* (on the lees). This is not racked but is bottled from the cask after short fermentation. It is easy to appreciate the popularity of Muscadet. It is reasonably fruity, makes no demands on purse or palate. It is a perfect accompaniment to the fish in which the adjacent Atlantic remains rich.

An important town of the Muscadet area is St Fiacre-sur-Maine. I mention this only as an odd sacramental connection between drinking and driving: St Fiacre is the patron saint of cab-drivers.

Anjou

The wines of this historic region are of great antiquity. Charlemagne, first Holy Roman Emperor, owned vineyards here. Later, Anjou came under English rule. The prestige of Anjou wines was such that in 1194 they could bear a tax four times that applied to other wines imported into England. Notable French monarchs recorded a liking for Anjou's products: Louis XVI showed his appreciation by allowing the Layon river to be canalised to give Dutch vessels easier access to wine cargoes. Britain's Edward VII, a great wine-drinker, made a personal friend of his Loire vintner.

Simple Anjou Blanc, without further attribution, is an inexpensive all-purpose medium-dry wine. Anjou is particularly associated with *rosé*: Anjou *rosé* was famous before nearly every white wine producer started making this style. That said, there is nothing very exciting about Anjou *rosé*: reliable light beverage wine, highly suitable for summer.

It is with sweeter and dessert wines that Anjou really scores, and it is almost certainly these which attracted the high and mighty in times past. Our forebears did not share the modern vogue for 'dryness', or 'lightness'. They liked wines rich and strong. The best Anjou sweet wines rival all but the top Sauternes and are much less costly. They come from grapes affected by *pourriture noble* (noble rot), the curious fungus that appears to destroy over-ripe grapes: yet in practice it absorbs moisture, thus concentrating the sugar in the fruit. The *Chenin Blanc*, much grown in the Loire, is particularly susceptible to 'noble rot' which readily occurs by nature in Anjou, whereas elsewhere it may be necessary to introduce it. The affected Chenin makes fine sweet wine. Look out for Coteaux du Layon for good value, or Coteaux de L'Aubance. Costlier, but worth every franc, are more specifically named Quarts de Chaume and Bonnezeaux.

Saumur

This region is part of Anjou but has claims for separate treatment. It produces the best, though not widely distributed, Anjou reds, led by Saumur-Champigny, and amongst *premiers crus* (first growths) is Parnay: it was the Parnay proprietor who was the king's friend mentioned above. There is also an outstanding white Parnay. Abroad, Saumur is best known for its sparklers, made, for the time being, by the 'champagne method', and also semi-sparkling *pétillant* varieties. Inevitably, there are also *rosé* and *créme* sparklers. I reckon you will do best with a Saumur AC *Brut*.

Touraine

The vinous virtues of Touraine were hymned by Rabelais, Balzac and Dumas, amongst other writers. It lies in the heart of the long Loire valley and its centre is gracious Tours. This used to – still does? – enjoy the reputation of being the home of the purest spoken French: once it was almost obligatory for aspirant entrants to the Foreign Office to study there for a spell! Touraine produces sound, reliable whites from the Sauvignon grape, so a Touraine Sauvignon in itself guarantees a superior *vin de table*. It is Vouvray and Montlouis that are associated with the better whites. Touraine makes the most widely distributed reds of the Loire, notably Bourgeuil and Chinon. These can stand considerable bottle-age. Touraine *rosé* wines are comparable to the more celebrated Anjou *rosés*. Sparkling Vouvray, very lively, has a considerable reputation.

Sancerre

Commercially, this district has some affinity to Muscadet. From an ancient, not much regarded – even declining – wine area, Sancerre has, in about a quarter-century, become not only popular but distinctly fashionable. Prices have risen accordingly. The dominant Sauvignon grape produces excellent, crisp whites. Look for 'Sancerre' with a *domaine* designation for the better types, though you will find straight Sancerre AC more than adequate; sometimes over-priced because of the vogue the name enjoys. Reuilly and Quincy are place-names to remember, plus the slightly lighter Menetou-Salon. Reuilly reds and *rosés* deserve serious attention.

Pouilly

Likes to consider itself separate from Sancerre. Do not confuse its basic Pouilly-sur-Loire with the much more special Pouilly-Fumé, a delicious, dry, yellowish white. It must be stressed that Pouilly-Fumé has absolutely no connection with Burgundy's Pouilly-Fuissé, a more acidic wine. Pouilly-Fumé is usually drunk young, though it does gain with some ageing.

A general merit of most Loire white wines is that they are as suitable before a meal as during it.

> *If the alchemists of old had known your wines, they would have had no need to seek further for gold one can drink.*
> King Edward VII, to M. Crystal,
> owner of Clos-des-Murs, Parnay (Saumur)

Condensed glossary of French wine and ancillary terminology

Abricotine – Generic apricot liqueur. Look for known brand-names.
Alcool blanc – Spirit distilled from fruit (not wine); not to be confused with fruit-flavoured cordials.
Aligoté – Burgundy wine (from grape of same name); light and dry.
Anis – Aniseed; much used in aperitifs of Pernod type.
Apéritif – Any drink taken as an appetiser (literally 'opener'). France has a huge range of proprietary aperitifs.
Appellation (d'Origine) Contrôlée – AC; see An Introduction to French Wines.
Armagnac – Superb brandy of the Gascon country, now achieving something of a rediscovery. See Hints on Spirits.
Barsac – Sweet Bordeaux wine (officially part of Sauternes); wide range from excellent to sickly boring.
Basserau – Sparkling red Burgundy; unusual if nothing else.
Beaune – Prestigious Burgundy name (red), the best very costly.
Blanc de Blancs – White wine from white grapes only. White wine is often made from black grapes, skins being removed before fermentation – as this is.
Blanc de Noirs – See immediately above: these are essentially type descriptions; some prestige accrues to *Blanc de Blancs*.
Bordeaux – See An Introduction to French Wines.
Bourgogne – Burgundy, see An Introduction to French Wines.
Brut – Very dry; particularly with good Champagne.
Cabernet – Noble grape, especially Cabernet-Sauvignon. Just its name on a label denotes a sound red wine.
Cacao – Cocoa; usually as *crème de cacao*.
Calvados – Apple brandy; see Hints on Spirits.
Cassis – Blackcurrant; *crème de cassis* widely favoured, notably in Kir (q.v.).
Cave – Cellar.
Cépage – Indication of grape variety; e.g. *cépage Sauvignon*.
Chai – Ground-level wine store, exclusively used in Cognac, frequently also in Bordeaux.
Champagne – See An Introduction to French Wines.
Clairet – Unimportant little-known Bordeaux wine, but probably origin of English word Claret (red Bordeaux).
Clos – Principally Burgundian word for vineyard enclosed, or formerly protected, by a wall.
Cognac – see Hints on Spirits.
Côte – Vineyard on a slope; no particular quality significance.
Coteau(x) – Hillside(s); much the same as *côte*.
Crème – Sweet, mildly alcoholic cordials of many flavours. Not rated as true liqueurs, but one exception is *crème de menthe* (mint). See also *cassis*.

Crémant – Sparkling wine, without lasting champagne-style effervescence.
Cru – Literally 'growth'. Somewhat complicated term. *Grand cru* only meaningful if allied to good name. *Grand cru classé* (officially classified great wine) covers greatest wines, but not all *cru classé* is *grand*.
Cuve close – Sealed vat; describes production of sparkling wine by bulk secondary fermentation as opposed to bottle fermentation of 'champagne method'.
Cuvée – Wine from one vat, unblended. Another confusing word; *cuvée spéciale* can have more than its literal meaning.
Demi-sec – Translates as 'medium dry'; in practice means sweet.
Domaine – Mainly Burgundian word; broadly equivalent to château.
Doux – Very sweet.
Eau-de-vie – Generic term for all distilled spirits.
Frappé – Drink served on finely crushed ice.
Glacé – Iced by immersion of bottle, or other refrigeration.
Goût – Taste. In some regions also describes rough local spirit.
Haut – 'High'; denotes upper part of wine district. Not necessarily a mark of quality, though Haut-Medoc produces notably better wines than its lower areas
Izarra – Ancient, Armagnac-based Basque liqueur.
Kir – Excellent, now very popular aperitif: very dry chilled white wine (properly *Bourgogne Aligoté*) with a teaspoon of *crème de cassis* (q.v.) added. Kir Royale employs champagne.
Liqueur – originally *liqueur de dessert*, denoting post-prandial digestive use. Always sweet, so to speak of a 'liqueur Cognac' is absurd.
Litre – 1.7 pints; 5 litres equals 1.1 gallons.
Méthode Champenoise – Wine made by the champagne method.
Marc – Usually roughish brandy distilled from wine residue, though a few *Marcs* (pronounced 'mar') – notably *Marc de Bourgogne* – have some status.
Marque – Brand or company name.
Mise – As in *mise en bouteilles au château* (bottled at the château) or . . . *dans nos caves* (in our own cellars), etc.
Moelleux – On the sweet side.
Mousseux – Semi-technical term for sparkling; applies to the greatest champagne and to artificially carbonated rubbish.
Nouveau – New wine, particularly Beaujolais; made for drinking within a few months of harvest.
Pastis – General description, once more specific, for strong anis/liquorice-flavoured aperitifs originating in Marseilles; Ricard is a prime example.
Pétillant – Gently effervescent; sometimes translated as 'prickly' or 'crackling'.
Pineau – Unfermented grape juice fortified with grape spirit. Made in many regions: *Pineau des Charantes* (Cognac area) is best known. Well chilled, an attractive aperitif.
Porto – Port wine. The French are very big consumers, often using it (chilled) as an aperitif.
Primeur – Basically the same as *nouveau*. However, much fine

Bordeaux and Burgundy is sold *'en primeur'* for long maturing by buyer.
Rosé – 'Pink wine'. Made by leaving skins of black grapes briefly in contact with juice; also by addition of red wine to white.
Sauvignon – Splendid white grape.
Sec – 'Dry', but wines thus marked will be sweetish. *Extra sec* may actually mean what it says.
Sirop – Syrup; akin to non-alcoholic *crème*.
Vermout – Vermouth.
Vin de Xérès – 'Vin de 'ereth'; sherry.

Glossary of cooking terms and dishes

(It would take another book to list comprehensively French cooking terms and dishes, but here are the ones most likely to be encountered)

Aigre-doux	bittersweet
Aiguillette	thin slice (aiguille – needle)
Aile	wing
Aïoli	garlic mayonnaise
Allemande (à l')	German style, i.e. with sausages and sauerkraut
Amuses-gueule	appetisers
Anglaise (à l')	plain boiled. Crème Anglaise – egg and cream sauce
Andouille	large boiling sausage
Andouillettes	ditto but made from smaller intestines, usually served hot after grilling
Anis	aniseed
Argenteuil	with asparagus
Assiette Anglaise	plate of cold meats
Baba au Rhum	yeast-based sponge macerated in rum
Baguette	long thin loaf
Ballotine	boned, stuffed and rolled meat or poultry, usually cold
Béarnaise	sauce made from egg yolks, butter, tarragon, wine, shallots
Beurre blanc	sauce from Nantes, with butter, reduction of shallot-flavoured vinegar or wine
Béchamel	white sauce flavoured with infusion of herbs
Beignets	fritters
Bercy	sauce with white wine and shallots
Beurre noir	browned butter
Bigarade	with oranges
Billy By	mussel soup
Bisque	creamy shellfish soup
Blanquette	stew with thick white creamy sauce, usually veal
Boeuf à la mode	braised beef
Bombe	ice cream mould
Bonne femme	with root vegetables
Bordelais	Bordeaux-style, with red or white wine, marrow bone fat
Bouchée	mouthful, i.e. vol au vent
Boudin	sausage or black pudding
Bourride	thick fish soup
Braisé	braised
Brandade (de morue)	dried salt cod pounded into a mousse
Broche	spit
Brochette	skewer
Brouillade	stew, using oil
Brouillé	scrambled
Brulé	burnt, i.e. crême brulée
Campagne	country style
Cannelle	cinnamon
Carbonade	braised in beer
Cardinal	red-coloured sauce, i.e. with lobster or in pâtisserie with redcurrant
Cassolette or cassoulette	small pan
Cassoulet	rich stew with goose, pork and haricot beans
Cervelas	pork garlic sausage
Cervelles	brains
Chantilly	whipped sweetened cream
Charcuterie	cold pork-butcher's meats
Charlotte	mould, as dessert lined with sponge fingers, as savoury lined with vegetable
Chasseur	with mushrooms, shallots, wine
Chausson	pastry turnover
Chemise	covering, i.e. pastry
Chiffonade	thinly cut, i.e. lettuce
Choron	tomato Béarnaise
Choucroute	Alsatian stew with sauerkraut and sausages
Civet	stew
Clafoutis	batter desert, usually with cherries
Clamart	with peas
Cocotte	covered casserole
Compôte	cooked fruit
Concassé	i.e. tomatoes concassées – skinned, chopped, juice extracted
Confit	preserved
Confiture	jam
Consommé	clear soup
Coque (à la)	i.e. oeufs – boiled eggs
Cou	neck

Coulis juice, purée (of vegetables or fruit)
Court-bouillon aromatic liquor for cooking meat, fish, vegetables
Couscous N. African dish with millet, chicken, vegetable variations
Crapaudine involving fowl, particularly pigeon, trussed
Crécy with carrots
Crême pâtissière thick custard filling
Crêpe pancake
Crépinette little flat sausage, encased in caul
Croque Monsieur toasted cheese and ham sandwich
Croustade pastry or baked bread shell
Croûte pastry crust
Croûton cube of fried or toasted bread
Cru raw
Crudités raw vegetables

Demi-glâce basic brown sauce
Doria with cucumber

Emincé thinly sliced
Entremets sweets
Etuvé stewed, i.e. vegetables in butter

Farci stuffed
Fines herbes parsley, thyme, bayleaf
Feuilleté leaves of flaky pastry
Flamande Flemish style, with beer
Flambé flamed in spirit
Flamiche flan
Florentine with spinach
Flute thinnest bread loaf
Foie gras goose liver
Fond (d'artichaut) heart (of artichoke)
Fondu melted
Forestière with mushrooms, bacon and potatoes
Four (au) baked in the oven
Fourré stuffed, usually sweets
Frais, fraiche fresh and cool
Frangipane almond crême pâtisserie
Fricadelle Swedish meat ball
Fricandeau veal, usually topside
Fricassée (usually of veal) in creamy sauce
Frit fried
Frites chips
Friture assorted small fish, fried in batter
Froid cold
Fumé smoked

Galatine loaf-shaped chopped meat, fish or vegetable, set in natural jelly
Galette Breton pancake, flat cake
Garbure thick country soup
Garni garnished, usually with vegetables
Gaufre waffle
Gelée aspic
Gésier gizzard
Gibier game
Gigôt leg
Glacé iced
Gougère choux pastry, large base
Goujons fried strips, usually of fish
Graine seed
Gratin baked dish of vegetables cooked in cream and eggs
Gratinée browned under grill
Grêcque (à la) cold vegetables served in oil
Grenouilles frogs; cuisses de grenouille – frogs' legs
Grillé grilled
Gros sel coarse salt

Hachis minced or chopped
Haricot slow cooked stew
Hochepot hotpot
Hollandaise sauce with egg, butter, lemon
Hongroise Hungarian, i.e. spiced with paprika
Hors d'oeuvres assorted starters
Huile oil

Île flottante floating island – soft meringue on egg custard sauce
Indienne Indian, i.e. with hot spices

Jambon ham
Jardinière from the garden, i.e. with vegetables
Jarret shin, i.e. jarret de veau
Julienne matchstick vegetables
Jus natural juice

Lait milk
Langue tongue
Lard bacon
Longe loin

Macedoine diced fruits or vegetables
Madeleine small sponge cake

Magret	breast (of duck)
Maïs	sweetcorn
Maître d'hôtel	sauce with butter, lemon, parsley
Marchand de vin	sauce with red wine, shallot
Marengo	sauce with tomatoes, olive oil, white wine
Marinière	seamen's style, i.e. moules marinières (mussels in white wine)
Marmite	deep casserole
Matelote	fish stew, i.e. of eel
Médaillon	round slice
Mélange	mixture
Meunière	sauce with butter, lemon
Miel	honey
Mille feuille	flaky pastry, lit. 1,000 leaves
Mirepoix	cubed carrot, onion, etc. used for sauces
Moëlle	beef marrow
Mornay	cheese sauce
Mouclade	mussel stew
Mousseline	Hollandaise sauce, lightened with egg white
Moutarde	mustard
Nage (à la)	poached in flavoured liquor (fish)
Nature	plain
Navarin (d'agneau)	stew of lamb with spring vegetables
Noisette	nut-brown, burned butter
Noix de veau	nut of veal (leg)
Normande	Normandy style, with cream, apple, cider, Calvados
Nouilles	noodles
Os	bone
Paillettes	straws (of pastry)
Panaché	mixed
Panade	flour crust
Papillote (en)	cooked in paper case
Parmentier	with potatoes
Pâté	paste, of meat or fish
Pâte	pastry
Pâte brisée	rich short crust pastry
Pâtisserie	pastries
Paupiettes	paper-thin slice
Pavé	thick slice
Paysan	country style
Perigueux	with truffles
Persillade	chopped parsley and garlic topping
Petit pain	bread roll
Petits fours	tiny cakes, sweetmeats
Piperade	peppers, onions, tomatoes in scrambled egg
Poché	poached
Poëlé	fried
Poitrine	breast
Poivre	pepper
Pommade	paste
Potage	thick soup
Pot-au-four	broth with meat and vegetables
Potée	country soup with cabbage
Pralines	caramelised almonds
Primeurs	young veg
Printanièr(e)	garnished with early vegetables
Profiteroles	choux pastry balls
Provençale	with garlic, tomatoes, olive oil, peppers
Purée	mashed and sieved
Quenelle	pounded fish or meat, bound with egg, poached
Queue	tail
Quiche	pastry flan, i.e. quiche Lorraine – egg, bacon, cream
Râble	saddle, i.e. rable de lièvre
Ragoût	stew
Ramequin	little pot
Rapé	grated
Ratatouille	Provençale stew of onions, garlic, peppers, tomatoes
Ravigote	highly seasoned white sauce
Rémoulade	mayonnaise with gherkins, capers, herbs and shallot
Rillettes	potted shredded meat, usually fat pork or goose
Riz	rice
Robert	sauce with mustard, vinegar, onion
Roquefort	ewe's milk blue cheese
Rossini	garnished with foie gras and truffle
Rôti	roast
Rouelle	nugget
Rouille	hot garlicky sauce for soupe de poisson
Roulade	roll
Roux	sauce base – flour and butter
Sabayon	sweet fluffy sauce, with eggs and wine
Safran	saffron
Sagou	sago
St.-Germain	with peas
Salade niçoise	with tunny, anchovies, tomatoes, beans, black olives

Salé	salted
Salmis	dish of game or fowl, with red wine
Sang	blood
Santé	lit. healthy, i.e. with spinach and potato
Salpicon	meat, fowl, vegetables, chopped fine, bound with sauce and used as fillings
Saucisse	fresh sausage
Saucisson	dried sausage
Sauté	cooked in fat in open pan
Sauvage	wild
Savarin	ring of yeast sponge, soaked in syrup and liquor
Sel	salt
Selle	saddle
Selon	according to, i.e. selon grosseur (according to size)
Smitane	with sour cream, white wine, onion
Soissons	with dried white beans
Sorbet	water ice
Soubise	with creamed onions
Soufflé	puffed, i.e. mixed with egg white and baked
Sucre	sugar (sucré – sugared)
Suprême	fillet of poultry breast or fish
Tartare	raw minced beef, flavoured with onion etc. and bound with raw egg
Tartare (sauce)	mayonnaise with capers, herbs, onions
Tarte Tatin	upside-down apple pie
Terrine	pottery dish/baked minced, chopped meat, veg., chicken, fish or fruit
Thé	tea
Tiède	lukewarm
Timbale	steamed mould
Tisane	infusion
Tourte	pie
Tranche	thick slice
Truffes	truffles
Tuile	tile, i.e. thin biscuit
Vacherin	meringue confection
Vallée d'Auge	with cream, apple, Calvados
Vapeur (au)	steamed
Velouté	white sauce, bouillon-flavoured
Véronique	with grapes
Vert(e)	green, i.e. sauce verte with herbs
Vessie	pig's bladder
Vichyssoise	chilled creamy leek and potato soup
Vierge	prime olive oil
Vinaigre	vinegar (lit. bitter wine)
Vinaigrette	wine vinegar and oil dressing
Volaille	poultry
Vol-au-vent	puff pastry case
Xérès	sherry
Yaourt	yoghurt

FISH – Les poissons, SHELLFISH – Les coquillages

Aiglefin	haddock – also Églefin
Alose	shad
Anchois	anchovy
Anguille	eel
Araignée de mer	spider crab
Bar	sea bass
Barbue	brill
Baudroie	monkfish, anglerfish
Belon	oyster – flat shelled
Bigorneau	winkle
Blanchaille	whitebait
Brochet	pike
Cabillaud	cod
Calmar	squid
Carrelet	plaice
Chapon de mer	scorpion fish
Claire	oyster
Clovisse	large clam
Colin	hake
Congre	conger eel
Coques	cockles
Coquille St. Jacques	scallop
Crabe	crab
Crevette grise	shrimp
Crevette rose	prawn
Daurade	sea bream
Donzelle or Girelle	a brightly coloured eel-like Mediterranean fish
Écrevisse	crayfish
Encornet	cuttlefish, squid
Éperlan	smelt
Espadon	swordfish
Etrille	baby crab
Favouille	spider crab
Fiecas	conger eel
Flétan	halibut
Fruits de mer	seafood
Gamba	large prawn
Grondin	red gurnet
Hareng	herring
Homard	lobster
Huitre	oyster
Julienne	ling
Laitance	soft herring roe
Lamproie	lamprey
Langouste	crawfish
Langoustine	Dublin Bay prawn
Lieu	ling
Limand	lemon sole
Lotte de mer	monkfish
Loup de mer	sea bass
Maquereau	mackerel
Merlan	whiting
Mérou	grouper
Morue	salt cod
Moule	mussel
Muge, mulet	grey mullet
Murène	moray eel
Nonat	tiny fish similar to whitebait
Ombre	grayling
Orade	gilt-headed bream
Oursin	sea urchin
Pageot	sea bream
Palourde	clam
Perche	perch
Petoncle	small scallop
Plie	plaice
Portugaise	oyster
Poulpe	octopus
Praire	small clam
Raie	skate
Rascasse	scorpion-fish
Rouget	red mullet
St. Pierre	John Dory
Sauclet	sand smelt
Saumon	salmon
Saumonette	rock salmon
Scipion	cuttlefish
Seiche	squid
Sole	sole
Soupion	inkfish
Sourdon	cockle
Thon	tunny
Tortue	turtle
Tourteau	large crab
Truite	trout
Turbot	turbot
Turbotin	chicken turbot
Vernis	clam
Violet	soft-shelled shellfish

FRUITS – Les fruits, VEGETABLES – Les légumes, NUTS – Les noix
HERBS – Les herbes, SPICES – Les épices

Ail	garlic
Algue	seaweed
Amande	almond
Ananas	pineapple
Aneth	dill
Abricot	apricot
Arachide	peanut
Artichaut	globe artichoke
Asperge	asparagus
Avocat	avocado
Banane	banana
Basilic	basil
Betterave	beetroot
Blette	Swiss chard
Brugnon	nectarine
Cassis	blackcurrant
Céleri	celery
Céleri-rave	celeriac
Cèpe	edible fungus
Cerfeuil	chervil
Cérise	cherry
Champignon	mushroom
Chanterelle	edible fungus
Chatâigne	chestnut
Chicorée	endive
Chou	cabbage
Choufleur	cauliflower
Choux de Bruxelles	Brussels sprout
Ciboulette	chive
Citron	lemon
Citron vert	lime
Coing	quince
Concombre	cucumber
Coriandre	coriander
Cornichon	gherkin
Courge	marrow, pumpkin
Courgette	courgette
Cresson	watercress
Échalotte	shallot
Endive	chicory
Épinard	spinach
Escarole	salad leaves
Estragon	tarragon
Fenouil	fennel
Fève	broad bean
Flageolet	small green bean
Fraise	strawberry
Framboise	raspberry
Genièvre	juniper
Gingembre	ginger
Girofle	clove
Girolle	edible fungus
Granade	pomegranate
Griotte	bitter red cherry
Groseille à maquereau	gooseberry
Groseille noire	blackcurrant
Groseille rouge	redcurrant
Haricot	dried white bean
Haricot vert	French bean
Laitue	lettuce
Mandarine	tangerine, mandarin
Mangetout	sugar pea
Marron	chestnut
Menthe	mint
Mirabelle	tiny gold plum
Morille	dark brown crinkly edible fungus
Mûre	blackberry
Muscade	nutmeg
Myrtille	bilberry, blueberry
Navet	turnip
Noisette	hazelnut
Oignon	onion
Oseille	sorrel
Palmier	palm
Pamplemousse	grapefruit
Panais	parsnip
Passe-Pierre	seaweed
Pastèque	water melon
Pêche	peach
Persil	parsley
Petit pois	pea
Piment doux	sweet pepper
Pissenlit	dandelion
Pistache	pistachio
Pleurote	edible fungi
Poire	pear
Poireau	leek
Poivre	pepper
Poivron	green, red and yellow peppers
Pomme	apple
Pomme-de-terre	potato
Prune	plum
Pruneau	prune
Quetsch	small dark plum
Radis	radish
Raifort	horseradish
Raisin	grape
Reine Claude	greengage
Romarin	rosemary
Safran	saffron
Salisifis	salsify
Thym	thyme
Tilleul	lime blossom
Tomate	tomato
Topinambour	Jerusalem artichoke
Truffe	truffle

MEAT – Les viandes

Le Boeuf	Beef	*Jambon cru*	raw smoked ham
Charolais	is the best	*Porcelet*	suckling pig
Chateaubriand	double fillet steak		
Contrefilet	sirloin	*Le Veau*	Veal
Entrecôte	rib steak	*Escalope*	thin slice cut from fillet
Faux filet	sirloin steak		
Filet	fillet	*Les Abats*	Offal
		Cervelles	brains
L'Agneau	Lamb	*Foie*	liver
Carré	neck cutlets	*Foie gras*	goose liver
Côte	chump chop	*Langue*	tongue
Epaule	shoulder	*Ris*	sweetbreads
Gigot	leg	*Rognons*	kidneys
Pré-Salé	is the best	*Tripes*	tripe
Le Porc	Pork		
Jambon	ham		

POULTRY– Volaille, GAME – Gibier

Abatis	giblets	*Lièvre*	hare
Bécasse	woodcock	*Oie*	goose
Bécassine	snipe	*Perdreau*	partridge
Caille	quail	*Pigeon*	pigeon
Canard	duck	*Pintade*	guineafowl
Caneton	duckling	*Pluvier*	plover
Chapon	capon	*Poularde*	chicken (boiling)
Chevreuil	roe deer	*Poulet*	chicken (roasting)
Dinde	young hen turkey	*Poussin*	spring chicken
Dindon	turkey	*Sanglier*	wild boar
Dindonneau	young turkey	*Sarcelle*	teal
Faisan	pheasant	*Venaison*	venison
Grive	thrush		

Other French Entrée Guides

French Entrée 8	The Loire	£6.95
French Entrée 10	The South of France	£6.95
French Entrée 11	Paris	£6.95
French Entrée 12	North of France	£6.95
French Entrée 13	Provence	£6.95
French Entrée 14	Brittany Encore	£6.95
French Entrée 16	Gardens of France	£9.95
French Entrée 17	Normandy	£7.95

Also Entrées to Majorca, Algarve, Malta, Florida, Catalunya, Halkidiki.